Learn Linux Shell Scripting Fundamentals of Bash 4.4

A comprehensive guide to automating administrative tasks with the Bash shell

Sebastiaan Tammer

BIRMINGHAM - MUMBAI

Learn Linux Shell Scripting – Fundamentals of Bash 4.4

Copyright © 2018 Packt Publishing

Commissioning Editor: Vijin Boricha
Acquisition Editor: Rohit Rajkumar
Content Development Editor: Abhishek Jadhav
Technical Editor: Prachi Sawant
Copy Editor: Safis Editing
Project Coordinator: Jagdish Prabhu
Proofreader: Safis Editing
Indexer: Priyanka Dhadke
Graphics: Tom Scaria
Production Coordinator: Tom Scaria

First published: December 2018

Production reference: 1281218

Published by Packt Publishing Ltd.
Livery Place
35 Livery Street
Birmingham
B3 2PB, UK.

ISBN 978-1-78899-559-7

www.packtpub.com

`mapt.io`

Mapt is an online digital library that gives you full access to over 5,000 books and videos, as well as industry leading tools to help you plan your personal development and advance your career. For more information, please visit our website.

Why subscribe?

- Spend less time learning and more time coding with practical eBooks and Videos from over 4,000 industry professionals

- Improve your learning with Skill Plans built especially for you

- Get a free eBook or video every month

- Mapt is fully searchable

- Copy and paste, print, and bookmark content

PacktPub.com

Did you know that Packt offers eBook versions of every book published, with PDF and ePub files available? You can upgrade to the eBook version at `www.PacktPub.com` and as a print book customer, you are entitled to a discount on the eBook copy. Get in touch with us at `service@packtpub.com` for more details.

At `www.PacktPub.com`, you can also read a collection of free technical articles, sign up for a range of free newsletters, and receive exclusive discounts and offers on Packt books and eBooks.

Contributors

About the author

Sebastiaan Tammer is a Linux enthusiast from the Netherlands. After attaining his BSc in information sciences, he graduated with an MSc in business informatics, both from Utrecht University. His professional career started in Java development, before he pivoted into a Linux opportunity. Because of this dual background, he feels most at home in a DevOps environment.

Besides working extensively with technologies such as Puppet, Chef, Docker, and Kubernetes, he has also attained the RHCE and OSCP certificates. He spends a lot of time in and around Bash. Whether it is creating complex scripting solutions or just automating simple tasks, there is hardly anything he hasn't done with Bash!

> *I would like to thank my girlfriend, Sanne, for all the help and support she has given me throughout the years. She has had to endure the late nights studying, me fixing stuff (which I had inevitably broken only hours earlier), and my endless storytelling about all those exciting new technologies. Thanks for the enormous amount of patience and love. I could not have done it without you!*

About the reviewer

Heathe Kyle Yeakley holds degrees in technical communications and network management. He began his IT career in 1999 doing entry-level help desk support. In 2003, he began his first enterprise data center job performing tape backup and recovery for the United States Federal Aviation Administration. He worked in the aerospace sector for several years, during which time he worked on a wide range of products, including HP Tru64 Unix, Red Hat Enterprise Linux, Solaris 10, Legato Networker, Symantec NetBackup, HP and NetApp storage arrays, Spectra Logic and ADIC tape libraries, VMware, and HP Blade servers.

He currently works for Agio, where he and his coworkers deliver managed IT services to some of the world's most prestigious companies.

Packt is searching for authors like you

If you're interested in becoming an author for Packt, please visit `authors.packtpub.com` and apply today. We have worked with thousands of developers and tech professionals, just like you, to help them share their insight with the global tech community. You can make a general application, apply for a specific hot topic that we are recruiting an author for, or submit your own idea.

Table of Contents

Preface

Shell scripts allow us to program commands in chains and have the system execute them as a scripted event, just like batch files. This book will start with an overview of Linux and Bash shell scripting, and then quickly deep dive into helping you set up your local environment, before introducing you to tools that are used to write shell scripts. The next set of chapters will focus on helping you understand Linux under the hood and what Bash provides the user. Soon, you will have embarked on your journey along the command line. You will now begin writing actual scripts instead of commands, and will be introduced to practical applications for scripts. The final set of chapters will deep dive into the more advanced topics in shell scripting. These advanced topics will take you from simple scripts to reusable, valuable programs that exist in the real world. The final chapter will leave you with some handy tips and tricks and, as regards the most frequently used commands, a cheat sheet containing the most interesting flags and options will also be provided.

After completing this book, you should feel confident about starting your own shell scripting projects, no matter how simple or complex the task previously seemed. We aim to teach you *how* to script and *what* to consider, to complement the clear-cut patterns that you can use in your daily scripting challenges.

Who this book is for

This book targets new and existing Linux system administrators, as well as Windows system administrators or developers who are interested in automating administrative tasks. No prior shell scripting experience is required, but if you do possess some experience, this book will quickly turn you into a pro. Readers should have a (very) basic understanding of the command line.

What this book covers

Chapter 1, *Introduction*, primes you for the remainder of the book. Aided by some background in Linux and Bash, you should be better able to understand how and why shell scripting can provide clear benefits to you.

Chapter 2, *Setting Up Your Local Environment*, helps you to prepare your local machine for the examples and exercises throughout the rest of the book. You will be shown how to set up an Ubuntu 18.04 Linux virtual machine on your local machine, using VirtualBox. This virtual machine will be used to write, run, and debug commands and scripts in this book.

Chapter 3, *Choosing the Right Tools*, introduces you to the tools that will be used to write shell scripts. Two different kinds of tools will be described: IDE editors (Atom, Notepad++), and terminal-based editors (vim and nano). You will be encouraged to initially write scripts in an IDE, and troubleshoot scripts in a terminal-based editor, to most resemble real-world use.

Chapter 4, *The Linux Filesystem*, coves how the Linux filesystem is organized by exploring the virtual machine created in the previous chapters. You will achieve this by performing your first command-line actions, such as cd, pwd, and ls. Context regarding the different structures will be provided so that you can use this information when writing scripts. And, most importantly, the concept of everything is a file will be explained.

Chapter 5, *Understanding the Linux Permissions Scheme*, gets you acquainted with permissions under Linux, once again by exploring the virtual machine. Commands such as sudo, chmod, and chown will be used to interactively learn about file and directory privileges. The skills acquired in this chapter will be heavily used in shell scripting, so it is imperative that you gain exposure to both the successful execution of commands as well as failure messages.

Chapter 6, *File Manipulation*, introduces you to the most relevant file manipulation commands, including the most commonly used flags and modifiers for those commands. This will be achieved by means of commands inside the virtual machine.

Chapter 7, *Hello World!*, educates you in terms of thinking ahead and developing good habits when it comes to writing scripts. You will write your first actual shell script during this chapter.

Chapter 8, *Variables and User Input*, introduces you to variables and user input. You will see how parameters are used by Bash, and where the differences lie between parameters and arguments. User input will be handled and used to produce new functions in your scripts. Finally, the difference between interactive and non-interactive scripts will be clarified and discussed.

Chapter 9, *Error Checking and Handling*, gets you familiar with (user) input, and error checking and handling. Introducing user input into a script is bound to result in more errors, unless the script specifically deals with the possibility of users submitting incorrect or unexpected input. You will learn how to best deal with this.

Chapter 10, *Regular Expressions*, gets you familiar with regular expressions, which are often used in shell scripting. The most common patterns and uses for these regular expressions will be presented. Basic usage of sed will be covered in this chapter, complementing regular expression explanations.

Chapter 11, *Conditional Testing and Scripting Loops*, discusses the different kind of loops and the relevant control structures that are used in shell scripting with Bash.

Chapter 12, *Using Pipes and Redirection in Scripts*, introduces you to redirection on Linux. This chapter will start with the basic input/output redirection, before continuing to stream redirection and pipes.

Chapter 13, *Functions*, introduces you to functions. Functions will be presented as blocks of code that are grouped together in such a way that they can be reused, often with different arguments, to produce a slightly different end result. You will learn to understand the benefit to reusing code, and planning scripts accordingly.

Chapter 14, *Scheduling and Logging*, teaches you how to schedule scripts and how to make sure these scheduled scripts perform the task they were intended for, by using the crontab and the at command, coupled with proper logging.

Chapter 15, *Parsing Bash Script Arguments with getopts,* helps you to improve your scripts by adding flags instead of positional parameters, thereby making the scripts much easier to use.

Chapter 16, *Bash Parameter Substitution and Expansion*, shows how previous patterns used in earlier scripts can be optimized by means of parameter expansion, substitution, and variable manipulation.

Chapter 17, *Tips and Tricks with Cheat Sheet*, provides you with some handy tips and tricks that are not necessarily used in Bash scripts, but that are very convenient when working on the terminal. For the most frequently used commands, a cheat sheet containing the most interesting flags and options will be provided so that you can use this chapter as reference while scripting.

To get the most out of this book

You will require an Ubuntu 18.04 Linux virtual machine to follow along with the book. We will guide you through setting this up during in the second chapter. You will only truly learn shell scripting if you **follow along with all code examples**. The entire book has been written with this in mind, so be sure to follow this advice!

Download the example code files

You can download the example code files for this book from your account at www.packtpub.com. If you purchased this book elsewhere, you can visit www.packtpub.com/support and register to have the files emailed directly to you.

You can download the code files by following these steps:

1. Log in or register at www.packtpub.com.
2. Select the **SUPPORT** tab.
3. Click on **Code Downloads & Errata**.
4. Enter the name of the book in the **Search** box and follow the onscreen instructions.

Once the file is downloaded, please make sure that you unzip or extract the folder using the latest version of:

- WinRAR/7-Zip for Windows
- Zipeg/iZip/UnRarX for Mac
- 7-Zip/PeaZip for Linux

The code bundle for the book is also hosted on GitHub at https://github.com/PacktPublishing/Learn-Linux-Shell-Scripting-Fundamentals-of-Bash-4.4. In case there's an update to the code, it will be updated on the existing GitHub repository.

We also have other code bundles from our rich catalog of books and videos available at https://github.com/PacktPublishing/. Check them out!

Download the color images

We also provide a PDF file that has color images of the screenshots/diagrams used in this book. You can download it here: https://www.packtpub.com/sites/default/files/downloads/9781788995597_ColorImages.pdf.

Conventions used

There are a number of text conventions used throughout this book.

CodeInText: Indicates code words in text, database table names, folder names, filenames, file extensions, pathnames, dummy URLs, user input, and Twitter handles. Here is an example: "Let's try to copy the /tmp/ directory into our home directory."

A block of code is set as follows:

```
#!/bin/bash

echo "Hello World!"
```

When we wish to draw your attention to a particular part of a code block, the relevant lines or items are set in bold:

```
reader@ubuntu:~/scripts/chapter_10$ grep 'use' grep-file.txt
We can use this regular file for testing grep.
but in the USA they use color (and realize)!
```

Any command-line input or output is written as follows:

```
reader@ubuntu:~/scripts/chapter_10$ grep 'e.e' character-class.txt
eee
e2e
e e
```

Bold: Indicates a new term, an important word, or words that you see on screen. For example, words in menus or dialog boxes appear in the text like this. Here is an example: "Click the **Install** button and watch the installation."

Warnings or important notes appear like this.

Tips and tricks appear like this.

Get in touch

Feedback from our readers is always welcome.

General feedback: Email `feedback@packtpub.com` and mention the book title in the subject of your message. If you have questions about any aspect of this book, please email us at `questions@packtpub.com`.

Errata: Although we have taken every care to ensure the accuracy of our content, mistakes do happen. If you have found a mistake in this book, we would be grateful if you would report this to us. Please visit `www.packtpub.com/submit-errata`, selecting your book, clicking on the Errata Submission Form link, and entering the details.

Piracy: If you come across any illegal copies of our works in any form on the internet, we would be grateful if you would provide us with the location address or website name. Please contact us at `copyright@packtpub.com` with a link to the material.

If you are interested in becoming an author: If there is a topic that you have expertise in, and you are interested in either writing or contributing to a book, please visit authors.packtpub.com.

Reviews

Please leave a review. Once you have read and used this book, why not leave a review on the site that you purchased it from? Potential readers can then see and use your unbiased opinion to make purchase decisions, we at Packt can understand what you think about our products, and our authors can see your feedback on their book. Thank you!

For more information about Packt, please visit packtpub.com.

Disclaimer

The information within this book is intended to be used only in an ethical manner. Do not use any information from the book if you do not have written permission from the owner of the equipment. If you perform illegal actions, you are likely to be arrested and prosecuted to the full extent of the law. Packt Publishing does not take any responsibility if you misuse any of the information contained within the book. The information herein must only be used while testing environments with proper written authorizations from appropriate persons responsible.

1
Introduction

Before we start writing shell scripts, we need to have some context about our two most relevant components: **Linux** and **Bash**. We'll give an explanation of Linux and Bash, look into the history behind the two technologies, and discuss the current state of both.

The following topics will be covered in this chapter:

- What is Linux?
- What is Bash?

What is Linux?

Linux is a generic term that refers to different open source operating systems that are based on the Linux kernel. The Linux kernel was originally created by Linus Torvalds in 1991, and open sourced in 1996. A kernel is a piece of software that is designed to act as an intermediate layer between low-level hardware (such as the processor, memory, and input/output devices) and high-level software, such as an operating system. Apart from the Linux kernel, most Linux operating systems rely heavily on GNU project utilities; for example, the Bash shell is a GNU program. Because of this, Linux operating systems are referred to by some as GNU/Linux. The GNU project, where GNU stands for *GNU's Not Unix!* (a recursive acronym), is a collection of free software, a lot of which is found in most Linux distributions. This collection includes many tools, but also an alternative kernel called GNU HURD (which is not as widespread as the Linux kernel).

Why do we need a kernel? Since a kernel sits between hardware and the operating system, it provides an abstraction for interacting with hardware. This is why the Linux ecosystem has grown so large: the kernel can be used freely, and it handles a lot of low-level operations on many types of hardware. Creators of an operating system can therefore spend their time making an easy-to-use, beautiful experience for their users, instead of having to worry about how the users' pictures are going to be written to the physical disk(s) attached to the system.

The Linux kernel is so-called **Unix-like** software. As you might suspect, this implies that it is similar to the original Unix kernel, which was created between 1971 and 1973 at Bell Labs, by Ken Thompson and Dennis Ritchie. However, the Linux kernel is only *based on* Unix principles and does not *share code* with Unix systems. Famous Unix systems include the BSDs (FreeBSD, OpenBSD, and so on) and macOS.

Linux operating systems are broadly used for one of two purposes: as a desktop or as a server. As a desktop, Linux can serve as a replacement for the more commonly used Microsoft Windows or macOS. However, most Linux usage is accounted for the server landscape. At the time of writing, it is estimated that around 70% of all servers on the internet use a Unix or Unix-like operating system. The next time you're browsing the news, reading your mail, or are scrolling through your favorite social media website, remember that there's a big chance the pages you are being shown have been processed by one or more Linux servers.

There are many distributions, or flavors, of Linux. Most Linux operating systems fall within distribution families. A distribution family is based on a common ancestor, and often use the same package management tools. One of the more well-known Linux distributions, **Ubuntu**, is based on the **Debian** distribution family. Another prominent Linux distribution, **Fedora**, is based on the **Red Hat** family. Other notable distribution families include **SUSE**, **Gentoo**, and **Arch**.

Not many people realize how many devices run the Linux kernel. For example, the most common smartphone operating system in use today, Android (with a market share of around 85%), uses a modified version of the Linux kernel. The same goes for many smart TVs, routers, modems, and various other (embedded) devices. If we were to include Unix and other Unix-like software, we can safely say that most of the devices in the world run on these kernels!

What is Bash?

The most commonly used shell in Linux systems is the **B**ourne-**a**gain **sh**ell, or Bash. The Bash shell is based on the **Bourne shell**, known as **sh**. But what is a shell?

A shell is, in essence, a user interface. Most often, it is used to refer to a text-based interface, also called a **command-line interface** (**CLI**). However, it is called a *shell* because it can be seen as a *shell around the kernel*; this means that it applies not just to CLIs, but just as well to **graphical user interfaces** (**GUIs**). When we refer to a shell in this book, we are talking about a CLI, and unless stating differently, we're talking about the Bash shell.

The purpose of a shell, both CLI and GUI, is to allow the user to interact with the system. After all, a system that does not offer interaction would be hard to justify, not too mention hard to use! Interaction in this context means many things: typing on your keyboard will make letters appear on your screen, moving your mouse will change the location of the cursor on screen, giving the command to delete a file (either with a CLI or GUI) will remove the bytes from the disk, and so on.

In the earliest days of Unix and computers, no GUIs were available, so all work was performed via a CLI. To connect to the shell on a running machine, a **video terminal** was used: often this would be a very simple monitor combined with a keyboard, which was connected with, for example, a RS-232 serial cable. Commands entered on this video terminal were processed by the shell running on the Unix machine.

Luckily for us, things have changed quite a bit since the first computers. Today, we no longer use dedicated hardware to connect to shells. A piece of software running in a GUI, a **terminal emulator**, is used for interaction with the shell. Lets take a quick look at how connecting to a Bash shell with a terminal emulator can look:

```
[root@caladan ~]# ssh reader@localhost -p 10022
reader@localhost's password:
Welcome to Ubuntu 18.04 LTS (GNU/Linux 4.15.0-23-generic x86_64)

 * Documentation:  https://help.ubuntu.com
 * Management:     https://landscape.canonical.com
 * Support:        https://ubuntu.com/advantage

  System information as of Fri Jun 22 14:20:02 UTC 2018

  System load:   0.13            Processes:           89
  Usage of /:    42.0% of 9.78GB Users logged in:     1
  Memory usage:  12%             IP address for enp0s3: 10.0.2.15
  Swap usage:    0%


0 packages can be updated.
0 updates are security updates.


Last login: Fri Jun 22 14:19:29 2018 from 10.0.2.2
reader@ubuntu:~$ █
```

In the preceding screenshot, we're connected to a Linux virtual machine (we'll be setting this up in the next chapter), using a terminal emulator (GNOME Terminal) via the **Secure Shell (SSH)** protocol. A few interesting things to note:

- We're on a CLI interface; we do not have access to, nor do we need, a mouse
- We're connected to an Ubuntu machine, but we're running this within another operating system (Arch Linux, in this case)
- We're presented with a welcome message by Ubuntu 18.04, showing some general information about the system

Besides using the Bash shell for direct system interaction, it provides another important functionality: the ability to execute multiple commands sequentially, with or without user interaction, tailored to a specific goal. This might sound complicated, but it's actually pretty simple: we're talking about **Bash scripts**, the subject of this book!

Summary

In this chapter, you've read about the GNU/Linux operating systems and the Linux kernel, what a kernel really is, and how big an impact Linux distributions have on daily life. You've also learned what a shell is, and that the most common Linux shell, Bash, can be both used to interact with a Linux system, and is also utilized to write shell scripts.

In the next chapter, we'll set up a local environment which we will use throughout the rest of the book, in both the examples and exercises.

Setting Up Your Local Environment

2

In the previous chapter, we ventured into some context for the wonderful world of Linux and Bash. Since this is a practical, exercise-driven book, we're going to use this chapter to set up a machine where you can follow along with the examples and perform the exercises at the end of each chapter. This can either be a virtual machine or a physical installation; that is up to you. We will discuss this in the first part of this chapter, before continuing with the installation of VirtualBox and, finally, creating an Ubuntu virtual machine.

The following command will be introduced in this chapter: `ssh` and `exit`.

The following topics will be covered in this chapter:

- Choosing between a virtual machine and a physical installation
- Setting up VirtualBox
- Creating an Ubuntu virtual machine

Technical requirements

To complete the exercises in this chapter (and the following chapters), you will need either a PC or laptop with at least 2 GHz of CPU power, 10 GB of hard disk space, and about 1 GB of RAM to spare. Pretty much all hardware created in the last 5 years should suffice.

Choosing between a virtual machine and a physical installation

A virtual machine is an emulation of a physical machine. This means it runs *inside* a physical machine, as opposed to *directly on the hardware*. A physical machine has direct access to all hardware, such as the CPU, the RAM, and other devices such as the mouse, the keyboard, and the monitor. It is, however, impossible to share the CPU or the RAM between multiple physical machines. Virtual machines do not directly get access to hardware, but through an emulation layer, which means resources can be shared between multiple virtual machines.

Because we're discussing Bash shell scripting in general, in theory it does not matter what kind of an installation is performed. As long as that installation runs a compatible Linux operating system with Bash 4.4 or later, all exercises should work. There are, however, many advantages to using a virtual machine over a physical installation:

- There is no need to remove your current preferred operating system, or set up a complicated dual-boot configuration
- Virtual machines can be snapshotted, which allows recovery from critical failures
- You are able to run (many) different operating systems on a single machine

Unfortunately, there are also drawbacks associated with virtual machine use:

- Because you're running a virtual operating system within an already running operating system, there is some overhead from the virtualization (in comparison to running a bare-metal installation)
- Since you're running multiple operating systems at the same time, you will need more resources than with a bare-metal installation

In our opinion, modern computers are fast enough to make the drawbacks almost trivial, while the advantages provided by running Linux in a virtual machine are very helpful. Because of this, we will only be explaining a virtual machine setup in the rest of this chapter. If you feel confident enough to run Linux as a physical installation (or perhaps you already have Linux running somewhere!), feel free to explore the rest of the book with that machine.

You might have a Raspberry Pi or another single-board computer running Linux in your house from a previous project. While these machines are indeed running a Linux distribution (Raspbian), they are probably running it on a different architecture: ARM instead of x86. Because this can cause unexpected results, we recommend only using x86 devices for this book.

If you want to be sure all examples and exercises work as seen in this book, run an Ubuntu 18.04 LTS virtual machine in VirtualBox with the recommended specifications of 1 CPU, 1 GB RAM, and a 10 GB hard disk: this setup is described in the rest of this chapter. Even if many other types of deployment should work, you would not want to be banging your head against the wall for hours when an exercise is not working, before discovering it was caused by your setup.

Setting up VirtualBox

To use virtual machines, we need software called a **hypervisor**. A hypervisor manages resources between the host machine and the virtual machines, provides access to disks, and has an interface to manage it all. There are two different types of hypervisors: type-1 and type-2. Type-1 hypervisors are the so-called bare-metal hypervisors. These are installed instead of a regular operating system such as Linux, macOS, or Windows, directly on the hardware. These types of hypervisors are used for corporate servers, cloud services, and so on. For this book, we will use a type-2 hypervisor (also called hosted hypervisors): these are installed within another operating system, as a piece of software not much different than, for example, a browser.

There are many type-2 hypervisors. The most popular choices at the time of writing are VirtualBox, VMware workstation player, or OS-specific variants such as QEMU/KVM on Linux, Parallels Desktop on macOS, and Hyper-V on Windows. Because we are going to use a virtual machine throughout this book, we do not assume anything about the host machine: you should work comfortably with whatever operating system you prefer. Because of this, we've chosen to use VirtualBox as our hypervisor, since it runs on Linux, macOS, and Windows (and even others!). Furthermore, VirtualBox is free and open source software, which means you can just download and use it.

Presently, VirtualBox is owned by Oracle. You can download the installer for VirtualBox from `https://www.virtualbox.org/`. Installation should not be hard; follow the instructions by the installer.

After installing a type-2 hypervisor such as VirtualBox, be sure to restart your computer. Hypervisors often need some kernel modules loaded, which is easiest to achieve by rebooting.

Creating an Ubuntu virtual machine

In this book, we're scripting with Bash, which means we do not need a GUI for our Linux installation. We have chosen to use **Ubuntu Server 18.04 LTS** as the virtual machine operating system, for a number of reasons:

- Ubuntu is considered a beginner-friendly Linux distribution
- The 18.04 is a **Long-Term Support** (**LTS**) release, which means it will receive updates until April 2023
- Because an Ubuntu server offers a CLI-only installation, it is easy on system resources and representative of real-life servers

At the time of writing, Ubuntu is maintained by Canonical. You can download the ISO image from `https://www.ubuntu.com/download/server`. Download the file now, and remember where you save this file, since you'll need it soon.

Should the preceding download link no longer work, you can go to your favorite search engine and search for `Ubuntu Server 18.04 ISO download`. You should find a reference to the Ubuntu archives, which will have the required ISO.

Creating the virtual machine in VirtualBox

First, we will start with creating the virtual machine to host our Ubuntu installation:

1. Open VirtualBox and choose **Machine** | **New** in the menu toolbar.
2. For reference, we have circled the **Machine** entry in the menu toolbar given in the following screenshot. Choose a name for the virtual machine (this can be a different name than the server name, but we like to keep it the same for simplicity), set the **Type** to **Linux**, and **Version** to **Ubuntu (64-bit)**. Click **Next**:

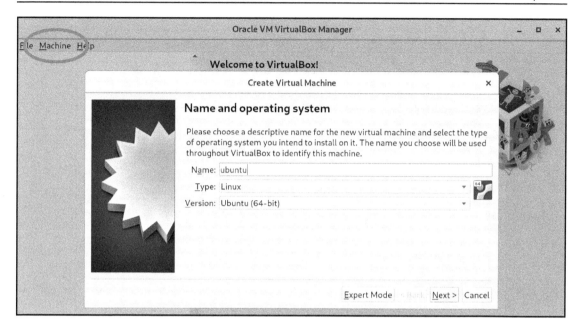

3. On this screen, we determine memory settings. For most servers, 1024 MB of RAM is a great start (and is recommended by VirtualBox for virtual machines as well). If you have beefy hardware, this can be set to 2048 MB, but 1024 MB should be fine. Make your selection and press **Next**:

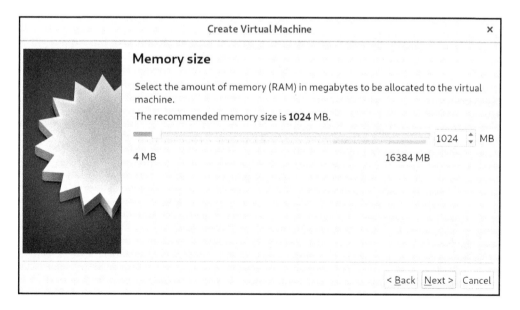

4. Once again, the recommended values by VirtualBox are perfect for our needs. Press **Create** to start the creation of the virtual hard disk:

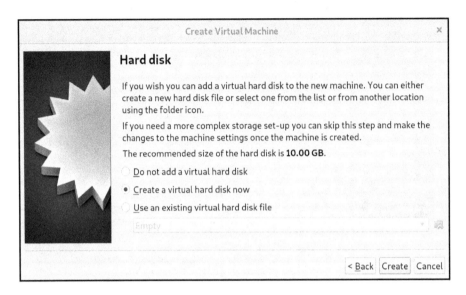

5. Virtual hard disks can be many different types. VirtualBox defaults to its own format, **VDI**, as opposed to **VMDK**, which is the format used by VMware (another popular virtualization provider). The last option is **VHD (Virtual Hard Disk)**, which is a more generic format usable by multiple virtualization providers. Since we'll be using VirtualBox exclusively in this book, keep the selection on **VDI (VirtualBox Disk Image)** and press **Next**:

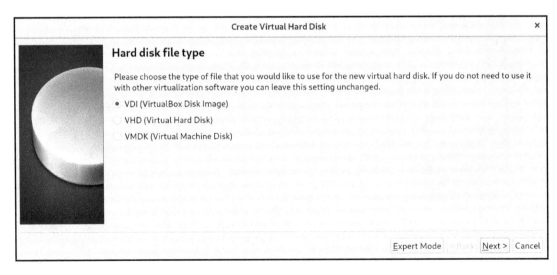

6. We have two options on this screen: we can allocate the full virtual hard disk on the physical hard disk right away, or we can use dynamic allocation, which does not reserve the full size of the virtual disk, but only what is used.

The difference between these options is often most relevant in situations where many virtual machines are running on a single host. Creating a total of disks larger than what is physically available, but assuming not all disks will be fully used, allows us to place more virtual machines on a single machine. This is called overprovisioning, and will only work if not all disks are filled up (because we can *never* have more virtual disk space than we have physical disk space). For us, this distinction does not matter since we'll be running a single virtual machine; we keep the default of **Dynamically allocated** and go to the next screen:

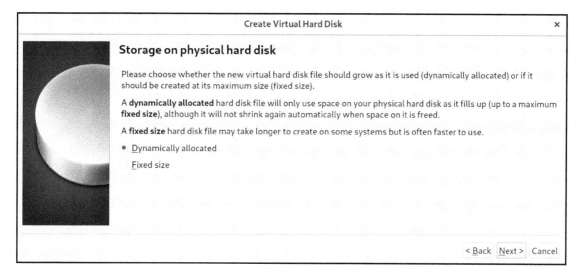

7. On this screen, we can do three things: name the virtual disk file, select the location, and specify the size. If you care about the location (it defaults to somewhere in your home/user directory), you can press the circled icon in the following screenshot. For the name, we like to keep it the same as the virtual machine name. Lastly, a size of 10 GB is sufficient for the exercises in this book. After you've set up the three values, press **Create**. Congratulations, you've just created your first virtual machine, as demonstrated in following screenshot:

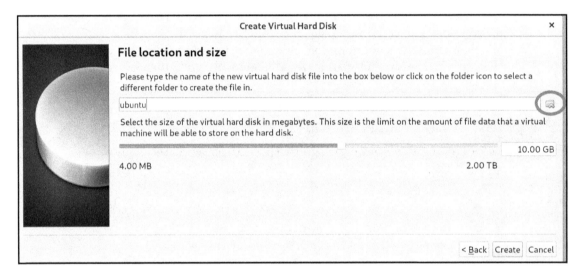

8. However, before we can start the installation of Ubuntu on our virtual machine, we need to do two more things: point the virtual machine to the installation ISO, and set up the networking. Select the newly created virtual machine and click **Settings**. Navigate to the **Storage** section:

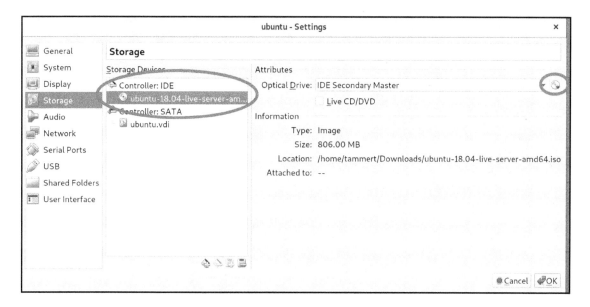

You should see a disk icon with the word **Empty** (in the location circled on the left in the preceding screenshot). Select it and mount an ISO file by clicking the select disk icon (circled on the right), choose virtual optical disk file, and then select the Ubuntu ISO that you downloaded earlier. If you do this correctly, your screen should resemble the preceding screenshot: you no longer see the word **Empty** next to the disk icon and the **Information** section should be filled in.

9. Once you have verified this, go to the **Network** section.

10. The configuration should default to the **NAT** type. If not, set it to **NAT** now. **NAT** stands for **Network Address Translation**. In this mode, the host machine acts as a router for the virtual machines. Finally, we're going to set up some port forwarding so we can use SSH tooling later on. Click on the **Port Forwarding** button:

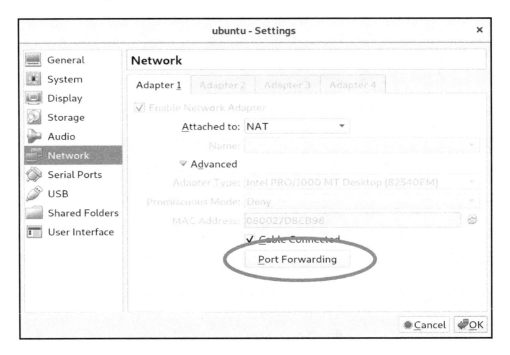

11. Set up the SSH rule just as we have done. This means that port 22 on the guest (which is the virtual machine) is exposed as port 2222 on the host (which is, surprise, the host machine). We've chosen port 2222 for two reasons: ports lower than 1024 require root/administrator permissions, which we might not have. Secondly, there is a chance an SSH process is already listening on the host machine, which would mean VirtualBox would not be able to use that port:

	Name	Protocol	Host IP	Host Port	Guest IP	Guest Port
SSH		TCP		2222		22

With this step, we've finished setting up the virtual machine!

Installing Ubuntu on the virtual machine

Now you can start your virtual machine from the VirtualBox main screen. Right click on the machine, select **Start** followed by **Normal Start**. If all goes well, a new window will pop up, showing you the virtual machine console. After a while, you should see the Ubuntu server installation screen in that window:

1. On the screen shown in the following screenshot, select your favorite language using the arrow keys (we're using **English**, so if you're not sure, English is a good choice) and press *Enter*:

2. Select the keyboard layout that you're using. If you're unsure, you can use the interactive **Identify keyboard** option to determine which layout is best for you. Once the proper layout is set, move the focus to **Done** and press *Enter*:

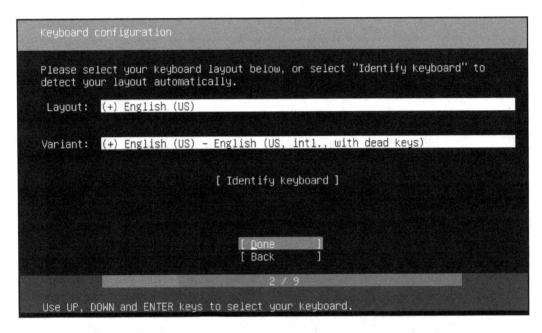

3. We now choose the type of installation. Because we're using the server ISO, we do not see any options related to the GUI. In the preceding screenshot, select **Install Ubuntu** (both other options use Canonical's **Metal-As-A-Server** (**MAAS**) cloud offering, which is not relevant for us) and press *Enter*:

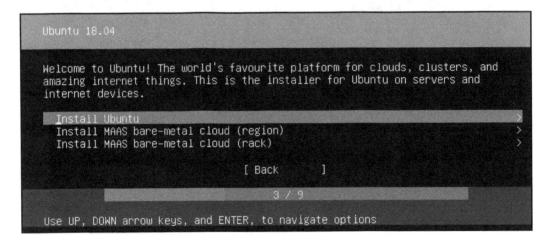

4. You will see the **Network connections** screen. The installer should default to using DHCP on the default network interface that was created with the virtual machine. Verify that an IP has been allocated to this interface, and press *Enter*:

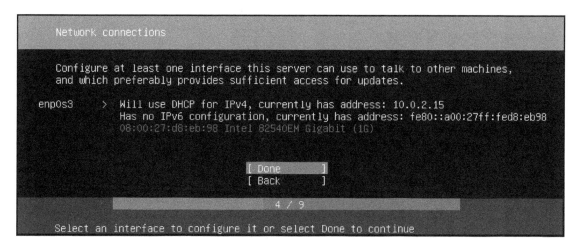

5. The **Configure proxy** screen is not relevant to us (unless you're running with a proxy setup, but there's a good chance you do not need our assistance with the installation in that case!). Leave the **Proxy address** blank and press *Enter*:

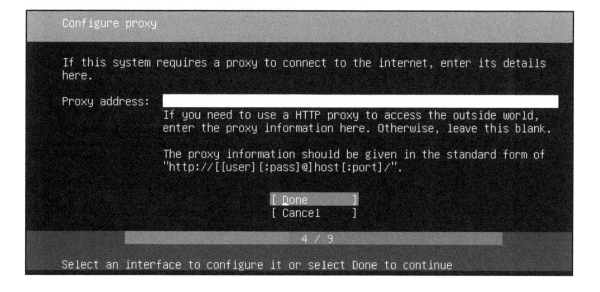

6. Sometimes it's helpful to manually partition your Linux disk to fit specific needs. In our case, the default value of **Use An Entire Disk** is a great fit, so press *Enter*:

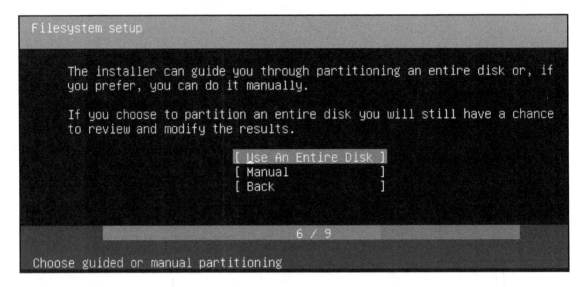

7. After having selected that we want to use an entire disk, we need to specify which disk to use. Since we only created one disk when we configured the virtual machine, select it and press *Enter*.
8. Now you will encounter a warning about performing a destructive action. Because we are using an entire (virtual!) disk, all information present on that disk will be erased. We created this disk when we created the virtual machine, so it does not contain any data. We can safely perform this action, so select **Continue** and press *Enter*:

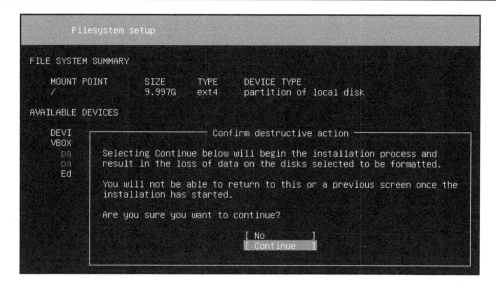

9. For the **Filesystem setup**, once again the default values are perfect for our needs. Verify that we have at least 10 GB of hard disk space (it might be a little less, like 9.997 GB in the following example: this is fine) and press *Enter*:

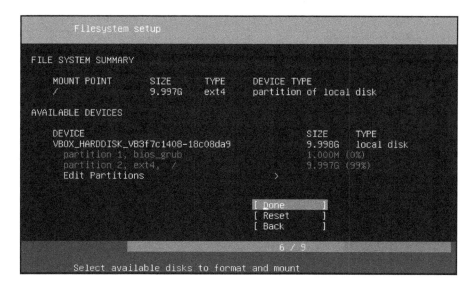

10. The Ubuntu server should now start installing to the virtual disk. In this step, we'll be setting the server name and creating an administrative user. We've chosen the server name `ubuntu`, the username `reader`, and the password `password`. Note that this is a *very weak* password that we will only use on this server for simplicity. This is acceptable because the server will only ever be accessible from our host machine. When configuring a server that accepts incoming traffic from the internet, never use a password as weak as this! Choose anything you like, as long as you can remember it. If you're unsure, we'd advise using the same values of `ubuntu`, `reader`, and `password`:

```
Profile setup

Enter the username and password (or ssh identity) you will use to log in to the
system.
                Your name:  Learn Linux Shell Scripting

        Your server's name:  ubuntu
                             The name it uses when it talks to other computers.

          Pick a username:  reader

        Choose a password:  ********

     Confirm your password:  ********

       Import SSH identity:  (+) No
                             You can import your SSH keys from Github or Launchpad.

          Import Username:

                             [ Done           ]
                                    8 / 9

Install complete
```

Now that you've chosen a server name and configured an administrative user, press *Enter* to finalize the installation.

11. Depending on how long it took to complete the previous screen and how fast the host machine is, Ubuntu will either still be installing or will have finished already. If you still see text moving around the screen, the installation is still running. Once the installation is completely finished, you will see the **Reboot Now** button appear. Press *Enter*:

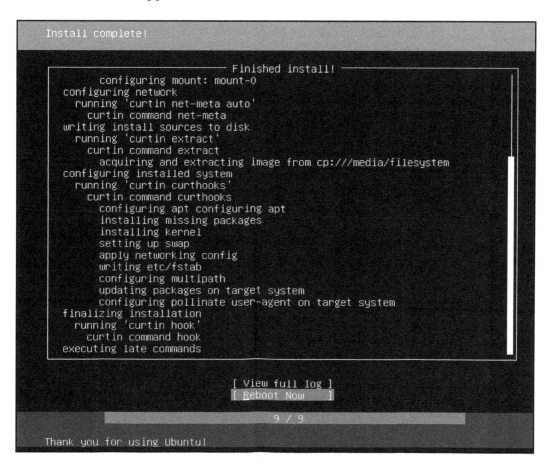

12. After a few seconds, a message stating `Please remove the installation medium, then press Enter` should appear. Follow the instructions and, if all goes well, you should be greeted with a terminal login prompt:

```
Ubuntu 18.04 LTS ubuntu tty1

ubuntu login: _
```

Normally, VirtualBox is intelligent enough to try a second boot from the hard disk instead of the ISO. If, after the previous steps, a reboot sends you back to the installation menu, power down the virtual machine from the VirtualBox main screen. Right-click on the machine, select **Close** followed by **Power Off**. After it's fully powered down, edit the machine and remove the ISO. This should force VirtualBox to boot from the disk, which contains your Ubuntu Server 18.04 LTS installation.

13. Now the moment of truth: try to log in with your created username and password. If successful, you should see a screen similar to the following:

```
Ubuntu 18.04 LTS ubuntu tty1

ubuntu login: reader
Password:
Welcome to Ubuntu 18.04 LTS (GNU/Linux 4.15.0-23-generic x86_64)

 * Documentation:  https://help.ubuntu.com
 * Management:     https://landscape.canonical.com
 * Support:        https://ubuntu.com/advantage

  System information as of Fri Jun 22 14:06:25 UTC 2018

  System load:  0.64              Processes:            85
  Usage of /:   39.7% of 9.78GB   Users logged in:      0
  Memory usage: 12%               IP address for enp0s3: 10.0.2.15
  Swap usage:   0%

90 packages can be updated.
43 updates are security updates.




The programs included with the Ubuntu system are free software;
the exact distribution terms for each program are described in the
individual files in /usr/share/doc/*/copyright.

Ubuntu comes with ABSOLUTELY NO WARRANTY, to the extent permitted by
applicable law.

To run a command as administrator (user "root"), use "sudo <command>".
See "man sudo_root" for details.

reader@ubuntu:~$ _
```

Give yourself a pat on the back: you have just created a virtual machine, installed Ubuntu Server 18.04 LTS, and logged in via the Terminal console. Well done! To exit, type `exit` or `logout` and press *Enter*.

Accessing the virtual machine via SSH

We have successfully connected to the Terminal console provided to us by VirtualBox. However, this Terminal connection is really basic: for example, we can't scroll up, we can't paste copied text, and we do not have colored syntax highlighting. Fortunately for us, we have a nice alternative: the **Secure Shell** (**SSH**) protocol. SSH is used to connect to the running shell on the virtual machine. Normally, this would be done over the network: this is how enterprises maintain their Linux servers. In our setup, we can actually use SSH within our host machine, using the power forwarding we set up earlier.

If you followed the installation guide, port 2222 on the host machine should be redirected to port 22 on the virtual machine, the port where the SSH process is running. From a Linux or macOS host machine, we can connect using the following command (substitute the username or port number if necessary):

```
$ ssh reader@localhost -p 2222
```

However, there is a good chance you're running Windows. In that case, you will probably not have access to a native SSH client application within Command Prompt. Luckily, there are many good (and free!) SSH clients. The simplest and most well-known client is **PuTTY**. PuTTY was created in 1999 and, while it's definitely a very stable client, its age is starting to show. We would recommend some newer SSH client software, such as **MobaXterm**. This provides you with more session management, a better GUI, and even a local Command Prompt!

Whichever software you decide on, be sure to use the following values (again, change the port or username if you deviated from the installation guide):

- **Host Name**: localhost
- **Port**: 2222
- **User Name**: reader

 If you're using SSH to connect to your virtual machine, you can start it **headless**. When you do this, VirtualBox will not create a new window with the Terminal console for you, but instead runs the virtual machine in the background where you can still connect via SSH (just like what happens on actual Linux servers). This option, **Headless Start**, is found right below the earlier **Normal Start**, when right clicking on the machine and selecting **Start.**

Summary

In this chapter, we have started preparing our local machine for the rest of the book. We now know about the differences between virtual and physical machines, and why we prefer to use a virtual machine for the remainder of this book. We've learned about the two different types of hypervisors. We have installed and configured VirtualBox with a virtual machine, on which we have installed the Ubuntu 18.04 operating system. Finally, we have connected to our running virtual machine using SSH instead of the VirtualBox terminal, which affords better usability and options.

The following command was introduced in this chapter: `ssh` and `exit`.

In the next chapter, we will finish setting up our local machine by looking at some different tools we can use that will help us with bash scripting, both on the GUI and on the virtual machine CLI.

Questions

1. What are some of the reasons running a virtual machine would be preferable to a bare-metal installation?
2. What are some of the downsides of running a virtual machine as opposed to a bare-metal installation?
3. What is the difference between a type-1 and type-2 hypervisor?
4. In which two ways can we start a virtual machine on VirtualBox?
5. What makes an Ubuntu LTS version special?
6. What should we do if, after the Ubuntu installation, the virtual machine boots to the Ubuntu installation screens again?
7. What should we do if we accidentally reboot during installation, and we never end up at the Ubuntu installation (but instead see an error)?
8. Why did we set up NAT forwarding for the virtual machine?

Further reading

The following resources might be interesting if you'd like to go deeper into the subjects of this chapter:

- *Getting Started with Oracle VM VirtualBox* by Pradyumna Dash, Packt: `https://www.packtpub.com/virtualization-and-cloud/getting-started-oracle-vm-virtualbox`
- *Mastering Ubuntu Server – Second Edition* by Jay LaCroix, Packt: `https://www.packtpub.com/networking-and-servers/mastering-ubuntu-server-second-edition`

3
Choosing the Right Tools

This chapter will introduce some tools that will help us when we're writing Bash scripts. We will focus on two types of tools: GUI-based editors (**Atom** and **Notepad++**) and Terminal-based editors (**Vim** and **nano**). We will describe the tools and how to use them, their strengths and weaknesses, and how to use both GUI- and Terminal-based editors together for the best results.

The following commands will be introduced in this chapter: `vim`, `nano`, and `ls`.

The following topics will be covered in this chapter:

- Using graphical editors for shell scripting
- Using command-line editors for shell scripting
- Combining graphical editors with command-line editors when writing shell scripts

Technical requirements

You will need the virtual machine we created in the previous chapter when using Vim or nano. If you want to use Notepad++, you will need a Windows host machine. For Atom, the host machine can run either Linux, macOS, or Windows.

Using graphical editors for shell scripting

Tooling has come a long way since the first Unix and Unix-like distributions. In the earliest days, writing shell scripts was significantly harder than today: the shells were less powerful, text editors were command-line only and things such as syntax highlighting and autocomplete were non-existent. Today, we have very powerful GUI editors that will help us in our scripting adventures. Why would we want to wait until we run a script to find an error, when a GUI editor could have already shown us the error in advance? Today, using an advanced editor for shell scripting is almost a necessity that we wouldn't want to live without.

We'll describe two text editors in the coming pages: Atom and Notepad++. Both are GUI-based, which we can use for efficient shell scripting. If you have a preference for either already, pick that one. If you're unsure, we would recommend using Atom.

Atom

The first graphical editor we will consider is Atom, made by GitHub. It's described as *A hackable text editor for the 21st Century*. Hackable, in this sense, means that while the default installation of Atom is as complete as any text editor, this application really shines because it is very configurable and extensible. Anything that has not been integrated by GitHub can be written as an extension package. By using these extensions, you can make your Atom installation fully your own; if you do not like something, change it. If it can't be changed out of the box, find a package that does it. And even if there's not a package that does what you're hoping, you still have the option to create your own package!

Another nice feature of Atom is the default integration with Git and GitHub. Git is currently the most popular version control system. Version control systems are used when writing code or scripts. They ensure that history of files is preserved, and make it possible for multiple, even many, contributors to work on the same files at the same time, without getting burdened down by conflict management. GitHub, as the name suggests, is currently the most prominent web-based Git provider for open source software.

The last great thing about Atom we want to mention is that, by default, it supports many scripting and programming languages. When we say *supports*, we mean that it can recognize file types by their extensions, and offer syntax highlighting (which makes for much easier scripting!). This functionality is provided through core packages, which work the same way as normal packages but are included from the start. For our purposes, the core package, **language-shellscript**, will help us in our shell scripting endeavors.

Atom installation and configuration

Let's go ahead and install Atom. As long as you're running Linux, macOS, or Windows, you can go to `https://atom.io/` and grab the installer. Run the installer and, if necessary, follow along with the prompts until Atom is installed. Now, start Atom and you'll be greeted by the welcome screen, which at the time of writing looks like the following:

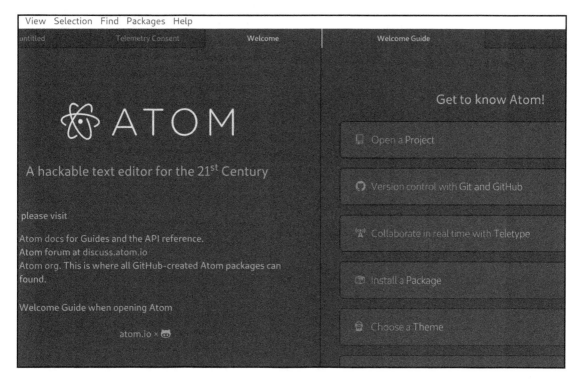

Be sure to look at all the screens Atom has to offer. When you feel like you've explored enough, let's add a package to Atom that will complement our shell scripting. If you have the **Welcome Guide** screen still open, select **Install a Package** from there. Otherwise, you can use the keyboard shortcut *Ctrl +* , to bring up the **Settings** screen. You will see an **Install** option there, which will take you to the **Install Packages** screen. Search for bash, and you should see the following package:

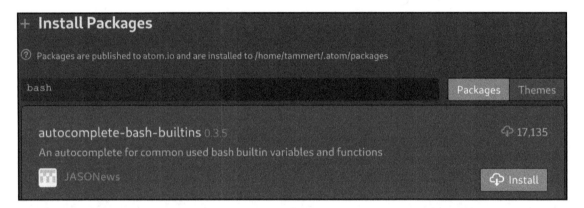

Click the **Install** button and watch the installation. You might be prompted to reboot Atom after the install; be sure to do so. If you're not prompted but see errors of any kind, a reboot of Atom is never a bad idea. After installing the package, you will now have autocomplete functionality when writing shell scripts. This means that you can start typing and Atom will try to predict what you want, in the following manner:

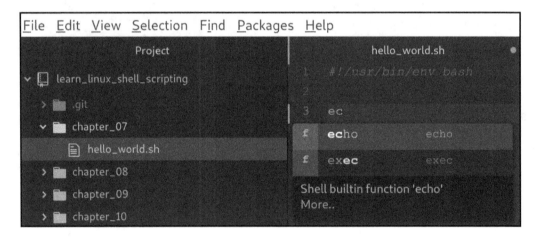

On the right-hand side, you can see we started typing the echo shell command, and after the first two letters, Atom presented us with two options that contain those two letters. Once it makes a suggestion, we can press *Enter* and the command is inserted fully. While it will not save much time in this instance, it can be great for two main reasons:

- If you're unsure what the command is called exactly, you might be able to find it with autocomplete.
- Once you start writing conditionals and loops (in the second part of this book), the autocomplete will span multiple lines, saving you from typing many words and remembering all the syntax.

Finally, let's look at how Atom looks when you've got a Git project open and are working on files:

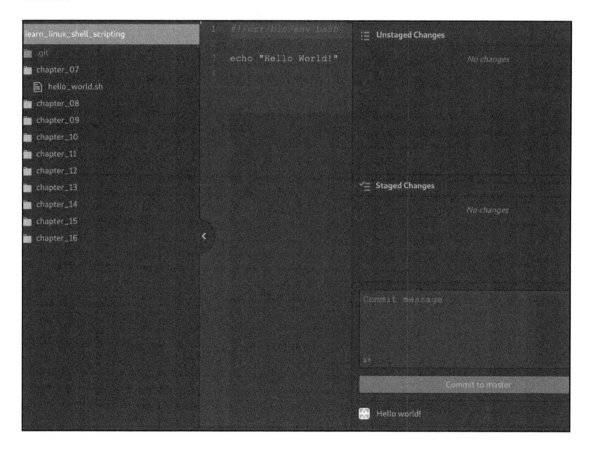

When working in Atom, the screen will mostly look like this. On the left-hand side, you'll see the **Tree View**, which you can toggle on/off by pressing *Ctrl + *. The Tree View contains all the files in your current project (which is the directory you've opened). All these files can be opened by double-clicking them, which causes them to appear in the middle: the **Editor View**. This is where you'll spend most of your time, working on the shell scripts. The Editor View will always be visible, even if there are currently no files open.

By default, there is one last view, the **Git View**, located on the right-hand side. This view can be toggled by pressing *Ctrl +Shift + 9*. The code for this book is hosted on GitHub, which you will download (or, as Git calls it, *clone*) once, without the need to edit it on the remote server. Because of this, the Git View is not needed in this book, but we mention it since you will probably use it for other projects.

Notepad++

Where Atom is closer to an **integrated development environment** (**IDE**) than a text editor, Notepad++ is pretty much what the name implies: good old Notepad with some added features. Some of these added features include being able to have multiple files open at the same time, syntax highlighting, and limited autocomplete. It was initially released in 2003 and only works on Windows.

Notepad++ is characterized by its simplicity. If you are familiar with any kind of Notepad software (who isn't?), Notepad++ should be instantly recognizable. While we recommend using Atom for this book, using a simple solution such as Notepad++ will definitely not hold you back. However, in a business environment, you would almost always create scripts in an already existing version-controlled repository, which is where the added features of Atom really shine.

If you would like to check out Notepad++, grab it from `https://notepad-plus-plus.org/download` and run the installer (remember, only if you're on Windows!). Keep the default options and run Notepad++ after the installation. You should be greeted by the following screen:

As you can see, when you open a file ending in `.sh`, you will see syntax highlighting. This is because the `.sh` extension is reserved for shell script files. This can help you immensely when writing scripts. The example of a missing quote messing up your script will become really apparent with color-based syntax highlighting, possibly saving you many minutes of troubleshooting.

Notepad++ has many other features that make it a great enhanced Notepad. You can use macros to perform scripted tasks, you can install plugins to extend functionality, and there are many more unique features that make Notepad++ an attractive option.

Using command-line editors

Being able to use command-line editors is a skill anyone working with Linux should learn sooner or later. For Linux installations with a GUI, this might be substituted with a GUI tool such as Atom or the distribution's built-in variant on Notepad. However, server installations will almost never have a GUI and you will have to rely on command-line text editors. While this might sound daunting, it's really not! To give you a small introduction to command-line editors, we'll go over two of the most popular applications that are present on most Linux distributions: **Vim** and **GNU nano**.

Vim

The first command-line text editor we will discuss is perhaps the most popular for Linux: **Vim**. Vim is derived from the term **Vi Improved**, as it is an updated clone of the Unix editor Vi. It was created and is still maintained by Bram Moolenaar, who first released Vim publicly in 1991. Vim (or, on *very* old systems, Vi) should be present on all Unix or Unix-like machines you will encounter.

Vim is considered a hard-to-learn tool. This is mainly caused by the fact it works very differently from text editors that most people are used to. However, once the initial learning curve is over, many agree that a lot of actions can be done in Vim much more quickly than in a *normal* text editor (such as Microsoft's Notepad++).

Let's jump in! Log in to your virtual machine:

```
$ ssh reader@localhost -p 2222
```

Once logged in, open Vim to an empty file:

```
$ vim
```

You should be greeted by something looking approximately like the following:

```
            VIM - Vi IMproved

            version 8.0.1453
          by Bram Moolenaar et al.
Modified by pkg-vim-maintainers@lists.alioth.debian.org
      Vim is open source and freely distributable

          Help poor children in Uganda!
    type  :help iccf<Enter>        for information

    type  :q<Enter>                to exit
    type  :help<Enter>  or  <F1>   for on-line help
    type  :help version8<Enter>    for version info



                                 0,0-1          All
```

Vim starts a new process that uses your entire Terminal (don't worry, everything will still be right where you left it once you exit Vim!). When you start up Vim, you will be placed in **normal** mode. Vim has a number of modes, of which normal and **insert** are the most interesting to explore. In normal mode, you can't just start typing like you would in Notepad or Word. Since Vim was designed to be used without a mouse, it needed a way to manipulate text as well. Where some applications decided on using modifiers for this (holding the *Shift* key in Notepad for example), Vim decided on modes. Let's first enter insert mode so we can start to type some text. Press the *I* key, and your screen should switch to insert mode:

```
File  Edit  View  Search  Terminal  Help
This is  insert  mode! We  can  now  enter  any text  we like,  since  our keyboard
actions  will  not  be  interpreted.☐
~
~
~
~
-- INSERT --                                            1,108          All
```

We've taken the liberty of typing some text while in insert mode. Be sure to do the same and when you're done, press *Esc* to go back to normal mode:

```
File  Edit  View  Search  Terminal  Help
This is  insert  mode! We  can  now  enter  any text  we like,  since  our keyboard
actions  will  not  be  interpreted▮
~
~
                                                        1,107          All
```

If you compare the two screenshots, you should a big difference: in the lower-left corner, the text -- INSERT -- is gone! When you're in a mode other than normal, that mode is clearly presented there. If you do not see anything, you can safely assume you're in normal mode. In normal mode, we can navigate using the arrow keys. We can also manipulate characters, words, and even (multiple) lines with a few key presses! For example, hit dd and notice that your whole line just got deleted. If you want to get it back, hit u for undo.

One challenge remains: exiting Vim. Normally, you might be tempted to use the *Esc* button to exit a program. If you're a little familiar with Linux, you might even know that a nice *Ctrl + C* will probably exit most programs as well. However, neither will work for Vim: *Esc* will just land you in normal mode, while *Ctrl + C* will not do anything. To quit Vim, make sure you are in normal mode and enter the following:

```
:q!
```

This exits your current document, without saving anything. If you want to *save and exit*, use the following:

```
:x filename.txt
```

This saves your current document as `filename.txt` and returns you to your Terminal. Note that normally you'll start Vim on an already existing file by using the following command:

```
$ vim filename.txt
```

In this case, you do not need to enter a filename when saving and exiting; using `:x` is enough in that case. `:x` is actually shorthand for `:wq`. `:w` is the *write* action, which you use to save a file, and `:q` is used to *quit*. Combined, they are used to *save and quit*. If you want to save your file at any other time during editing, you can just use `:w` to accomplish this.

Vim summary

Vim has many commands that power users appreciate. For now, remember that there are two important modes, normal and insert. You can go from normal to insert by pressing *I*, and you can go back to normal mode by pressing *Esc*. When in insert mode, Vim behaves just like Notepad or Word, but in normal mode you can perform easy text manipulation, for example deleting the whole line currently selected. If you want to exit Vim, go to normal mode and enter either `:q!` or `:x`, depending on whether you want to save the changes or not.

Don't be afraid to start using Vim. While it might seem daunting at first, once you get the hang of it you can really perform file-related tasks on servers much more quickly. If you want to get a head start, take 30 minutes of your time and work through **vimtutor**. This command-line tool will get you up to speed with the basic usage of Vim really quickly! To start, simply navigate to your virtual machine, type `vimtutor`, and press *Enter*.

.vimrc

The `.vimrc` file can be used to set some persistent options for Vim. Using this file, you can customize your Vim experience. There are many possibilities for customization: popular examples include setting the color scheme, converting between tabs and spaces, and setting search options.

To create a `.vimrc` file that will be used when starting Vim, do the following:

```
$ cd
$ vim .vimrc
```

The first command places you in your `home` directory (don't worry, this will be explained in greater detail later in this book). The second starts a Vim editor for the `.vimrc` file. Don't forget the dot in front, as this is how Linux deals with hidden files (again, more on this later on). We're using the following configuration in our `.vimrc` file:

```
set expandtab
set tabstop=2
syntax on
colo peachpuff
set ignorecase
set smartcase
set number
```

In order, the following things are achieved with this configuration:

- `set expandtab`: Converts tabs to spaces.
- `set tabstop=2`: Each tab is converted to two spaces.
- `syntax on`: Turns on syntax highlighting (by using different colors).
- `colorscheme peachpuff`: Uses the peachpuff color scheme.
- `set ignorecase`: Ignores case when searching.
- `set smartcase`: Doesn't ignore case when searching with one or more uppercase letters.
- `set number`: shows line numbers.

Vim cheat sheet

To get you started off with some great-to-know commands for Vim, we've incorporated a cheat sheet. After working through **vimtutor**, having this cheat sheet nearby almost guarantees you can properly use Vim!

Keystrokes are entered directly. Note that the keystrokes are case sensitive, so *a* is different from *A*. You can either hold *Shift* for the capital letters or use the *Caps Lock* key. However, the most practical approach would be to use *Shift*:

Keystroke	Effect
Esc	Exit insert mode, go back to command mode.
i	Enter insert mode before the current location of the cursor.
a	Enter insert mode after the current location of the cursor.
I	Enter insert mode at the beginning of the current line.
A	Enter insert mode at the end of the current line.

o	Enter insert mode with a new line below the current line.
O	Enter insert mode with a new line above the current line.
dd	Delete the current line.
u	Undo the changes made in the previous insert mode.
Ctrl + r	Redo an undo.
yy	'Yank' the current line (=copy).
p	Paste the last yanked line below the current line.
P	Paste the last yanked line above the current line.
H	Navigate to the beginning of the file.
M	Navigate to the middle of the file.
G	Navigate to the end of the file.
dH	Delete all lines until the beginning of the file (including the current line).
dG	Delete all lines until the end of the file (including the current line).

nano

GNU nano, commonly referred to as just nano, is another command-line editor that is present by default on most Linux installations. As the name might suggest, it is part of the GNU project, no different than many other parts that make up a Linux distribution (remember, Bash is also GNU project software). Nano was first released in 1999, with the intention of replacing the Pico text editor, a simple text editor created for Unix systems.

Nano is much more than a **What You See Is What You Get** (WYSIWYG) tool, definitely when compared to Vim. Similar to Notepad and Word, nano does not use different modes; it's always ready to start typing your documents or scripts.

On your virtual machine, open a nano editor screen:

```
$ nano
```

A screen similar to the following should come up:

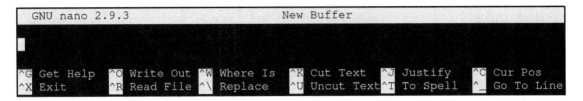

Feel free to start typing something. It should look something like the following:

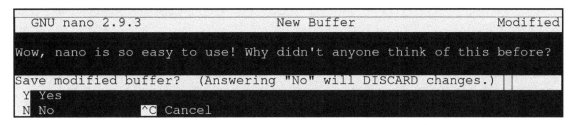

As you can see, the bottom of the screen is reserved for presenting what nano calls **control keys**. While it might not be obvious at first, the ^ is shorthand for *Ctrl*. If you want to exit, you hold down *Ctrl* and press *X*:

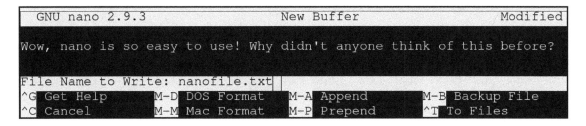

You will be prompted whether you'd like to exit with or without saving your file. In this case, we press *Y* for Yes. If we started nano with a filename, the save and exit would be completed right away, but because we started nano without a filename, another choice will be presented to us:

```
  GNU nano 2.9.3                    New Buffer                    Modified
Wow, nano is so easy to use! Why didn't anyone think of this before?



File Name to Write: nanofile.txt
^G Get Help        M-D DOS Format   M-A Append      M-B Backup File
^C Cancel          M-M Mac Format   M-P Prepend     ^T To Files
```

Enter a filename and press *Enter*. You will be back in your previous Terminal screen, in the directory where you started nano. If everything went well, you can see the file with the following command:

```
$ ls -l
```

```
File  Edit  View  Search  Terminal  Help
reader@ubuntu:~$ ls -l
total 4
-rw-rw-r-- 1 reader reader 69 Jul 14 13:18 nanofile.txt
reader@ubuntu:~$ 
```

While nano has more advanced features, for basic usage we have discussed the most important features. While it's initially easier to use than Vim, it's also not as powerful. Simply said, nano is simple, Vim is powerful.

If you do not have any experience and/or preference, our recommendation would be to spend a little bit of time learning Vim and stick with it. After spending more time with Linux and Bash scripting, the advanced features of Vim become hard to live without. However, if you can't get used to Vim, don't be ashamed to use nano: it's a fine editor that will get most jobs done without too much hassle!

Combining graphical editors with command-line editors when writing shell scripts

To give you an impression of how we like to combine GUI tools with command-line editors, we've given the following example workflow. Don't worry about not understanding all steps yet; at the end of the book, you should come back to this example and understand exactly what we're talking about.

When you're writing shell scripts, you normally go through a few phases:

1. Gather requirements for the shell script.
2. Design the shell script.
3. Write the shell script.
4. Test and adjust the shell script.
5. (Optional) Submit the working shell scripts to your version control system.

Phases 1 and 2 are often done without writing actual code. You think about the purpose of the script, how it could be implemented, and what is gained by creating the script. These steps often involve research and looking for best practices. When you feel like you have a good idea about why, what, and how you're going to write your shell script, you move on to phase 3: writing the script. At this point, you would open your favorite GUI-based editor and start typing away. Because the GUI editor has autocomplete, syntax highlighting, and other productivity features built in, you can efficiently write most of the shell script code. After you feel like your script is ready for testing, you need to move away from your GUI: the script has to be tested on the system it's been designed for.

Phase 4 begins. You copy and paste the script to the server, using either Vim or nano. Once the script is on the server, you run it. Most of the time, it will not actually do everything you expected it to do. Tiny mistakes are easy to make and easy to fix, but it would be a small hassle to go back to the GUI editor, change it, save it, transfer it to the server, and run it again! Luckily, we can use either Vim or nano to make minor changes to fix the script right there on the server and try again. A missing ; or " will make a shell script unusable, but it's fixed quickly (although errors like that are often highlighted in the GUI editors, so those are unlikely to make it onto the server, even for the first version).

Finally, after a number of iterations, your script will work as expected. Now you have to make sure the full and correct script is uploaded to your version control system. It's recommended to transfer the script from the GUI to the server one last time, to see whether you have applied all the changes you made on the server to your GUI session as well. Once that is done, commit it, and you're finished!

Summary

In this chapter, we discussed four text editing tools, divided into two types: GUI-based editors (Atom and Notepad++) and command-line editors (Vim and GNU nano), before showing how to use these tools together.

Atom is a powerful text editor that can be configured exactly how you want . By default, it has support for many different coding languages, including shell. It also comes with Git and GitHub integration. We also briefly discussed Notepad++. While not as powerful as Atom, it is also suitable for our purposes, as it is basically an enhanced Notepad with all the important features for shell scripting.

Vim and nano are the two most popular Linux command-line text editors. We have learned that while Vim is very powerful, it is also harder to learn than nano. However, learning how to properly use Vim will speed up many things you do on a Linux system and is a very valuable skill to have. For a great hands-on introduction to Vim, go through the vimtutor. Nano is much easier to use, as it more closely resembles the WYSIWYG editing style also found in Microsoft Word and Notepad.

We ended the chapter with an example of a shell scripting journey. We gave a brief overview of how to use GUI-based editors in combination with command-line editors.

The following commands were introduced in this chapter: `vim`, `nano`, and `ls`.

Questions

1. Why is syntax highlighting an important feature for text editors?
2. How can we extend the functionality already provided by Atom?
3. What are the benefits of autocomplete when writing shell scripts?
4. How could we describe the difference between Vim and GNU nano?
5. Which are the two most interesting modes in Vim?
6. What is the `.vimrc` file?
7. What do we mean when we call nano a WYSIWYG editor?
8. Why would we want to combine GUI editors with command-line editors?

Further reading

The following resource might be interesting if you'd like to go deeper into the subjects of this chapter:

- *Hacking Vim 7.2* by Kim Schulz, Packt Publishing: `https://www.packtpub.com/application-development/hacking-vim-72`

The Linux Filesystem

4

In this chapter, we'll spend some time exploring the Linux filesystem. We will explain what a filesystem is and what makes the Linux filesystem unique. We will describe the structure of the Linux filesystem and how, under Linux, (almost) everything is a file. We will do this interactively, giving your the first closer look at some common Linux commands which will be used in scripting later on.

The following commands will be introduced in this chapter: `pwd`, `cd`, `df`, `echo`, `type`, `cat`, and `less`.

The following topics will be covered in this chapter:

- The Linux filesystem explained
- The structure of the Linux filesystem
- Everything is a file

Technical requirements

We will explore the Linux filesystem using the virtual machine we created in `Chapter 2`, *Setting Up Your Local Environment*.

 If you run into issues with connecting to your virtual machine, make sure that VirtualBox is running and the virtual machine has been started. While there are many things that can cause issues, making sure the hypervisor and virtual machine are running should always be your first step in troubleshooting.

The Linux filesystem explained

This chapter will present the basics of the Linux filesystem. Because filesystems are complicated, we will not be delving too deeply into the guts of the technology; instead, we'll present just enough information that's still relevant for shell scripting.

What is a filesystem?

A filesystem is, in essence, the way data is stored and retrieved on a physical medium (which can be a hard disk, solid state drive, or even RAM). It is a software implementation that manages where and how the bits are written and found again, and may include various advanced features which enhance reliability, performance, and functionality.

The concept of a filesystem is abstract: there are many filesystem *implementations*, which are confusingly often referred to as filesystems. We find it easiest to grasp by ordering the filesystems in families, just as with Linux distributions: there are Linux filesystems, Windows filesystems, macOS filesystems, and many others. The Windows filesystem family spans from the earliest filesystem of **FAT** up until the newest **ReFS**, with the most widely used currently being **NTFS**.

At the time of writing, the most important filesystems in the Linux family are the following implementations:

- **ext4**
- **XFS**
- **Btrfs**

The most commonly used Linux filesystem implementation is currently ext4. It is the fourth iteration in the **extended file system** (**ext**) series of Linux filesystems. It was released in 2008 and is considered *very* stable, but it is not state-of-the-art; reliability is the most important consideration.

XFS is most famously used in Red Hat distributions (Red Hat Enterprise Linux, CentOS, and Fedora). It contains some features that are more advanced than ext4, such as parallel I/O, larger file size support, and better handling of large files.

Finally, there is Btrfs. This filesystem implementation was initially designed at Oracle and is considered stable as of 2014. Btrfs has many advanced features that could make it preferable to ext4 and XFS; the principal developer of ext4 even stated that ext4 should eventually be replaced by Btrfs. The most interesting feature of Btrfs is that it uses the **copy-on-write** (**COW**) principle: files that are copied aren't actually written out to the physical medium fully, but only a new pointer to the same data is created. Only when either the copy or the original gets modified is new data written.

As you might have guessed, a filesystem implementation is nothing more than software. For Linux, the three implementations previously described are present in all newer Linux kernels. This means that, as long as the correct drivers are installed in the operating system, these can all be used. Even better, all of these can even be used *concurrently*! We will discuss this further later in this chapter.

Another interesting thing to note is that, while ext4 is native to Linux, with the help of drivers it can be used under, for example, Windows as well. You would not use ext4 as the filesystem for the primary drive under Windows, but you could *mount* a Linux-formatted ext4 filesystem under Windows and interact with the contents. The other way around, mounting a Windows filesystem under Linux, is also supported for most implementations. And while we used ext4 as the example here, the same goes for XFS and Btrfs.

What makes the Linux filesystem unique?

As should be clear by now, in reality, there is no such thing as *the* Linux filesystem. However, these filesystems share certain characteristics that make them viable as Linux filesystems.

A Linux filesystem adheres to the **Filesystem Hierarchy Standard** (**FHS**). This FHS is maintained by The Linux Foundation and is currently up to version 3.0. As with many things in the Linux ecosystem, it is based on a Unix predecessor: the **Unix Filesystem Standard** (**UFS**). It specifies the **directory structure** and its contents. We'll explore this structure together in the next part of this chapter.

Since Linux is most commonly used in servers, Linux filesystem implementations (often) have very advanced features on the topic of file integrity and disaster recovery. An example of such a disaster would be a system experiencing a power outage when it was in the middle of writing a business-critical file. If the write operation was stored in memory and aborted halfway through, the file would be in an inconsistent state. When the system is brought up again, the operating system does not have the write operation in memory anymore (since memory is cleared on each reboot), and only a part of the file will be written. Obviously, this is unwanted behavior and can lead to problems. Because of the properties of COW, Btrfs does not have this problem. However, ext4 and XFS are not COW filesystems. They both handle this issue in another way: with **journaling**:

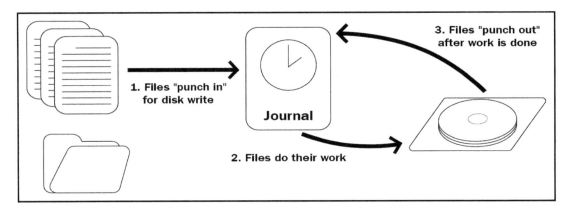

As the preceding diagram shows, files are written to disk in three steps:

1. Filesystem requests disk write from journal
2. Journal writes on disk
3. After file write, journal is updated

If the server crashes between steps 2 and 3, the write will be done again after power up, because the journal still contains the entry. The journal only contains some metadata about the operation, not the entire file. Since the journal contains a reference to the *actual* location on disk (the drive sectors), it will overwrite what was previously written, in this case, part of the file. If it finished successfully this time, the journal entry will be removed and the state of the file/disk is guaranteed. Should the server fail between steps 1 and 2, the actual instruction to write to disk has never been given and the software giving the instruction should account for that possibility.

Full disclosure: This part about journaling is a bit of an oversimplification, but again filesystems are complicated and we want to focus on things that are relevant for shell scripting. If you're interested in how filesystems work on a lower level, be sure to pick up another book since it really is a very interesting subject!

Structure of the Linux filesystem

While there are many more advanced filesystem features that are very interesting, we want to focus on what makes the Linux filesystem distinctively Linux: the filesystem structure. If you're used to Windows, this will probably be the single most confusing difference between the two operating systems. If you're coming from macOS, the difference is still noticeable, but much smaller: this is a result of macOS being a Unix operating system, which has obvious similarities with the Unix-like Linux structure.

We're going to be interactively exploring the Linux filesystem from this point on. We advise you to follow along with the code examples that follow, since this increases information retention significantly. Besides that, your system might look differently from the one we use, should you have chosen not to use Ubuntu 18.04 LTS for this book. In any case, start up that virtual machine and start exploring with us!

Tree structure

Let's start by logging in to our virtual machine via SSH:

```
ssh -p 2222 reader@localhost
```

Enter your password at the prompt and you should arrive at the default Ubuntu 18.04 login banner, which should look similar to the following:

```
reader@localhost's password:
Welcome to Ubuntu 18.04.1 LTS (GNU/Linux 4.15.0-29-generic x86_64)
<SNIPPED>
  System information as of Sat Jul 28 14:15:19 UTC 2018

  System load:   0.09            Processes:            87
  Usage of /:    45.6% of 9.78GB  Users logged in:     0
  Memory usage:  15%             IP address for enp0s3: 10.0.2.15
  Swap usage:    0%
<SNIPPED>
Last login: Sat Jul 28 14:13:42 2018 from 10.0.2.2
reader@ubuntu:~$
```

When logging in (either via SSH or the Terminal console) you will end up at the home directory of the user. You can always find out where you are exactly by using the pwd command. pwd stands for **p**rint **w**orking **d**irectory:

```
reader@ubuntu:~$ pwd
/home/reader
```

So, we've ended up in the /home/reader/ directory. This is the default for most Linux distributions: /home/$USERNAME/. Since we created the primary user reader, this is where we expect to be. For those of you coming from Windows, this might look very foreign: where is the drive name (C:, D:, and so on) and why are we using (forward) slashes instead of backslashes?

Linux, as well as Unix and other Unix-like systems, uses a **tree structure**. It is referred to as a tree because it starts at a single origin point, the root (found at /). Directories are nested from there (like **branches** from a tree), not much differently from other operating systems. Finally, the tree structure ends in files that are considered the **leaves** of the tree. This might sound terribly complicated still, but it's actually relatively simple. Let's keep exploring to make sure we fully understand this structure! Under Linux, we use the cd command to change directories. It works by entering cd, followed by the location on the filesystem where we want to go as the *argument to the command*. Navigate to the filesystem root:

```
reader@ubuntu:~$ cd /
reader@ubuntu:/$
```

As you can see, nothing much seems to have happened. However, there is one tiny difference in your Terminal prompt: the ~ character has been replaced by /. Under Ubuntu, the default configuration shows the location on the filesystem without needing to use the pwd command. The prompt is built as follows: <username>@<hostname>:<location>**$**. Why the ~ then? Simple: the tilde character is shorthand for the user's home directory! If the shorthand wasn't there, the prompt at login would be reader@ubuntu:/home/reader$.

Since we have navigated to the root of the filesystem, let's check out what we can find there. To list the contents of the current directory, we use the ls command:

```
reader@ubuntu:/$ ls
bin dev home initrd.img.old lib64 media opt root sbin srv sys usr vmlinuz
boot etc initrd.img lib lost+found mnt proc run snap swap.img tmp var
vmlinuz.old
```

If you're using SSH, you'll most likely have some colors to differentiate between files and directories (and even permissions on directories, if you see `tmp` in a different manner; this will be discussed in the next chapter). However, even with color assistance, this still feels unclear. Let's clean it up a bit by using an **option** on the `ls` command:

```
reader@ubuntu:/$ ls -l
total 2017372
drwxr-xr-x  2 root root       4096 Jul 28 10:31 bin
drwxr-xr-x  3 root root       4096 Jul 28 10:32 boot
drwxr-xr-x 19 root root       3900 Jul 28 10:31 dev
drwxr-xr-x 90 root root       4096 Jul 28 10:32 etc
drwxr-xr-x  3 root root       4096 Jun 30 18:20 home
lrwxrwxrwx  1 root root         33 Jul 27 11:39 initrd.img ->
boot/initrd.img-4.15.0-29-generic
lrwxrwxrwx  1 root root         33 Jul 27 11:39 initrd.img.old ->
boot/initrd.img-4.15.0-23-generic
drwxr-xr-x 22 root root       4096 Apr 26 19:09 lib
drwxr-xr-x  2 root root       4096 Apr 26 19:07 lib64
drwx------  2 root root      16384 Jun 30 17:58 lost+found
drwxr-xr-x  2 root root       4096 Apr 26 19:07 media
drwxr-xr-x  2 root root       4096 Apr 26 19:07 mnt
drwxr-xr-x  2 root root       4096 Apr 26 19:07 opt
dr-xr-xr-x 97 root root          0 Jul 28 10:30 proc
drwx------  3 root root       4096 Jul  1 09:40 root
drwxr-xr-x 26 root root        920 Jul 28 14:15 run
drwxr-xr-x  2 root root      12288 Jul 28 10:31 sbin
drwxr-xr-x  4 root root       4096 Jun 30 18:20 snap
drwxr-xr-x  2 root root       4096 Apr 26 19:07 srv
-rw-------  1 root root 2065694720 Jun 30 18:00 swap.img
dr-xr-xr-x 13 root root          0 Jul 28 10:30 sys
drwxrwxrwt  9 root root       4096 Jul 28 14:32 tmp
drwxr-xr-x 10 root root       4096 Apr 26 19:07 usr
drwxr-xr-x 13 root root       4096 Apr 26 19:10 var
lrwxrwxrwx  1 root root         30 Jul 27 11:39 vmlinuz ->
boot/vmlinuz-4.15.0-29-generic
lrwxrwxrwx  1 root root         30 Jul 27 11:39 vmlinuz.old ->
boot/vmlinuz-4.15.0-23-generic
```

The option -l (hyphen lowercase l, as in *long*) to `ls` gives the **long listing format**. Among other things, this prints the permissions, the owner of the file/directory, the type of file, and its size. Remember, permissions and ownership are discussed in the next chapter, so no need to worry about this for now. The most important thing to take away from this is that each file/directory is printed on its own line, where the first character of that line denotes the type of file: `d` for directory, `-` for regular file, and `l` for symlinks (which are shortcuts under Linux).

Let's navigate deeper into the tree structure, back *toward* our home directory. At this point, you have two options. You can use a **relative path** (as in: relative to the current location) or a **fully qualified path** (which is *not* relative to the current directory). Let's try both:

```
reader@ubuntu:/$ cd home
reader@ubuntu:/home$
```

The preceding is an example of changing directories into a relative directory. We were positioned in the root directory, /, and we navigated to home from there, effectively ending up in /home. We could have navigated there from anywhere by using the fully qualified path:

```
reader@ubuntu:/$ cd /home
reader@ubuntu:/home$
```

Did you spot the difference? In the fully qualified example, the argument to cd started with a slash, but in the relative example it did not. Let's see what happens if you use both types incorrectly:

```
reader@ubuntu:/home$ ls
reader
reader@ubuntu:/home$ cd /reader
-bash: cd: /reader: No such file or directory
```

We listed the contents of the /home directory with ls. As expected, we saw (at least) the current user's home directory, reader. However, when we tried to navigate to it using cd /reader, we got the infamous error No such file or directory. This is not surprising though: there isn't actually a directory /reader. The directory we're looking for is /home/reader, which would be reached fully qualified with the command cd /home/reader:

```
reader@ubuntu:/home$ cd home
-bash: cd: home: No such file or directory
reader@ubuntu:/home$
```

The same error is presented if we try to use an incorrect relative path. In the preceding example, we are currently located in the /home directory and we use the cd home command. Effectively, this would put us in /home/home, which, as we saw when we used ls in the /home directory, does not exist!

The safest way to navigate around Linux is fully qualified: as long as you have the correct directory, it always works, no matter where you are currently located on the filesystem. However, especially when you get deeper into the filesystem, you're typing a lot more. We always recommend beginning users to start with fully qualified navigation and switch to relative once they're comfortable with the cd, ls, and pwd commands.

Even though fully qualified is safer, it's much less efficient then relative. You saw how we can move deeper into the branches of the tree structure, but what if you had to go down a level, back toward the root? Luckily for us, that does not force us to use fully qualified paths. We can use the .. notation, which means as much as go up a level toward /:

```
reader@ubuntu:/home$ cd ..
reader@ubuntu:/$
```

A note on terminology is in order here. While we conceptualized the filesystem as a tree, when talking about the root directory, we consider this as the *highest point* in the filesystem. So when moving from / to /home, we're moving *down*. If we use the command cd .. to move back to /, we're moving *up*. While we think that this doesn't really match with the picture of a tree (where the root is actually the *lowest* point), please remember this convention!

Using cd .. to move up lands us back at the root of the filesystem. At this point, you might think *If I do this again while I'm on the highest level of the filesystem, what would happen?*. Give it a try:

```
reader@ubuntu:/$ cd ..
reader@ubuntu:/$
```

Fortunately for us, we do not get an error nor a crashing machine; instead, we just end up (or, depending on how you look at it, stay) on the root of the filesystem.

A source of confusion among new users of Linux is often the term **root**. It can stand for any of three things:

1. The lowest point in the filesystem, at /
2. The default superuser, named just `root`
3. The default superuser's home directory, at `/root/`

Often, it is left to the reader to use context to determine which of the three is meant. When talking in the context of filesystems, it will probably be:

1. If it seems to be referring to a *user*, you can expect it to mean the **root** user
2. Only when talking about the root user's home directory or `/root/` should you think of
3. Most often, you will encounter root to mean either 1 or 2!

Overview of top-level directories

Now that we've got the basics of moving around using `cd` and listing directory contents using `ls` under control, let's start exploring other parts of the filesystem. Let's begin with an overview of every directory directly under the root filesystem, as specified by the FHS:

Location	Purpose
/bin/	Contains essential **bin**aries (=tools) used by normal users
/boot/	Contains files used in the **boot** process: `kernel, initramfs, bootloader`
/dev/	Contains special files used to access **dev**ices
/etc/	Default location for software configuration files
/home/	Contains the **home** directories for normal users
/lib/	Contains system **lib**raries
/lib64/	Contains **64**bit system **lib**raries
/media/	Removable devices such as USB and DVDs can be found here
/mnt/	Empty by default, can be used to **mount** other filesystems
/opt/	Directory where **opt**ional software can be installed
/proc/	Directory where information about **proc**esses is stored
/root/	The home directory of the **root** user

`/run/`	Contains variable data about **run**-time data, different each boot
`/sbin/`	Contains essential **s**ystem **bin**aries (=tools) used by administrative users
`/srv/`	Directory to place data to be **serv**ed by the server
`/sys/`	Contains information about the **sys**tem, such as drivers and kernel features
`/tmp/`	Directory intended for **temp**orary files, often cleared on reboot (because it is stored in RAM, instead of on disk)
`/usr/`	Contains non-essential files and binaries as read-only **user** data
`/var/`	Contains **var**iable files, such as logs

While each and every **top-level directory** has an important function, there are a few we're going to examine more closely since we're undoubtedly going to encounter them in our shell scripting. These are `/bin/`, `/sbin/`, `/usr/`, `/etc/`, `/opt/`, `/tmp/`, and `/var/`.

What about multiple partitions?

But first, we'd like to briefly address something you might have found confusing, especially if you're coming from a Windows background where you're used to multiple disks/partitions in the form of `C:\`, `D:\`, `E:\`, and so on. With the preceding directory structure, and the information that the highest point in the filesystem is at `/`, how does Linux deal with multiple disks/partitions?

The answer is actually pretty simple. Linux *mounts* filesystems somewhere within the tree structure. The first mount is found on the primary partition we have already covered: it is mounted on `/`! Let's see how this looks while we check out a new `df` tool:

```
reader@ubuntu:~$ df -hT
Filesystem      Type       Size  Used Avail Use% Mounted on
udev            devtmpfs   464M     0  464M   0% /dev
tmpfs           tmpfs       99M  920K   98M   1% /run
/dev/sda2       ext4       9.8G  4.4G  5.0G  47% /
tmpfs           tmpfs      493M     0  493M   0% /dev/shm
tmpfs           tmpfs      5.0M     0  5.0M   0% /run/lock
tmpfs           tmpfs      493M     0  493M   0% /sys/fs/cgroup
/dev/loop0      squashfs    87M   87M     0 100% /snap/core/4917
/dev/loop1      squashfs    87M   87M     0 100% /snap/core/4486
/dev/loop2      squashfs    87M   87M     0 100% /snap/core/4830
tmpfs           tmpfs       99M     0   99M   0% /run/user/1000
```

While this is a lot of output by df (which *reports filesystem disk space usage*), the most interesting was highlighted previously: the partition /dev/sda2 of type ext4 (remember?) is mounted on /. You're getting a preview of the *everything is a file* later in this chapter: /dev/sda2 is handled as a file, but it is actually a reference to a partition on the disk (which is, in this case, a virtual disk). Another example from our Arch Linux host gives even more information (don't worry if you don't have a Linux host, we'll explain later):

```
[root@caladan ~]# df -hT
Filesystem                            Type       Size  Used Avail Use% Mounted
on
dev                                   devtmpfs   7.8G     0  7.8G   0% /dev
run                                   tmpfs      7.8G  1.5M  7.8G   1% /run
/dev/mapper/vg_caladan-lv_arch_root   ext4        50G   29G   19G  60% /
tmpfs                                 tmpfs      7.8G  287M  7.5G   4%
/dev/shm
tmpfs                                 tmpfs      7.8G     0  7.8G   0%
/sys/fs/cgroup
tmpfs                                 tmpfs      7.8G  212K  7.8G   1% /tmp
/dev/sda1                             vfat       550M   97M  453M  18% /boot
tmpfs                                 tmpfs      1.6G   16K  1.6G   1%
/run/user/120
tmpfs                                 tmpfs      1.6G   14M  1.6G   1%
/run/user/1000
/dev/sdc1       vfat        15G  552M   14G   4% /run/media/tammert/ARCH_201803
/dev/mapper/vg_caladan-lv_data        btrfs       10G   17M  9.8G   1% /data
```

You can see I have an ext4 filesystem mounted as my root. However, I also have an extra btrfs partition mounted on /data/ and a vfat boot partition (which is needed on bare-metal installations, but not on virtual machines) on /boot/. To top it off, there's also a vfat USB device with the Arch Linux installer connected, which was automatically mounted under /run/media/. So not only does Linux handle multiple partitions or disks gracefully, even different types of filesystems can be used side by side under the same tree structure!

/bin/, /sbin/, and /usr/

Let's get back to top-level directories. We'll discuss /bin/, /sbin/, and /usr/ first, because they are really similar. As stated in the overview, all of these directories contain binaries used by normal users and administrators of the system. Let's see where those binaries are and how our user session knows how to find them in the process. We'll manage this by using the echo command. Its short description is simply display a line of text. Let's see how it works:

```
reader@ubuntu:~$ echo

reader@ubuntu:~$ echo 'Hello'
Hello
reader@ubuntu:~$
```

If we use echo without passing an argument, an empty line of text is displayed (pretty much just as promised by the short description!). If we pass text, which we enclose in single quotes, that text is printed instead. In this context, a bit of text which contains either letters, numbers, or other characters is referred to as a **string**. So, any string we pass to echo will be printed in our Terminal. While this might not seem that interesting, it is interesting when you start to consider **variables**. A variable is a string which value is, as the name implies, variable from time to time. Let's use echo to print the current value of the variable BASH_VERSION:

```
reader@ubuntu:~$ echo BASH_VERSION
BASH_VERSION
reader@ubuntu:~$ echo $BASH_VERSION
4.4.19(1)-release
reader@ubuntu:~$
```

You should notice we did not use the echo BASH_VERSION command, since that would print the literal text BASH_VERSION, but we instead started the variable name with a $. In Bash, the $ denotes the fact that we're using a variable (we will explain *variables* and *variable interpolation* further in Chapter 8, *Variables and User Input*). Why are we telling you this? Because the binaries we can use from our Terminal are found by using a variable, specifically the PATH variable:

```
reader@ubuntu:~$ echo $PATH
/usr/local/sbin:/usr/local/bin:/usr/sbin:/usr/bin:/sbin:/bin <SNIPPED>
reader@ubuntu:~$
```

As you can see here, binaries need to be in the `/usr/local/sbin/`, `/usr/local/bin/`, `/usr/sbin/`, `/usr/bin/`, `/sbin/`, or `/bin/` directory for us to be able to use them (with the current value of `PATH`, which we can change, but that's out of scope for now). That would mean that binaries we've been using up until now (cd, ls, pwd, and echo) would need to be in one of these directories so that we can use them, right? Unfortunately, this is where things get slightly complicated. On Linux, we basically use two types of binaries: those that are found on disk (in a directory as specified by the `PATH` variable), or they can be built into the shell we're using, then called a *shell builtin*. A good example is actually the echo command we just learned, which is both! We can see what type of command we're dealing with by using `type`:

```
reader@ubuntu:~$ type -a echo
echo is a shell builtin
echo is /bin/echo
reader@ubuntu:~$ type -a cd
cd is a shell builtin
reader@ubuntu:~$
```

If a command is both built-in and a binary within the `PATH`, the binary is used. If it is only present as a built-in, such as cd, the built-in is used. As a general rule, most commands you use will be binaries on disk, as found in your `PATH`. Furthermore, most of these will be present in the `/usr/bin/` directory (on our Ubuntu virtual machine, more than half of the total binaries are present in `/usr/bin/`!).

So, the overall goal of the binary directories should be clear: to provide us with the tools we need to perform our work. The question remains, why are there (at least) six different directories, and why are they divided between `bin` and `sbin`? The answer to the last part of the question is easy: `bin` has normal utilities used by users, while `sbin` has utilities used by system administrators. In that last category, tools related to disk maintenance, network configuration, and firewalling, for example, are found. The `bin` directories contain utilities that are used for filesystem operations (such as creating and removing files/directories), archiving, and listing information about the system, among others.

The difference between the top-level `/(s)bin/` and `/usr/(s)bin/` is a bit more vague. In general, the rule is that essential tools are found in `/(s)bin`, while system-specific binaries are placed in the `/usr/(s)bin` directories. So if you installed a package to run a web server, it would be placed in either `/usr/bin/` or `/usr/sbin/`, since it is system-specific. Finally, the `/usr/local/(s)bin/` directories are, in our experience, most often used for binaries that are installed manually, instead of from a package manager. But you could place them in either directory of the `PATH` to work; it's mostly a matter of convention.

As a final note, `/usr/` contains more than just binaries. Among these are some libraries (which have the same relation to the `/lib/` and `/lib64/` top-level directories) and some miscellaneous files. If you're curious, we would definitely recommend checking out the rest of the `/usr/` directory using `cd` and `ls`, but the most important thing to remember is that **binaries** and **libraries** can be located here.

/etc/

On to the next interesting top-level directory within the Linux filesystem: the `/etc/` directory. Pronounced *et-c* as in *et-cetera*, it is used to store configuration files for both system software as well as user software. Let's see what it contains:

```
reader@ubuntu:/etc# ls
acpi console-setup ethertypes inputrc logrotate.conf network python3 shadow
ucf.conf
...<SNIPPED>:
```

We snipped the preceding output to only the top line of our system. If you followed along with the example (and you should!) you will see well over 150 files and directories. We will print a particularly interesting one using the `cat` command:

```
reader@ubuntu:/etc$ cat fstab
UUID=376cd784-7c8f-11e8-a415-080027a7d0ea / ext4 defaults 0 0
/swap.img    none    swap    sw    0    0
reader@ubuntu:/etc$
```

What we're seeing here is the **file systems table**, or `fstab` file. It contains the instructions for Linux to mount the filesystems at each start. As we can see here, we're referencing a partition by its **Universally Unique Identifier** (**UUID**) and we're mounting it on /, so as the root filesystem. It's of type `ext4`, mounted using options `defaults`. The last two zeros deal with backups and checks at the start of the system. On the second line, we see we're using a file as swap space. Swap is used in case there isn't enough memory available to the system, which can be compensated for by writing it to disk (but incurring a hefty performance penalty, since a disk is much slower than RAM).

Another interesting configuration file in the `/etc/` directory is the `passwd` file. While it sounds like *password*, don't worry, those aren't stored there. Let's check the contents using the `less` command:

```
reader@ubuntu:/etc$ less passwd
```

This will open the file in a so-called pager, in read-only mode. `less` uses Vim commands, so you can quit by pressing the *Q* on your keyboard. If the file is larger than your screen, you can navigate up and down with the Vim keystrokes: either the arrow keys or by using *J* and *K*. When in the `less`, the screen should look something like the following:

```
root:x:0:0:root:/root:/bin/bash
daemon:x:1:1:daemon:/usr/sbin:/usr/sbin/nologin
...<SNIPPED>:
sshd:x:110:65534::/run/sshd:/usr/sbin/nologin
reader:x:1000:1004:Learn Linux Shell Scripting:/home/reader:/bin/bash
```

This file contains information about all users on the system. In order, the fields separated by the : denote the following:

Username	Password	User ID (UID)	Group ID (GID)	User real name	Home directory	Users' default shell

While there is a password field here, this is because of legacy reasons; the (hashed!) password has been moved to the `/etc/shadow` file, which can only be read by the root superuser. We will cover the UID and GID in the next chapter; the other fields should be clear by now.

These are just two examples of configuration files found in the `/etc/` directory (important ones though!).

/opt/, /tmp/, and /var/

On a fresh installation of Ubuntu, the `/opt/` directory is empty. While it is again a matter of convention, in our experience, this directory is most often used to install software that comes from outside the distribution's package manager. However, some applications that are installed with the package manager do use `/opt/` for their files; it's all a matter of preference by the package maintainer. In our case, we will be using this directory *to save the shell scripts* we'll be creating, as these definitely classify as optional software.

The `/tmp/` directory is used for temporary files (who would have guessed?). In some Linux distributions, `/tmp/` is not part of the root partition but mounted as a separate **tmpfs** filesystem. This type of filesystem is allocated within the RAM, which means the contents of `/tmp/` do not survive a reboot. Since we're dealing with temporary files, this is sometimes not only a nice feature, but a prerequisite for particular uses. For a desktop Linux user, this could for example be used to save a note which is only needed during the active session, without having to worry about cleaning it up after you're done.

Finally, the `/var/` directory is a little more complex. Let's have a look:

```
reader@ubuntu:~$ cd /var/
reader@ubuntu:/var$ ls -l
total 48
drwxr-xr-x  2 root root    4096 Jul 29 10:14 backups
drwxr-xr-x 10 root root    4096 Jul 29 12:31 cache
drwxrwxrwt  2 root root    4096 Jul 28 10:30 crash
drwxr-xr-x 35 root root    4096 Jul 29 12:30 lib
drwxrwsr-x  2 root staff   4096 Apr 24 08:34 local
lrwxrwxrwx  1 root root       9 Apr 26 19:07 lock -> /run/lock
drwxrwxr-x 10 root syslog  4096 Jul 29 12:30 log
drwxrwsr-x  2 root mail    4096 Apr 26 19:07 mail
drwxr-xr-x  2 root root    4096 Apr 26 19:07 opt
lrwxrwxrwx  1 root root       4 Apr 26 19:07 run -> /run
drwxr-xr-x  3 root root    4096 Jun 30 18:20 snap
drwxr-xr-x  4 root root    4096 Apr 26 19:08 spool
drwxrwxrwt  4 root root    4096 Jul 29 15:04 tmp
drwxr-xr-x  3 root root    4096 Jul 29 12:30 www
reader@ubuntu:/var$
```

As you should see, `/var/` contains many subdirectories and some symlinks (which are denoted by the `->` characters). In this case, `/var/run/` is actually a shortcut to the top-level directory `/run`. The most interesting subdirectories within `/var/` (for now) are `log/` and `mail/`.

`/var/log/` is conventionally used to save log files for most system and user processes. In our experience, most third-party software installed on a Linux system will adhere to this convention and will output log files to the `/var/log/` directory, or create a subdirectory in `/var/log/`. Let's look at an example of a log file using `less` with a fully qualified path:

```
reader@ubuntu:~$ less /var/log/kern.log
```

In the `less` pager, you'll encounter something which looks similar to the following:

```
Jun 30 18:20:32 ubuntu kernel: [    0.000000] Linux version 4.15.0-23-
generic (buildd@lgw01-amd64-055) (gcc version 7.3.0 (Ubuntu
7.3.0-16ubuntu3)) #25-Ubuntu SMP Wed May 23 18:02:16 UTC 2018 (Ubuntu
4.15.0-23.25-generic 4.15.18)
Jun 30 18:20:32 ubuntu kernel: [    0.000000] Command line:
BOOT_IMAGE=/boot/vmlinuz-4.15.0-23-generic root=UUID=376cd784-7c8f-11e8-
a415-080027a7d0ea ro maybe-ubiquity
Jun 30 18:20:32 ubuntu kernel: [    0.000000] KERNEL supported cpus:
Jun 30 18:20:32 ubuntu kernel: [    0.000000]   Intel GenuineIntel
Jun 30 18:20:32 ubuntu kernel: [    0.000000]   AMD AuthenticAMD
...<SNIPPED>:
```

This log file contains information about the kernel boot process. You can see a reference to the actual kernel on disk, `/boot/vmlinuz-4.15.0-23-generic`, and the UUID of the filesystem being mounted at root, `UUID=376cd784-7c8f-11e8-a415-080027a7d0ea`. This file would be something you would check if your system has trouble booting or if some functionality does not seem to be working!

In the earliest days of Unix and Linux, sending mail was something that wasn't only used over the internet (which was in its mere infancy at that time), but also to relay messages between servers or users on the same server. On your new Ubuntu virtual machine, the `/var/mail/` directory and its symlink, `/var/spool/mail/`, will be empty. However, once we start talking about scheduling and logging, we will see that this directory will be used to store messages.

That concludes the short description about the top-level directories in the default Linux filesystem. We discussed the most important ones, in our eyes, when relating to shell scripting. However, in time, you will get a feeling for all directories and finding anything on the Linux filesystem will surely get a lot easier, as difficult as it might sound right now.

Everything is a file

Under Linux, there is a well-known expression:

On a Linux system, everything is a file; if something is not a file, it is a process.

While this is not strictly 100% true, it is true for at least 90% of things you will encounter on Linux, definitely if you're not very advanced yet. Even though, in general, this rule works out, it has some extra notes. While most stuff on Linux is a file, there are different file types, seven to be exact. We'll discuss them all in the coming pages. You will probably not use all seven; however, having basic knowledge about them all gives you a better understanding about Linux in general, something which is never a bad thing!

Different types of files

The seven types of files are as follows, denoted with the character used by Linux to represent them:

Type	Explanation
–: Normal file	A regular file, containing text or bytes
d: Directory	A directory, which can contain other directories and regular files

l: Symlink	Symbolic link, used as a shortcut
s: Socket	A channel used for communication
c: Special file	Mostly used for device handlers
b: Block device	The type that represents storage hardware, such as disk partitions
p: Named pipe	Used between processes to talk to each other

Out of these seven file types, you will first encounter just the regular files (–) and the directories (d). Next, you will probably interact some more with symlinks (l), block devices (b), and special files (c). Very rarely will you use the last two: sockets (s) and named pipes (p).

A good place to encounter the most common file types is in /dev/. Let's use ls to see what it contains:

```
reader@ubuntu:/dev$ ls -l /dev/
total 0
crw-r--r-- 1 root root     10, 235 Jul 29 15:04 autofs
drwxr-xr-x 2 root root         280 Jul 29 15:04 block
drwxr-xr-x 2 root root          80 Jul 29 15:04 bsg
crw-rw---- 1 root disk     10, 234 Jul 29 15:04 btrfs-control
drwxr-xr-x 3 root root          60 Jul 29 15:04 bus
lrwxrwxrwx 1 root root           3 Jul 29 15:04 cdrom -> sr0
drwxr-xr-x 2 root root        3500 Jul 29 15:04 char
crw------- 1 root root      5,   1 Jul 29 15:04 console
lrwxrwxrwx 1 root root          11 Jul 29 15:04 core -> /proc/kcore
...<SNIPPED>:
brw-rw---- 1 root disk      8,   0 Jul 29 15:04 sda
brw-rw---- 1 root disk      8,   1 Jul 29 15:04 sda1
brw-rw---- 1 root disk      8,   2 Jul 29 15:04 sda2
crw-rw---- 1 root cdrom    21,   0 Jul 29 15:04 sg0
crw-rw---- 1 root disk     21,   1 Jul 29 15:04 sg1
drwxrwxrwt 2 root root          40 Jul 29 15:04 shm
crw------- 1 root root     10, 231 Jul 29 15:04 snapshot
drwxr-xr-x 3 root root         180 Jul 29 15:04 snd
brw-rw---- 1 root cdrom    11,   0 Jul 29 15:04 sr0
lrwxrwxrwx 1 root root          15 Jul 29 15:04 stderr -> /proc/self/fd/2
lrwxrwxrwx 1 root root          15 Jul 29 15:04 stdin -> /proc/self/fd/0
lrwxrwxrwx 1 root root          15 Jul 29 15:04 stdout -> /proc/self/fd/1
crw-rw-rw- 1 root tty       5,   0 Jul 29 17:58 tty
crw--w---- 1 root tty       4,   0 Jul 29 15:04 tty0
crw--w---- 1 root tty       4,   1 Jul 29 15:04 tty1
...<SNIPPED>:
reader@ubuntu:/dev$
```

As you saw from your output, /dev/ contains a lot of files, with most of the types as outlined above. Ironically, it does not contain the most common file type: regular files. However, because we have been interacting with regular files until now, you should have an idea about what they are (and otherwise the rest of the book will *definitely* give you an idea).

So, let's look at anything other than a regular file. Let's start with the most familiar: directories. Any line that starts with a d is a directory, and, if you're using SSH, will most probably be represented in a different color as well. Do not underestimate how important this visual aid is, as it will save you a lot of time when you're navigating a Linux machine. Remember, you can move into a directory by using either cd with a relative path or a fully qualified path, which always starts from the root of the filesystem.

Next, you will see files starting with the b. These files are used to represent block devices, the most common usage being a disk device or partition. Under most Linux distributions, disks are often called /dev/sda, /dev/sdb, and so on. Partitions on those disks are referred to with a number: /dev/sda1, /dev/sda2, and further. As you can see in the preceding output, our system has a single disk (only /dev/sda). That disk does, however, have two partitions: /dev/sda1 and /dev/sda2. Try using df -hT again, and you will notice /dev/sda2 mounted as the root filesystem (unless your virtual machine was configured differently, in which case it might be /dev/sda1 or even /dev/sda3).

Symlinks are often used on Linux. Look in the preceding output for the entry cdrom, which you will see starts with an l. The term cdrom has contextual meaning: it refers to the CD (or more probably, in a newer system, the DVD) drive. However, it is linked to the actual block device that handles the interaction, /dev/sr0, which starts with the b for block device. Using a symlink makes it easy to find the item you need (the disk drive) while still preserving the Linux configuration which calls the device handler sr0.

Finally, you should see a long list of files called tty. These are denoted by a c at the beginning of the line, indicating a special file. To keep it simple, you should consider a tty as a Terminal you use to connect to your Linux server. These are a kind of virtual device that Linux uses to allow interaction from the user with the system. Many virtual and physical devices use the special file handlers when they appear on your Linux filesystem.

This chapter introduced you to many commands. Perhaps you have gotten sick of typing everything already, perhaps not. In any case, we have some good news: Bash has something called autocomplete. It is something we did not want to introduce to early as to avoid confusion, but it is something that is used so extensively when working with a Linux system that we would be cheating you if we had not explained it.

It's actually pretty simple: if you hit the *Tab* key after the first part of a command (such as cd or ls), it will complete your command if it has a single choice, or if you hit *Tab* again, it will present you a list of options. Go to /, type cd, and press *Tab* twice to see this in action. Moving into the /home/ directory and pressing *Tab* once (after entering cd) will make it autocomplete with the only directory there is, saving you time!

Summary

In this chapter, we presented an overview of the Linux filesystem. We started with a short introduction on filesystems in general, before explaining what is unique about the Linux filesystem. Ext4, XFS, and Btrfs filesystem implementations were discussed, together with the journaling feature of these filesystems. Next, the FHS that Linux adheres to was explained in high level, before focusing on the more important parts of the Linux filesystem in detail. This was done by exploring parts of the tree structure that makes up the Linux filesystem. We explained that different filesystems can be used side by side, by mounting them somewhere inside the tree. We ended the chapter by explaining that (almost) everything on Linux is handled as a file, and we discussed the different file types that are used.

The following commands were introduced in this chapter: pwd, cd, df, echo, type, cat, and less. As a tip, the Bash autocomplete feature was explained.

Questions

1. What is a filesystem?
2. Which Linux-specific filesystems are most common?
3. True or false: multiple filesystem implementations can be used concurrently on Linux?
4. What is the journaling feature present on most Linux filesystem implementations?
5. On which point in the tree is the root filesystem mounted?
6. What is the PATH variable used for?
7. In which top-level directory are configuration files stored according to the FHS?
8. Where are process logs commonly saved?
9. How many file types does Linux have?
10. How does the Bash autocomplete function work?

Further reading

The following resource might be interesting if you'd like to go deeper into the subjects of this chapter:

- **General overview of the Linux filesystem**: https://www.tldp.org/LDP/intro-linux/html/sect_03_01.html

5
Understanding the Linux Permissions Scheme

In this chapter, we will explore how the Linux permission scheme is implemented. Read, write, and execute permissions for files and directories will be discussed, and we will see how they affect files and directories differently. We will see how multiple users can work together using groups, and how some files and directories are available to others as well.

The following commands will be introduced in this chapter: `id`, `touch`, `chmod`, `umask`, `chown`, `chgrp`, `sudo`, `useradd`, `groupadd`, `usermod`, `mkdir`, and `su`.

The following topics will be covered in this chapter:

- Read, write, and execute
- Users, groups, and others
- Working with multiple users
- Advanced permissions

Technical requirements

We will explore the Linux permissions scheme using the virtual machine we created in Chapter 2, *Setting Up Your Local Environment*. During this chapter, we will add new users to this system, but only having access as the first user (which has administrative, or *root* privileges) is sufficient at this point.

Read, write, and execute

In the previous chapter, we discussed the Linux filesystem and the different types with which Linux implements the *everything is a file* philosophy. However, we did not look at permissions on those files. As you might have guessed, in a multi-user system such as a Linux server, it is not a particularly great idea that users can access files which are owned by other users. Where would the privacy be in that?

The Linux permissions scheme is actually at the heart of the Linux experience, as far as we are concerned. Just as (almost) everything is handled as a file in Linux, all of those files have a distinct set of permissions accompanying them. While exploring the file system in the previous chapter, we limited ourselves to files that were viewable by either everyone or by the currently logged in user. However, there are many files that are only viewable or writable by the `root` user: often, these are sensitive files such as `/etc/shadow` (which contains the *hashed* passwords for all users), or files which are used when starting the system, such as `/etc/fstab` (which determines which file systems are mounted at boot). If everyone could edit those files, it could result in an unbootable system very quickly!

RWX

File permissions under Linux are handled by three attributes: **r**ead, **w**rite, and e**x**ecute, or RWX. While there are other permissions (some of which we will discuss later in this chapter), most interactions with regards to permissions will be handled by these three. Even though the names seem to speak for themselves, they behave differently with regards to (normal) files and directories. The following table should illustrate this:

Allows the user to see the contents of the file with any command that supports this, such as `vim`, `nano`, `less`, `cat`, and so on.

Permission	On normal files	On directories
Read	Allows the user to list the contents of the directory using the `ls` command. This will even list files in the directory on which the user has no other privileges!	Allows the user to list the contents of the directory using the ls command. This will even list files in directory on which the user has no other privileges!
Write	Allows the user to make changes to the file.	Allows the user to replace or delete files within the directory, even if the user has no direct permissions on that file. However, this does not include read permissions on all files within the directory!

	Allows the user to execute the file. This is only relevant when the file is something that is supposed to be executed, such as a binary or script; otherwise, this attribute does nothing.	Allows the user to traverse into the directory by using cd. This is a separate permission from the listing of contents, but they are almost always used together; being able to list without being able to navigate into it (and vice versa) is mostly an ineffective configuration.
Execute		

This overview should provide a basis for the three different permissions. Please take a good look and see whether you can fully understand what is presented there.

Now, it's about to get a little more complicated. While these permissions on both files and directories show what can and cannot be done for a user, how does Linux deal with multiple users? How does Linux keep track of file *ownership*, and how are files shared by multiple users?

Users, groups, and others

Under Linux, every file is *owned* by exactly one user and one group. Every user has an identifying number, the **User ID (UID)**. The same applies for a group: it is resolved by a **Group ID (GID)**. Every user has exactly one UID and one *primary* GID; however, users can be members of multiple groups. In that case, the user will have one or more supplementary GIDs. You can see this for yourself by running the id command on your Ubuntu machine:

```
reader@ubuntu:~$ id
uid=1000(reader) gid=1004(reader)
groups=1004(reader),4(adm),24(cdrom),27(sudo),30(dip),46(plugdev),108(lxd),
1000(lpadmin),1001(sambashare),1002(debian-tor),1003(libvirtd)
reader@ubuntu:~$
```

In the preceding output, we can see the following things:

- The uid for the reader user is 1000; Linux typically starts numbering normal users at 1000
- The gid is 1004, which corresponds to the reader group; by default, Linux creates a group with the same name as the user (unless told specifically not to)
- Other groups include adm, sudo, and others

What does this mean? The current logged-in user has a uid of 1000, a primary gid of 1004, and a few supplementary groups, which makes sure that it has other privileges. For example, under Ubuntu, the cdrom group allows the user to have access to the disk drive. The sudo group allows the user to perform administrative commands, and the adm group allows the user to read administrative files.

While we typically refer to users and groups by name, this is just a representation for the UIDs and GIDs that Linux provides us with. On a system level, only the UID and GIDs are important for permissions. This makes it possible, for example, to have two users with the same username but different UIDs: the permissions for those users will not be the same. The other way around is also possible: two different usernames with the same UID—this causes the permissions for both users to be the same, at least on the UID level. However, both situations are terribly confusing and should not be used! As we'll see later on, using groups to share permissions is by far the best solution for sharing files and directories.

Another thing to keep in mind is that UIDs and GIDs are *local to the machine*. So if I have a user named **bob** with UID 1000 on machine A, and UID 1000 is mapped to user **alice** on machine B, transferring **bob**'s files from machine A to machine B would result in the files being owned by **alice** on system B!

The RWX permissions explained previously relate to the users and groups we're discussing now. In essence, every file (or directory, which is just a different type of file), has the following attributes:

- The file is owned by a *user*, which has (part of) the RWX permissions
- The file is also owned by a *group*, which again, has (part of) the RWX permissions
- The file finally has RWX permissions for *others*, which means all different users that don't share the group

To determine if a user can read, write, or execute a file or directory, we need to look at the following attributes (not necessarily in this order):

- Is the user the owner of the file? What RWX permissions does the owner have?
- Is the user part of the group that owns the file? What RWX permissions have been set for the group?
- Does the file have enough permissions on the *others* attribute?

Let's look at some simple examples before it gets too abstract. On your virtual machine, follow along with the following commands:

```
reader@ubuntu:~$ pwd
/home/reader
reader@ubuntu:~$ ls -l
total 4
-rw-rw-r-- 1 reader reader 69 Jul 14 13:18 nanofile.txt
```

```
reader@ubuntu:~$ touch testfile
reader@ubuntu:~$
```

First, we ensure that we are in the home directory for the reader user. If not, we can move back there by using the cd /home/reader command or, alternatively, by just entering cd (without an argument, cd defaults to the user's home directory!). We proceed by listing the contents of the directory in the long format, using ls -l, which shows us one file: nanofile.txt, from Chapter 2, *Setting Up Your Local Environment* (don't worry if you didn't follow along there and do not have the file; we'll be creating and manipulating files in a little bit). We use a new command, touch, to create an empty file. The argument we specify for touch is interpreted as the file name, as we can see when we list the files again:

```
reader@ubuntu:~$ ls -l
total 4
-rw-rw-r-- 1 reader reader 69 Jul 14 13:18 nanofile.txt
-rw-rw-r-- 1 reader reader  0 Aug  4 13:44 testfile
reader@ubuntu:~$
```

You'll see the permission followed by two names: the username and the group name (in that order!). For our testfile, the user reader and members of the reader group can both read and write to the file, but cannot execute (on the position of the x, there is instead a –, indicating an absence of that permission). All other users, such as those that are neither *readers* nor part of the *reader* group (which, in this case, is really all other users), can only read the file due to the permission of others. This is also described in the following table:

File type (1st character)	User permissions (2nd to 4th characters)	Group permissions (5th to 7th characters)	Others permissions (8th to 10th characters)	User ownership	Group ownership
- (normal file)	rw–, read and write, no execute	rw–, read and write, no execute	r––, only read	reader	reader

If a **file** had full permissions for everyone, it would look like this: -rwxrwxrwx. For files that have all permissions for the owner and the group, but none for others, it would be –rwxrwx---. **Directories** with full permissions on user and group, but none for others, are represented as drwxrwx---.

Let's look at another example:

```
reader@ubuntu:~$ ls -l /
<SNIPPED>
dr-xr-xr-x 98 root root         0 Aug  4 10:49 proc
drwx------  3 root root      4096 Jul  1 09:40 root
```

```
drwxr-xr-x 25 root root        900 Aug  4 10:51 run
<SNIPPED>
reader@ubuntu:~$
```

The `home` directory for the systems' superuser is `/root/`. We can see from the first character on the line that it is a `d`, for *directory*. It has RWX (one last time: read, write, execute) permissions for the owner `root`, and no permissions for the group (also `root`), nor for others (as denoted by `---`). These permissions can only mean one thing: **only the user root can enter or manipulate this directory!** Let's see if our assumption is correct. Remember, *entering* a directory requires the `x` permission, while *listing* the directory contents the `r` permission. We should not be able to do either, since we're neither the `root` user or in the root group. In this case, the permissions of others will be applied, this being `---`:

```
reader@ubuntu:~$ cd /root/
-bash: cd: /root/: Permission denied
reader@ubuntu:~$ ls /root/
ls: cannot open directory '/root/': Permission denied
reader@ubuntu:~$
```

Manipulating file permissions and ownership

After reading the first part of this chapter, you should have a decent understanding of Linux file permissions, and how read, write, and executed are used on a user, group, and other levels to ensure that files are exposed exactly as required. However, up until this point, we've been dealing with static permissions. When administering a Linux system, you will most likely spend a fair bit of time adjusting and troubleshooting permissions. In this part of the book, we'll be exploring the commands we can use to manipulate the permissions on files.

chmod, umask

Let's circle back to our `testfile`. It has the following permissions: `-rw-rw----`. Read/writable by user and group, readable by others. While these permissions might be fine for most files, they are definitely not a great fit for all files. What about private files? You would not want those to be readable by everyone, perhaps not even by group members.

The Linux command to change permissions on a file or directory is chmod, which we like to read as **ch**ange file **mod**e. chmod has two operating modes: symbolic mode and numeric/octal mode. We will begin by explaining symbolic mode (which is easier to understand), before we move to octal mode (which is faster to use).

 Something we have not yet introduced is the command to view manuals for commands. The command is simply man, followed by the command for which you'd like to see the manual of. In this case, man chmod will place us into the chmod manual pager, which uses the same navigation controls as you learned for Vim. Remember, quitting is done by entering : q. In this case, just q is enough. Take a look at the chmod manual now and read at least the **description** header; it will make the explanation that follows clearer.

Symbolic mode uses the RWX construct we saw before with the UGOA letters. This might seem new, but it actually isn't! **U**sers, **G**roups, **O**thers, and **A**ll are used to denote which permissions we're changing.

To add permissions, we tell chmod who (users, groups, others, or all) we are doing this for, followed by the permission we want to add. chmod u+x <filename>, for example, will add the execute permission for the user. Similarly, removing permissions with chmod is done as follows: chmod g-rwx <filename>. Notice that we use the + sign to add permissions and the – sign to remove permissions. If we do not specify user, group, others, or all, **all** is used by default. Let's try this out on our Ubuntu machine:

```
reader@ubuntu:~$ cd
reader@ubuntu:~$ pwd
/home/reader
reader@ubuntu:~$ ls -l
total 4
-rw-rw-r-- 1 reader reader 69 Jul 14 13:18 nanofile.txt
-rw-rw-r-- 1 reader reader  0 Aug  4 13:44 testfile
reader@ubuntu:~$ chmod u+x testfile
reader@ubuntu:~$ ls -l
total 4
-rw-rw-r-- 1 reader reader 69 Jul 14 13:18 nanofile.txt
-rwxrw-r-- 1 reader reader  0 Aug  4 13:44 testfile
reader@ubuntu:~$ chmod g-rwx testfile
reader@ubuntu:~$ ls -l
total 4
-rw-rw-r-- 1 reader reader 69 Jul 14 13:18 nanofile.txt
-rwx---r-- 1 reader reader  0 Aug  4 13:44 testfile
reader@ubuntu:~$ chmod -r testfile
reader@ubuntu:~$ ls -l
total 4
```

```
-rw-rw-r-- 1 reader reader 69 Jul 14 13:18 nanofile.txt
--wx------ 1 reader reader  0 Aug  4 13:44 testfile
reader@ubuntu:~$
```

First, we added the execute permission for the user to the testfile. Next, we removed read, write, and execute from the group, resulting in -rwx---r--. In this scenario, group members are still able to read the file, however, *because everyone can still read the file*. Not the perfect permissions for privacy, to say the least. Lastly, we do not specify anything before the -r, which effectively removes read access for the user, group, and others, causing the file to end up as --wx------.

Being able to write and execute a file you can't read is a bit weird. Let's fix it and look at how octal permissions work! We can use the **verbose** option on chmod to make it print more information by using the -v flag:

```
reader@ubuntu:~$ chmod -v u+rwx testfile
mode of 'testfile' changed from 0300 (-wx------) to 0700 (rwx------)
reader@ubuntu:~$
```

As you can see, we now get output from chmod! Specifically, we can see the octal mode. Before we changed the file, the mode was 0300, and after adding read for the user, it jumped up to 0700. What do these numbers mean?

It all has to do with the binary implementation of the permission. For all three levels (user, group, others), there are 8 different possible permissions when combining read, write, and execute, as follows:

Symbolic	Octal
---	0
--x	1
-w-	2
-wx	3
r--	4
r-x	5
rw-	6
rwx	7

Basically, the octal value is between 0 and 7, for a total of 8 values. This is the reason it's called octal: from the Latin/Greek representation of 8, **octo**. The read permission is given the value of 4, write permission the value of 2, and the execute permission the value of 1.

By using this system, the value of 0 to 7 can always be uniquely related to an RWX value. RWX is *4+2+1 = 7*, RX is *4+1 = 5*, and so on.

Now that we know how octal representations work, we can use them to modify the file permissions with chmod. Let's give the test file full permissions (RWX or 7) for user, group, and others in a single command:

```
reader@ubuntu:~$ chmod -v 0777 testfile
mode of 'testfile' changed from 0700 (rwx------) to 0777 (rwxrwxrwx)
reader@ubuntu:~$ ls -l
total 4
-rw-rw-r-- 1 reader reader 69 Jul 14 13:18 nanofile.txt
-rwxrwxrwx 1 reader reader  0 Aug  4 13:44 testfile
reader@ubuntu:~$
```

In this case, chmod accepts four numbers as the argument. The first number is in regards to a special type of permission called the sticky bit; we won't be discussing this, but we have included material in the *Further reading* section for those interested. In these examples, it is always set to 0, so no special bits are set. The second number maps to the user permissions, the third to group permissions, and the fourth, unsurprisingly, to the others permissions.

If we wanted to do this using symbolic representation, we could have used the chmod a+rwx command. So, why is octal faster than, as we said earlier on? Let's see what happens if we want to have different permissions for each level, for example, -rwxr-xr--. If we want to do this with symbolic representation, we'd need to use either three commands or one chained command (another function of chmod):

```
reader@ubuntu:~$ chmod 0000 testfile
reader@ubuntu:~$ ls -l
total 4
-rw-rw-r-- 1 reader reader 69 Jul 14 13:18 nanofile.txt
---------- 1 reader reader  0 Aug  4 13:44 testfile
reader@ubuntu:~$ chmod u+rwx,g+rx,o+r testfile
reader@ubuntu:~$ ls -l
total 4
-rw-rw-r-- 1 reader reader 69 Jul 14 13:18 nanofile.txt
-rwxr-xr-- 1 reader reader  0 Aug  4 13:44 testfile
reader@ubuntu:~$
```

As you can see from the chmod u+rwx,g+rx,o+r testfile command, things have gotten a bit complicated. Using octal notation, however, the command is much simpler:

```
reader@ubuntu:~$ chmod 0000 testfile
reader@ubuntu:~$ ls -l
total 4
-rw-rw-r-- 1 reader reader 69 Jul 14 13:18 nanofile.txt
```

```
---------- 1 reader reader  0 Aug  4 13:44 testfile
reader@ubuntu:~$ chmod 0754 testfile
reader@ubuntu:~$ ls -l
total 4
-rw-rw-r-- 1 reader reader 69 Jul 14 13:18 nanofile.txt
-rwxr-xr-- 1 reader reader  0 Aug  4 13:44 testfile
reader@ubuntu:~$
```

Basically, the difference is mainly using *imperative* notation (add or remove permissions) versus *declarative* notation (set it to these values). In our experience, declarative is almost always the better/safer option. With imperative, we need to first check the current permissions and mutate them; with declarative, we can just specify in a single command exactly what we want.

 It might be obvious by now, but we prefer to use the octal notation. Besides the benefits from shorter, simpler commands that are handled declaratively, another benefit is that most examples you will find online use the octal notation as well. To fully understand these examples, you will need to at least understand octals. And, if you need to understand them anyway, nothing beats using them in your day to day life!

Earlier, when we used the touch command, we ended up with a file that could be read and written to by both the user and group, and was readable to others. These seem to be default permissions, but where do they come from? And how can we manipulate them? Let's meet umask:

```
reader@ubuntu:~$ umask
0002
reader@ubuntu:~$
```

The umask session is used to determine the file permissions for newly created files and directories. For files, the following is done: take the maximum octal value for files, 0666, and subtract the umask (in this case, 0002), which gives us 0664. This would mean that newly created files are -rw-rwr--, which is exactly what we saw for our testfile. Why do we take 0666 and not 0777, you might ask? This is a protection that Linux provides; if we were to use 0777, most files would be created as executable. Executable files can be dangerous, and the design decision was made that files should only be executable when explicitly set that way. So, with the current implementation, there is no such thing as *accidentally* creating an executable file. For directories, the normal octal value of 0777 is used, which means that directories are created with 0775, -rwxrwxr-x permissions. We can check this out by creating a new directory with the mkdir command:

```
reader@ubuntu:~$ ls -l
total 4
```

```
-rw-rw-r-- 1 reader reader 69 Jul 14 13:18 nanofile.txt
-rwxr-xr-- 1 reader reader  0 Aug  4 13:44 testfile
reader@ubuntu:~$ umask
0002
reader@ubuntu:~$ mkdir testdir
reader@ubuntu:~$ ls -l
total 8
-rw-rw-r-- 1 reader reader   69 Jul 14 13:18 nanofile.txt
drwxrwxr-x 2 reader reader 4096 Aug  4 16:16 testdir
-rwxr-xr-- 1 reader reader    0 Aug  4 13:44 testfile
reader@ubuntu:~$
```

Because the execute permission on a directory is much less dangerous (remember, it is used to determine if you can move into the directory), this implementation differs from files.

We have one last trick we'd like to showcase with regards to umask. In specific cases, we'd like to determine default values for files and directories ourselves. We can also do this using the umask command:

```
reader@ubuntu:~$ umask
0002
reader@ubuntu:~$ umask 0007
reader@ubuntu:~$ umask
0007
reader@ubuntu:~$ touch umaskfile
reader@ubuntu:~$ mkdir umaskdir
reader@ubuntu:~$ ls -l
total 12
-rw-rw-r-- 1 reader reader   69 Jul 14 13:18 nanofile.txt
drwxrwxr-x 2 reader reader 4096 Aug  4 16:16 testdir
-rwxr-xr-- 1 reader reader    0 Aug  4 13:44 testfile
drwxrwx--- 2 reader reader 4096 Aug  4 16:18 umaskdir
-rw-rw---- 1 reader reader    0 Aug  4 16:18 umaskfile
reader@ubuntu:~$
```

In the preceding example, you can see that running the umask command without arguments prints the current umask. Running it with a valid umask value as an argument changes umask to that value, which is then used when creating new files and directories. Compare umaskfile and umaskdir with the earlier testfile and testdir in the preceding output. This is very useful if we want to create files that are private by default!

sudo, chown, and chgrp

So far, we have seen how we can manipulate the (basic) permissions for files and directories. However, we haven't dealt with changing either the owner or the group for a file. It would be a little impractical to always have to work with users and groups as they were at creation time. For Linux, we can use two tools to change the owner and group: **change own**er (chown) and **change group** (chgrp). However, there is one very important thing to note: these commands can only be executed for someone with root permissions (which will, typically, be the root user). So, before we introduce you to chown and chgrp, let's look at sudo!

sudo

The sudo command was originally named for **s**uper**u**ser **do**, which, as the name implies, gives you a chance to perform an action as the root superuser. The sudo command uses the /etc/sudoers file to determine if users are allowed to elevate to superuser permissions. Let's see how it works!

```
reader@ubuntu:~$ cat /etc/sudoers
cat: /etc/sudoers: Permission denied
reader@ubuntu:~$ ls -l /etc/sudoers
-r--r----- 1 root root 755 Jan 18  2018 /etc/sudoers
reader@ubuntu:~$ sudo cat /etc/sudoers
[sudo] password for reader:
#
# This file MUST be edited with the 'visudo' command as root.
#
# Please consider adding local content in /etc/sudoers.d/ instead of
# directly modifying this file.
#
# See the man page for details on how to write a sudoers file.
#
Defaults       env_reset
Defaults       mail_badpass
Defaults
secure_path="/usr/local/sbin:/usr/local/bin:/usr/sbin:/usr/bin:/sbin:/bin:/
snap/bin"
<SNIPPED>
# User privilege specification
root    ALL=(ALL:ALL) ALL

# Members of the admin group may gain root privileges
%admin ALL=(ALL) ALL
```

```
# Allow members of group sudo to execute any command
%sudo    ALL=(ALL:ALL) ALL
<SNIPPED>
reader@ubuntu:~$
```

We first try to look at the contents of /etc/sudoers as a normal user. When that gives us a
Permission denied error, we look at the permissions on the file. From the -r--r-----
1 root root line, it becomes obvious that only the root user or members of the root
group can read the file. To elevate to root privileges, we use the sudo command *in front of*
the command we want to run, which is cat /etc/sudoers. For verification, Linux will
always ask the user for their password. This password is then kept in memory for about 5
minutes by default, so you do not have to type your password every time if you've recently
entered it.

After entering the password, the /etc/sudoers file is printed for us! It seems that sudo
did indeed provide us with superuser permissions. How that works is also explained by the
/etc/sudoers file. The # Allow members of group sudo to execute any
command line is a comment (since it starts with a #; more on this later) and tells us that the
line below gives all users of the sudo group permissions for any commands. On Ubuntu,
the default created user is considered an administrator and is a member of this group. Use
the id command to verify this:

```
reader@ubuntu:~$ id
uid=1000(reader) gid=1004(reader)
groups=1004(reader),4(adm),24(cdrom),27(sudo),30(dip),46(plugdev),108(lxd),
1000(lpadmin),1001(sambashare),1002(debian-tor),1003(libvirtd)
reader@ubuntu:~$
```

The sudo command has another excellent use: switching to the root user! For this, use
the --login flag, or its shorthand, -i:

```
reader@ubuntu:~$ sudo -i
[sudo] password for reader:
root@ubuntu:~#
```

In the prompt, you will see that the username has changed from reader to root.
Furthermore, the last character in your prompt is now a # instead of a $. This is also used to
denote the current elevated permissions. You can exit this elevated position by using the
built-in exit shell:

```
root@ubuntu:~# exit
logout
reader@ubuntu:~$
```

Remember, the `root` user is the superuser of the system that can do everything. And with everything, we really mean everything! Unlike other operating systems, if you tell Linux to delete the root file system and everything below it, it will happily oblige (right up until the point it has destroyed too much to work properly anymore). Do not expect an `Are you sure?` prompt either. Be very, very careful with `sudo` commands or anything in a root prompt.

chown, chgrp

After the little `sudo` detour, we can get back to file permissions: how do we change the ownership of files? Let's start with changing the group using `chgrp`. The syntax is as follows: `chgrp <groupname> <filename>`:

```
reader@ubuntu:~$ ls -l
total 12
-rw-rw-r-- 1 reader reader   69 Jul 14 13:18 nanofile.txt
drwxrwxr-x 2 reader reader 4096 Aug  4 16:16 testdir
-rwxr-xr-- 1 reader reader    0 Aug  4 13:44 testfile
drwxrwx--- 2 reader reader 4096 Aug  4 16:18 umaskdir
-rw-rw---- 1 reader reader    0 Aug  4 16:18 umaskfile
reader@ubuntu:~$ chgrp games umaskfile
chgrp: changing group of 'umaskfile': Operation not permitted
reader@ubuntu:~$ sudo chgrp games umaskfile
reader@ubuntu:~$ ls -l
total 12
-rw-rw-r-- 1 reader reader   69 Jul 14 13:18 nanofile.txt
drwxrwxr-x 2 reader reader 4096 Aug  4 16:16 testdir
-rwxr-xr-- 1 reader reader    0 Aug  4 13:44 testfile
drwxrwx--- 2 reader reader 4096 Aug  4 16:18 umaskdir
-rw-rw---- 1 reader games    0 Aug  4 16:18 umaskfile
reader@ubuntu:~$
```

First, we list the contents using `ls`. Next, we try to use `chgrp` to change the group of the `umaskfile` file to games. However, since this is a privileged operation and we did not start the command with `sudo`, it fails with the `Operation not permitted` error message. Next, we use the correct `sudo chgrp games umaskfile` command, which does not give us feedback; generally, this is a good sign in Linux. We list the files again to make sure that this is the case, and we can see that the group has changed to `games` for the `umaskfile`!

Let's do the same, but now for the user, by using the `chown` command. The syntax is the same as `chgrp`: `chown <username> <filename>`:

```
reader@ubuntu:~$ sudo chown pollinate umaskfile
reader@ubuntu:~$ ls -l
total 12
-rw-rw-r-- 1 reader    reader   69 Jul 14 13:18 nanofile.txt
drwxrwxr-x 2 reader    reader 4096 Aug  4 16:16 testdir
-rwxr-xr-- 1 reader    reader    0 Aug  4 13:44 testfile
drwxrwx--- 2 reader    reader 4096 Aug  4 16:18 umaskdir
-rw-rw---- 1 pollinate games    0 Aug  4 16:18 umaskfile
reader@ubuntu:~$
```

As we can see, we have now changed the file ownership from `reader:reader` to `pollinate:games`. However, there is one little trick that's so convenient that we'd like to show you it right away! You can actually use `chown` to change both users and groups by using the following syntax: `chown <username>:<groupname> <filename>`. Let's see if this can restore the `umaskfile` to its original ownership:

```
reader@ubuntu:~$ ls -l
total 12
-rw-rw-r-- 1 reader    reader   69 Jul 14 13:18 nanofile.txt
drwxrwxr-x 2 reader    reader 4096 Aug  4 16:16 testdir
-rwxr-xr-- 1 reader    reader    0 Aug  4 13:44 testfile
drwxrwx--- 2 reader    reader 4096 Aug  4 16:18 umaskdir
-rw-rw---- 1 pollinate games    0 Aug  4 16:18 umaskfile
reader@ubuntu:~$ sudo chown reader:reader umaskfile
reader@ubuntu:~$ ls -l
total 12
-rw-rw-r-- 1 reader reader   69 Jul 14 13:18 nanofile.txt
drwxrwxr-x 2 reader reader 4096 Aug  4 16:16 testdir
-rwxr-xr-- 1 reader reader    0 Aug  4 13:44 testfile
drwxrwx--- 2 reader reader 4096 Aug  4 16:18 umaskdir
-rw-rw---- 1 reader reader    0 Aug  4 16:18 umaskfile
reader@ubuntu:~$
```

 We used random users and groups in the preceding examples. If you want to see which groups are present on the system, inspect the `/etc/group` file. For users, the same information can be found in `/etc/passwd`.

Working with multiple users

As we've stated before, Linux is inherently a multi-user system, especially in the context of a Linux server, where these systems are often administered not by a single user, but often a (large) team. Each user on a server has it own set of permissions. Imagine, for example, a server where three departments need to be development, operations, and security. Development and operations both have their own stuff there, but also need to share some other things. The security department needs to be able to view everything to ensure proper compliance and adherence to security guidelines. How could we arrange such a structure? Let's make it happen!

First, we need to create some users. For each department, we will create a single user, but since we're going to ensure permissions on the group level, this will work just as well for 5, 10, or 100 users in each department. We can create users with the useradd command. In its basic form, we can just use useradd <username>, and Linux will handle the rest via default values. Obviously, as with almost everything in Linux, this is highly customizable; check the man page (man useradd) for more information.

As was the case with chown and chgrp, useradd (and later usermod) is a privileged command, which we will execute with sudo:

```
reader@ubuntu:~$ useradd dev-user1
useradd: Permission denied.
useradd: cannot lock /etc/passwd; try again later.
reader@ubuntu:~$ sudo useradd dev-user1
[sudo] password for reader:
reader@ubuntu:~$ sudo useradd ops-user1
reader@ubuntu:~$ sudo useradd sec-user1
reader@ubuntu:~$ id dev-user1
uid=1001(dev-user1) gid=1005(dev-user1) groups=1005(dev-user1)
reader@ubuntu:~$ id ops-user1
uid=1002(ops-user1) gid=1006(ops-user1) groups=1006(ops-user1)
reader@ubuntu:~$ id sec-user1
uid=1003(sec-user1) gid=1007(sec-user1) groups=1007(sec-user1)
reader@ubuntu:~$
```

As a last reminder, we've showed you what happens when you forget sudo. While the error message is technically fully correct (you need root permissions to edit /etc/passwd, where user information is stored), it might not be fully obvious why the command is failing, especially because of the misleading try again later! error.

With `sudo`, however, we are able to add three users: `dev-user1`, `ops-user1`, and `sec-user1`. When we inspect these users in order, we can see that their `uid` goes up by one each time. We can also see that a group with the same name as the user is created, and that that is the sole group of which the users are a member. Groups also have their `gid`, which is incremented by one for each next user.

So, now we have the users in place, but we need shared groups. For this, we have a similar command (both in name and operation): `groupadd`. Check the man page for `groupadd` and add three groups corresponding to our departments:

```
reader@ubuntu:~$ sudo groupadd development
reader@ubuntu:~$ sudo groupadd operations
reader@ubuntu:~$ sudo groupadd security
reader@ubuntu:~$
```

To see which groups are already available, you can check out the `/etc/group` file (with, for example, `less` or `cat`). Once you're satisfied, we now have the users and groups in place. But how do we make the users members of the groups? Enter `usermod` (which stands for **user mod**ify). The syntax to set a user's primary group is as follows: `usermod -g <groupname> <username>`:

```
reader@ubuntu:~$ sudo usermod -g development dev-user1
reader@ubuntu:~$ sudo usermod -g operations ops-user1
reader@ubuntu:~$ sudo usermod -g security sec-user1
reader@ubuntu:~$ id dev-user1
uid=1001(dev-user1) gid=1008(development) groups=1008(development)
reader@ubuntu:~$ id ops-user1
uid=1002(ops-user1) gid=1009(operations) groups=1009(operations)
reader@ubuntu:~$ id sec-user1
uid=1003(sec-user1) gid=1010(security) groups=1010(security)
reader@ubuntu:~$
```

What we have accomplished now is closer to our goal, but we're not there yet. So far, we have only ensured that multiple developers can share files by all being in the development group. But how about the shared folder between development and operations? And how can security monitor everything? Let's create some directories (using `mkdir`, which stands for **make dir**ectory) with the correct groups and see how far we can get:

```
reader@ubuntu:~$ sudo mkdir /data
[sudo] password for reader:
reader@ubuntu:~$ cd /data
reader@ubuntu:/data$ sudo mkdir dev-files
reader@ubuntu:/data$ sudo mkdir ops-files
reader@ubuntu:/data$ sudo mkdir devops-files
reader@ubuntu:/data$ ls -l
```

```
total 12
drwxr-xr-x 2 root root 4096 Aug 11 10:03 dev-files
drwxr-xr-x 2 root root 4096 Aug 11 10:04 devops-files
drwxr-xr-x 2 root root 4096 Aug 11 10:04 ops-files
reader@ubuntu:/data$ sudo chgrp development dev-files/
reader@ubuntu:/data$ sudo chgrp operations ops-files/
reader@ubuntu:/data$ sudo chmod 0770 dev-files/
reader@ubuntu:/data$ sudo chmod 0770 ops-files/
reader@ubuntu:/data$ ls -l
total 12
drwxrwx--- 2 root development 4096 Aug 11 10:03 dev-files
drwxr-xr-x 2 root root        4096 Aug 11 10:04 devops-files
drwxrwx--- 2 root operations  4096 Aug 11 10:04 ops-files
reader@ubuntu:/data
```

We now have the following structure: a /data/ top level directory, which contains the directories dev-files and ops-files, which are owned by the development and operations groups, respectively. Now, let's fulfill the requirement that security can go into both directories and manage the files! Apart from using usermod to change the main groups, we can also append users to extra groups. In this case, the syntax is usermod -a -G <groupnames> <username>. Let's add sec-user1 to the development and operations groups:

```
reader@ubuntu:/data$ id sec-user1
uid=1003(sec-user1) gid=1010(security) groups=1010(security)
reader@ubuntu:/data$ sudo usermod -a -G development,operations sec-user1
reader@ubuntu:/data$ id sec-user1
uid=1003(sec-user1) gid=1010(security)
groups=1010(security),1008(development),1009(operations)
reader@ubuntu:/data$
```

The user from the security department is now a member of all new groups: security, development, and operations. Since both /data/dev-files/ and /data/ops-files/ do not have permissions for *others*, our current user should not be able to enter either, but sec-user1 should be. Let's see if this is correct:

```
reader@ubuntu:/data$ sudo su - sec-user1
No directory, logging in with HOME=/
$ cd /data/
$ ls -l
total 12
drwxrwx--- 2 root development 4096 Aug 11 10:03 dev-files
drwxr-xr-x 2 root root        4096 Aug 11 10:04 devops-files
drwxrwx--- 2 root operations  4096 Aug 11 10:04 ops-files
$ cd dev-files
$ pwd
```

```
/data/dev-files
$ touch security-file
$ ls -l
total 0
-rw-r--r-- 1 sec-user1 security 0 Aug 11 10:16 security-file
$ exit
reader@ubuntu:/data$
```

If you followed along with this example, you should see that we introduced a new command: su. Short for **s**witch **u**ser, it allows us to, well, switch between users. If you prefix it with sudo, you can switch to a user without needing the password for that user, as long as you have those privileges. Otherwise, you will have to enter the password (which is hard in this case, since we haven't set a password for the user). As you might have noticed, the shell is different for the new user. That's because we haven't loaded any configuration (which is automatically done for the default user). Don't worry about that, though—it's still a fully functioning shell! Our test succeeded: we were able to move into the dev-files directory, even though we are not a developer. We were even able to create a file. If you want, verify that the same is possible for the ops-files directory.

Finally, let's create a new group, devops, which we will use to share files between developers and operations. After creating the group, we will add both dev-user1 and ops-user1 to this group, in the same way we added sec-user1 to the development and operations groups:

```
reader@ubuntu:/data$ sudo groupadd devops
reader@ubuntu:/data$ sudo usermod -a -G devops dev-user1
reader@ubuntu:/data$ sudo usermod -a -G devops ops-user1
reader@ubuntu:/data$ id dev-user1
uid=1001(dev-user1) gid=1008(development)
groups=1008(development),1011(devops)
reader@ubuntu:/data$ id ops-user1
uid=1002(ops-user1) gid=1009(operations)
groups=1009(operations),1011(devops)
reader@ubuntu:/data$ ls -l
total 12
drwxrwx--- 2 root development 4096 Aug 11 10:16 dev-files
drwxr-xr-x 2 root root        4096 Aug 11 10:04 devops-files
drwxrwx--- 2 root operations  4096 Aug 11 10:04 ops-files
reader@ubuntu:/data$ sudo chown root:devops devops-files/
reader@ubuntu:/data$ sudo chmod 0770 devops-files/
reader@ubuntu:/data$ ls -l
total 12
drwxrwx---  2 root development 4096 Aug 11 10:16 dev-files/
drwxrwx---  2 root devops      4096 Aug 11 10:04 devops-files/
drwxrwx---  2 root operations  4096 Aug 11 10:04 ops-files/
reader@ubuntu:/data$
```

We now have a shared directory, `/data/devops-files/`, where both `dev-user1` and `ops-user1` can enter and create files.

As an exercise, do any of the following:

- Add `sec-user1` to the `devops` group, so that it can also audit the shared files
- Verify that both `dev-user1` and `ops-user1` can write files in the shared directories
- Understand why `dev-user1` and `ops-user1` can only read each other's files in the `devops` directory, but cannot edit them (hint: the next section of this chapter, *Advanced permissions*, will tell you how to solve this with SGID)

Advanced permissions

This covers the basic permissions for Linux. There are, however, some advanced topics that we'd like to point out, but we will not be discussing them at length. For more information on these topics, check the *Further reading* section at the end of this chapter. We have included a reference for file attributes, special file permissions, and access control lists.

File attributes

Files can also have attributes that are expressed in another way than the permissions we have seen so far. An example of this is making a file immutable (a fancy word, which means it cannot be changed). An immutable file still has normal ownership and group and RWX permissions, but it will not allow the user to change it, even if it contains the writable permission. Another characteristic of this is that the file cannot be renamed.

Other file attributes include *undeletable, append only,* and *compressed*. For more information on file attributes, check the man pages for the `lsattr` and `chattr` commands (`man lsattr` and `man chattr`).

Special file permissions

As you might have noticed in the part about octal notation, we always start the notation with a zero (0775, 0640, and so on). Why do we include the zero if we do not use it? That position is reserved for special file permissions: SUID, SGID, and the sticky bit. They have a similar octal notation (where SUID is 4, SGID is 2, and the sticky bit is 1) and are used in the following manner:

	Files	Directories
SUID	Files are executed with the permissions of the owner, regardless of which user executes it.	Does nothing.
SGID	Files are executed with the permissions of the group, regardless of which user executes it.	Files that are created in this directory get the same group as the directory.
Sticky bit	Does nothing.	User can only delete their own files within this directory. See the /tmp/ directory for its most famous use.

Access Control Lists (ACLs)

ACLs are a way to increase the flexibility of the UGO/RWX system. Using setfacl (**set file acl**) and getfacl (**get file acl**), you can set additional permissions for files and directories. So, for example, using ACLs, you could say that, while the /root/ directory is normally only accessible by the root user, it could also be read by the reader user. The other way to accomplish this, which is by adding the reader user to the root group, also gives the reader user many other privileges on the system (anything that has permissions on the root group has then been granted to the reader user!). While ACLs are not often used in practice in our experience, for edge cases they can be the difference between a complex solution and a simple one.

Summary

In this chapter, we have looked at the Linux permissions scheme. We have learned that there are two main axes on which permissions are arranged: file permissions and file ownership. For file permissions, each file has an allowance (or disallowance) on *read*, *write*, and *execute* permissions. How these permissions work differs for files and directories. Permissions are applied by using ownership: a file is always owned by a user and a group. Besides the *user* and *group*, there are also file permissions present for everyone else, called the *others* ownership. If the user is either the owner or a member of the file's group, those permissions are available to the user. Otherwise, there need to be permissions for others to allow interaction with the file.

Next, we learned how to manipulate file permissions and ownership. By using chmod and umask, we were able to get the file permissions in the way we needed. Using sudo, chown, and chgrp, we manipulated the owner and group of a file. A warning was given about the usage of sudo and the root user, since both can render a Linux system inoperable with very little effort.

We continued with an example of working with multiple users. We added three additional users to the system using useradd, and gave them the correct groups with usermod. We saw how those users can be members of the same groups and, in that way, share access to files.

Finally, we touched on some basics of advanced permissions under Linux. The *Further reading* section contains more information for those subjects.

The following commands were introduced in this chapter: id, touch, chmod, umask, chown, chgrp, sudo, useradd, groupadd, usermod, mkdir, and su.

Questions

1. Which three permissions are used for Linux files?
2. Which three types of ownership are defined for Linux files?
3. Which command is used to change the permissions on a file?
4. What mechanism controls the default permissions for newly created files?
5. How is the following symbolic permission described in octal: `rwxrw-r--`?
6. How is the following octal permission described symbolically: `0644`?
7. Which command allows us to gain superuser privileges?
8. Which commands can we use to change ownership for a file?
9. How can we arrange for multiple users to share access to files?
10. Which types of advanced permissions does Linux have?

Further reading

The following resources might be interesting if you'd like to go deeper into the subjects of this chapter:

- **Fundamentals of Linux** by *Oliver Pelz*, Packt: `https://www.packtpub.com/networking-and-servers/fundamentals-linux`
- **File attributes**: `https://linoxide.com/how-tos/howto-show-file-attributes-in-linux/`
- **Special file permissions**: `https://thegeeksalive.com/linux-special-permissions/`
- **Access Control Lists**: `https://www.tecmint.com/secure-files-using-acls-in-linux/`

6
File Manipulation

This chapter is dedicated to file manipulation. As in *everything is a file*system, file manipulation is considered one of the most important aspects of working with Linux. We will start by exploring common file operations, such as creating, copying, and deleting files. We will continue with a bit on archiving, another important tool when working on the command line. The last part of this chapter will be devoted to finding files on the file system, another important skill in the toolset of a shell scripter.

The following commands will be introduced in this chapter: cp, rm, mv, ln, tar, locate, and find.

The following topics will be covered in this chapter:

- Common file operations
- Archiving
- Finding files

Technical requirements

We will practice file manipulation using the virtual machine we created in Chapter 2, *Setting Up Your Local Environment*. No further resources are needed at this point.

Common file operations

So far, we have mainly introduced commands related to navigation on the Linux filesystem. In earlier chapters, we already saw that we can use mkdir and touch to create directories and empty files, respectively. If we want to give a file some meaningful (text) content, we use vim or nano. However, we have not yet talked about removing files or directories, or copying, renaming, or creating shortcuts. Let's start with copying files.

Copying

In essence, copying a file on Linux is really simple: use the `cp` command, followed by the filename-to-be-copied to the filename-to-copy-to. It looks something like this:

```
reader@ubuntu:~$ ls -l
total 12
-rw-rw-r-- 1 reader reader   69 Jul 14 13:18 nanofile.txt
drwxrwxr-x 2 reader reader 4096 Aug  4 16:16 testdir
-rwxr-xr-- 1 reader reader    0 Aug  4 13:44 testfile
drwxrwx--- 2 reader reader 4096 Aug  4 16:18 umaskdir
-rw-rw---- 1 reader games    0 Aug  4 16:18 umaskfile
reader@ubuntu:~$ cp testfile testfilecopy
reader@ubuntu:~$ ls -l
total 12
-rw-rw-r-- 1 reader reader   69 Jul 14 13:18 nanofile.txt
drwxrwxr-x 2 reader reader 4096 Aug  4 16:16 testdir
-rwxr-xr-- 1 reader reader    0 Aug  4 13:44 testfile
-rwxr-xr-- 1 reader reader    0 Aug 18 14:00 testfilecopy
drwxrwx--- 2 reader reader 4096 Aug  4 16:18 umaskdir
-rw-rw---- 1 reader games    0 Aug  4 16:18 umaskfile
reader@ubuntu:~$
```

As you can see, in this example we copied an (empty) *file* that was already *owned by us*, while we were *in the same directory* as the file. This might raise some questions, such as:

- Do we always need to be in the same directory as the source and destination file?
- What about the permissions of the file?
- Can we also copy directories with `cp`?

As you might expect, as with many things under Linux, the `cp` command is also very versatile. We can indeed copy files not owned by us; we do not need to be in the same directory as the file, and we can also copy directories! Let's try a few of these things out:

```
reader@ubuntu:~$ cd /var/log/
reader@ubuntu:/var/log$ ls -l
total 3688
<SNIPPED>
drwxr-xr-x  2 root       root                4096 Apr 17 20:22 dist-upgrade
-rw-r--r--  1 root       root              550975 Aug 18 13:35 dpkg.log
-rw-r--r--  1 root       root               32160 Aug 11 10:15 faillog
<SNIPPED>
-rw-------  1 root       root               64320 Aug 11 10:15 tallylog
<SNIPPED>
reader@ubuntu:/var/log$ cp dpkg.log /home/reader/
reader@ubuntu:/var/log$ ls -l /home/reader/
```

```
total 552
-rw-r--r-- 1 reader reader 550975 Aug 18 14:20 dpkg.log
-rw-rw-r-- 1 reader reader     69 Jul 14 13:18 nanofile.txt
drwxrwxr-x 2 reader reader   4096 Aug  4 16:16 testdir
-rwxr-xr-- 1 reader reader      0 Aug  4 13:44 testfile
-rwxr-xr-- 1 reader reader      0 Aug 18 14:00 testfilecopy
drwxrwx--- 2 reader reader   4096 Aug  4 16:18 umaskdir
-rw-rw---- 1 reader games      0 Aug  4 16:18 umaskfile
reader@ubuntu:/var/log$ cp tallylog /home/reader/
cp: cannot open 'tallylog' for reading: Permission denied
reader@ubuntu:/var/log$
```

So, what happened? We used `cd` to change the directory to `/var/log/`. We listed the files there using `ls` with the *long* option. We copied a file with a relative path that we were able to read, but that was owned by `root:root`, to the fully qualified `/home/reader/` directory. When we listed `/home/reader/` with the fully qualified path, we saw that the copied file was now owned by `reader:reader`. When we tried to do the same for the `tallylog` file, we got the error `cannot open 'tallylog' for reading: Permission denied`. This should not be unexpected, since we do not have any read permissions on that file, so copying would be hard.

This should answer two of the three questions. But what about directories? Let's try to copy the `/tmp/` directory into our `home` directory:

```
reader@ubuntu:/var/log$ cd
reader@ubuntu:~$ cp /tmp/ .
cp: -r not specified; omitting directory '/tmp/'
reader@ubuntu:~$ ls -l
total 552
-rw-r--r-- 1 reader reader 550975 Aug 18 14:20 dpkg.log
-rw-rw-r-- 1 reader reader     69 Jul 14 13:18 nanofile.txt
drwxrwxr-x 2 reader reader   4096 Aug  4 16:16 testdir
-rwxr-xr-- 1 reader reader      0 Aug  4 13:44 testfile
-rwxr-xr-- 1 reader reader      0 Aug 18 14:00 testfilecopy
drwxrwx--- 2 reader reader   4096 Aug  4 16:18 umaskdir
-rw-rw---- 1 reader games      0 Aug  4 16:18 umaskfile
reader@ubuntu:~$ cp -r /tmp/ .
cp: cannot access '/tmp/systemd-private-72bcf47b69464914b021b421d5999bbe-
systemd-timesyncd.service-LeF05x': Permission denied
cp: cannot access '/tmp/systemd-private-72bcf47b69464914b021b421d5999bbe-
systemd-resolved.service-ApdzhW': Permission denied
reader@ubuntu:~$ ls -l
total 556
-rw-r--r-- 1 reader reader 550975 Aug 18 14:20 dpkg.log
-rw-rw-r-- 1 reader reader     69 Jul 14 13:18 nanofile.txt
drwxrwxr-x 2 reader reader   4096 Aug  4 16:16 testdir
```

```
-rwxr-xr-- 1 reader reader        0 Aug  4 13:44 testfile
-rwxr-xr-- 1 reader reader        0 Aug 18 14:00 testfilecopy
drwxrwxr-t 9 reader reader     4096 Aug 18 14:38 tmp
drwxrwx--- 2 reader reader     4096 Aug  4 16:18 umaskdir
-rw-rw---- 1 reader games        0 Aug  4 16:18 umaskfile
reader@ubuntu:~$
```

For such a simple exercise, a lot actually happened! First, we navigate back to our home directory using cd without any arguments; a neat little trick in itself. Next, we try to copy the entire /tmp/ directory to . (which, as you should remember, is shorthand for *current directory*). However, this fails with the error -r not specified; omitting directory '/tmp/'. We list the directory to check this, and indeed, it seems like nothing happened. When we add the -r, as specified by the error, and retry the command, we get some Permission denied errors. This is not unexpected, since not all files *inside* the /tmp/ directory will be readable to us. Even though we got the errors, when we now check the contents of our home directory, we can see the tmp directory there! So, using the -r option, which is short for --recursive, allows us to copy directories and everything that's in them.

Removing

After copying some files and directories into our home directory (which is a safe bet, because we know for sure that we can write there!), we're left with a little mess. Instead of only creating files, let's use the rm command to remove some duplicate items:

```
reader@ubuntu:~$ ls -l
total 556
-rw-r--r-- 1 reader reader 550975 Aug 18 14:20 dpkg.log
-rw-rw-r-- 1 reader reader     69 Jul 14 13:18 nanofile.txt
drwxrwxr-x 2 reader reader   4096 Aug  4 16:16 testdir
-rwxr-xr-- 1 reader reader      0 Aug  4 13:44 testfile
-rwxr-xr-- 1 reader reader      0 Aug 18 14:00 testfilecopy
drwxrwxr-t 9 reader reader   4096 Aug 18 14:38 tmp
drwxrwx--- 2 reader reader   4096 Aug  4 16:18 umaskdir
-rw-rw---- 1 reader games      0 Aug  4 16:18 umaskfile
reader@ubuntu:~$ rm testfilecopy
reader@ubuntu:~$ rm tmp/
rm: cannot remove 'tmp/': Is a directory
reader@ubuntu:~$ rm -r tmp/
reader@ubuntu:~$ ls -l
total 552
-rw-r--r-- 1 reader reader 550975 Aug 18 14:20 dpkg.log
-rw-rw-r-- 1 reader reader     69 Jul 14 13:18 nanofile.txt
drwxrwxr-x 2 reader reader   4096 Aug  4 16:16 testdir
```

```
-rwxr-xr-- 1 reader reader       0 Aug  4 13:44 testfile
drwxrwx--- 2 reader reader    4096 Aug  4 16:18 umaskdir
-rw-rw---- 1 reader games        0 Aug  4 16:18 umaskfile
reader@ubuntu:~$
```

Using `rm` followed by a filename deletes it. As you might notice, there is no **Are you sure?** prompt. This can actually be enabled by using the `-i` flag, but by default this is not the case. Consider that `rm` also allows you to use wildcards, such as `*` (which matches everything), which will delete every file that is matched (and can be deleted by the user). In short, this is a great way to lose your files really quickly! When we tried to use `rm` with the name of a directory, however, it gave the error `cannot remove 'tmp/': Is a directory`. This is very similar to the `cp` command, and luckily for us, the remediation is also the same: add `-r` for a *recursive* delete! Again, this is a great way to lose files; a single command lets you delete your entire `home` directory and everything in it, without so much as a warning. Consider **this** your warning! Especially when using in combination with the `-f` flag, which is short for `--force`, which will ensure that `rm` *never prompts* and starts deleting right away.

Renaming, moving, and linking

Sometimes, we do not just want to create or delete a file, we might need to rename one. Weirdly, Linux does not have anything that sounds like rename; however, the `mv` command (for **m**ove) does accomplish the functionality that we want. Similar to the `cp` command, it takes a source file and destination file as arguments, and looks like this:

```
reader@ubuntu:~$ ls -l
total 552
-rw-r--r-- 1 reader reader 550975 Aug 18 14:20 dpkg.log
-rw-rw-r-- 1 reader reader     69 Jul 14 13:18 nanofile.txt
drwxrwxr-x 2 reader reader   4096 Aug  4 16:16 testdir
-rwxr-xr-- 1 reader reader      0 Aug  4 13:44 testfile
drwxrwx--- 2 reader reader   4096 Aug  4 16:18 umaskdir
-rw-rw---- 1 reader games       0 Aug  4 16:18 umaskfile
reader@ubuntu:~$ mv testfile renamedtestfile
reader@ubuntu:~$ mv testdir/ renamedtestdir
reader@ubuntu:~$ ls -l
total 552
-rw-r--r-- 1 reader reader 550975 Aug 18 14:20 dpkg.log
-rw-rw-r-- 1 reader reader     69 Jul 14 13:18 nanofile.txt
drwxrwxr-x 2 reader reader   4096 Aug  4 16:16 renamedtestdir
-rwxr-xr-- 1 reader reader      0 Aug  4 13:44 renamedtestfile
drwxrwx--- 2 reader reader   4096 Aug  4 16:18 umaskdir
-rw-rw---- 1 reader games       0 Aug  4 16:18 umaskfile
reader@ubuntu:~$
```

As you can see, the `mv` command is really simple to use. It even works for directories, without needing a special option such as the `-r` we saw for `cp` and `rm`. It does, however, get a little more complex when we introduce wildcards, but don't worry about that for now. The commands we used in the preceding code are relative, but they work just as well fully qualified or mixed.

Sometimes, you'll want to move a file from one directory into another. If you think about it, this is actually a rename of the fully qualified file name! No data is being touched, but you just want to reach the file somewhere else. So, using `mv umaskfile umaskdir/` will move the `umaskfile` into `umaskdir/`:

```
reader@ubuntu:~$ ls -l
total 16
-rw-r--r-- 1 reader reader 550975 Aug 18 14:20 dpkg.log
-rw-rw-r-- 1 reader reader     69 Jul 14 13:18 nanofile.txt
drwxrwxr-x 2 reader reader   4096 Aug  4 16:16 renamedtestdir
-rwxr-xr-- 1 reader reader      0 Aug  4 13:44 renamedtestfile
drwxrwx--- 2 reader reader   4096 Aug  4 16:18 umaskdir
-rw-rw---- 1 reader games      0 Aug  4 16:18 umaskfile
reader@ubuntu:~$ mv umaskfile umaskdir/
reader@ubuntu:~$ ls -l
total 16
-rw-r--r-- 1 reader reader 550975 Aug 18 14:20 dpkg.log
-rw-rw-r-- 1 reader reader     69 Jul 14 13:18 nanofile.txt
drwxrwxr-x 2 reader reader   4096 Aug  4 16:16 renamedtestdir
-rwxr-xr-- 1 reader reader      0 Aug  4 13:44 renamedtestfile
drwxrwx--- 2 reader reader   4096 Aug 19 10:37 umaskdir
reader@ubuntu:~$ ls -l umaskdir/
total 0
-rw-rw---- 1 reader games 0 Aug  4 16:18 umaskfile
reader@ubuntu:~$
```

Finally, we have the `ln` command, which stands for **lin**king. This is the Linux way of creating links between files, which are closest to the shortcuts that Windows uses. There are two types of links: symbolic links (also called soft links) and hard links. The difference is found deeper in the filesystem workings: a symbolic link refers to the filename (or directory name), whereas a hard link links to *inode* that stores the contents of the file or directory. For scripting, if you're using links, you're probably using symbolic links, so let's see those in action:

```
reader@ubuntu:~$ ls -l
total 552
-rw-r--r-- 1 reader reader 550975 Aug 18 14:20 dpkg.log
-rw-rw-r-- 1 reader reader     69 Jul 14 13:18 nanofile.txt
drwxrwxr-x 2 reader reader   4096 Aug  4 16:16 renamedtestdir
-rwxr-xr-- 1 reader reader      0 Aug  4 13:44 renamedtestfile
```

```
drwxrwx--- 2 reader reader    4096 Aug  4 16:18 umaskdir
-rw-rw---- 1 reader games        0 Aug  4 16:18 umaskfile
reader@ubuntu:~$ ln -s /var/log/auth.log
reader@ubuntu:~$ ln -s /var/log/auth.log link-to-auth.log
reader@ubuntu:~$ ln -s /tmp/
reader@ubuntu:~$ ln -s /tmp/ link-to-tmp
reader@ubuntu:~$ ls -l
total 552
lrwxrwxrwx 1 reader reader      17 Aug 18 15:07 auth.log ->
/var/log/auth.log
-rw-r--r-- 1 reader reader 550975 Aug 18 14:20 dpkg.log
lrwxrwxrwx 1 reader reader      17 Aug 18 15:08 link-to-auth.log ->
/var/log/auth.log
lrwxrwxrwx 1 reader reader       5 Aug 18 15:08 link-to-tmp -> /tmp/
-rw-rw-r-- 1 reader reader      69 Jul 14 13:18 nanofile.txt
drwxrwxr-x 2 reader reader    4096 Aug  4 16:16 renamedtestdir
-rwxr-xr-- 1 reader reader       0 Aug  4 13:44 renamedtestfile
lrwxrwxrwx 1 reader reader       5 Aug 18 15:08 tmp -> /tmp/
drwxrwx--- 2 reader reader    4096 Aug  4 16:18 umaskdir
-rw-rw---- 1 reader games        0 Aug  4 16:18 umaskfile
reader@ubuntu:~$
```

We created two types of symbolic link using `ln -s` (which is short for `--symbolic`): to the `/var/log/auth.log` file first, and to the `/tmp/` directory after. We are seeing two different ways of using `ln -s`: without a second argument, it creates the link with the same name as the thing we're linking to; otherwise, we can give our own name for the link as the second argument (as can be seen with the `link-to-auth.log` and `link-to-tmp/` links). We can now read the contents of `/var/log/auth.log` by either interacting with `/home/reader/auth.log` or `/home/reader/link-to-auth.log`. If we want to navigate to `/tmp/`, we can now use either `/home/reader/tmp/` or `/home/reader/link-to-tmp/` in combination with `cd`. While this example isn't particularly useful in your day to day work (unless typing `/var/log/auth.log` instead of `auth.log` saves you tons of time), linking prevents duplicate copies of files while maintaining easy access.

An important concept in linking (and Linux filesystems in general) is the **inode**. Every file (whatever the type, so including directories) has an inode, which describes the attributes and *disk block locations* of that file. In this context, attributes include things like ownership and permissions, as well as last change, access and modification timestamps. In linking, *soft links* have their own inodes, while *hard links* refer to the same inode.

Before continuing with the next part of this chapter, clean up the four links and the copied `dpk.log` file by using `rm`. If you're in doubt about how to do this, check out the man page for `rm`. A little tip: removing symbolic links is as simple as `rm <name-of-link>`!

Archiving

Now that we have a grasp on common file operations in Linux, we'll move on to archiving. While it might sound fancy, archiving refers simply to **creating archives**. An example most of you will be familiar with is creating a ZIP file, which is an archive. ZIP is not Windows-specific; it is an *archive file format* with different implementations for Windows, Linux, macOS, and so on.

As you might expect, there are many archive file formats. On Linux, the most commonly used is the **tarball**, which is created by using the `tar` command (which is derived from the term **tar**chive). A tarball file, which ends in `.tar`, is uncompressed. In practice, tarballs will almost always be compressed with Gzip, which stands for **GNU zip**. This can be done either directly with the `tar` command (most common) or afterwards using the `gzip` command (less common, but can be used to compress files other than tarballs as well). Since `tar` is a complicated command, we'll explore the most commonly used flags in more detail (descriptions are taken from the `tar` manual page):

`-c, --create`	Create a new archive. Arguments supply the names of the files to be archived. Directories are archived recursively, unless the `--no-recursion` option is given.
`-x, --extract, --get`	Extract files from an archive. Arguments are optional. When given, they specify names of the archive members to be extracted.
`-t, --list`	List the contents of an archive. Arguments are optional. When given, they specify the names of the members to list.
`-v, --verbose`	Verbosely list files processed.
`-f, --file=ARCHIVE`	Use archive file or device ARCHIVE.
`-z, --gzip, --gunzip, --ungzip`	Filter the archive through Gzip.
`-C, --directory=DIR`	Change to DIR before performing any operations. This option is order-sensitive, that is, it affects all options that follow.

The `tar` command is pretty flexible about how we specify these options. We can present them one by one, all together, with and without a hyphen, or with the long or short option. This means that the following ways to create an archive are all correct and would all work:

- `tar czvf <archive name> <file1> <file2>`
- `tar -czvf <archive name> <file1> <file2>`
- `tar -c -z -v -f <archive name> <file1> <file2>`
- `tar --create --gzip --verbose --file=<archive name> <file1> <file2>`

While this seems to be helpful, it can also be confusing. Our suggestion: pick one of the formats and stick with it. In this book, we will use the shortest form, so this is all short options without dashes. Let's use this form to create our first archive!

```
reader@ubuntu:~$ ls -l
total 12
-rw-rw-r-- 1 reader reader   69 Jul 14 13:18 nanofile.txt
drwxrwxr-x 2 reader reader 4096 Aug  4 16:16 renamedtestdir
-rwxr-xr-- 1 reader reader    0 Aug  4 13:44 renamedtestfile
drwxrwx--- 2 reader reader 4096 Aug  4 16:18 umaskdir
reader@ubuntu:~$ tar czvf my-first-archive.tar.gz \
nanofile.txt renamedtestfile
nanofile.txt
renamedtestfile
reader@ubuntu:~$ ls -l
total 16
-rw-rw-r-- 1 reader reader  267 Aug 19 10:29 my-first-archive.tar.gz
-rw-rw-r-- 1 reader reader   69 Jul 14 13:18 nanofile.txt
drwxrwxr-x 2 reader reader 4096 Aug  4 16:16 renamedtestdir
-rwxr-xr-- 1 reader reader    0 Aug  4 13:44 renamedtestfile
drwxrwx--- 2 reader reader 4096 Aug  4 16:18 umaskdir
-rw-rw---- 1 reader games    0 Aug  4 16:18 umaskfile
reader@ubuntu:~$
```

With this command, we verbosely created a gzipped file with the name `my-first-archive.tar.gz`, containing the files `nanofile.txt` `umaskfile`, and `renamedtestfile`.

In this example, we only archived files. In practice, it is often nice to archive an entire directory. The syntax for this is exactly the same, only instead of a filename you will give a directory name. The whole directory will be archived (and, in the case of the `-z` option, compressed as well). When you unpack a tarball that archived a directory, the entire directory will be extracted again, not just the contents.

Now, let's see if unpacking it gives us back our files! We move the gzipped tarball to `renamedtestdir`, and use the `tar xzvf` command to unpack it there:

```
reader@ubuntu:~$ ls -l
total 16
-rw-rw-r-- 1 reader reader  226 Aug 19 10:40 my-first-archive.tar.gz
-rw-rw-r-- 1 reader reader   69 Jul 14 13:18 nanofile.txt
drwxrwxr-x 2 reader reader 4096 Aug  4 16:16 renamedtestdir
-rwxr-xr-x 1 reader reader    0 Aug  4 13:44 renamedtestfile
drwxrwx--- 2 reader reader 4096 Aug 19 10:37 umaskdir
reader@ubuntu:~$ mv my-first-archive.tar.gz renamedtestdir/
reader@ubuntu:~$ cd renamedtestdir/
reader@ubuntu:~/renamedtestdir$ ls -l
total 4
-rw-rw-r-- 1 reader reader 226 Aug 19 10:40 my-first-archive.tar.gz
reader@ubuntu:~/renamedtestdir$ tar xzvf my-first-archive.tar.gz
nanofile.txt
renamedtestfile
reader@ubuntu:~/renamedtestdir$ ls -l
total 8
-rw-rw-r-- 1 reader reader 226 Aug 19 10:40 my-first-archive.tar.gz
-rw-rw-r-- 1 reader reader  69 Jul 14 13:18 nanofile.txt
-rwxr-xr-- 1 reader reader   0 Aug  4 13:44 renamedtestfile
reader@ubuntu:~/renamedtestdir$
```

As we can see, we got our files back in the `renamedtestdir`! Actually, we never removed the original files, so these are copies. You might want to know what's inside a tarball before you go to the trouble of extracting it and cleaning up everything. This can be accomplished by using the `-t` option instead of `-x`:

```
reader@ubuntu:~/renamedtestdir$ tar tzvf my-first-archive.tar.gz
-rw-rw-r-- reader/reader 69 2018-08-19 11:54 nanofile.txt
-rw-rw-r-- reader/reader  0 2018-08-19 11:54 renamedtestfile
reader@ubuntu:~/renamedtestdir$
```

The last interesting option that's widely used for `tar` is the `-C`, or `--directory` option. This command ensures that we do not have to move the archive around before we extract it. Let's use it to extract `/home/reader/renamedtestdir/my-first-archive.tar.gz` into `/home/reader/umaskdir/` from our `home` directory:

```
reader@ubuntu:~/renamedtestdir$ cd
reader@ubuntu:~$ tar xzvf renamedtestdir/my-first-archive.tar.gz -C
umaskdir/
nanofile.txt
renamedtestfile
reader@ubuntu:~$ ls -l umaskdir/
total 4
```

```
-rw-rw-r-- 1 reader reader 69 Jul 14 13:18 nanofile.txt
-rwxr-xr-- 1 reader reader  0 Aug  4 13:44 renamedtestfile
-rw-rw---- 1 reader games   0 Aug  4 16:18 umaskfile
reader@ubuntu:~$
```

By specifying -C with a directory argument after the archive name, we made sure that tar extracts the contents of the gzipped tarball into that specified directory.

That covers the most important aspects of the tar command. However, one little thing remains: cleaning up! We've made a nice mess of our home directory, and we do not have any files there that actually do anything. The following is a practical example showing how dangerous the wildcard with the rm -r command can be:

```
reader@ubuntu:~$ ls -l
total 12
-rw-rw-r-- 1 reader reader   69 Jul 14 13:18 nanofile.txt
drwxrwxr-x 2 reader reader 4096 Aug 19 10:42 renamedtestdir
-rwxr-xr-- 1 reader reader    0 Aug  4 13:44 renamedtestfile
drwxrwx--- 2 reader reader 4096 Aug 19 10:47 umaskdir
reader@ubuntu:~$ rm -r *
reader@ubuntu:~$ ls -l
total 0
reader@ubuntu:~$
```

One simple command, no warning, and all files, including directories with more files, are gone! And should you be wondering: no, Linux does not have a Recycle Bin either. These files are gone; only advanced hard disk recovery techniques *might* still be able to recover these files.

Make sure that you perform the preceding command, just to get a feeling for how destructive rm can be. Before you do, however, ensure that you are in your home directory and that you do not accidentally have any files there that you do not want to delete. If you followed our examples, this should not be the case, but if you've done anything else, be sure about what you're doing!

Finding files

After learning about common file operations and archiving, there is one vital skill in file manipulation we have not yet covered: finding files. It's very neat that you know how to copy or archive files, but if you cannot find the file you want to manipulate, you're going to have a hard time completing your task. Fortunately, there are tools devoted to finding and locating files on a Linux filesystem. And, to keep things simple, these are called `find` and `locate`. The `find` command is more complex, but more powerful, while the `locate` command is easier to use when you know exactly what you're looking for. First, we'll show you how to use `locate`, before moving on to the more extensive capabilities of `find`.

locate

On the man page for locate, the description could not be more fitting: `locate - find files by name`. The `locate` command is installed by default on your Ubuntu machine and the basic functionality is as simple as using `locate <filename>`. Let's see how this works:

```
reader@ubuntu:~$ locate fstab
/etc/fstab
/lib/systemd/system-generators/systemd-fstab-generator
/sbin/fstab-decode
/usr/share/doc/mount/examples/fstab
/usr/share/doc/mount/examples/mount.fstab
/usr/share/doc/util-linux/examples/fstab
/usr/share/doc/util-linux/examples/fstab.example2
/usr/share/man/man5/fstab.5.gz
/usr/share/man/man8/fstab-decode.8.gz
/usr/share/man/man8/systemd-fstab-generator.8.gz
/usr/share/vim/vim80/syntax/fstab.vim
reader@ubuntu:~$
```

In the preceding example, we looked for the filename `fstab`. We might have remembered that we need to edit this file for filesystem changes, but we were not sure where we could find it. `locate` presented us with all locations on disk which contain `fstab`. As you can see, it does not have to be an exact match; everything that contains the `fstab` string will be printed.

You might have noticed that the `locate` command completes almost instantly. That is because it uses a database for all files which is updated periodically, instead of going through the whole filesystem at runtime. Because of this, the information is not always accurate, since changes are not synchronized to the database in real-time. To ensure that you are talking to the database with the latest state of the filesystem, be sure to run `sudo updatedb` (requires root privileges) before running `locate`. This is also required before the first run of `locate` on a system, because otherwise there is no database to query!

Locate has some options, but in our experience, you only use it if you know the exact (or an exact part of the) filename. For other searches, defaulting to the `find` command is a much better idea.

find

Find is a very powerful, but complicated command. You can do any of the following things with `find`:

- Search on a filename
- Search on permissions (both user and group)
- Search on ownership
- Search on file type
- Search on file size
- Search on timestamps (created, last-modified, last-accessed)
- Search only in certain directories

It would take a full chapter to explain all of the functionality in the `find` command. We will only be describing the most common use cases. The real lesson here is being aware of the advanced functionalities of `find`; if you ever need to look for files with a specific set of attributes, always think of the `find` command first and check out the `man file` page to see if you can utilize find for your search (spoiler alert: this is **almost always** the case!).

Let's start with the basic use of find: `find <location> <options and arguments>`. Without any options and arguments, find will print every file it finds within the location:

```
reader@ubuntu:~$ find /home/reader/
/home/reader/
/home/reader/.gnupg
/home/reader/.gnupg/private-keys-v1.d
/home/reader/.bash_logout
```

```
/home/reader/.sudo_as_admin_successful
/home/reader/.profile
/home/reader/.bashrc
/home/reader/.viminfo
/home/reader/.lesshst
/home/reader/.local
/home/reader/.local/share
/home/reader/.local/share/nano
/home/reader/.cache
/home/reader/.cache/motd.legal-displayed
/home/reader/.bash_history
reader@ubuntu:~$
```

You might have been under the impression that your home directory was empty. It actually contains quite a number of hidden files or directories (which start with a dot), which find has found for us. Now, let's apply a filter with the −name option:

```
reader@ubuntu:~$ find /home/reader/ -name bash
reader@ubuntu:~$ find /home/reader/ -name *bash*
/home/reader/.bash_logout
/home/reader/.bashrc
/home/reader/.bash_history
reader@ubuntu:~$ find /home/reader/ -name .bashrc
/home/reader/.bashrc
reader@ubuntu:~$
```

Contrary to what you might have expected, find works differently from locate with regards to partly matched files. Unless you add wildcards around the argument to −name, it will only match on the full filename, not on partly matched files. This is definitely something to keep in mind. Now, what about looking only for files, instead of directories as well? For this, we can use the −type option with the d argument for directories or f for files:

```
reader@ubuntu:~$ find /home/reader/ -type d
/home/reader/
/home/reader/.gnupg
/home/reader/.gnupg/private-keys-v1.d
/home/reader/.local
/home/reader/.local/share
/home/reader/.local/share/nano
/home/reader/.cache
reader@ubuntu:~$ find /home/reader/ -type f
/home/reader/.bash_logout
/home/reader/.sudo_as_admin_successful
/home/reader/.profile
/home/reader/.bashrc
/home/reader/.viminfo
```

```
/home/reader/.lesshst
/home/reader/.cache/motd.legal-displayed
/home/reader/.bash_history
reader@ubuntu:~$
```

The first result presents all directories within /home/reader/ (including /home/reader/!), while the second result prints all files. As you can see, there is no overlap, since a file under Linux is *always of only one type*. We can also combine multiple options, such as -name and -type:

```
reader@ubuntu:~$ find /home/reader/ -name *cache* -type f
reader@ubuntu:~$ find /home/reader/ -name *cache* -type d
/home/reader/.cache
reader@ubuntu:~$
```

We start by looking for *files* in /home/reader/ which contain the string cache. The find command does not print anything, which means we did not find anything. If we look for *directories* with the cache string, however, we are shown the /home/reader/.cache/ directory.

As a last example, let's look at how we can use find to distinguish between files of different sizes. To do this, we'll create an empty file using touch and a non-empty file using vim (or nano):

```
reader@ubuntu:~$ ls -l
total 0
reader@ubuntu:~$ touch emptyfile
reader@ubuntu:~$ vim textfile.txt
reader@ubuntu:~$ ls -l
total 4
-rw-rw-r-- 1 reader reader  0 Aug 19 11:54 emptyfile
-rw-rw-r-- 1 reader reader 23 Aug 19 11:54 textfile.txt
reader@ubuntu:~
```

As you can see from the 0 and 23 on-screen, emptyfile contains 0 bytes, whereas textfile.txt contains 23 bytes (which, not entirely coincidental, contains a sentence of 23 characters). Let's see how we can use the find command to find both files:

```
reader@ubuntu:~$ find /home/reader/ -size 0c
/home/reader/.sudo_as_admin_successful
/home/reader/.cache/motd.legal-displayed
/home/reader/emptyfile
reader@ubuntu:~$ find /home/reader/ -size 23c
/home/reader/textfile.txt
reader@ubuntu:~$
```

To do this, we use the -size option. We give it the number we're looking for, followed by a letter which indicates which range we're dealing with. c is used for bytes, k for kilobytes, M for megabytes, and so on. You can find these values on the manual page. As the results show, there are three files which are exactly 0 bytes: our emptyfile is one of them. These is one file which is exactly 23 bytes: our textfile.txt. You might think: 23 bytes, that's very specific! How will we ever know how many bytes a file is exactly? Well, you won't. The creators of find have also implemented a *greater than* and *lower than* construct, which we can use to give us a little more flexibility:

```
reader@ubuntu:~$ find /home/reader/ -size +10c
/home/reader/
/home/reader/.gnupg
/home/reader/.gnupg/private-keys-v1.d
/home/reader/.bash_logout
/home/reader/.profile
/home/reader/.bashrc
/home/reader/.viminfo
/home/reader/.lesshst
/home/reader/textfile.txt
/home/reader/.local
/home/reader/.local/share
/home/reader/.local/share/nano
./home/reader/.cache
/home/reader/.bash_history
reader@ubuntu:~$ find /home/reader/ -size +10c -size -30c
/home/reader/textfile.txt
reader@ubuntu:~$
```

Let's say we're looking for a file that's at least larger than 10 bytes. We use the + option on the argument, which only prints the files that are larger than 10 bytes. However, we still see too many files. Now, we expect the file to also be smaller than 30 bytes. We add another -size option, this time specifying -30c, meaning that the file will be less than 30 bytes. And, not entirely unexpectedly, our 23 byte testfile.txt is found!

All of the preceding options and more can be combined to form a very powerful search query. Are you looking for a *file*, which is *at least* 100 KB but *not more than* 10 MB, located *somewhere in* /var/, that was created *in the last week*, and is *readable* to you? Just combine the options in find and you will definitely find that file in no time!

Summary

This chapter described file manipulation in Linux. We started with common file operations. We explained how to we can copy files in Linux with cp and how we can move or rename files with mv. Next, we discussed how we can remove files and directories with rm and how we can create *shortcuts* under Linux with symbolic links by using the ln -s command.

In the second part of this chapter, we discussed archiving. While there are many different tools that allow archiving, we focused on the most commonly used one in Linux: tar. We showed you how to create and extract archives, both in the current working directory and to somewhere else on the filesystem. We described that both files and whole directories can be archived by tar, and that we can see what's inside a tarball without actually extracting it by using the -t option.

We ended this chapter with finding files using file and locate. We explained that locate is a simple command that is useful under certain circumstances, while find is a more complicated but very powerful command that can provide great benefits to those who master it.

The following commands were introduced in this chapter: cp, rm, mv, ln, tar, locate, and find.

Questions

1. Which command do we use to copy files in Linux?
2. What is the difference between moving and renaming files?
3. Why is the rm command, which is used to remove files under Linux, potentially dangerous?
4. What is the difference between a hard link and a symbolic (soft) link?
5. What are the three most important operating modes of tar?
6. Which option is used by tar to select the output directory?
7. What is the biggest difference between locate and find when searching on filenames?
8. How many options of find can be combined?

Further reading

The following resources might be interesting if you'd like to go deeper into the subjects of this chapter:

- **File manipulation**: `https://ryanstutorials.net/linuxtutorial/filemanipulation.php`
- **Tar tutorial**: `https://www.poftut.com/linux-tar-command-tutorial-with-examples/`
- **Find practical examples**: `https://www.tecmint.com/35-practical-examples-of-linux-find-command/`

7
Hello World!

In this chapter, we will finally start writing shell scripts. After writing and running our very own `Hello World!` script, we will look at some best practices for all future scripts. We will use many techniques to increase the readability of our scripts, and we will follow the KISS principle (Keep It Simple, Stupid) where possible.

The following commands will be introduced in this chapter: `head`, `tail`, and `wget`.

The following topics will be covered in this chapter:

- First steps
- Readability
- KISS

Technical requirements

We will create our shell scripts directly on our virtual machine; we will not be using Atom/Notepad++ just yet.

All scripts for this chapter can be found on GitHub: `https://github.com/PacktPublishing/Learn-Linux-Shell-Scripting-Fundamentals-of-Bash-4.4/tree/master/Chapter07`.

First steps

After getting some background information on Linux, preparing our system, and getting an overview of important concepts for scripting in Linux, we have finally arrived at the point where we will be writing actual shell scripts!

To recap, a shell script is nothing more than multiple Bash commands in sequence. Scripts are often used to automate repetitive tasks. They can be run interactively or non-interactively (meaning with or without user input) and can be shared with others. Let's create our `Hello World` script! We'll create a folder in our `home` directory where we will store all scripts, sorted by each chapter:

```
reader@ubuntu:~$ ls -l
total 4
-rw-rw-r-- 1 reader reader  0 Aug 19 11:54 emptyfile
-rw-rw-r-- 1 reader reader 23 Aug 19 11:54 textfile.txt
reader@ubuntu:~$ mkdir scripts
reader@ubuntu:~$ cd scripts/
reader@ubuntu:~/scripts$ mkdir chapter_07
reader@ubuntu:~/scripts$ cd chapter_07/
reader@ubuntu:~/scripts/chapter_07$ vim hello-world.sh
```

Next, in the `vim` screen, enter the following text (note how we use an empty line *between* the two lines):

```
#!/bin/bash

echo "Hello World!"
```

As we explained before, the `echo` command prints text to the Terminal. Let's run the scripts using the `bash` command:

```
reader@ubuntu:~/scripts/chapter_07$ bash hello-world.sh
Hello World!
reader@ubuntu:~/scripts/chapter_07
```

Congratulations, you are now a shell scripter! Perhaps not a very good or well-rounded one *yet*, but a shell scripter nonetheless.

Remember, if `vim` is not doing the trick for you yet, you can always fall back to `nano`. Or, even better, run `vimtutor` again and refresh those `vim` actions!

The shebang

You are probably wondering about that first line. The second (or third, if you count the empty line) should be clear, but that first one is new. It is called the **shebang**, but is sometimes also referred to as a *sha-bang*, *hashbang*, *pound-bang*, and/or *hash-pling*. Its function is pretty simple: it tells the system which binary to use to execute the script. It is always in the format of `#!<binary path>`. For our purposes, we will always use the `#!/bin/bash` shebang, but for Perl or Python scripts it would be `#!/usr/bin/perl` and `#!/usr/bin/python3` respectively. It might seem unnecessary at first sight. We create the script named `hello-world.sh`, whereas a Perl or Python script would use `hello-world.pl` and `hello-world.py`. Why, then, do we need the shebang?

For Python, it allows us to easily distinguish between Python 2 and Python 3. You would normally expect people to switch to a newer version of a programming language as soon as it's there, but for Python this seems to require a lot more effort, which is why you see both Python 2 and Python 3 in use today.

Bash scripts do not end in `.bash`, but in `.sh`, the general acronym for *shell*. So, unless we specify the shebang for Bash, we will end up in a *normal* shell execution. While this is fine for some scripts (the `hello-world.sh` script would work fine), when we use the advanced functions of Bash, we will run into issues.

Running scripts

If you were really paying attention, you will have noticed we executed a script that was not executable, using the `bash` command. Why would we need the shebang, if we specify how to run it anyway? In this case, we would not need the shebang. However, we would need to know exactly which kind of script it is and find the correct binary on the system to run it, which can be kind of a hassle, especially once you have many scripts. Thankfully, there is a better way for us to run these scripts: using the executable permission. Let's see how we can run our `hello-world.sh` script by setting the executable permission:

```
reader@ubuntu:~/scripts/chapter_07$ ls -l
total 4
-rw-rw-r-- 1 reader reader 33 Aug 26 12:08 hello-world.sh
reader@ubuntu:~/scripts/chapter_07$ ./hello-world.sh
-bash: ./hello-world.sh: Permission denied
reader@ubuntu:~/scripts/chapter_07$ chmod +x hello-world.sh
reader@ubuntu:~/scripts/chapter_07$ ./hello-world.sh
Hello World!
reader@ubuntu:~/scripts/chapter_07$ /home/reader/scripts/chapter_07/hello-world.sh
```

```
Hello World!
reader@ubuntu:~/scripts/chapter_07$ ls -l
total 4
-rwxrwxr-x 1 reader reader 33 Aug 26 12:08 hello-world.sh
reader@ubuntu:~/scripts/chapter_07$
```

We can execute a script (or any file, really, if it makes sense for the file to be executed) by either running it *fully qualified* or using ./ in the same directory, as long as it has the executable permission set. We need the prefix ./ because of security: normally when we execute a command the PATH variable is explored for that name. Now imagine someone putting a malicious binary called ls in your home directory. If ./ rule wasn't in place, running the ls command would result in the binary being run, instead of /bin/ls (which is on your PATH).

Because we are running a script by just using ./hello-world.sh, we now need the shebang again. Otherwise, Linux would default to using /bin/sh, which is not what we want in a **Bash** scripting book, right?

Readability

When writing shell scripts, you should always aim to make sure the code is as readable as possible. When you're in the process of creating a script, all the logic, commands, and flow of the script will be obvious to you, but if you look at the script after putting it down for a little while, this isn't a given anymore. Even worse, you'll most likely work together with other people on scripts; these people have never had the same considerations you had when writing the script (and the same goes for the other way around). How can we promote better readability in our scripts? Comments and verbosity are two ways in which we can achieve this.

Comments

As any good software engineer could tell you, placing relevant comments in your code increases the quality of the code. A comment is nothing more than a bit of text explaining what you're doing, prefixed by a special character that ensures the language you're coding in does not interpret the text. For Bash, this character is the *number sign* # (currently more famous for its use in #HashTags). When you're reading other sources, it may also be referred to as the *pound sign* or the *hash*. Other examples of comment characters are // (Java, C++), -- (SQL), and <!-- comment here --> (HTML, XML). The # character is also used as a comment for Python and Perl.

A comment can either be used at the beginning of a line, which ensures the entire line does not get interpreted, or further in a line. In that case, everything up until # will be processed. Let's look at an example of both of these in a revised `Hello World` script:

```
#!/bin/bash

# Print the text to the Terminal.
echo "Hello World!"
```

Alternatively, we can use the following syntax:

```
#!/bin/bash

echo "Hello World!" # Print the text to the Terminal.
```

In general, we prefer putting comments on their own line directly above the command. However, once we introduce loops, redirection, and other advanced constructs, an *inline comment* can ensure better readability than an entire line. The most important thing to remember, though, is: **any relevant comment is always better than no comment, whether full line or inline**. By convention, we always prefer to keep comments either really short (one to three words) or use a full sentence with proper punctuation. In cases where a full sentence would be overkill, use a few keywords; otherwise, opt for the full sentence. We guarantee it will make your scripts look much more professional.

Script header

In our scripting endeavors, we always include a *header* at the beginning of the script. While this is not necessary for the functioning of the script, it can help greatly when other people are working with your scripts (or, again, when you're working with other people's scripts). A header can include any information you think is needed, but in general we always start with the following fields:

- Author
- Version
- Date
- Description
- Usage

By implementing a simple header using comments, we can give someone who stumbles upon the script an idea of when it was written and by whom (should they have questions). Furthermore, a simple description gives a goal to the script, and usage information ensures there is no trial and error when using a script for the first time. Let's create a copy of our `hello-world.sh` script, call it `hello-world-improved.sh`, and implement both a header and a comment for the functionality:

```
reader@ubuntu:~/scripts/chapter_07$ ls -l
total 4
-rwxrwxr-x 1 reader reader 33 Aug 26 12:08 hello-world.sh
reader@ubuntu:~/scripts/chapter_07$ cp hello-world.sh hello-world-
improved.sh
reader@ubuntu:~/scripts/chapter_07$ vi hello-world-improved.sh
```

Make sure the script looks like the following, but be sure to enter the *current date* and *your own name*:

```
#!/bin/bash

###################################
# Author: Sebastiaan Tammer
# Version: v1.0.0
# Date: 2018-08-26
# Description: Our first script!
# Usage: ./hello-world-improved.sh
###################################

# Print the text to the Terminal.
echo "Hello World!"
```

Now, doesn't that look nice? The only thing that might stick out is that we now have a script of 12 lines, where only a single line contains any functionality. In this case, indeed, it seems a bit much. However, we're trying to learn good practices. As soon as scripts become more complicated, these 10 lines we're using for the shebang and the header will not make a difference, but the usability increases notably. While we're at it, we're introducing a new `head` command.

```
reader@ubuntu:~/scripts/chapter_07$ head hello-world-improved.sh
#!/bin/bash

###################################
# Author: Sebastiaan Tammer
# Version: v1.0.0
```

```
# Date: 2018-08-26
# Description: Our first script!
# Usage: ./hello-world-improved.sh
####################################

reader@ubuntu:~/scripts/chapter_07$
```

The `head` command is like `cat`, but it does not print the whole file; by default, it only prints the first 10 lines. Which, not entirely coincidentally, is exactly as long as we created our header to be. So, anybody that wants to use your script (and, let's be honest, **you** after 6 months are also *anybody*) can just use `head` to print the header and get all the information needed to start using the script.

While we're introducing `head`, we would be negligent if we did not introduce `tail` as well. As the name might imply, while `head` prints the top of the file, `tail` prints the end of the file. While this does not help us with our script headers, it is very useful when looking at log files for errors or warnings:

```
reader@ubuntu:~/scripts/chapter_07$ tail /var/log/auth.log
Aug 26 14:45:28 ubuntu systemd-logind[804]: Watching system buttons on
/dev/input/event1 (Sleep Button)
Aug 26 14:45:28 ubuntu systemd-logind[804]: Watching system buttons on
/dev/input/event2 (AT Translated Set 2 keyboard)
Aug 26 14:45:28 ubuntu sshd[860]: Server listening on 0.0.0.0 port 22.
Aug 26 14:45:28 ubuntu sshd[860]: Server listening on :: port 22.
Aug 26 15:00:02 ubuntu sshd[1079]: Accepted password for reader from
10.0.2.2 port 51752 ssh2
Aug 26 15:00:02 ubuntu sshd[1079]: pam_unix(sshd:session): session opened
for user reader by (uid=0)
Aug 26 15:00:02 ubuntu systemd: pam_unix(systemd-user:session): session
opened for user reader by (uid=0)
Aug 26 15:00:02 ubuntu systemd-logind[804]: New session 1 of user reader.
Aug 26 15:17:01 ubuntu CRON[1272]: pam_unix(cron:session): session opened
for user root by (uid=0)
Aug 26 15:17:01 ubuntu CRON[1272]: pam_unix(cron:session): session closed
for user root
reader@ubuntu:~/scripts/chapter_07$
```

Verbosity

Back to how we can improve the readability of our scripts. While commenting is a great way to improve our understanding of a script, if the commands in the script use many obscure flags and options, we need many words in our comments to explain everything. And, as you might expect, if we need five lines of comments to explain our commands, the readability becomes lower instead of higher! Verbosity is the balancing act between not too much but also not too little explanation. For example, you will probably not have to explain to anyone if and why you are using an `ls` command, since that is very basic. However, the `tar` command can be quite complex so it might be worthwhile to give a short comment about what you're trying to achieve.

In this context, there are three types of verbosity we want to discuss. These are the following:

- Verbosity in comments
- Verbosity of commands
- Verbosity of command output

Verbosity in comments

The issue with verbosity is that it's hard to give definitive rules. Almost always it's very dependent on the context. So, while we can say that, indeed, we do not have to comment on `echo` or `ls`, this might not always be the case. Let's say we use the output of the `ls` command to iterate over some files; perhaps we want to mention this in a comment? Or perhaps even this situation is so clear for our perceived readers that a short comment on the entire loop would suffice?

The answer is, very unsatisfactorily, *it depends*. If you're unsure, it's often a good idea to include the comment anyway, but you might want to keep it more sparse. Instead of *This instance of ls lists all the files, which we can then use to iterate over for the rest of the scripts*, you might choose *Builds list for iteration with ls.* instead. This is mostly a practiced skill, so be sure to at least start practicing it: you will most certainly get better as you shell-script more.

Verbosity of commands

Command verbosity is an interesting one. In the previous chapters you were introduced to a lot of commands, sometimes with accompanying flags and options that alter the functioning of that command. Most options have both a short and long syntax that accomplishes the same thing. The following is an example:

```
reader@ubuntu:~$ ls -R
.:
emptyfile    scripts    textfile.txt
./scripts:
chapter_07
./scripts/chapter_07:
hello-world-improved.sh   hello-world.sh
reader@ubuntu:~$ ls --recursive
.:
emptyfile    scripts    textfile.txt
./scripts:
chapter_07
./scripts/chapter_07:
hello-world-improved.sh   hello-world.sh
reader@ubuntu:~$
```

We use `ls` to recursively print the files in our home directory. We first use the shorthand option `-R`, and right after the long `--recursive` variant. As you can see from the output, the command is exactly the same, even `-R` is much shorter and faster to type. However, the `--recursive` option is more verbose, since it gives us a much better hint about what we're doing than just `-R`. So, when do you use which? The short answer: **use shorthand options in your daily work, but use long options when scripting**. While this works great for most situations, it isn't a foolproof rule. Some shorthand commands are so prevalent that using the long option might be more confusing for the reader, as counterintuitive as it sounds. For example, when working with SELinux or AppArmor, the `-Z` command for `ls` prints the security context. The long option for this is `--context`, but this is not as well known as the `-Z` option (in our experience). In this case, using shorthand would be better.

There is, however, a command we have already seen that is complicated, but a lot more readable when we use long options: `tar`. Let's look at two ways of creating an archive:

```
reader@ubuntu:~/scripts/chapter_07$ ls -l
total 8
-rwxrwxr-x 1 reader reader 277 Aug 26 15:13 hello-world-improved.sh
-rwxrwxr-x 1 reader reader  33 Aug 26 12:08 hello-world.sh
reader@ubuntu:~/scripts/chapter_07$ tar czvf hello-world.tar.gz hello-world.sh
hello-world.sh
```

```
reader@ubuntu:~/scripts/chapter_07$ tar --create --gzip --verbose --file
hello-world-improved.tar.gz hello-world-improved.sh
hello-world-improved.sh
reader@ubuntu:~/scripts/chapter_07$ ls -l
total 16
-rwxrwxr-x 1 reader reader 277 Aug 26 15:13 hello-world-improved.sh
-rw-rw-r-- 1 reader reader 283 Aug 26 16:28 hello-world-improved.tar.gz
-rwxrwxr-x 1 reader reader  33 Aug 26 12:08 hello-world.sh
-rw-rw-r-- 1 reader reader 317 Aug 26 16:26 hello-world.tar.gz
reader@ubuntu:~/scripts/chapter_07$
```

The first command, `tar czvf`, uses only shorthand. A command like this would be great for either a full-line comment or inline comment:

```
#!/bin/bash
<SNIPPED>
# Verbosely create a gzipped tarball.
tar czvf hello-world.tar.gz hello-world.sh
```

Alternatively, you could use the following:

```
#!/bin/bash
<SNIPPED>
# Verbosely create a gzipped tarball.
tar czvf hello-world.tar.gz hello-world.sh
```

The `tar --create --gzip --verbose --file` command, however, is verbose enough *in itself* and would not warrant a comment, because an appropriate comment would literally say the same as what the long options are saying!

Shorthand is used to save time. For daily tasks, this is a great way to interact with your system. However, when shell scripting, it's much more important to be clear and verbose. Using long options is a better idea, since you can prevent the need for extra comments when using these options. However, some commands are used so often that the longer flag can actually be more confusing; use your best judgement here and learn from experience.

Verbosity of command output

Lastly, when running a shell script, you will see output from the commands in the script (unless you want to remove that output with *redirection*, which will be explained in Chapter 12, *Using Pipes and Redirection in Scripts*). Some commands are verbose by default. Good examples of these are the `ls` and `echo` commands: their entire function is to print something on screen.

If we circle back to the `tar` command, we can ask ourselves if we need to see all the files that are being archived. If the logic in our script is correct, we can assume the correct files are being archived and a list of these files will only clutter up the rest of the output from the script. By default, `tar` does not print anything; we have used the `-v/--verbose` option for this up until now. But, for a script, this is often not desirable behavior, so we can safely omit this option (unless we have a good reason not to).

Most commands have appropriate verbosity by default. The output of `ls` is printed, but `tar` is hidden by default. For most commands, it is possible to reverse the verbosity by using either a `--verbose` or `--quiet` option (or the corresponding shorthands, often `-v` or `-q`). A good example of this is `wget`: this command is used to grab a file from the internet. By default, it gives a lot of output about the connection, hostname resolution, download progress, and download destination. Many times, however, all these things are not interesting at all! In this case, we use the `--quiet` option for `wget`, because for that situation that is the **appropriate verbosity** of the command.

When shell scripting, always consider the verbosity of the commands you are using. If it is not enough, check the man page for a way to increase the verbosity. If it is too much, check that same man page for a quieter option. Most commands we have encountered have either or both options present, sometimes in different levels (`-q` and `-qq` for even quieter operation!).

Keep It Simple, Stupid (KISS)

The KISS principle is a great way to approach shell scripting. While it might come across as a bit harsh, the spirit in which it is given is important: it should only be considered great advice. Further advice is given in the *Zen of Python*, the design principles on which Python rests:

- Simple is better than complex
- Complex is better than complicated
- Readability counts

There are about 17 more aspects in the *Zen of Python*, but these three are the most relevant for Bash scripting as well. The last one, '*Readability counts*', should be obvious by now. However, the first two, '*Simple is better than complex*' and '*Complex is better than complicated*' are closely related to the KISS principle. Keeping things simple is a great goal, but if that is not possible, a complex solution is always better than a complicated one (no one likes complicated scripts!).

There are a few things you can keep in mind when writing scripts:

- If the solution you're cooking up seems to get very complicated, do either of the following things:
  - Research your problem; perhaps there is another tool you can use instead of what you are using now.
  - See whether you can split things into discrete steps, so it gets more complex but less complicated.
- Ask yourself if you need everything on a single line, or if it is perhaps possible to split the command over multiple lines to increase readability. When using pipes or other forms of redirection, as explained in greater detail in Chapter 12, *Using Pipes and Redirection in Scripts*, this becomes something to keep in mind.
- If it works, it's *probably* not a bad solution. However, make sure that the solution is not *too* simple, since edge cases might cause trouble later on.

Summary

We started this chapter off by creating and running our very first shell script. As is almost mandatory when learning a new software language, we printed **Hello World!** onto our Terminal. Continuing, we explained the shebang: the first line of a script, it is an instruction to the Linux system about the interpreter it should use when running the script. For a Bash script, the convention is to have the file name end in **.sh**, with a shebang of **#!/bin/bash**.

We explained that there are multiple ways in which we can run a script. We can start with the interpreter and pass the script name as the argument (for example: bash hello-world.sh). In this case, the shebang is not needed because we're specifying the interpreter on the command line. However, normally, we run the file by setting the executable permission and calling it directly; in this case, the shebang is used to determine which interpreter to use. Because you cannot be sure about how a user will run your script, including a shebang should be considered mandatory.

To increase the quality of our scripts, we described how to increase the readability of our shell scripts. We explained how and when to use comments in our scripts, and how we can use comments to create a script header that we can easily view by using the head command. The tail command, which is closely related to head, was briefly introduced. Besides comments, we also explained the concept of **verbosity**.

Verbosity can be found in multiple levels: verbosity in comments, verbosity in commands, and verbosity in command output. We argued that using long options for commands in scripts is almost always a better idea than shorthand, as it increases readability and can prevent the need for extra comments, even though we established that too many comments are almost always better than no comments.

We ended the chapter with a short description of the KISS principle, which we linked to some design principles in Python. The reader should realize that, if there is a simple solution to a problem, it will most often be the best one. If a simple solution isn't an option, a complex solution should be preferred over a complicated one.

The following commands were introduced in this chapter: `head`, `tail`, and `wget`.

Questions

1. What do we, by convention, do as the first thing when we learn a new programming or scripting language?
2. What is the shebang for Bash?
3. Why is the shebang needed?
4. In what three ways can we run a script?
5. Why do we place such emphasis on readability when creating shell scripts?
6. Why do we use comments?
7. Why do we recommend including a script header for all shell scripts you write?
8. Which three types of verbosity have we discussed?
9. What is the KISS principle?

Further reading

The following resources might be interesting if you'd like to go deeper into the subjects of this chapter:

- **Hello World (long tutorial)**: `https://bash.cyberciti.biz/guide/Hello,_World!_Tutorial`
- **Bash coding style guide**: `https://bluepenguinlist.com/2016/11/04/bash-scripting-tutorial/`
- **KISS**: `https://people.apache.org/%7Efhanik/kiss.html`

8
Variables and User Input

In this chapter, we'll begin by describing what variables are, and why we want and need them. We'll explain the difference between variables and constants. Next, we'll provide some possibilities with regard to variable naming and introduce some best practices on naming conventions. Finally, we'll discuss user input and how to properly deal with it: either with positional arguments or with interactive scripts. We'll end the chapter with an introduction to `if-then` constructs and exit codes, which we'll use to combine positional arguments and interactive prompts.

The following commands will be introduced in this chapter: `read`, `test`, and `if`.

The following topics will be covered in this chapter:

- What is a variable?
- Variable naming
- Dealing with user input
- Interactive versus non-interactive scripts

Technical requirements

Other than the Ubuntu virtual machine with files from the previous chapters, no other resources are needed.

All scripts for this chapter can be found on GitHub: `https://github.com/PacktPublishing/Learn-Linux-Shell-Scripting-Fundamentals-of-Bash-4.4/tree/master/Chapter08`. For the **name-improved.sh** script only the final version is found online. Be sure to verify the script version in the header before executing it on your system.

What is a variable?

Variables are a standard building block used in many (if not all) programming and scripting languages. Variables allow us to store information, so we can reference and use it later, often multiple times. We can, for example, use the `textvariable` variable to store the sentence `This text is contained in the variable`. In this case, the variable name of `textvariable` is referred to as the key, and the content of the variable (the text) is referred to as the value, in the key-value pair that makes up the variable.

In our program, we always reference the `textvariable` variable when we need the text. This might be a bit abstract now, but we're confident that after seeing the examples in the rest of the chapter, the usefulness of variables will become clear.

We've actually already seen Bash variables in use. Remember, in `Chapter 4`, *The Linux Filesystem*, we looked at both the `BASH_VERSION` and `PATH` variables. Let's see how we can use variables in shell scripting. We'll take our `hello-world-improved.sh` script, and instead of using the `Hello world` text directly, we'll first put it in a variable and reference it:

```
reader@ubuntu:~/scripts/chapter_08$ cp ../chapter_07/hello-world-
improved.sh hello-world-variable.sh
reader@ubuntu:~/scripts/chapter_08$ ls -l
total 4
-rwxrwxr-x 1 reader reader 277 Sep  1 10:35 hello-world-variable.sh
reader@ubuntu:~/scripts/chapter_08$ vim hello-world-variable.sh
```

First, we copy the `hello-world-improved.sh` script from the `chapter_07` directory into the newly created `chapter_08` directory, with the name `hello-world-variable.sh`. Then, we use `vim` to edit it. Give it the following contents:

```
#!/bin/bash

#####################################
# Author: Sebastiaan Tammer
# Version: v1.0.0
# Date: 2018-09-01
# Description: Our first script using variables!
# Usage: ./hello-world-variable.sh
#####################################

hello_text="Hello World!"

# Print the text to the terminal.
echo ${hello_text}
```

```
reader@ubuntu:~/scripts/chapter_08$ ./hello-world-variable.sh
Hello World!
reader@ubuntu:~/scripts/chapter_08$
```

Congratulations, you've just used your first variable in a script! As you can see, you can use the content of a variable by wrapping its name inside the `${...}` syntax. Technically, just putting `$` in front of the name is enough (for example, `echo $hello_text`). However, in that situation, it is hard to differentiate where the variable name ends and the rest of the program begins—if you use the variable in the middle of a sentence, for example (or, even better, in the middle of a word!). If you use `${..}`, it's clear that the variable name ends at `}`.

At runtime, the variable we defined will be replaced with the actual content instead of the variable name: this process is called *variable interpolation* and is used in all scripting/programming languages. We'll never see or directly use the value of a variable within a script, since in most cases the value is dependent on runtime configurations.

You will also see that we edited the information in the header. While it's easy to forget it, if a header does not contain correct information, you reduce readability. Always make sure you have an up-to-date header!

If we further dissect the script, you can see the `hello_text` variable is the first functional line after the header. We call this **assigning a value to a variable**. In some programming/scripting languages, you first have to *declare* a variable before you can *assign* it (most of the time, these languages have shorthand in which you can declare and assign as a single action).

The need for declaration comes from the fact that some languages are *statically typed* (the variable type—for example, string or integer—should be declared before a value is assigned, and the compiler will check that you're doing it correctly—for example, not assigning a string to an integer typed variable), while other languages are *dynamically typed*. For dynamically typed languages, the language just assumes the type of the variable from what is assigned to it. If it is assigned a number, it will be an integer; if it is assigned text, it will be a string, and so on.

 Basically, variables can be **assigned** a value, **declared**, or **initialized**. While, technically, these are different things, you will often see the terms being used interchangeably. Do not get too hung up on this; the most important thing to remember is you're *creating the variable and its content*!

Bash does not *really* follow either approach. Bash's simple variables (excluding arrays, which we will explain later) are always considered strings, unless the operation explicitly specifies that we should be doing arithmetic. Look at the following script and result (we omitted the header for brevity):

```
reader@ubuntu:~/scripts/chapter_08$ vim hello-int.sh
reader@ubuntu:~/scripts/chapter_08$ cat hello-int.sh
#/bin/bash

# Assign a number to the variable.
hello_int=1

echo ${hello_int} + 1
reader@ubuntu:~/scripts/chapter_08$ bash hello-int.sh
1 + 1
```

You might have expected that we would get the number 2 printed. However, as stated, Bash considers everything a string; it just prints the value of the variable, followed by the space, the plus sign, another space, and the number 1. If we want to have the actual arithmetic performed, we need a specialized syntax so that Bash knows that it is dealing with numbers:

```
reader@ubuntu:~/scripts/chapter_08$ vim hello-int.sh
reader@ubuntu:~/scripts/chapter_08$ cat hello-int.sh
#/bin/bash

# Assign a number to the variable.
hello_int=1

echo $(( ${hello_int} + 1 ))

reader@ubuntu:~/scripts/chapter_08$ bash hello-int.sh
2
```

By including the `variable + 1` inside `$((...))`, we tell Bash to evaluate it as arithmetic.

Why do we need variables?

Hopefully, you understand how to use variables now. However, you might not yet grasp why we would *want* or *need* to use variables. It might just seem like extra work for a small payoff, right? Consider the next example:

```
reader@ubuntu:~/scripts/chapter_08$ vim name.sh
reader@ubuntu:~/scripts/chapter_08$ cat name.sh
#!/bin/bash
```

```
#####################################
# Author: Sebastiaan Tammer
# Version: v1.0.0
# Date: 2018-09-01
# Description: Script to show why we need variables.
# Usage: ./name.sh
#####################################

# Assign the name to a variable.
name="Sebastiaan"

# Print the story.
echo "There once was a guy named ${name}. ${name} enjoyed Linux and Bash so
much that he wrote a book about it! ${name} really hopes everyone enjoys
his book."

reader@ubuntu:~/scripts/chapter_08$ bash name.sh
There once was a guy named Sebastiaan. Sebastiaan enjoyed Linux and Bash so
much that he wrote a book about it! Sebastiaan really hopes everyone enjoys
his book.
reader@ubuntu:~/scripts/chapter_08$
```

As you can see, we used the name variable not once, but three times. If we did not have the variable in place, and we needed to edit the name, we would need to search for every place in the text that the name was used.

Furthermore, if we made a spelling mistake in one of the places, writing *Sebastian* instead of *Sebastiaan* (which, if you're interested, happens *a lot*), both reading the text and editing it would take much more effort. Moreover, this was a simple example: often, variables are used many times (many more than three times at least).

Furthermore, variables are often used to store the *state* of a program. For a Bash script, you could imagine creating a temporary directory in which you'll perform some operations. We can store the location of this temporary directory in a variable, and anything we need to do in the temporary directory will make use of the variable to find the location. After the program finishes, the temporary directory should be cleaned up and the variable will no longer be needed. For every run of the program, the temporary directory will be named differently, so the content of the variable will be different, or *variable*, as well.

Another advantage of variables is that they have a name. Because of this, if we create a descriptive name, we can make the application easier to read and easier to use. We've determined that readability is always a must-have for shell scripting, and the use of properly named variables helps us with this.

Variables or constants?

In the examples up to now, we have actually used variables as **constants**. The term variable implies that it can change, whereas our examples have always assigned a variable at the start of the script, and used it throughout. While that has merits of its own (as stated before, for consistency or easier editing), it does not yet utilize the full power of variables.

A constant is a variable, but a special type. Simply put, a constant is *a variable defined at the start of the script that is not affected by user input and does not change value during execution.*

Later in this chapter, when we discuss dealing with user input, we'll see true variables. There, the content of the variables is supplied by the caller of the script, which means the output of the script will be different, or *varied*, each time the script is called. Later in the book, when we describe conditional testing, we will even change the value of a variable during the script itself, according to logic in that same script.

Variable naming

On to the subject of naming. You might have noticed something about the variables we've seen up to now: the Bash variables PATH and BASH_VERSION are written fully uppercase, but in our examples we used lowercase, with words separated by an underscore (hello_text). Consider the following example:

```bash
#!/bin/bash

#####################################
# Author: Sebastiaan Tammer
# Version: v1.0.0
# Date: 2018-09-08
# Description: Showing off different styles of variable naming.
# Usage: ./variable-naming.sh
#####################################

# Assign the variables.
name="Sebastiaan"
home_type="house"
LOCATION="Utrecht"
_partner_name="Sanne"
animalTypes="gecko and hamster"

# Print the story.
echo "${name} lives in a ${home_type} in ${LOCATION}, together with
${_partner_name} and their two pets: a ${animalTypes}."
```

If we run this, we get a nice little story:

```
reader@ubuntu:~/scripts/chapter_08$ bash variable-naming.sh
Sebastiaan lives in a house in Utrecht, together with Sanne and their two
pets: a gecko and hamster.
```

So, our variables are working great! Technically, everything we did in this example was fine. However, they look a mess. We used four different naming conventions: lowercase_with_underscores, UPPERCASE, _lowercase, and finally camelCase. While these are technically valid, remember that readability counts: it's best to pick one way of naming your variables, and stick with this.

As you might expect, there are many opinions about this (probably as many as in the tabs versus spaces debate!). Obviously, we also have an opinion, which we would like to share: use **lowercase_separated_by_underscores** for regular variables, and **UPPERCASE** for constants. From now on, you'll see this practice in all further scripts.

The previous example would look like this:

```
reader@ubuntu:~/scripts/chapter_08$ cp variable-naming.sh variable-naming-
proper.sh
reader@ubuntu:~/scripts/chapter_08$ vim variable-naming-proper.sh
vim variable-naming-proper.sh
reader@ubuntu:~/scripts/chapter_08$ cat variable-naming-proper.sh
#!/bin/bash

######################################
# Author: Sebastiaan Tammer
# Version: v1.0.0
# Date: 2018-09-08
# Description: Showing off uniform variable name styling.
# Usage: ./variable-naming-proper.sh
######################################

NAME="Sebastiaan"
HOME_TYPE="house"
LOCATION="Utrecht"
PARTNER_NAME="Sanne"
ANIMAL_TYPES="gecko and hamster"

# Print the story.
echo "${NAME} lives in a ${HOME_TYPE} in ${LOCATION}, together with
${PARTNER_NAME} and their two pets: a ${ANIMAL_TYPES}."
```

We hope you agree this looks *much better*. Later in this chapter, when we introduce user input, we will be working with normal variables as well, as opposed to the constants we've been using so far.

 Whatever you decide upon when naming your variables, there is only one thing in the end that really matters: consistency. Whether you prefer lowercase, camelCase, or UPPERCASE, it has no impact on the script itself (except for certain readability pros and cons, as discussed). However, using multiple naming conventions at the same time greatly confuses things. Always make sure to pick a convention wisely, and then **stick to it!**

To keep things clean, we generally avoid using UPPERCASE variables, except for constants. The main reason for this is that (almost) all *environment variables* in Bash are written in uppercase. If you do use uppercase variables in your scripts, there is one important thing to keep in mind: **make sure the names you choose do not conflict with pre-existing Bash variables**. These include PATH, USER, LANG, SHELL, HOME, and so on. Should you use the same names in your script, you might get some unexpected behavior.

It is a much better idea to avoid these conflicts and choose unique names for your variables. You could, for example, choose the SCRIPT_PATH variable instead of PATH.

Dealing with user input

So far, we've been dealing with really static scripts. While it's fun to have a story available for everyone to print out, it hardly qualifies as a functional shell script. At the very least, it's not something you are going to use often! So, we'd like to introduce a very important concept in shell scripting: **user input**.

Basic input

At a very basic level, everything that you put on the command line right after calling the script can be used as input. However, it is up to the script to use it! For example, consider the following situation:

```
reader@ubuntu:~/scripts/chapter_08$ ls
hello-int.sh hello-world-variable.sh name.sh variable-naming-proper.sh
variable-naming.sh
reader@ubuntu:~/scripts/chapter_08$ bash name.sh
There once was a guy named Sebastiaan. Sebastiaan enjoyed Linux and Bash so
much that he wrote a book about it! Sebastiaan really hopes everyone enjoys
his book.
```

```
reader@ubuntu:~/scripts/chapter_08$ bash name.sh Sanne
There once was a guy named Sebastiaan. Sebastiaan enjoyed Linux and Bash so
much that he wrote a book about it! Sebastiaan really hopes everyone enjoys
his book
```

When we called `name.sh` the first time, we used the originally intended functionality. The second time we called it, we supplied an extra argument: `Sanne`. However, because the script does not parse user input at all, the output we saw was exactly the same.

Let's revise the `name.sh` script so that it actually uses the extra input we specify when calling the script:

```
reader@ubuntu:~/scripts/chapter_08$ cp name.sh name-improved.sh
reader@ubuntu:~/scripts/chapter_08$ vim name-improved.sh
reader@ubuntu:~/scripts/chapter_08$ cat name-improved.sh
#!/bin/bash

#####################################
# Author: Sebastiaan Tammer
# Version: v1.0.0
# Date: 2018-09-08
# Description: Script to show why we need variables; now with user input!
# Usage: ./name-improved.sh <name>
#####################################

# Assign the name to a variable.
name=${1}

# Print the story.
echo "There once was a guy named ${name}. ${name} enjoyed Linux and Bash so
much that he wrote a book about it! ${name} really hopes everyone enjoys
his book."

reader@ubuntu:~/scripts/chapter_08$ bash name-improved.sh Sanne
There once was a guy named Sanne. Sanne enjoyed Linux and Bash so much that
he wrote a book about it! Sanne really hopes everyone enjoys his book.
```

Now, that looks much better! The script now accepts user input; specifically, the name of the person. It does this by using the $1 construct: this is the *first positional argument*. We call these arguments positional because the position matters: the first one will always be written to $1, the second to $2, and so on. There is no way for us to swap these around. Only once we start looking into making our script compatible with flags will we get more flexibility. If we provide even more arguments to the script, we can grab them using $3, $4, and so on.

There is a limit to the number of arguments you can provide. However, it is sufficiently high that you never have to really worry about it. If you get to that point, your script will be unwieldy enough that no one will ever use it anyway!

You might want to pass a sentence to a Bash script, as **one** argument. In this case, you need to enclose the entire sentence in single or double quotes if you want to have it interpreted as a *single positional argument*. If you do not, Bash will consider each space in your sentence the delimiter between the arguments; passing the sentence **This Is Cool** will result in three arguments to the script: This, Is, and Cool.

Notice how, again, we updated the header to include the new input under *Usage*. Functionally, however, the script isn't that great; we used male pronouns with a female name! Let's fix that real quick and find out what happens if we now *omit the user input*:

```
reader@ubuntu:~/scripts/chapter_08$ vim name-improved.sh
reader@ubuntu:~/scripts/chapter_08$ tail name-improved.sh
# Date: 2018-09-08
# Description: Script to show why we need variables; now with user input!
# Usage: ./name-improved.sh
#####################################

# Assign the name to a variable.
name=${1}

# Print the story.
echo "There once was a person named ${name}. ${name} enjoyed Linux and Bash
so much that he/she wrote a book about it! ${name} really hopes everyone
enjoys his/her book."

reader@ubuntu:~/scripts/chapter_08$ bash name-improved.sh
There once was a person named .  enjoyed Linux and Bash so much that he/she
wrote a book about it!  really hopes everyone enjoys his/her book.
```

So, we've made the text a little more unisex. However, when we called the script without providing a name as an argument, we messed up the output. In the next chapter we'll dive deeper into error checking and input validation, but for now remember that Bash **will not provide an error if variables are missing/empty**; you are fully responsible for handling this. We will discuss this further in the next chapter, as this is another very important topic in shell scripting.

Parameters and arguments

We need to take a small step back and discuss some terminology—parameters and arguments. It's not terribly complicated, but it can be a bit confusing, and they are sometimes used incorrectly.

Basically, an argument is something you pass to a script. What you define in the script is considered the parameter. Look at the following example to see how this works:

```
reader@ubuntu:~/scripts/chapter_08$ vim arguments-parameters.sh
reader@ubuntu:~/scripts/chapter_08$ cat arguments-parameters.sh
#!/bin/bash

#####################################
# Author: Sebastiaan Tammer
# Version: v1.0.0
# Date: 2018-09-08
# Description: Explaining the difference between argument and parameter.
# Usage: ./arguments-parameters.sh <argument1> <argument2>
#####################################

parameter_1=${1}
parameter_2=${2}

# Print the passed arguments:
echo "This is the first parameter, passed as an argument: ${parameter_1}"
echo "This is the second parameter, also passed as an argument:
${parameter_2}"

reader@ubuntu:~/scripts/chapter_08$ bash arguments-parameters.sh 'first-
arg' 'second-argument'
This is the first parameter, passed as an argument: first-arg
This is the second parameter, also passed as an argument: second-argument
```

Variables we use in this manner are called parameters inside the scripts, but are referred to as arguments when passing them to the script. In our `name-improved.sh` script, the parameter is the `name` variable. This is static and bound to the script version. The argument, however, is different each time the script is run: it can be `Sebastiaan`, or `Sanne`, or any other name.

 Remember, when we are talking about an argument, you can read that as a *runtime argument*; something that can be different each run. If we're talking about a parameter of the script, we're referring to the static piece of information expected by a script (which is often provided by a runtime argument, or some logic in the script).

Interactive versus non-interactive scripts

The script we have created so far uses user input, but it can't really be called interactive. As soon as the script is fired off, with or without arguments to the parameters, the script runs and completes.

But what if we do not want to use a long list of arguments, instead prompting the user for the information that is needed?

Enter the `read` command. The basic usage of `read` looks at input from the command line, and stores it in the `REPLY` variable. Try it out yourself:

```
reader@ubuntu:~$ read
This is a random sentence!
reader@ubuntu:~$ echo $REPLY
This is a random sentence!
reader@ubuntu:~$
```

After you start the `read` command, your terminal will go down a line and allow you to type anything you want. As soon as you hit *Enter* (or, actually, until Bash encounters the *newline* key), the input will be saved into the `REPLY` variable. You can then echo this variable to verify it has actually stored your text.

`read` has a few interesting flags which make it more usable in shell scripting. We can use the `-p` flag with an argument (the text to display, surrounded by quotes) to present the user with a prompt, and we can supply the name of the variable in which we want to store the response as the last argument:

```
reader@ubuntu:~$ read -p "What day is it? "
What day is it? Sunday
reader@ubuntu:~$ echo ${REPLY}
Sunday
reader@ubuntu:~$ read -p "What day is it? " day_of_week
What day is it? Sunday
reader@ubuntu:~$ echo ${day_of_week}
Sunday
```

In the previous example, we first used `read -p` without specifying a variable where we want to save our response. In this case, `read`'s default behavior places it in the `REPLY` variable. A line later, we ended the `read` command with the text `day_of_week`. In this case, the full response is saved into a variable with this name, as can be seen in the echo `${day_of_week}` right after.

Let's use `read` in an actual script now. We'll first create the script using `read`, and then using positional arguments as we have up to now:

```
reader@ubuntu:~/scripts/chapter_08$ vim interactive.sh
reader@ubuntu:~/scripts/chapter_08$ cat interactive.sh
#!/bin/bash

#####################################
# Author: Sebastiaan Tammer
# Version: v1.0.0
# Date: 2018-09-09
# Description: Show of the capabilities of an interactive script.
# Usage: ./interactive.sh
#####################################

# Prompt the user for information.
read -p "Name a fictional character: " character_name
read -p "Name an actual location: " location
read -p "What's your favorite food? " food

# Compose the story.
echo "Recently, ${character_name} was seen in ${location} eating ${food}!

reader@ubuntu:~/scripts/chapter_08$ bash interactive.sh
Name a fictional character: Donald Duck
Name an actual location: London
What's your favorite food? pizza
Recently, Donald Duck was seen in London eating pizza!
```

That worked out pretty well. The user could just call the script without looking at how to use it, and is further prompted for information. Now, let's copy and edit this script and use positional arguments to supply the information:

```
reader@ubuntu:~/scripts/chapter_08$ cp interactive.sh interactive-
arguments.sh
reader@ubuntu:~/scripts/chapter_08$ vim interactive-arguments.sh
reader@ubuntu:~/scripts/chapter_08$ cat interactive-arguments.sh
#!/bin/bash

#####################################
# Author: Sebastiaan Tammer
# Version: v1.0.0
# Date: 2018-09-09
# Description: Show of the capabilities of an interactive script,
# using positional arguments.
# Usage: ./interactive-arguments.sh <fictional character name>
# <actual location name> <your favorite food>
#####################################
```

```
# Initialize the variables from passed arguments.
character_name=${1}
location=${2}
food=${3}

# Compose the story.
echo "Recently, ${character_name} was seen in ${location} eating ${food}!"

reader@ubuntu:~/scripts/chapter_08$ bash interactive-arguments.sh "Mickey
Mouse" "Paris" "a hamburger"
Recently, Mickey Mouse was seen in Paris eating a hamburger!
```

First, we copied the `interactive.sh` script to `interactive-arguments.sh`. We edited this script to no longer use `read`, but instead to grab the values from the arguments passed to the script. We edited the header with *the new name and the new usage*, and we ran it by supplying another set of arguments. Once again, we were presented with a nice little story.

So, you might be wondering, when should you use which method? Both methods ended with the same result. However, as far as we're concerned, both scripts aren't equally readable or simple to use. Look at the following table for pros and cons for each method:

	Pros	Cons
Read	• User does not need to be aware of arguments to supply; they can just run the script and be prompted for any information needed • It is not possibly to forget to supply information	• If you want to repeat the script multiple times, you need to type the responses every time • Cannot be run non-interactively; for example, in a scheduled job
Arguments	• Can be repeated easily • Can be run non-interactively as well	• User needs to be aware of arguments to supply **before** attempting to run the script • It is much easier to forget to supply part of the information needed

Basically, the pros for one method are the cons for the other, and vice-versa. It seems as though we can't win by using either method. So, how would we create a robust interactive script that we can also run non-interactively?

Combining positional arguments and read

By combining both methods, of course! Before we start executing the actual functionality of the script, we need to verify whether all necessary information has been supplied. If it has not, we can then prompt the user for the missing information.

We're going to look ahead slightly to `Chapter 11`, *Conditional Testing and Scripting Loops*, and explain the basic use of `if-then` logic. We'll combine this with the `test` command, which we can use to check if a variable contains a value or is empty. *If* that is the case, *then* we can prompt the user with `read` to supply the missing information.

At its heart, `if-then` logic is nothing more than saying `if <something>, then do <something>`. In our example, `if` the variable of `character_name` is empty, `then` use `read` to prompt for this information. We'll do this for all three parameters in our script.

Because the arguments we're supplying are positional, we cannot supply the first and the third only; the script would interpret that as the first and second argument, with a missing third argument. With our current knowledge, we're limited by this. In `Chapter 15`, *Parsing Bash Script Arguments with getopts*, we'll explore how to supply information using flags. In this case, we can supply all information separately, without worrying about the order. For now, however, we'll have to live with the limitation!

Before we can explain the `test` command, we need to go back a little bit and explain **exit codes**. Basically, every program that runs and exits returns a code to the parent process that originally started it. Normally, if a process is done and execution was successful, it exits with **code 0**. If execution of the program was not successful, it exits with *any other code*; however, this is usually **code 1**. While there are conventions for exit codes, often you will just encounter 0 for good exits and 1 for bad exits.

When we use the `test` command, it generates exit codes conforming to the guidelines as well: if the test is successful, we see exit code 0. If it is not, we see another code (probably 1). You can see the exit code of the previous command with the `echo $?` command.

Let's look at an example:

```
reader@ubuntu:~/scripts/chapter_08$ cd
reader@ubuntu:~$ ls -l
total 8
-rw-rw-r-- 1 reader reader    0 Aug 19 11:54 emptyfile
drwxrwxr-x 4 reader reader 4096 Sep  1 09:51 scripts
-rwxrwxr-x 1 reader reader   23 Aug 19 11:54 textfile.txt
reader@ubuntu:~$ mkdir scripts
mkdir: cannot create directory 'scripts': File exists
reader@ubuntu:~$ echo $?
1
reader@ubuntu:~$ mkdir testdir
reader@ubuntu:~$ echo $?
0
```

```
reader@ubuntu:~$ rmdir testdir/
reader@ubuntu:~$ echo $?
0
reader@ubuntu:~$ rmdir scripts/
rmdir: failed to remove 'scripts/': Directory not empty
reader@ubuntu:~$ echo $?
1
```

A lot happened in the previous example. First, we tried to create a directory that was already present. Since we can't have two directories with the same name (in the same location), the mkdir command failed. When we printed the exit code using $?, we were returned 1.

Moving on, we successfully created a new directory, testdir. When we printed the exit code after that command, we saw the number for success: 0. After successfully removing the empty testdir, we saw an exit code of 0 again. When we tried to remove the not-empty scripts directory with rmdir (which isn't allowed), we got an error message and saw that the exit code was again 1.

Let's get back to test. What we need to do is verify whether a variable is empty. If it is, we want to start a read prompt to have it filled by user input. First we'll try this on the ${PATH} variable (which will never be empty), and then on the empty_variable, which will be indeed empty. To test whether a variable is empty, we use test -z <variable name>:

```
reader@ubuntu:~$ test -z ${PATH}
reader@ubuntu:~$ echo $?
1
reader@ubuntu:~$ test -z ${empty_variable}
reader@ubuntu:~$ echo $?
0
```

While this might seem like the wrong way around at first, think about it. We're testing whether a variable **is empty**. Since $PATH is not empty, the test fails and produces an exit code of 1. For ${empty_variable} (which we have never created), we are sure it is indeed empty, and an exit code of 0 confirms this.

If we want to combine the Bash if with test, we need to know that if expects a test that ends in an exit code of 0. So, if the test is successful, we can do something. This fits our example perfectly, since we're testing for empty variables. If you wanted to test it the other way around, you'd need to test for a non-zero length variable, which is the -n flag for test.

Let's look at the `if` syntax first. In essence, it looks like this: `if <exit code 0>; then <do something>; fi`. You can choose to have this on multiple lines, but using `;` on a line terminates it as well. Let's see whether we can manipulate this for our needs:

```
reader@ubuntu:~$ if test -z ${PATH}; then read -p "Type something: " PATH;
fi
reader@ubuntu:~$ if test -z ${empty_variable}; then read -p "Type
something: " empty_variable; fi
Type something: Yay!
reader@ubuntu:~$ echo ${empty_variable}
Yay!
reader@ubuntu:~$ if test -z ${empty_variable}; then read -p "Type
something: " empty_variable; fi
reader@ubuntu:~
```

First, we used our constructed `if-then` clause on the `PATH` variable. Since it is not empty, we did not expect a prompt: a good thing we did not get one! We used the same construct, but now with the `empty_variable`. Behold, since the `test -z` returned exit code 0, the `then` part of the `if-then` clause was executed and prompted us for a value. After inputting the value, we could echo it out. Running the `if-then` clause again did not give us the `read` prompt, because at that point the variable `empty_variable` was no longer empty!

Finally, let's incorporate this `if-then` logic into our new `interactive-ultimate.sh` script:

```
reader@ubuntu:~/scripts/chapter_08$ cp interactive.sh interactive-
ultimate.sh
reader@ubuntu:~/scripts/chapter_08$ vim interactive-ultimate.sh
reader@ubuntu:~/scripts/chapter_08$ cat interactive-ultimate.sh
#!/bin/bash

#####################################
# Author: Sebastiaan Tammer
# Version: v1.0.0
# Date: 2018-09-09
# Description: Show the best of both worlds!
# Usage: ./interactive-ultimate.sh [fictional-character-name] [actual-
# location] [favorite-food]
#####################################

# Grab arguments.
character_name=$1
location=$2
food=$3
```

```
# Prompt the user for information, if it was not passed as arguments.
if test -z ${character_name}; then read -p "Name a fictional character: "
character_name; fi
if test -z ${location}; then read -p "Name an actual location: " location;
fi
if test -z ${food}; then read -p "What's your favorite food? " food; fi

# Compose the story.
echo "Recently, ${character_name} was seen in ${location} eating ${food}!"

reader@ubuntu:~/scripts/chapter_08$ bash interactive-ultimate.sh
"Goofy"

Name an actual location: Barcelona
What's your favorite food? a hotdog
Recently, Goofy was seen in Barcelona eating a hotdog!
```

Success! We were prompted for `location` and `food`, but `character_name` was
successfully resolved from the argument that we passed. We've created a script that we can
use both fully interactive, without supplying arguments, but also non-interactive with
arguments.

 While this script is informative, it is not really efficient. It would be better
to combine the `test` looking directly at the passed arguments ($1, $2, $3),
so we only need one line. Later on in the book, we will start using such
optimizations, but for now it is more important to write things out in full,
so you can more easily understand them!

Summary

At the start of this chapter, we explained what a variable was: a standard building block
that allows us to store information, which we can reference later. We prefer to use variables
for a number of reasons: we can store a value once and reference it multiple times, and if
we need to change the value, we only have to change it once and the new value will be
used everywhere.

We explained that a constant is a special type of variable: it is defined only once in the
beginning of a script, it is not affected by user input, and it does not change during the
course of the script execution.

We continued with some notes on variable naming. We demonstrated that Bash is very flexible with regard to variables: it allows many different styles of variable naming. However, we explained that readability suffers if you use multiple different naming conventions in the same script, or between multiple scripts. The best idea is to choose one way of naming variables, and stick with it. We recommended using UPPERCASE for constants, and lowercase_separated_by_underscores for all other variables. This will lessen the chance of conflicts between local and environment variables.

Next, we explored user input and how to deal with it. We gave users of our scripts the ability to alter the outcome of our scripts, a function that is almost mandatory for most real-life functional scripts. We described two different methods of user interaction: basic input using positional arguments, and interactive input using the `read` construct.

We ended the chapter with a brief introduction to if–then logic and the `test` command. We used these concepts to create a robust way to handle user input, combining positional arguments with a `read` prompt for missing information, after presenting the pros and cons of each method used alone. This created a script that could be used both interactively and non-interactively, depending on the use case.

The following commands were introduced in this chapter: `read`, `test`, and `if`.

Questions

1. What is a variable?
2. Why do we need variables?
3. What is a constant?
4. Why are naming conventions especially important for variables?
5. What are positional arguments?
6. What is the difference between a parameter and an argument?
7. How can we make a script interactive?
8. How can we create a script that we can use both non-interactively and interactively?

Further reading

The following resources might be interesting if you'd like to go deeper into the subjects of this chapter:

- **Bash variables**: `https://ryanstutorials.net/bash-scripting-tutorial/bash-variables.php`
- **Google Shell Style Guide**: `https://google.github.io/styleguide/shell.xml`

Error Checking and Handling

9

In this chapter, we will describe how we can check for errors and handle them gracefully. We will start by explaining the exit status concept, followed by a number of functional checks with the `test` command. After that, we will start using shorthand notation for `test` command. The next part of this chapter is dedicated to error handling: we will use `if-then-exit` and `if-then-else` to handle simple errors. In the final part of this chapter, we will present some ways in which we can prevent errors from occurring in the first place, since prevention is better than remediation.

The following commands will be introduced in this chapter: `mktemp`, `true`, and `false`.

The following topics will be covered in this chapter:

- Error checking
- Error handling
- Error prevention

Technical requirements

Only the Ubuntu virtual machine is needed for this chapter. If you have never updated your machine, now might be a good time! The `sudo apt update && sudo apt upgrade -y` command upgrades your machine with all tools completely. If you choose to do this, make sure that you reboot your machine so that upgraded kernels are loaded. On Ubuntu, if the `/var/log/reboot-required` file is present, you can be sure a reboot is, well, *required*.

All scripts for this chapter can be found on GitHub: `https://github.com/PacktPublishing/Learn-Linux-Shell-Scripting-Fundamentals-of-Bash-4.4/tree/master/Chapter09`.

Error checking

In the previous chapter, we spent some time explaining how we could capture and use *user input* in our scripts. While this makes our scripts much more dynamic and, by extension, much more practical, we also introduce a new concept: **human error.** Let's say you're writing a script where you want to present the user with a yes/no question. You might expect a reasonable user to use any of the following as an answer:

- y
- n
- Y
- N
- Yes
- No
- yes
- no
- YES
- NO

While Bash allows us to check for all values we can think of, sometimes a user will still be able to *break* the script by supplying input you do not expect. An example of this would be the user answering the yes/no question in their native language: `ja`, `si`, `nei`, or any of the countless other possibilities. In practice, you will find that you can *never* think of every possible input a user will provide. That being the way it is, the best solution is to handle the most common expected input, and catch all other input with a generic error message which tells the user *how to correctly supply the answer*. We'll see how we can do that later on in this chapter, but first, we'll start by looking at how we can even determine if an error has occurred by checking the **exit status** of a command.

Exit status

The exit status, commonly also referred to as *exit codes* or *return codes*, is the way Bash communicates the successful or unsuccessful termination of a process to its parent. In Bash, all processes are *forked* from the shell that calls them. The following diagram illustrates this:

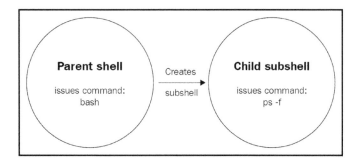

When a command runs, such as ps -f in the preceding diagram, the current shell is copied (including the environment variables!), and the command runs in the copy, called the *fork*. After the command/process is done, it terminates the fork and returns the exit status to the shell that it was initially forked from (which, in the case of an interactive session, will be your user session). At that point, you can determine whether the process was executed successfully by looking at the exit code. As explained in the previous chapter, an exit code of 0 is considered OK, while all other codes should be treated as NOT OK. Because the fork is terminated, we need the return code, otherwise we will have no way of communicating the status back to our session!

Because we have already seen how to grab the exit status in an interactive session in the previous chapter (hint: we looked at the content of the $? variable!), let's see how we can do the same in a script:

```
reader@ubuntu:~/scripts/chapter_09$ vim return-code.sh
reader@ubuntu:~/scripts/chapter_09$ cat return-code.sh
#!/bin/bash

####################################
# Author: Sebastiaan Tammer
# Version: v1.0.0
# Date: 2018-09-29
# Description: Teaches us how to grab a return code.
# Usage: ./return-code.sh
####################################

# Run a command that should always work:
mktemp
mktemp_rc=$?

# Run a command that should always fail:
mkdir /home/
mkdir_rc=$?

echo "mktemp returned ${mktemp_rc}, while mkdir returned ${mkdir_rc}!"
```

```
reader@ubuntu:~/scripts/chapter_09$ bash return-code.sh
/tmp/tmp.DbxKK1s4aV
mkdir: cannot create directory '/home': File exists
mktemp returned 0, while mkdir returned 1!
```

Going through the script, we start with the shebang and header. Since we don't use user input in this script, the usage is just the script name. The first command we run is `mktemp`. This command is used to create a temporary *file* with a random name, which could be useful is we needed to have a place on disk for some temporary data. Alternatively, if we supplied the `-d` flag to `mktemp`, we would create a temporary *directory* with a random name. Because the random name is sufficiently long and we should always have write permissions in `/tmp/`, we would expect the `mktemp` command to almost always succeed and thus return an exit status of 0. We save the return code to the `mktemp_rc` variable by running the variable assignment **directly after the command**. In that lies the biggest weakness with return codes: we only have them available directly after the command completes. If we do anything else after, the return code will be set for that action, overwriting the previous exit status!

Next, we run a command which we expect to always fail: `mkdir /home/`. The reason we expect this to fail is because on our system (and on pretty much every Linux system), the `/home/` directory already exists. In this case, it cannot be created again, which is why the command fails with an exit status of 1. Again, directly after the `mkdir` command, we save the exit status into the `mkdir_rc` variable.

Finally, we need to check to see whether our assumptions are correct. Using `echo`, we print the values of both variables along with some text so that we know where we printed which value. One last thing to note here: we used *double quotes* for our sentence containing variables. If we used *single quotes*, the variables would not be *expanded* (the Bash term for substituting the variable name with its value). Alternatively, we could omit the quotes altogether, and `echo` would perform as desired as well, however that could start presenting issues when we start working with redirection, which is why we consider it good form to always use double quotes when dealing with strings containing variables.

Functional checks

Now, we know how we can check the exit status of a process to determine if it was successful. However, that is not the only way we can validate the success/failure of commands. For most commands that we run, we could also perform a functional check to see if we were successful. In the previous script, we tried to create the `/home/` directory. But what if we were more concerned with the existence of the `/home/` directory, instead of the exit status of the process?

The following script shows how we can perform *functional checks* on the state of our system:

```
reader@ubuntu:~/scripts/chapter_09$ vim functional-check.sh
reader@ubuntu:~/scripts/chapter_09$ cat functional-check.sh
#!/bin/bash

#####################################
# Author: Sebastiaan Tammer
# Version: v1.0.0
# Date: 2018-09-29
# Description: Introduces functional checks.
# Usage: ./functional-check.sh
#####################################

# Create a directory.
mkdir /tmp/temp_dir
mkdir_rc=$?

# Use test to check if the directory was created.
test -d /tmp/temp_dir
test_rc=$?

# Check out the return codes:
echo "mkdir resulted in ${mkdir_rc}, test resulted in ${test_rc}."

reader@ubuntu:~/scripts/chapter_09$ bash functional-check.sh
mkdir resulted in 0, test resulted in 0.
reader@ubuntu:~/scripts/chapter_09$ bash functional-check.sh
mkdir: cannot create directory '/tmp/temp_dir': File exists
mkdir resulted in 1, test resulted in 0.
```

We start the preceding script with the usual plumbing. Next, we want to create a directory with mkdir. We grab the exit status and store it in a variable. Next, we use the test command (which we briefly explored in the previous chapter) to validate whether /tmp/temp_dir/ is a directory (and thus, if it was created **sometime**). We then print the return codes with echo, in the same fashion as we did for **return-code.sh**.

Next, we run the script twice. Here is where something interesting happens. The first time we run the script, the /tmp/temp_dir/ directory does not exist on the filesystem and is created. Because of this, the exit code for the mkdir command is 0. Since it was successfully created, test -d also succeeds and gives us back an exit status of **0**, as expected.

Now, in the second run of the script, the `mkdir` command does not successfully complete. This is expected, because the first run of the script already created the directory. Since we did not delete it in between the runs, the second run of `mkdir` is unsuccessful. However, `test -d` still runs fine: **the directory exists**, even though it was not created in that run of the script.

 When creating scripts, make sure you think long and hard about how you want to check for errors. Sometimes, return codes will be what you need: this is the case when you need to be sure that the command has been run successfully. Other times, however, a functional check might be a better fit. This is often the case when it is the end result that matters (for example, a directory must exist), but it does not matter so much what caused the desired state.

Test shorthand

The `test` command is one of the most important commands we have in our shell scripting arsenal. Because shell scripts can often be fragile, especially where user input is concerned, we want to make these as robust as possible. While explaining every aspect of the `test` command would take a whole chapter, the following are the things `test` can do:

- Check whether a file exists
- Check whether a directory exists
- Check whether a variable is not empty
- Check whether two variables have the same values
- Check whether FILE1 is older than FILE2
- Check whether INTEGER1 is greater than INTEGER2

And so on and on and on—this should give you at least an impression of things you can check with `test`. In the *Further reading* section, we have included an extensive source on test. Make sure to give it a look, as it will definitely help in your shell scripting adventures!

For most scripting and programming languages, there is no such thing as a `test` command. Obviously, tests are just as important in those languages but, unlike Bash, tests are often directly integrated with the `if-then-else` logic (which we will discuss in the next part of this chapter). Luckily for us, Bash has a shorthand for the `test` command, which brings it a lot closer to the syntax of other languages: `[` and `[[`.

Look at the following code to get a better idea of how we can replace the `test` command with this shorthand:

```
reader@ubuntu:~/scripts/chapter_09$ vim test-shorthand.sh
reader@ubuntu:~/scripts/chapter_09$ cat test-shorthand.sh
#!/bin/bash

####################################
# Author: Sebastiaan Tammer
# Version: v1.0.0
# Date: 2018-09-29
# Description: Write faster tests with the shorthand!
# Usage: ./test-shorthand.sh
####################################

# Test if the /tmp/ directory exists using the full command:
test -d /tmp/
test_rc=$?

# Test if the /tmp/ directory exists using the simple shorthand:
[ -d /tmp/ ]
simple_rc=$?

# Test if the /tmp/ directory exists using the extended shorthand:
[[ -d /tmp/ ]]
extended_rc=$?

# Print the results.
echo "The return codes are: ${test_rc}, ${simple_rc}, ${extended_rc}."

reader@ubuntu:~/scripts/chapter_09$ bash test-shorthand.sh
The return codes are: 0, 0, 0.
```

As you can see, after the plumbing we started with the previously introduced `test` syntax. Next, we replaced the word test with `[`, and ended the line with `]`. This is the part that Bash has in common with other scripting/programming languages. Note that, unlike most languages, Bash requires a **whitespace after [and before]**! Finally, we used the extended shorthand syntax, starting with `[[` and ending with `]]`. When we print the return codes, they all return 0, which means that all tests succeeded, even with the different syntaxes.

The difference between [ ] and [[ ]] is minor, but can be very important. Simply said, the simple shorthand syntax of [ ] can introduce problems when variables or paths have whitespace in them. In this case, the test considers the whitespace the delimiter, which means the string `hello there` becomes two arguments instead of one (`hello` + `there`). There are other differences, but in the end our advice is really simple: **use the extended shorthand syntax of [[ ]]**. For more information, see the *Further reading* section on test.

Variable refresher

As a little bonus, we have a slight improvement for the `test-shorthand.sh` script. In the previous chapter, we explained that, if we have to use the same value multiple times in a script, we're better off making it a variable. If the value of the variable does not change during the script's execution and is not influenced by user input, we use a CONSTANT. Take a look at how we would incorporate that in our previous script:

```
reader@ubuntu:~/scripts/chapter_09$ cp test-shorthand.sh test-shorthand-
variable.sh
reader@ubuntu:~/scripts/chapter_09$ vim test-shorthand-variable.sh
reader@ubuntu:~/scripts/chapter_09$ cat test-shorthand-variable.sh
#!/bin/bash

#####################################
# Author: Sebastiaan Tammer
# Version: v1.0.0
# Date: 2018-09-29
# Description: Write faster tests with the shorthand, now even better
# with a CONSTANT!
# Usage: ./test-shorthand-variable.sh
#####################################

DIRECTORY=/tmp/

# Test if the /tmp/ directory exists using the full command:
test -d ${DIRECTORY}
test_rc=$?

# Test if the /tmp/ directory exists using the simple shorthand:
[ -d ${DIRECTORY} ]
simple_rc=$?

# Test if the /tmp/ directory exists using the extended shorthand:
[[ -d ${DIRECTORY} ]]
extended_rc=$?
```

```
# Print the results.
echo "The return codes are: ${test_rc}, ${simple_rc}, ${extended_rc}."

reader@ubuntu:~/scripts/chapter_09$ bash test-shorthand-variable.sh
The return codes are: 0, 0, 0.
```

While the end result is the same, this script is more robust if we ever want to change it. Furthermore, it shows us that we can use variables in the `test` shorthand, which will automatically be expanded by Bash.

Bash debugging

We have one more trick up our sleeve to prove that values are expanded properly: running the Bash script **with debug logging**. Look at the following execution:

```
reader@ubuntu:~/scripts/chapter_09$ bash -x test-shorthand-variable.sh
+ DIRECTORY=/tmp/
+ test -d /tmp/
+ test_rc=0
+ '[' -d /tmp/ ']'
+ simple_rc=0
+ [[ -d /tmp/ ]]
+ extended_rc=0
+ echo 'The return codes are: 0, 0, 0.'
The return codes are: 0, 0, 0.
```

If you compare this to the actual script, you will see that the script text `test -d ${DIRECTORY}` is resolved to `test -d /tmp/` at runtime. This is because, instead of running `bash test-shorthand-variable.sh`, we're running `bash -x test-shorthand-variable.sh`. In this case, the `-x` flag tells Bash to *print commands and their arguments as they are executed*—a very handy thing to remember if you're ever building scripts and unsure why the script is not doing what you expect it to do!

Error handling

So far, we have looked at how we can check for errors. However, besides checking for errors, there is an aspect to this which is just as important: handling errors. We'll initially combine our previous experience with `if` and `test` to exit on errors, before we go on to introduce much smarter ways to handle errors!

if-then-exit

As you might recall from the previous chapter, the `if-then` construct used by Bash is common to (almost) all programming languages. In its basic form, the idea is that you test for a condition (IF), and if that condition is true, you do something (THEN).

Here's a very basic example: if `name` is longer than or equal to 2 characters, then `echo` `"hello ${name}"`. In this case, we assume that a name has to be, at the very least, 2 characters. If it is not, the input is invalid and we do not give it a "hello".

In the following script, `if-then-exit.sh`, we will see that our goal is to print the contents of a file using `cat`. However, before we do that, we check if the file exists, and if it doesn't, we exit the script with a message to the caller that specifies what went wrong:

```
reader@ubuntu:~/scripts/chapter_09$ vim if-then-exit.sh
reader@ubuntu:~/scripts/chapter_09$ cat if-then-exit.sh
#!/bin/bash

#####################################
# Author: Sebastiaan Tammer
# Version: v1.0.0
# Date: 2018-09-30
# Description: Use the if-then-exit construct.
# Usage: ./if-then-exit.sh
#####################################

FILE=/tmp/random_file.txt

# Check if the file exists.
if [[ ! -f ${FILE} ]]; then
  echo "File does not exist, stopping the script!"
  exit 1
fi

# Print the file content.
cat ${FILE}

reader@ubuntu:~/scripts/chapter_09$ bash -x if-then-exit.sh
+ FILE=/tmp/random_file.txt
+ [[ ! -f /tmp/random_file.txt ]]
+ echo 'File does not exist, stopping the script!'
File does not exist, stopping the script!
+ exit 1
```

Most of this script should be clear by now. We used the *extended shorthand syntax* for the test, as we will do in the rest of this book. The -f flag is described in the man page of test as *FILE exists and is a regular file*. However, we ran into a little issue here: we want to print the file (with cat), but only if the file exists; otherwise, we want to print the message with echo. Later in this chapter, when we introduce if-then-else, we'll see how we can do this with a positive test. At the moment though, we want the test to give us a TRUE if the file we're checking **is not** an existing file. In this case, semantically speaking, we're doing the following: IF the file does not exist, THEN print a message and EXIT. The test syntax in Bash does not have a flag for this. There is, luckily, one powerful construct we can use: the exclamation mark, !, which negates/reverses the test!

Some examples of this are as follows:

- if [[-f /tmp/file]]; then *do-something* -> *do-something* is executed if the file /tmp/file exists
- if [[! -f /tmp/file]]; then *do-something* -> *do-something* is executed if the file /tmp/file **does not** exist
- if [[-n ${variable}]]; then *do-something* -> *do-something* is executed if the variable ${variable} is not empty
- if [[! -n ${variable}]]; then *do-something* -> *do-something* is executed if the variable ${variable} is **not** not empty (so, the double negative means do-something is only executed if the variable is in fact empty)
- if [[-z ${variable}]]; then *do-something* -> *do-something* is executed if the variable ${variable} is empty
- if [[! -z ${variable}]]; then *do-something* -> *do-something* is executed if the variable ${variable} is **not** empty

As you should be aware, the last four examples overlap. This is because the flags −n (nonzero) and −z (zero) are already each other's opposites. Since we can negate the test with !, this means that −z is equal to ! −n, and ! −z is the same as −n. In this case, it would not matter if you used −n or ! −z. We would advise you to use the specific flag if it is available, before using a negation with another flag.

Let's get back to our script. When we found that the file did not exist by using the negated file exists test, we then printed the helpful message to the caller and exited the script. In this case, we never reached the cat command, but since the file does not exist anyway, the cat would never have succeeded. If we'd let the execution continue to that point, we would be presented with an error message by cat. In the case of cat, this message is no worse than our own message, but for some other commands, error messages are definitely not always as clear as we'd like; in this case, a check of our own with a clear message is not a bad thing!

Here's another example, where we use if and test to look at the status code which we'll catch in a variable:

```
reader@ubuntu:~/scripts/chapter_09$ vim if-then-exit-rc.sh
reader@ubuntu:~/scripts/chapter_09$ cat if-then-exit-rc.sh
#!/bin/bash

####################################
# Author: Sebastiaan Tammer
# Version: v1.0.0
# Date: 2018-09-30
# Description: Use return codes to stop script flow.
# Usage: ./if-then-exit-rc.sh
####################################

# Create a new top-level directory.
mkdir /temporary_dir
mkdir_rc=$?

# Test if the directory was created successfully.
if [[ ${mkdir_rc} -ne 0 ]]; then
  echo "mkdir did not successfully complete, stop script execution!"
  exit 1
fi

# Create a new file in our temporary directory.
touch /temporary_dir/tempfile.txt

reader@ubuntu:~/scripts/chapter_09$ bash if-then-exit-rc.sh
mkdir: cannot create directory '/temporary_dir': Permission denied
mkdir did not successfully complete, stop script execution!
```

In the first functional part of this script, we tried to create the top-level directory /temporary_dir/. Since only root has these privileges, and we're neither running this as the root user nor with sudo, the mkdir fails. When we catch the exit status in the mkdir_rc variable, we do not know the exact value (we could print it if we wanted it), but we know one thing for sure: it is not 0, which is reserved for successful execution. So, we have two options here: we can check if the exit status *is not equal to 0*, or if the status code *is equal to 1* (which is actually what mkdir reports back to the parent shell in this case). We generally prefer **checking for the absence of success**, instead of checking for a specific type of failure (as denoted by different return codes, such as 1, 113, 127, 255, and so on). If we only stop on an exit code of 1, we would continue the script in all cases where we do not get a 1: this would hopefully be a 0, but we're not sure of that. And, in general, anything that is not successful warrants stopping a script!

For this situation, checking if the return code is not 0, we're using an integer (remember, a fancy word for *number*) comparison. If we check man test, we can see that the -ne flag is described as INTEGER1 -ne INTEGER2: INTEGER1 is not equal to INTEGER2. So, for our logic, that would mean that, if the return code caught in the variable is **n**ot **e**qual to 0, the command did not succeed successfully and we should stop. Remember that we could also use the -eq (**eq**ual to) flag and negate it with ! for the same effect.

In its current form, the script is a little longer than it strictly needs to be. We first store the return code in a variable, and then we compare that variable. What we can also do is directly use the exit status in the if-test construction, like so:

```
reader@ubuntu:~/scripts/chapter_09$ cp if-then-exit-rc.sh if-then-exit-rc-
improved.sh
reader@ubuntu:~/scripts/chapter_09$ vim if-then-exit-rc-improved.sh
reader@ubuntu:~/scripts/chapter_09$ cat if-then-exit-rc-improved.sh
#!/bin/bash

#####################################
# Author: Sebastiaan Tammer
# Version: v1.0.0
# Date: 2018-09-30
# Description: Use return codes to stop script flow.
# Usage: ./if-then-exit-rc-improved.sh
#####################################

# Create a new top-level directory.
mkdir /temporary_dir

# Test if the directory was created successfully.
if [[ $? -ne 0 ]]; then
  echo "mkdir did not successfully complete, stop script execution!"
  exit 1
fi

# Create a new file in our temporary directory.
touch /temporary_dir/tempfile.txt

reader@ubuntu:~/scripts/chapter_09$ bash if-then-exit-rc-improved.sh
mkdir: cannot create directory '/temporary_dir': Permission denied
mkdir did not successfully complete, stop script execution!
```

While this *only* saves us a single line (the variable assignment), it also saves us an unnecessary variable. You can see that we changed the test to comparing **0** to **$?**. We know that we want to check the execution anyway, so we might as well do it right away. Should we need to do it later, we would still need to save it in a variable, because remember: the exit status is only available directly after running a command. After that point, it has been overridden by the exit status of later commands.

if-then-else

By now, you'll hopefully have a feeling for how useful `if-then` logic is. However, you might feel like something is missing still. If that is the case, you would be right! An `if-then` construct is not complete without the ELSE statement. The `if-then-else` construct allows us to specify what should happen if the test in the if-clause does **not** equal true. Semantically, it could be translated as:

IF condition, THEN do-something, ELSE (otherwise) do-something-else

We can illustrate this very easily by taking one of our earlier scripts, `if-then-exit.sh`, and optimizing both the flow of the script and the code:

```
reader@ubuntu:~/scripts/chapter_09$ cp if-then-exit.sh if-then-else.sh
reader@ubuntu:~/scripts/chapter_09$ vim if-then-else.sh
reader@ubuntu:~/scripts/chapter_09$ cat if-then-else.sh
#!/bin/bash

####################################
# Author: Sebastiaan Tammer
# Version: v1.0.0
# Date: 2018-09-30
# Description: Use the if-then-else construct.
# Usage: ./if-then-else.sh
####################################

FILE=/tmp/random_file.txt

# Check if the file exists.
if [[ ! -f ${FILE} ]]; then
  echo "File does not exist, stopping the script!"
  exit 1
else
  cat ${FILE} # Print the file content.
fi

reader@ubuntu:~/scripts/chapter_09$ bash if-then-else.sh
```

```
File does not exist, stopping the script!
reader@ubuntu:~/scripts/chapter_09$ touch /tmp/random_file.txt
reader@ubuntu:~/scripts/chapter_09$ bash -x if-then-else.sh
+ FILE=/tmp/random_file.txt
+ [[ ! -f /tmp/random_file.txt ]]
+ cat /tmp/random_file.txt
```

Now, this is starting to look like something! We moved our `cat` command into the `if-then-else` logic block. Now, it feels (and is!) like a single command: if the file does not exist, print an error message and exit, otherwise, print its contents. It is a little weird that we used the then block for the error situation, though; by convention, that is reserved for the success condition. We can make our script a little more intuitive by swapping the then and else blocks; however, we will also need to invert our test condition. Let's take a look:

```
reader@ubuntu:~/scripts/chapter_09$ cp if-then-else.sh if-then-else-
proper.sh
reader@ubuntu:~/scripts/chapter_09$ vim if-then-else-proper.sh
reader@ubuntu:~/scripts/chapter_09$ cat if-then-else-proper.sh
#!/bin/bash

####################################
# Author: Sebastiaan Tammer
# Version: v1.0.0
# Date: 2018-09-30
# Description: Use the if-then-else construct, now properly.
# Usage: ./if-then-else-proper.sh file-name
####################################

file_name=$1

# Check if the file exists.
if [[ -f ${file_name} ]]; then
  cat ${file_name} # Print the file content.
else
  echo "File does not exist, stopping the script!"
  exit 1
fi

reader@ubuntu:~/scripts/chapter_09$ bash -x if-then-else-proper.sh
/home/reader/textfile.txt
+ FILE=/home/reader/textfile.txt
+ [[ -f /home/reader/textfile.txt ]]
+ cat /home/reader/textfile.txt
Hi, this is some text.
```

The changes we made in this script are as follows:

- We replaced the hard-coded FILE constant with a user input variable `file_name`
- We removed the `!` which inverts the `test`
- We swapped the then and else execution blocks

As it is now, the script first checks if the file exists, and if it does, it prints its contents (success scenario). If the file does not exist, the script prints an error message and exits with an exit code of 1 (failure scenario). In practice, `else` is often reserved for failure scenarios, and `then` for the success scenario. However, these are not golden rules and could differ, based on the types of test you have available. If you're ever writing a script and you want to use the else block for the success scenario, go right ahead: as long as you're sure it's the right choice for your situation, there is definitely no shame in it!

 You might have noticed that within an `if-then-else` block, the commands we execute in then or else are always preceded by two whitespaces. In scripting/programming, this is called indenting. It serves only a single function in Bash: to improve readability. By indenting those commands with two spaces, we know they're part of the then-else logic. In that same manner, it is much easier to see where the `then` ends and the `else` begins. Note that, in some languages, notably Python, whitespace is part of the programming language syntax and cannot be omitted!

Until this point, we have only used `if-then-else` logic for error detection, followed by an exit `1`. However, in some cases, both *then* and *else* can be used to accomplish the goal of the script, instead of one of them being used for error handling. Take a look at the following script:

```
reader@ubuntu:~/scripts/chapter_09$ vim empty-file.sh
reader@ubuntu:~/scripts/chapter_09$ cat empty-file.sh
#!/bin/bash

#####################################
# Author: Sebastiaan Tammer
# Version: v1.0.0
# Date: 2018-10-02
# Description: Make sure the file given as an argument is empty.
# Usage: ./empty-file.sh <file-name>
#####################################

# Grab the first argument.
file_name=$1

# If the file exists, overwrite it with the always empty file
```

```
# /dev/null; otherwise, touch it.
if [[ -f ${file_name} ]]; then
  cp /dev/null ${file_name}
else
  touch ${file_name}
fi

# Check if either the cp or touch worked correctly.
if [[ $? -ne 0 ]]; then
  echo "Something went wrong, please check ${file_name}!"
  exit 1
else
  echo "Succes, file ${file_name} is now empty."
fi

reader@ubuntu:~/scripts/chapter_09$ bash -x empty-file.sh /tmp/emptyfile
+ file_name=/tmp/emptyfile
+ [[ -f /tmp/emptyfile ]]
+ touch /tmp/emptyfile
+ [[ 0 -ne 0 ]]
+ echo 'Succes, file /tmp/emptyfile is now empty.'
Succes, file /tmp/emptyfile is now empty.
reader@ubuntu:~/scripts/chapter_09$ bash -x empty-file.sh /tmp/emptyfile
+ file_name=/tmp/emptyfile
+ [[ -f /tmp/emptyfile ]]
+ cp /dev/null /tmp/emptyfile
+ [[ 0 -ne 0 ]]
+ echo 'Succes, file /tmp/emptyfile is now empty.'
Succes, file /tmp/emptyfile is now empty.
```

We use this script to make sure that a file exists and is empty. Basically, there are two scenarios: the file exists (and *might* not be empty) or it does not exist. In our **if** test, we check to see if the file exists. If it does, we replace it with an empty file by copying /dev/null (which is always empty) to the location given by the user. Otherwise, if the file does not exist, we simply create it using touch.

As you can see in the script's execution, the first time we run this script, the file does not exist and is created with touch. In the next run of the script, directly after, the file does exist (since it was created in the first run). This time, we can see in the debug that cp is used. Because we want to make sure whether either of these actions succeeded, we include an extra **if** block, which handles exit status checking, as we have seen before.

Shorthand syntax

By now, we've seen a few uses of an if block to see if our previous commands ran successfully. While the functionality is great, using 5-7 lines after each command where you suspect errors could occur really adds to the total script length! Even more of an issue will be readability: if half the script is error checking, it might be very hard to get to the bottom of the code. Fortunately, there is a way in which we can check for errors directly after a command. We can accomplish this with the || command, which is the Bash version of a logical OR. Its counterpart, **&&**, is the implementation of a logical AND. To illustrate this, we'll introduce two new commands: `true` and `false`. If you take a look at the respective man pages, you'll find the clearest answer you can possibly get:

- true: Do nothing, successfully
- false: Do nothing, unsuccessfully

The following script illustrates how we use || and **&&** to create a logical application flow. If logical operators are unfamiliar terrain, check out the link in the *Further reading* section under *Logical operators* first:

```
reader@ubuntu:~/scripts/chapter_09$ vim true-false.sh
reader@ubuntu:~/scripts/chapter_09$ cat true-false.sh
#!/bin/bash

#####################################
# Author: Sebastiaan Tammer
# Version: v1.0.0
# Date: 2018-10-02
# Description: Shows the logical AND and OR (&& and ||).
# Usage: ./true-false.sh
#####################################

# Check out how an exit status of 0 affects the logical operators:
true && echo "We get here because the first part is true!"
true || echo "We never see this because the first part is true :("

# Check out how an exit status of 1 affects the logical operators:
false && echo "Since we only continue after && with an exit status of 0,
this is never printed."
false || echo "Because we only continue after || with a return code that is
not 0, we see this!"

reader@ubuntu:~/scripts/chapter_09$ bash -x true-false.sh
+ true
+ echo 'We get here because the first part is true!'
We get here because the first part is true!
+ true
```

```
+ false
+ false
+ echo 'Because we only continue after || with a return code that is not 0,
we see this!'
Because we only continue after || with a return code that is not 0, we see
this!
```

As we expect, the code after **&&** is only executed if the command before returns an exit code of **0**, while the code after || is only executed if the exit code is **not 0** (so, most often, **1**). If you look closely, you can actually see this happening in the debug of the script. You can see `true` being executed twice, as well as `false`. However, the first `echo` we actually end up seeing is after the first **true**, whereas the second `echo` we see is after the second **false**! We've highlighted this in the preceding code for your convenience.

Now, how can we use this to handle errors? An error will give an exit status that is anything other than 0, so this is comparable to the `false` command. In our example, the code after the logical operator || was printed after the false. This makes sense, because either `false` OR `echo` should succeed. In this case, since `false` (by default) fails, `echo` is executed. In the following simple example, we'll show you how we would use the || operator in a script:

```
reader@ubuntu:~/scripts/chapter_09$ vim logical-or.sh
reader@ubuntu:~/scripts/chapter_09$ cat logical-or.sh
#!/bin/bash

#####################################
# Author: Sebastiaan Tammer
# Version: v1.0.0
# Date: 2018-10-02
# Description: Use the logical OR for error handling.
# Usage: ./logical-or.sh
#####################################

# This command will surely fail because we don't have the permissions
needed:
cat /etc/shadow || exit 123

reader@ubuntu:~/scripts/chapter_09$ cat /etc/shadow
cat: /etc/shadow: Permission denied
reader@ubuntu:~/scripts/chapter_09$ echo $?
1
reader@ubuntu:~/scripts/chapter_09$ bash logical-or.sh
cat: /etc/shadow: Permission denied
reader@ubuntu:~/scripts/chapter_09$ echo $?
123
```

We try to `cat` a file that we do not have permissions to (which is a good thing, since `/etc/shadow` contains the hash passwords for all users on the system). When we do this normally, we receive the exit status of **1**, as you can see from our manual `cat`. However, in our script, we use `exit 123`. If our logical operator does its job, we will not exit with the default 1, but instead with exit status 123. When we call the script, we get the same `Permission denied` error, but this time when we print the return code, we see the expected 123.

> If you really want to confirm that the code after || is only executed if the first part fails, run the script with `sudo`. In this case, you will see the contents of `/etc/shadow`, since root has those permissions and the exit code will be 0 instead of the earlier 1 and 123.

Similarly, you can also use **&&** if you only want to execute code when you're entirely sure the first command has finished successfully. To handle potential errors in a really graceful manner, it would be best to combine `echo` and `exit` after the ||. In the next example, on one of the next few pages, you will see how this is achieved! We will use that way of handling errors in the rest of this book, so don't worry about the syntax just yet – you will encounter it many more times before this book is over.

Error prevention

At this point, you should have a firm grasp on how we can handle (user input) error. Obviously, context is everything here: depending on the situation, some errors are handled in different ways. There is one more important subject in this chapter, and that is *error prevention*. While knowing how to handle errors is one thing, it would be even better if we can prevent errors during script execution altogether.

Checking arguments

As we noted in the previous chapter, when you're dealing with positional arguments passed to your script, a few things are very important. One of them is whitespace, which signifies the boundary between arguments. If we need to pass an argument to our script that contains whitespace, we need to wrap that argument in single or double quotes, otherwise it will be interpreted as multiple arguments. Another important aspect of positional arguments is getting exactly the right number of arguments: not too few, but definitely not too many either.

By starting our scripts (that use positional arguments) with a check on the number of arguments passed, we can validate if the user called the script correctly. Otherwise, we can instruct the user on how to correctly call it! The following example shows you how we can do this:

```
reader@ubuntu:~/scripts/chapter_09$ vim file-create.sh
reader@ubuntu:~/scripts/chapter_09$ cat file-create.sh
#!/bin/bash

#####################################
# Author: Sebastiaan Tammer
# Version: v1.0.0
# Date: 2018-10-01
# Description: Create a file with contents with this script.
# Usage: ./file-create.sh <directory_name> <file_name> <file_content>
#####################################

# We need exactly three arguments, check how many have been passed to
# the script.
if [[ $# -ne 3 ]]; then
  echo "Incorrect usage!"
  echo "Usage: $0 <directory_name> <file_name> <file_content>"
  exit 1
fi
# Arguments are correct, lets continue.

# Save the arguments into variables.
directory_name=$1
file_name=$2
file_content=$3

# Create the absolute path for the file.
absolute_file_path=${directory_name}/${file_name}

# Check if the directory exists; otherwise, try to create it.
if [[ ! -d ${directory_name} ]]; then
  mkdir ${directory_name} || { echo "Cannot create directory, exiting
script!"; exit 1; }
fi

# Try to create the file, if it does not exist.
if [[ ! -f ${absolute_file_path} ]]; then
  touch ${absolute_file_path} || { echo "Cannot create file, exiting
script!"; exit 1; }
fi

# File has been created, echo the content to it.
echo ${file_content} > ${absolute_file_path}
```

```
reader@ubuntu:~/scripts/chapter_09$ bash -x file-create.sh /tmp/directory/
newfile "Hello this is my file"
+ [[ 3 -ne 3 ]]
+ directory_name=/tmp/directory/
+ file_name=newfile
+ file_content='Hello this is my file'
+ absolute_file_path=/tmp/directory//newfile
+ [[ ! -d /tmp/directory/ ]]
+ mkdir /tmp/directory/
+ [[ ! -f /tmp/directory//newfile ]]
+ touch /tmp/directory//newfile
+ echo Hello this is my file
reader@ubuntu:~/scripts/chapter_09$ cat /tmp/directory/newfile
Hello this is my file
```

To properly illustrate this principle and some others we have seen before, we've created a rather large and complicated script (compared to what you have seen before). To make it easy to understand this, we'll cut it up into pieces and discuss each piece sequentially. We'll start with the header:

```
#!/bin/bash

####################################
# Author: Sebastiaan Tammer
# Version: v1.0.0
# Date: 2018-10-01
# Description: Create a file with contents with this script.
# Usage: ./file-create.sh <directory_name> <file_name> <file_content>
####################################
...
```

The shebang and most fields should feel natural right now. When specifying positional parameters, however, we like to enclose them within <> if they're **required**, and [] if they're **optional** (which they are if they have a default value, for instance, which we will see at the end of this chapter). This is a common pattern in scripting and you would do well to follow it! The next part of the script is the actual check for the number of arguments:

```
...
# We need exactly three arguments, check how many have been passed to the
script.
if [[ $# -ne 3 ]]; then
  echo "Incorrect usage!"
  echo "Usage: $0 <directory_name> <file_name> <file_content>"
  exit 1
fi
# Arguments are correct, lets continue.
...
```

The magic in this section comes from the **$#** combination. Similar to the **$?** exit status construct, **$#** is resolved to the number of arguments that have been passed to the script. Because this is an integer, we can compare it, using the -ne and -eq flags of test, to the number of arguments we need: three. Anything that is *not three* will not work for this script, which is why we build the check in this manner. If the *test is positive* (which means a negative result!), we perform the then-logic, which tells the user that they called the script incorrectly. To prevent that from happening again, the correct way to use the script is passed as well. We use one more trick here, the $0 signs. This resolves to the script name, which is why, in the case of incorrect calling, the script name is printed nicely next to the actual expected arguments, like so:

```
reader@ubuntu:~/scripts/chapter_09$ bash file-create.sh 1 2 3 4 5
Incorrect usage!
Usage: file-create.sh <directory_name> <file_name> <file_content>
```

Because of this check and the hint to the user, we would expect the user to call this script incorrectly only once. Because we have not started processing the script's functionality yet, we will not have a situation where half the tasks in the script have been completed, even though we would know **at the start of the script** that it would never complete, since it is missing information that the script needs. Let's move on to the next part of the script:

```
...
# Save the arguments into variables.
directory_name=$1
file_name=$2
file_content=$3

# Create the absolute path for the file.
absolute_file_path=${directory_name}/${file_name}
...
```

As a recap, we can see that we assigned positional user input to a variable name we chose to represent the thing it is saving. Because we need to use the absolute path of the final file more than once, we combine two of the variables based on user input to form the absolute path to the file. The next part of the script contains the actual functionality:

```
...
# Check if the directory exists; otherwise, try to create it.
if [[ ! -d ${directory_name} ]]; then
  mkdir ${directory_name} || { echo "Cannot create directory, exiting
script!"; exit 1; }
fi

# Try to create the file, if it does not exist.
if [[ ! -f ${absolute_file_path} ]]; then
    touch ${absolute_file_path} || { echo "Cannot create file, exiting
```

```
script!"; exit 1; }
fi

# File has been created, echo the content to it.
echo ${file_content} > ${absolute_file_path}
```

For both the file and the directory, we do a similar check: we check if the directory/file is already there, or if we need to create it. By using the || shorthand with echo and exit, we check if mkdir and touch return an exit status of **0**. Remember, if they return *anything other than 0*, everything after the || and within the curly braces will be executed, in this case exiting the script!

The last part contains the *redirection* of the echo to the file. Simply said, the output of echo is redirected into a file. Redirection will be discussed in depth in Chapter 12, *Using Pipes and Redirection in Scripts*. For now, accept that the text we used for ${file_content} will be written to the file (as you can check yourself).

Managing absolute and relative paths

There is an issue we have not discussed yet: running scripts with absolute and relative paths. This might seem like a trivial difference, but it most certainly is not. Most commands you run, while directly interactive or from within a script you call, use your current working directory as their current working directory. You might have expected commands in a script to default to the directory where the script is, but since the script is nothing more than a fork of your current shell (as explained at the beginning of this chapter), it also inherits the current working directory. We can best illustrate this by creating a script which copies a file to a relative path:

```
reader@ubuntu:~/scripts/chapter_09$ vim log-copy.sh
reader@ubuntu:~/scripts/chapter_09$ cat log-copy.sh
#!/bin/bash

#####################################
# Author: Sebastiaan Tammer
# Version: v1.0.0
# Date: 2018-10-02
# Description: Copy dpkg.log to a local directory.
# Usage: ./log-copy.sh
#####################################

# Create the directory in which we'll store the file.
if [[ ! -d dpkg ]]; then
  mkdir dpkg || { echo "Cannot create the directory, stopping script.";
exit 1; }
```

```
fi

# Copy the log file to our new directory.
cp /var/log/dpkg.log dpkg || { echo "Cannot copy dpkg.log to the new
directory."; exit 1; }
```

```
reader@ubuntu:~/scripts/chapter_09$ ls -l dpkg
ls: cannot access 'dpkg': No such file or directory
reader@ubuntu:~/scripts/chapter_09$ bash log-copy.sh
reader@ubuntu:~/scripts/chapter_09$ ls -l dpkg
total 632
-rw-r--r-- 1 reader reader 643245 Oct  2 19:39 dpkg.log
reader@ubuntu:~/scripts/chapter_09$ cd /tmp
reader@ubuntu:/tmp$ ls -l dpkg
ls: cannot access 'dpkg': No such file or directory
reader@ubuntu:/tmp$ bash /home/reader/scripts/chapter_09/log-copy.sh
reader@ubuntu:/tmp$ ls -l dpkg
total 632
-rw-r--r-- 1 reader reader 643245 Oct  2 19:39 dpkg.log
```

The script itself is pretty easy – check if a directory is present, otherwise create it. You can check for errors on `mkdir` by using our shorthand error handling. Next, copy a known file (`/var/log/dpkg.log`) to the `dpkg` directory. The first time we run it, we're in the same directory as the script. We can see the `dpkg` directory that was created there and the file copied inside it. Then, we move our current working directory to `/tmp/` and we run the script again, this time using the absolute path instead of the relative path of the first call. Now, we can see that the `dpkg` directory is created at `/tmp/dpkg/`! Not really unexpected, but how could we `avoid` this? Just a single line at the beginning of the script will fix this:

```
reader@ubuntu:~/scripts/chapter_09$ cp log-copy.sh log-copy-improved.sh
reader@ubuntu:~/scripts/chapter_09$ vim log-copy-improved.sh
reader@ubuntu:~/scripts/chapter_09$ cat log-copy-improved.sh
#!/bin/bash

#####################################
# Author: Sebastiaan Tammer
# Version: v1.0.0
# Date: 2018-10-02
# Description: Copy dpkg.log to a local directory.
# Usage: ./log-copy-improved.sh
#####################################

# Change directory to the script location.
cd $(dirname $0)

# Create the directory in which we'll store the file.
if [[ ! -d dpkg ]]; then
```

```
    mkdir dpkg || { echo "Cannot create the directory, stopping script.";
exit 1; }
fi

# Copy the log file to our new directory.
cp /var/log/dpkg.log dpkg || { echo "Cannot copy dpkg.log to the new
directory."; exit 1; }

reader@ubuntu:~/scripts/chapter_09$ cd /tmp/
reader@ubuntu:/tmp$ rm -rf /tmp/dpkg/
reader@ubuntu:/tmp$ rm -rf /home/reader/scripts/chapter_09/dpkg/
reader@ubuntu:/tmp$ bash -x /home/reader/scripts/chapter_09/log-copy-
improved.sh
++ dirname /home/reader/scripts/chapter_09/log-copy-improved.sh
+ cd /home/reader/scripts/chapter_09
+ [[ ! -d dpkg ]]
+ mkdir dpkg
+ cp /var/log/dpkg.log dpkg
reader@ubuntu:/tmp$ ls -l dpkg
ls: cannot access 'dpkg': No such file or directory
```

As the code execution should show, we now do everything relative to the script location. This is made possible by a little bit of Bash magic combined with the `dirname` command. This command is pretty simple as well: it prints the directory name from whatever we pass, in this case, **$0**. As you might remember, **$0** resolves to the script name as it is called. From **/tmp/**, this is the absolute path; if we call it from another directory, it might be a relative path. If we are in the same directory as the script, `dirname`, **$0** will result in **.**, which means we `cd` to the current directory. This is not really needed, but it does not do any harm either. This seems like a small payoff for a much more robust script, which we can now call from wherever we want!

> For now, we won't go into details regarding the `$(...)` syntax. We will further discuss this in `Chapter 12`, *Using Pipes and Redirection in Scripts*. At this point, remember that this allows us to get a value which we can pass to `cd` in a single line.

Dealing with y/n

At the beginning of this chapter, we presented you with something to think about: asking the user to agree or disagree with something by stating yes or no. As we discussed, there are many possible answers we can expect a user to give. Realistically, there are five ways a user could give us a *yes*: y, Y, yes, YES, and Yes.

The same goes for *no*. Let's see how we could check this without using any tricks:

```
reader@ubuntu:~/scripts/chapter_09$ vim yes-no.sh
reader@ubuntu:~/scripts/chapter_09$ cat yes-no.sh
#!/bin/bash

######################################
# Author: Sebastiaan Tammer
# Version: v1.0.0
# Date: 2018-10-01
# Description: Dealing with yes/no answers.
# Usage: ./yes-no.sh
######################################

read -p "Do you like this question? " reply_variable

# See if the user responded positively.
if [[ ${reply_variable} = 'y' || ${reply_variable} = 'Y' ||
${reply_variable} = 'yes' || ${reply_variable} = 'YES' || ${reply_variable}
= 'Yes' ]]; then
  echo "Great, I worked really hard on it!"
  exit 0
fi

# Maybe the user responded negatively?
if [[ ${reply_variable} = 'n' || ${reply_variable} = 'N' ||
${reply_variable} = 'no' || ${reply_variable} = 'NO' || ${reply_variable} =
'No' ]]; then
  echo "You did not? But I worked so hard on it!"
  exit 0
fi

# If we get here, the user did not give a proper response.
echo "Please use yes/no!"
exit 1

reader@ubuntu:~/scripts/chapter_09$ bash yes-no.sh
Do you like this question? Yes
Great, I worked really hard on it!
reader@ubuntu:~/scripts/chapter_09$ bash yes-no.sh
Do you like this question? n
You did not? But I worked so hard on it!
reader@ubuntu:~/scripts/chapter_09$ bash yes-no.sh
Do you like this question? maybe
Please use yes/no!
```

While this works, it is not really a very workable solution. Even worse, if the user happens to have Caps Lock on while they're trying to type *Yes*, we will end up with *yES*! Do we need to include that as well? The answer is, of course, no. Bash has a nifty little feature called **parameter expansion**. We will explain this in much more depth in Chapter 16, *Bash Parameter Substitution and Expansion*, but for now, we can give you a preview of what it is capable of:

```
reader@ubuntu:~/scripts/chapter_09$ cp yes-no.sh yes-no-optimized.sh
reader@ubuntu:~/scripts/chapter_09$ vim yes-no-optimized.sh
reader@ubuntu:~/scripts/chapter_09$ cat yes-no-optimized.sh
#!/bin/bash

#####################################
# Author: Sebastiaan Tammer
# Version: v1.0.0
# Date: 2018-10-01
# Description: Dealing with yes/no answers, smarter this time!
# Usage: ./yes-no-optimized.sh
#####################################

read -p "Do you like this question? " reply_variable

# See if the user responded positively.
if [[ ${reply_variable,,} = 'y' || ${reply_variable,,} = 'yes' ]]; then
  echo "Great, I worked really hard on it!"
  exit 0
fi

# Maybe the user responded negatively?
if [[ ${reply_variable^^} = 'N' || ${reply_variable^^} = 'NO' ]]; then
  echo "You did not? But I worked so hard on it!"
  exit 0
fi

# If we get here, the user did not give a proper response.
echo "Please use yes/no!"
exit 1

reader@ubuntu:~/scripts/chapter_09$ bash yes-no-optimized.sh
Do you like this question? YES
Great, I worked really hard on it!
reader@ubuntu:~/scripts/chapter_09$ bash yes-no-optimized.sh
Do you like this question? no
You did not? But I worked so hard on it!
```

Instead of five checks for each answer, we now use two: one for the full word (yes/no) and one for the short one-letter answer (y/n). But, how does the answer *YES* work, when we have only specified *yes*? The solution to this question lies in the ,, and ^^, which we have included inside the variable. So, instead of **${reply_variable}**, we used **${reply_variable,,}** and **${reply_variable^^}**. In the case of ,, the variable is first resolved to its value and then converted to *all lowercase letters*. Because of this, all three answers – *YES, Yes, and yes* – can be compared with *yes*, as that is how Bash will expand them. You might take a guess at what ^^ does: it converts the content of the string to uppercase, which is why we can compare it to NO, even though we give the answer no.

Always try to place yourself in the users' shoes. They are dealing with many different tools and commands. In most of these cases, logic as given for dealing with different ways of writing yes/no has been integrated. This can make even the most friendly system administrator a bit lazy and train them to go for the one-letter answer. But you wouldn't want to punish the sysadmin that actually listens to you, either! So, make a point of dealing with the most *reasonable* answers in a friendly manner.

Summary

In this chapter, we discussed many aspects of errors in Bash scripts. First, error **checking** was described. To start with, we explained that an exit status is a way for commands to communicate whether their execution was considered a success or failure. The `test` command and its shorthand `[[...]]` notation were introduced. This command allows us to perform functional checks in our scripts. Examples of this are comparing strings and integers, and checking if a file or directory is created and accessible/writable. We gave a quick refresher on variables, followed by a short introduction to running a script with the debug flag, `-x`, set.

The second part of this chapter dealt with error **handling**. We described the (unofficial) `if-then-exit` construct, which we use to check command execution and exit if it failed. In the examples that followed, we saw that we do not always have to write return code to variables when we want to check them; we can use **$?** directly in a test case. Going on, we gave a preview of how we can use `if-then-else` logic to handle errors in a better way. We ended the second part of this chapter by presenting the shorthand syntax for error handling, which we will continue to use throughout the rest of this book.

In the third and final part of this chapter, we explained error **prevention**. We learned how we can check if the arguments are correct and how we can avoid issues with absolute and relative paths when calling our script. In the final part of this chapter, we answered the question we posed at the beginning: How can we best deal with yes/no input from the user? By using some simple Bash parameter expansions (which will be further explained in the last chapter of this book), we were able to simply facilitate multiple answering styles for the users of our script.

The following commands were introduced in this chapter: `mktemp`, `true`, and `false`.

Questions

1. Why do we need an exit status?
2. What is the difference between exit status, exit code, and return code?
3. Which flag do we use with test to test for the following?
   - An existing directory
   - A writable file
   - An existing symbolic link
4. What is the preferred shorthand syntax for `test -d /tmp/`?
5. How can we print debug information in a Bash session?
6. How can we check whether a variable has content?
7. What is the Bash format for grabbing a return code?
8. Of `||` and `&&`, which is the logical AND and which is the OR?
9. What is the Bash format for grabbing the number of arguments?
10. How can we make sure that it does not matter from which working directory the user calls the script?
11. How do Bash parameter expansions help us when dealing with user input?

Further reading

The following resources might be interesting if you'd like to go deeper into the subjects of this chapter:

- **The test command**: http://wiki.bash-hackers.org/commands/classictest
- **Bash debugging**: http://tldp.org/LDP/Bash-Beginners-Guide/html/sect_02_03.html
- **Logical operators**: https://secure.php.net/manual/en/language.operators.logical.php

10
Regular Expressions

This chapter introduces regular expressions, and the main commands that we can use to leverage their power. We'll first look at the theory behind regular expressions, before moving deeper into practical examples of using regular expressions with `grep` and `sed`.

We will also explain globbing, and how it is used on the command line.

The following commands will be introduced in this chapter: `grep`, `set`, `egrep`, and `sed`.

The following topics will be covered in this chapter:

- What are regular expressions?
- Globbing
- Using regular expressions with `egrep` and `sed`

Technical requirements

All scripts for this chapter can be found on GitHub: `https://github.com/tammert/learn-linux-shell-scripting/tree/master/chapter_10`. Other than this, the Ubuntu virtual machine is still our way of testing and running the scripts in this chapter.

Introducing regular expressions

You might have heard the term *regular expression*, or *regex*, before. For many people, a regular expression is something that seems very complicated, and is often plucked somewhere from the internet or a textbook, without fully grasping what it does.

While that is fine for completing a set task, understanding regular expressions better than the average systems administrator really allows you to differentiate yourself, both in creating scripts and working on the Terminal.

A nicely tailored regular expression can really help you keep your scripts short, simple, and robust to changes in the future.

What is a regular expression?

In essence, a regular expression is a *piece of text* that functions as a *search pattern* for other text. Regular expressions make it possible to easily say, for example, that I want to select all lines that contain a word that is five characters in length, or look for all files that end in .log.

An example might help with your understanding. First, we need a command that we can use to explore regular expressions. The most famous command used in Linux with regular expressions is grep.

grep is an acronym meaning *global regular expression print*. As you can see, this seems like a good candidate for explaining the concept!

grep

We are going to dive right in as follows:

```
reader@ubuntu:~/scripts/chapter_10$ vim grep-file.txt
reader@ubuntu:~/scripts/chapter_10$ cat grep-file.txt
We can use this regular file for testing grep.
Regular expressions are pretty cool
Did you ever realise that in the UK they say colour,
but in the USA they use color (and realize)!
Also, New Zealand is pretty far away.
reader@ubuntu:~/scripts/chapter_10$ grep 'cool' grep-file.txt
Regular expressions are pretty cool
reader@ubuntu:~/scripts/chapter_10$ cat grep-file.txt | grep 'USA'
but in the USA they use color (and realize)!
```

First of all, let's explore the basic functionality of grep, before we move on to regular expressions. What grep does is really simple, as stated in man grep: *print lines matching a pattern*.

In the preceding example, we created a file with some sentences. Some of these start with capital letters; they mostly end differently; and they use some words that are similar, but not really the same. These and more characteristics will be used in further examples.

To start, we use grep to match a single word (the search is case-sensitive by default), and print that. grep has two operating modes:

- grep <pattern> <file>
- grep <pattern> (which needs input in the form of a pipe, or |)

The first operating mode lets you specify a filename from which you want to specify the lines that need to be printed, if they match the pattern you specify. The grep 'cool' grep-file.txt command is an example of this.

There is another way of using grep: in streams. A stream is something *in transit* to your Terminal, but which can be changed while on the move. In this case, a cat of the file would normally print all lines to your Terminal.

However, with the pipe symbol (|) we redirect the output of cat to grep; in this case, we only need to specify the pattern to match. Any line that does not match will be discarded, and will not be shown in your Terminal.

As you can see, the full syntax for this is cat grep-file.txt | grep 'USA'.

Piping is a form of redirection that we will further discuss in Chapter 12, *Using Pipes and Redirection in Scripts*. For now, keep in mind that by using the pipe, the *output* of cat is used as *input* for grep, in the same manner as the filename is used as input. While discussing grep, we will (for now) use the method explained first, which does not use redirection.

Because the words *cool* and *USA* are only found in a single line, both instances of grep print just that line. But if a word is found in multiple lines, all of them are printed in the order grep encounters them (which is normally from top to bottom):

```
reader@ubuntu:~/scripts/chapter_10$ grep 'use' grep-file.txt
We can use this regular file for testing grep.
but in the USA they use color (and realize)!
```

With `grep`, it is possible to specify that instead of the default case-sensitive approach, we would like the search to be case-insensitive. This is, for example, a great way of finding errors in a log file. Some programs use the word *error*, others *ERROR*, and we've even come across the occasional *Error*. All of these results can be returned by supplying the `-i` flag to `grep`:

```
reader@ubuntu:~/scripts/chapter_10$ grep 'regular' grep-file.txt
We can use this regular file for testing grep.
reader@ubuntu:~/scripts/chapter_10$ grep -i 'regular' grep-file.txt
We can use this regular file for testing grep.
Regular expressions are pretty cool
```

By supplying `-i`, we see now that both 'regular' and 'Regular' have been matched, and their lines have been printed.

Greediness

By default, regular expressions are considered greedy. This might seem a strange term to describe a technical concept, but it does fit really well. To illustrate why regular expressions are considered greedy, look at this example:

```
reader@ubuntu:~/scripts/chapter_10$ grep 'in' grep-file.txt
We can use this regular file for testing grep.
Did you ever realise that in the UK they say colour,
but in the USA they use color (and realize)!
reader@ubuntu:~/scripts/chapter_10$ grep 'the' grep-file.txt
Did you ever realise that in the UK they say colour,
but in the USA they use color (and realize)!
```

As you can see, `grep` does not by default look for full words. It looks at the characters in the file, and if a string matches the search (regardless of what comes before or after them), the line is printed.

In the first example, `in` matches both the normal word **in**, but also test**in**g. In the second example, both lines have two matches, both **the** and **the**y.

If you want to return whole words only, be sure to include the spaces in your `grep` search pattern:

```
reader@ubuntu:~/scripts/chapter_10$ grep ' in ' grep-file.txt
Did you ever realise that in the UK they say colour,
but in the USA they use color (and realize)!
reader@ubuntu:~/scripts/chapter_10$ grep ' the ' grep-file.txt
Did you ever realise that in the UK they say colour,
but in the USA they use color (and realize)!
```

As you can see, the search for ' in ' now does not return the line with the word **testing**, since the string of characters **in** isn't surrounded by spaces there.

 A regular expression is just a definition of a particular search pattern, which is implemented differently by individual scripting/programming languages. The regular expressions we are using with Bash are different from those in Perl or Java, for example. While in some languages, greediness can be tuned or even turned off, regular expressions under `grep` and `sed` are always greedy. This is not really an issue, just something to consider when defining your search patterns.

Character matching

We now know how we can search for whole words, even if we're not entirely sure about uppercase and lowercase yet.

We've also seen that regular expressions under (most) Linux applications are greedy, so we need to be sure that we're dealing with this properly by specifying whitespace and character anchors, which we will explain shortly.

In both these cases, we knew what we were looking for. But what if we do not really know what we are looking for, or perhaps only part of it? The answer to this dilemma is character matching.

In regular expressions, there are two characters we can use as substitutes for other characters:

- . (dot) matches any one character (except a newline)
- * (asterisk) matches any number of repeats of the character before (even zero instances)

An example will help in understanding this:

```
reader@ubuntu:~/scripts/chapter_10$ vim character-class.txt
reader@ubuntu:~/scripts/chapter_10$ cat character-class.txt
eee
e2e
e e
aaa
a2a
a a
aabb
reader@ubuntu:~/scripts/chapter_10$ grep 'e.e' character-class.txt
eee
```

```
e2e
e e
reader@ubuntu:~/scripts/chapter_10$ grep 'aaa*' character-class.txt
aaa
aabb
reader@ubuntu:~/scripts/chapter_10$ grep 'aab*' character-class.txt
aaa
aabb
```

A lot of things happened there, some of which may feel very counter-intuitive. We'll walk through them one by one and go into detail on what is happening:

```
reader@ubuntu:~/scripts/chapter_10$ grep 'e.e' character-class.txt
eee
e2e
e e
```

In this example, we use the dot to substitute for *any character*. As we can see, this includes both letters (e**e**e) and numbers (e**2**e). However, it also matches the space character between the two es on the last line.

Here's another example:

```
reader@ubuntu:~/scripts/chapter_10$ grep 'aaa*' character-class.txt
aaa
aabb
```

When we use the * substitution, we're looking for **zero or more** instances of the preceding character. In the search pattern aaa*, this means the following strings are valid:

- aa
- aaa
- aaaa
- aaaaa

... and so on. While everything after the first result should be clear, why does aa also match aaa*? Because of the zero in *zero or more!* In that case, if the last a is zero, we're left with only aa.

The same thing happens in the last example:

```
reader@ubuntu:~/scripts/chapter_10$ grep 'aab*' character-class.txt
aaa
aabb
```

The pattern aab* matches the aa within **aa**a, since the b* can be zero, which makes the pattern end up as aa. Of course, it also matches one or more bs (aabb is fully matched).

These wildcards are great when you have only a general idea about what you're looking for. Sometimes, however, you will have a more specific idea of what you need.

In this case, we can use brackets, [...], to narrow our substitution to a certain character set. The following example should give you a good idea of how to use this:

```
reader@ubuntu:~/scripts/chapter_10$ grep 'f.r' grep-file.txt
We can use this regular file for testing grep.
Also, New Zealand is pretty far away.
reader@ubuntu:~/scripts/chapter_10$ grep 'f[ao]r' grep-file.txt
We can use this regular file for testing grep.
Also, New Zealand is pretty far away.
reader@ubuntu:~/scripts/chapter_10$ grep 'f[abcdefghijklmnopqrstuvwxyz]r'
grep-file.txt
We can use this regular file for testing grep.
Also, New Zealand is pretty far away.
reader@ubuntu:~/scripts/chapter_10$ grep 'f[az]r' grep-file.txt
Also, New Zealand is pretty far away.
reader@ubuntu:~/scripts/chapter_10$ grep 'f[a-z]r' grep-file.txt
We can use this regular file for testing grep.
Also, New Zealand is pretty far away.
reader@ubuntu:~/scripts/chapter_10$ grep 'f[a-k]r' grep-file.txt
Also, New Zealand is pretty far away.
reader@ubuntu:~/scripts/chapter_10$ grep 'f[k-q]r' grep-file.txt
We can use this regular file for testing grep
```

First, we demonstrate using . (dot) to replace any character. In this scenario, the pattern **f.r** matches both **for** and **far**.

Next, we use the bracket notation in f[ao]r to convey that we'll accept a single character between f and r, which is in the character set of ao. As expected, this again returns both **far** and **for**.

If we do this with the f[az]r pattern, we can only match with **far** and **fzr**. Since the string fzr isn't in our text file (and not a word, obviously), we only see the line with **far** printed.

Next, let's say you wanted to match with a letter, but not a number. If you used . (dot) to search, as in the first example, this would return both letters and numbers. So, you would also get, for example, **f2r** as a match (should that be in the file, which it is not).

If you used the bracket notation, you could use the following notation: f[abcdefghijklmnopqrstuvwxyz]r. That matches on any letter, a-z, between f and r. However, it's not great to type that out on a keyboard (trust me on this).

Luckily, the creators of POSIX regular expressions introduced a shorthand for this: [a-z], as shown in the previous example. We can also use a subset of the alphabet, as shown: f[a-k]r. Since the letter **o** is not between a and k, it does not match on **for**.

A last example demonstrates that this is a powerful, and also practical, pattern:

```
reader@ubuntu:~/scripts/chapter_10$ grep reali[sz]e grep-file.txt
Did you ever realise that in the UK they say colour,
but in the USA they use color (and realize)!
```

Hopefully, this still all makes sense. Before moving on to line anchors, we're going to go one step further by combining notations.

In the preceding example, you see that we can use bracket notation to handle some of the differences between American and British English. However, this only works when the difference in spelling is a single letter, as with realise/realize.

In the case of color/colour, there is an extra letter we need to deal with. This sounds like a case for zero or more, does it not?

```
reader@ubuntu:~/scripts/chapter_10$ grep 'colo[u]*r' grep-file.txt
Did you ever realise that in the UK they say colour,
but in the USA they use color (and realize)!
```

By using the pattern colo[u]*r, we're searching for a line containing a word that starts with **colo**, may or may not contain any number of **us**, and ends with an **r**. Since both color and colour are acceptable for this pattern, both lines are printed.

You might be tempted to use the dot character with the zero-or-more * notation. However, look closely at what happens in that case:

```
reader@ubuntu:~/scripts/chapter_10$ grep 'colo.*r' grep-file.txt
Did you ever realise that in the UK they say colour,
but in the USA they use color (and realize)!
```

Again, both lines are matched. But, since the second line contains another **r** further on, the string color (and r is matched, as well as colour and color.

This is a typical instance where the regular expression pattern is too greedy for our purposes. While we cannot tell it to be less greedy, there is an option in grep that lets us only look for single words that match.

The notation –w evaluates whitespaces and line endings/beginnings to find only whole words. This is how it is used:

```
reader@ubuntu:~/scripts/chapter_10$ grep -w 'colo.*r' grep-file.txt
Did you ever realise that in the UK they say colour,
but in the USA they use color (and realize)!
```

Now, only the words colour and color are matched. Earlier, we put whitespace around our word to facilitate this behavior, but as the word colour is at the end of the line, it is not followed by a whitespace.

Try for yourself and see why enclosing the colo.*r search pattern does not work with whitespace, but does work with the –w option.

> Some implementations of regular expressions have the {3} notation, to supplement the * notation. In this notation, you can specify exactly how often a pattern should be present. The search pattern [a-z]{3} would match all lowercase strings of exactly three characters. In Linux, this can only be done with extended regular expressions, which we will see later in this chapter.

Line anchors

We've already briefly mentioned line anchors. With the explanations we have presented up until now, we were only able to search for words in a line; we weren't yet able to set expectations on *where* those words were in the line. For this, we use line anchors.

In regular expressions, the ^ (caret) character signifies the beginning of a line, and a $ (dollar) represents the end of a line. We can use these within a search pattern, for example, in the following scenarios:

- Look for the word error, but only at the beginning of a line: ^error
- Look for lines ending in a dot: \.$
- Look for an empty line: ^$

The first usage, looking for something at the beginning of a line, should be pretty clear. The following example, which uses `grep -i` (remember, this allows us to search without case sensitivity), shows how we can use this to filter by line position:

```
reader@ubuntu:~/scripts/chapter_10$ grep -i 'regular' grep-file.txt
We can use this regular file for testing grep.
Regular expressions are pretty cool
reader@ubuntu:~/scripts/chapter_10$ grep -i '^regular' grep-file.txt
Regular expressions are pretty cool
```

In the first search pattern, `regular`, we are returned two lines. This is not unexpected, since both lines contain the word *regular* (albeit with different casing).

Now, to just select the line that starts with the word *Regular*, we use the caret character ^ to form the pattern `^regular`. This only returns the line where the word is in the first position on that line. (Note that if we did not choose to include `-i` on `grep`, we could have used `[Rr]egular` instead.)

The next example, where we look for lines ending in a dot, is a little bit more tricky. As you recall, the dot in regular expressions is considered a special character; it is a substitute for any other one character. If we use it normally, we will see all lines in the file return (since all lines end in *any one character*).

To actually search for a dot in the text, we need to **escape** the dot by prefixing it with a backslash; this tells the regular expression engine to not interpret the dot as a special character, but to search for it instead:

```
reader@ubuntu:~/scripts/chapter_10$ grep '.$' grep-file.txt
We can use this regular file for testing grep.
Regular expressions are pretty cool
Did you ever realise that in the UK they say colour,
but in the USA they use color (and realize)!
Also, New Zealand is pretty far away.
reader@ubuntu:~/scripts/chapter_10$ grep '\.$' grep-file.txt
We can use this regular file for testing grep.
Also, New Zealand is pretty far away.
```

Since the \ is used to escape special characters, you might encounter a situation where you are looking for a backslash in the text. In that case, you can use the backslash to escape the special functionality of the backslash! Your pattern will be \\ in this case, which matches with the \ strings.

In this example, we run into one other issue. So far, we have always quoted all patterns with single quotes. However, this isn't always needed! For example, `grep cool grep-file.txt` works just as well as `grep 'cool' grep-file.txt`.

So, why are we doing it? Hint: try the previous example, with the dot line endings, without quotes. Then remember that a dollar character in Bash is also used to denote variables. If we quote it, the `$` will not be expanded on by Bash, which returns problematic results.

We will discuss Bash expansion in `Chapter 16`, *Bash Parameter Substitution and Expansion*.

Finally, we presented the `^$` pattern. This searches for a line beginning, followed directly by a line ending. There is only one situation where that occurs: an empty line.

To illustrate why you would want to find empty lines, let's look at a new `grep` flag: `-v`. This flag is shorthand for `--invert-match`, which should give a nice clue about what it actually does: instead of printing lines that match, it prints lines that do not match.

By using `grep -v '^$' <file name>`, you can print a file without empty lines. Give it a go on a random configuration file:

```
reader@ubuntu:/etc$ cat /etc/ssh/ssh_config

# This is the ssh client system-wide configuration file.  See
# ssh_config(5) for more information.  This file provides defaults for
# users, and the values can be changed in per-user configuration files
# or on the command line.

# Configuration data is parsed as follows:
<SNIPPED>
reader@ubuntu:/etc$ grep -v '^$' /etc/ssh/ssh_config
# This is the ssh client system-wide configuration file.  See
# ssh_config(5) for more information.  This file provides defaults for
# users, and the values can be changed in per-user configuration files
# or on the command line.
# Configuration data is parsed as follows:
<SNIPPED>
```

As you can see, the `/etc/ssh/ssh_config` file starts with an empty line. Then, in between comment blocks, there is another empty line. By using `grep -v '^$'`, these empty lines are removed. While this is a nice exercise, this does not really save us that many lines.

There is, however, one search pattern that is widely used and very powerful: filtering out comments from a configuration file. This operation gives us a quick overview of what is actually configured, and omits all comments (which have their own merit, but can be obstructive when you just want to see which options are configured).

To do this, we combine the beginning-of-line caret with a hashtag, which denotes a comment:

```
reader@ubuntu:/etc$ grep -v '^#' /etc/ssh/ssh_config

Host *
    SendEnv LANG LC_*
    HashKnownHosts yes
    GSSAPIAuthentication yes
```

This still prints all empty lines, but no longer prints the comments. In this particular file, out of the 51 lines, only four lines contain actual configuration directives! All other lines are either empty or contain comments. Pretty cool, right?

With `grep`, it is also possible to use multiple patterns at the same time. By using this, you can combine the filtering of empty lines and comment lines for a condensed, quick overview of configuration options. Multiple patterns are defined using the `-e` option. The full command in this case is `grep -v -e '^$' -e '^#' /etc/ssh/ssh_config`. Try it!

Character classes

We've now seen many examples of how to use regular expressions. While most things are pretty intuitive, we have also seen that if we want to filter for both uppercase and lowercase strings, we'd either have to specify the `-i` option for `grep`, or change the search pattern from `[a-z]` to `[a-zA-z]`. For numbers, we would need to use `[0-9]`.

Some might find this fine to work with, but others might disagree. In this case, there is an alternative notation that can be used: `[[:pattern:]]`.

The next example uses both this new double bracket notation, and the old single bracket one:

```
reader@ubuntu:~/scripts/chapter_10$ grep [[:digit:]] character-class.txt
e2e
a2a
reader@ubuntu:~/scripts/chapter_10$ grep [0-9] character-class.txt
e2e
a2a
```

As you can see, both patterns result in the same lines: those with a digit. The same can be done with uppercase characters:

```
reader@ubuntu:~/scripts/chapter_10$ grep [[:upper:]] grep-file.txt
We can use this regular file for testing grep.
Regular expressions are pretty cool
Did you ever realise that in the UK they say colour,
but in the USA they use color (and realize)!
Also, New Zealand is pretty far away.
reader@ubuntu:~/scripts/chapter_10$ grep [A-Z] grep-file.txt
We can use this regular file for testing grep.
Regular expressions are pretty cool
Did you ever realise that in the UK they say colour,
but in the USA they use color (and realize)!
Also, New Zealand is pretty far away.
```

At the end of the day, it is a matter of preference which notation you use. There is one thing to be said for the double bracket notation, though: it is much closer to implementations of other scripting/programming languages. For example, most regular expression implementations use \w (word) to select letters, and \d (digit) to search for digits. In the case of \w, the uppercase variant is intuitively \W.

For your convenience, here is a table with the most common POSIX double-bracket character classes:

Notation	Description	Single bracket equivalent
[[:alnum:]]	Matches lowercase and uppercase letters or digits	[a-z A-Z 0-9]
[[:alpha:]]	Matches lowercase and uppercase letters	[a-z A-Z]
[[:digit:]]	Matches digits	[0-9]
[[:lower:]]	Matches lowercase letters	[a-z]
[[:upper:]]	Matches uppercase letters	[A-Z]
[[:blank:]]	Matches spaces and tabs	[\t]

We prefer to use the double bracket notation, as it maps better to other regular expression implementations. Feel free to use either in your scripting! However, as always: make sure you choose one, and stick with it; not following a standard results in sloppy scripts that are confusing to readers. The rest of the examples in this book will use the double bracket notation.

Globbing

We now have the basics of regular expressions under control. There is another subject closely related to regular expressions on Linux: *globbing*. Even though you probably didn't realize it, you've already seen examples of globbing in this book.

Even better, there is actually a good chance you've used a *glob pattern* in practice. If, when working on the command line, you've ever used the wildcard character, *, you've been globbing!

What is globbing?

Simply said, a glob pattern describes injecting a wildcard character into a file path operation. So, when you do a `cp * /tmp/`, you copy all files (not directories!) in the current working directory to the `/tmp/` directory.

The * expands to all regular files inside the working directory, and then all of those are copied to `/tmp/`.

Here's a simple example:

```
reader@ubuntu:~/scripts/chapter_10$ ls -l
total 8
-rw-rw-r-- 1 reader reader  29 Oct 14 10:29 character-class.txt
-rw-rw-r-- 1 reader reader 219 Oct  8 19:22 grep-file.txt
reader@ubuntu:~/scripts/chapter_10$ cp * /tmp/
reader@ubuntu:~/scripts/chapter_10$ ls -l /tmp/
total 20
-rw-rw-r-- 1 reader reader  29 Oct 14 16:35 character-class.txt
-rw-rw-r-- 1 reader reader  219 Oct 14 16:35 grep-file.txt
<SNIPPED>
```

Instead of executing both `cp grep-file.txt /tmp/` and `cp character-class.txt /tmp/`, we used * to select both of them. The same glob pattern can be used with `rm`:

```
reader@ubuntu:/tmp$ ls -l
total 16
-rw-rw-r-- 1 reader reader   29 Oct 14 16:37 character-class.txt
-rw-rw-r-- 1 reader reader  219 Oct 14 16:37 grep-file.txt
drwx------ 3 root   root   4096 Oct 14 09:22 systemd-private-c34c8acb350...
drwx------ 3 root   root   4096 Oct 14 09:22 systemd-private-c34c8acb350...
reader@ubuntu:/tmp$ rm *
rm: cannot remove 'systemd-private-c34c8acb350...': Is a directory
rm: cannot remove 'systemd-private-c34c8acb350...': Is a directory
```

```
reader@ubuntu:/tmp$ ls -l
total 8
drwx------ 3 root root 4096 Oct 14 09:22 systemd-private-c34c8acb350...
drwx------ 3 root root 4096 Oct 14 09:22 systemd-private-c34c8acb350...
```

By default, `rm` only deletes files and not directories (as you can see from the errors in the previous example). As stated in `Chapter 6`, *File Manipulation*, adding a `-r` will delete directories *recursively* too.

Again, do think about how destructive this is: without warning, you could delete every file within the current tree location (if you have the permissions, of course). The preceding example shows how powerful the `*` glob pattern is: it expands to every file it can find, whatever the type.

Similarities with regular expressions

As stated, glob commands achieve a similar effect to regular expressions. There are some differences though. For example, the `*` character in regular expressions stood for *zero or more occurrences of the preceding character*. For globbing, it is a wildcard for any and all characters, more similar to the `.*` notation of regular expressions.

As with regular expressions, a glob pattern can consist of normal characters, combined with special characters. Take a look at an example where `ls` is used with different arguments/globbing patterns:

```
reader@ubuntu:~/scripts/chapter_09$ ls -l
total 68
-rw-rw-r-- 1 reader reader  682 Oct  2 18:31 empty-file.sh
-rw-rw-r-- 1 reader reader 1183 Oct  1 19:06 file-create.sh
-rw-rw-r-- 1 reader reader  467 Sep 29 19:43 functional-check.sh
<SNIPPED>
reader@ubuntu:~/scripts/chapter_09$ ls -l *
-rw-rw-r-- 1 reader reader  682 Oct  2 18:31 empty-file.sh
-rw-rw-r-- 1 reader reader 1183 Oct  1 19:06 file-create.sh
-rw-rw-r-- 1 reader reader  467 Sep 29 19:43 functional-check.sh
<SNIPPED>
reader@ubuntu:~/scripts/chapter_09$ ls -l if-then-exit.sh
-rw-rw-r-- 1 reader reader 416 Sep 30 18:51 if-then-exit.sh
reader@ubuntu:~/scripts/chapter_09$ ls -l if-*.sh
-rw-rw-r-- 1 reader reader 448 Sep 30 20:10 if-then-else-proper.sh
-rw-rw-r-- 1 reader reader 422 Sep 30 19:56 if-then-else.sh
-rw-rw-r-- 1 reader reader 535 Sep 30 19:44 if-then-exit-rc-improved.sh
-rw-rw-r-- 1 reader reader 556 Sep 30 19:18 if-then-exit-rc.sh
-rw-rw-r-- 1 reader reader 416 Sep 30 18:51 if-then-exit.sh
```

In the `scripts` directory for the previous chapter, we first run a normal `ls -l`. As you know, this prints all files in the directory. Now, if we use `ls -l *`, we get the exact same result. It would seem that, given an absence of arguments, `ls` will inject a wildcard glob for us.

Next, we use the alternative mode of `ls`, which is where we present a filename as the argument. In this case, because filenames are unique for each directory, we only see a single line returned.

But, what if we wanted all *scripts* (ending in `.sh`) that *start with* `if-`? We use the globbing pattern of `if-*.sh`. In this pattern, the `*` wildcard is expanded to match, as `man glob` says, *any string, including the empty string.*

More globbing

Globbing is very present in Linux. If you're dealing with a command that handles files (which, under the *everything is a file principle*, is most commands), there is a good chance that you can use globbing. To give you an impression of this, consider the following examples:

```
reader@ubuntu:~/scripts/chapter_10$ cat *
eee
e2e
e e
aaa
a2a
a a
aabb
We can use this regular file for testing grep.
Regular expressions are pretty cool
Did you ever realise that in the UK they say colour,
but in the USA they use color (and realize)!
Also, New Zealand is pretty far away.
```

The `cat` command, combined with the wildcard glob pattern, prints the contents of **all files** in the current working directory. In this case, since all files are ASCII text, this was not really a problem. As you can see, the files are printed right after each other; there's not so much as an empty line in between.

Should you `cat` a binary file, your screen will look something like this:

```
reader@ubuntu:~/scripts/chapter_10$ cat /bin/chvt
@H!@8    @@@�888�� �� �  H 88 8 �TTTDDP�td\\\llQ�tdR�td�� �
/lib64/ld-linux-x86-64.so.2GNUGNU��H������)�!�@`��a*�K��9���X'
Q��/9'~���C J
```

The worst case scenario is that the binary file contains a certain character sequence that makes temporary changes to your Bash shell, which will make it unusable (yes, this has happened to us many times). The lesson here should be simple: **watch out when globbing!**

Other commands we've seen up until now that can deal with globbing patterns include `chmod`, `chown`, `mv`, `tar`, `grep`, and so on. Perhaps the most interesting for now is `grep`. We've used regular expressions with `grep` on a single file, but we can also select files using a glob.

Let's look at the most ridiculous example of `grep` with globbing: finding *anything* in *everything*.

```
reader@ubuntu:~/scripts/chapter_10$ grep .* *
grep: ..: Is a directory
character-class.txt:eee
character-class.txt:e2e
character-class.txt:e e
character-class.txt:aaa
character-class.txt:a2a
character-class.txt:a a
character-class.txt:aabb
 grep-file.txt:We can use this regular file for testing grep.
 grep-file.txt:Regular expressions are pretty cool
 grep-file.txt:Did you ever realise that in the UK they say colour,
 grep-file.txt:but in the USA they use color (and realize)!
 grep-file.txt:Also, New Zealand is pretty far away.
```

Here, we used the regular expression `.*` search pattern (anything, zero or more times) with the glob pattern of `*` (any file). As you might expect, this should match every line in every file.

When we use `grep` in this manner, it has pretty much the same functionality as the earlier `cat *`. However, when `grep` is used on multiple files, the output includes the filename (so you know where the line was found).

Make a note: a globbing pattern is always related to files, whereas a regular expression is used *inside* the files, on the actual content. Since the syntax is similar, you will probably not be too confused about this, but if you ever run into a situation where your pattern is not working as you'd expect, it would be good to take a moment and consider whether you're globbing or regexing!

Advanced globbing

Basic globbing is done mainly with the wildcard, sometimes combined with part of a filename. However, just as regular expressions allow us to substitute a single character, so do globs.

Regular expressions achieve this with the dot; in globbing patterns, the question mark is used:

```
reader@ubuntu:~/scripts/chapter_09$ ls -l if-then-*
-rw-rw-r-- 1 reader reader 448 Sep 30 20:10 if-then-else-proper.sh
-rw-rw-r-- 1 reader reader 422 Sep 30 19:56 if-then-else.sh
-rw-rw-r-- 1 reader reader 535 Sep 30 19:44 if-then-exit-rc-improved.sh
-rw-rw-r-- 1 reader reader 556 Sep 30 19:18 if-then-exit-rc.sh
-rw-rw-r-- 1 reader reader 416 Sep 30 18:51 if-then-exit.sh
reader@ubuntu:~/scripts/chapter_09$ ls -l if-then-e???.sh
-rw-rw-r-- 1 reader reader 422 Sep 30 19:56 if-then-else.sh
-rw-rw-r-- 1 reader reader 416 Sep 30 18:51 if-then-exit.sh
```

The globbing pattern if-then-e???.sh should speak for itself now. Where the ? is present, any character (letter, digit, special character) is a valid substitute.

In the preceding example, all three question marks are replaced by letters. As you might have deduced, the regular expression . character serves the same function as the globbing pattern ? character: it is valid for exactly one character.

Finally, the single bracket notation we use for regular expressions can also be used in globbing. A quick example shows how we can use this with cat:

```
reader@ubuntu:/tmp$ echo ping > ping # Write the word ping to the file
ping.
reader@ubuntu:/tmp$ echo pong > pong # Write the word pong to the file
pong.
reader@ubuntu:/tmp$ ls -l
total 16
-rw-rw-r-- 1 reader reader      5 Oct 14 17:17 ping
-rw-rw-r-- 1 reader reader      5 Oct 14 17:17 pong
```

```
reader@ubuntu:/tmp$ cat p[io]ng
ping
pong
reader@ubuntu:/tmp$ cat p[a-z]ng
ping
pong
```

Disabling globbing, and other options

As powerful as globbing is, this is also what makes it dangerous. For that reason, you might want to take drastic measures and turn globbing off. While this is possible, we have not seen it in practice. However, for some work or scripts, turning off globbing might be a good safeguard.

Using the set command, we can, as the man page states, *change the value of a shell option*. In this case, using -f will turn off globbing, as we can see when we try to repeat our previous example:

```
reader@ubuntu:/tmp$ cat p?ng
ping
pong
reader@ubuntu:/tmp$ set -f
reader@ubuntu:/tmp$ cat p?ng
cat: 'p?ng': No such file or directory
reader@ubuntu:/tmp$ set +f
reader@ubuntu:/tmp$ cat p?ng
ping
pong
```

Options are turned off by prefixing a minus (-), and turned on by prefixing a plus (+). As you might remember, this is not the first time you're using this functionality. When we debugged our Bash scripts, we started those not with bash, but with bash -x.

In this case, the Bash subshell executes a set -x command before calling the scripts. If you use set -x in your current terminal, your commands would start to look like this:

```
reader@ubuntu:/tmp$ cat p?ng
ping
pong
reader@ubuntu:/tmp$ set -x
reader@ubuntu:/tmp$ cat p?ng
+ cat ping pong
ping
pong
reader@ubuntu:/tmp$ set +x
```

```
+ set +x
reader@ubuntu:/tmp$ cat p?ng
ping
pong
```

Note that we can now see how the globbing pattern is resolved: from `cat p?ng` to `cat ping pong`. Try to remember this functionality; if you're ever at the point of pulling your hair out because you have no idea why a script isn't doing what you want, a simple `set -x` might make all the difference! And if it doesn't, you can always revert to normal behavior with `set +x`, as shown in the example.

> `set` has many interesting flags that can make your life easier. To see an overview of the capabilities of `set` in your Bash version, use the `help set` command. Because `set` is a shell builtin (which you can verify with `type set`), looking for a man page with `man set` does not work, unfortunately.

Using regular expressions with egrep and sed

We have now discussed both regular expressions and globbing. As we saw, they were very similar, but still had differences to be aware of. In our examples for regular expressions, and a little for globbing, we have already seen how `grep` can be used.

In this part, we'll introduce another command, which is very handy when combined with regular expressions: `sed` (not to be confused with `set`). We'll start with some advanced uses for `grep`.

Advanced grep

We have already discussed a few popular options for `grep` to alter its default behavior: `--ignore-case` (`-i`), `--invert-match` (`-v`), and `--word-regexp` (`-w`). As a reminder here's what they do:

- `-i` allows us to search case-insensitively
- `-v` only prints lines that are *not* matched, instead of matched lines
- `-w` only matches on full words that are surrounded by spaces and/or line anchors and/or punctuation marks

There are three other options we'd like to share with you. The first new option, --only-matching (-o) prints only the matching words. If your search pattern does not contain any regular expressions, this will probably be a pretty boring option, as you can see in this example:

```
reader@ubuntu:~/scripts/chapter_10$ grep -o 'cool' grep-file.txt
cool
```

It does exactly as you expected: it printed the word you were looking for. However, unless you just wanted to confirm this, it is probably not that interesting.

Now, if we do the same thing when using a more interesting search pattern (containing a regular expression), this option makes more sense:

```
reader@ubuntu:~/scripts/chapter_10$ grep -o 'f.r' grep-file.txt
for
far
```

In this (simplified!) example, you actually get new information: whichever words fell within your search pattern are now printed. While this might not seem impressive for such a short word in such a small file, imagine a more complex search pattern on a much larger file!

This brings up another point: grep is *fast*. Because of the Boyer-Moore algorithm, grep can search very fast even in very large files (100 MB+).

The second extra option, --count (-c), does not return any lines. It does, however, return a single digit: the number of lines for which the search pattern matched. A well-known example of when this comes in handy is when looking at log files for package installations:

```
reader@ubuntu:/var/log$ grep 'status installed' dpkg.log
2018-04-26 19:07:29 status installed base-passwd:amd64 3.5.44
2018-04-26 19:07:29 status installed base-files:amd64 10.1ubuntu2
2018-04-26 19:07:30 status installed dpkg:amd64 1.19.0.5ubuntu2
<SNIPPED>
2018-06-30 17:59:37 status installed linux-headers-4.15.0-23:all
4.15.0-23.25
2018-06-30 17:59:37 status installed iucode-tool:amd64 2.3.1-1
2018-06-30 17:59:37 status installed man-db:amd64 2.8.3-2
<SNIPPED>
2018-07-01 09:31:15 status installed distro-info-data:all 0.37ubuntu0.1
2018-07-01 09:31:17 status installed libcurl3-gnutls:amd64
7.58.0-2ubuntu3.1
2018-07-01 09:31:17 status installed libc-bin:amd64 2.27-3ubuntu1
```

In the regular `grep` here, we see log lines that show which package was installed on which date. But what if we just wanted to know *how many packages were installed on a certain date?* – `-count` to the rescue!

```
reader@ubuntu:/var/log$ grep 'status installed' dpkg.log | grep
'2018-08-26'
2018-08-26 11:16:16 status installed base-files:amd64 10.1ubuntu2.2
2018-08-26 11:16:16 status installed install-info:amd64 6.5.0.dfsg.1-2
2018-08-26 11:16:16 status installed plymouth-theme-ubuntu-text:amd64
0.9.3-1ubuntu7
<SNIPPED>
reader@ubuntu:/var/log$ grep 'status installed' dpkg.log | grep -c
'2018-08-26'
40
```

We perform this `grep` operation in two stages. The first `grep 'status installed'` filters out all lines related to successful installations, skipping intermediate steps such as *unpacked* and *half-configured*.

We use the alternative form of `grep` behind a pipe (which we will discuss further in `Chapter 12`, *Using Pipes and Redirection in Scripts*) to match another search pattern to the already-filtered data. This second `grep '2018-08-26'` filters on the date.

Now, without the `-c` option, we would see 40 lines. If we were curious about the packages, this might have been a good option, but otherwise, just the printed number is better than counting the lines by hand.

Alternatively, we could have written this as a single grep search pattern, using regular expressions. Try it yourself: `grep '2018-08-26 .* status installed' dpkg.log` (be sure to replace the date with some day on which you have run updates/installations).

The final option, which is very interesting, especially for scripting, is the `--quiet` (`-q`) option. Imagine a situation where you want to know if a certain search pattern is present in a file. If you find the search pattern, you delete the file. If you do not find the search pattern, you'll add it to the file.

As you know, you can use a nice `if-then-else` construct to accomplish that. However, if you use a normal `grep`, you will see the text printed in the Terminal when you run your script.

This is not really that big an issue, but once your scripts get sufficiently large and complicated, a lot of output to the screen will make a script hard to use. For this, we have the `--quiet` option. Look at this example script to see how you would do this:

```
reader@ubuntu:~/scripts/chapter_10$ vim grep-then-else.sh
reader@ubuntu:~/scripts/chapter_10$ cat grep-then-else.sh
#!/bin/bash

#####################################
# Author: Sebastiaan Tammer
# Version: v1.0.0
# Date: 2018-10-16
# Description: Use grep exit status to make decisions about file
manipulation.
# Usage: ./grep-then-else.sh
#####################################

FILE_NAME=/tmp/grep-then-else.txt

# Touch the file; creates it if it does not exist.
touch ${FILE_NAME}

# Check the file for the keyword.
grep -q 'keyword' ${FILE_NAME}
grep_rc=$?

# If the file contains the keyword, remove the file. Otherwise, write
# the keyword to the file.
if [[ ${grep_rc} -eq 0 ]]; then
  rm ${FILE_NAME}
else
  echo 'keyword' >> ${FILE_NAME}
fi

reader@ubuntu:~/scripts/chapter_10$ bash -x grep-then-else.sh
+ FILE_NAME=/tmp/grep-then-else.txt
+ touch /tmp/grep-then-else.txt
+ grep --quiet keyword /tmp/grep-then-else.txt
+ grep_rc='1'
+ [[ '1' -eq 0 ]]
+ echo keyword
reader@ubuntu:~/scripts/chapter_10$ bash -x grep-then-else.sh
+ FILE_NAME=/tmp/grep-then-else.txt
+ touch /tmp/grep-then-else.txt
+ grep -q keyword /tmp/grep-then-else.txt
+ grep_rc=0
+ [[ 0 -eq 0 ]]
+ rm /tmp/grep-then-else.txt
```

As you can see, the trick is in the exit status. If grep finds one or more matches of the search pattern, an exit code of **0** is given. If grep does not find anything, this return code will be **1**.

You can see this for yourself on the command line:

```
reader@ubuntu:/var/log$ grep -q 'glgjegeg' dpkg.log
reader@ubuntu:/var/log$ echo $?
1
reader@ubuntu:/var/log$ grep -q 'installed' dpkg.log
reader@ubuntu:/var/log$ echo $?
0
```

In grep-then-else.sh, we suppress all output from grep. Still, we can achieve what we want: each run of the script changes between the *then* and *else* condition, as our bash -x debug output clearly shows.

Without the --quiet, the non-debug output of the script would be as follows:

```
reader@ubuntu:/tmp$ bash grep-then-else.sh
reader@ubuntu:/tmp$ bash grep-then-else.sh
keyword
reader@ubuntu:/tmp$ bash grep-then-else.sh
reader@ubuntu:/tmp$ bash grep-then-else.sh
keyword
```

It doesn't really add anything to the script, does it? Even better, a lot of commands have a --quiet, -q, or equivalent option.

When you're scripting, always consider whether the output of a command is relevant. If it is not, and you can use the exit status, this almost always makes for a cleaner output experience.

Introducing egrep

Until now, we've seen grep used with various options that alter its behavior. There is one final important option we'd like to share with you: --extended-regexp (-E). As the man grep page states, this means *interpret PATTERN as an extended regular expression*.

In contrast to the default regular expressions found in Linux, extended regular expressions have search patterns that are a lot closer to regular expressions in other scripting/programming languages (should you already have experience with those).

Specifically, the following constructs are available when using extended regular expressions over default regular expressions:

?	Matches a repeat of the previous character *zero or more times*
+	Matches a repeat of the previous character *one or more times*
{n}	Matches a repeat of the previous character *exactly n times*
{n,m}	Matches a repeat of the previous character *between n and m times*
{,n}	Matches a repeat of the previous character *n or fewer times*
{n,}	Matches a repeat of the previous character *n or more times*
(xx|yy)	Alternation character, allows us to find xx *OR* yy in the search pattern (great for patterns with more than one character, otherwise, [xy] notation would suffice)

As you might have seen, the man page for grep contains a dedicated section on regular expressions and search patterns, which you may find very convenient as a quick reference.

Now, before we start using the new ERE search patterns, we'll look at a *new* command: egrep. If you tried to find out what it does, you might start with a which egrep, which would result in /bin/egrep. This might lead you to think it was a separate binary from grep, which you've used so much by now.

However, in the end, egrep is nothing more than a small wrapper script:

```
reader@ubuntu:~/scripts/chapter_10$ cat /bin/egrep
#!/bin/sh
exec grep -E "$@"
```

As you can see, it's just a shell script, but without the customary .sh extension. It uses the exec command to *replace the current process image with a new process image.*

You might recall that normally, a command is executed in a fork of the current environment. In this case, since we use this script to *wrap* (hence why it is called a wrapper script) grep -E as egrep, it makes sense to replace it instead of forking it again.

The "$@" construct is new as well: it is an *array* (if you aren't familiar with this term, think of an ordered list) of arguments. In this case, it essentially passes all arguments received by egrep into grep -E.

So, if the full command was egrep -w [[:digit:]] grep-file.txt, it would be wrapped and finally executed in place as grep -E -w [[:digit:]] grep-file.txt.

In practice, it does not matter whether you use egrep or grep -E. We prefer using egrep so we know for sure that we're dealing with extended regular expressions (since the extended functionality is often used in practice, in our experience). For simple search patterns, however, there is no need for ERE.

We advise you to find your own system for when to use each one.

Now for some examples of the extended regular expression search pattern capabilities:

```
reader@ubuntu:~/scripts/chapter_10$ egrep -w '[[:lower:]]{5}' grep-file.txt
but in the USA they use color (and realize)!
reader@ubuntu:~/scripts/chapter_10$ egrep -w '[[:lower:]]{7}' grep-file.txt
We can use this regular file for testing grep.
Did you ever realise that in the UK they say colour,
but in the USA they use color (and realize)!
reader@ubuntu:~/scripts/chapter_10$ egrep -w '[[:alpha:]]{7}' grep-file.txt
We can use this regular file for testing grep.
Regular expressions are pretty cool
Did you ever realise that in the UK they say colour,
but in the USA they use color (and realize)!
Also, New Zealand is pretty far away.
```

The first command, egrep -w [[:lower:]]{5} grep-file.txt, shows us all words that are exactly five characters long, using lowercase letters. Don't forget we need the -w option here, because otherwise, any five letters in a row match as well, ignoring word boundaries (in this case, the **prett** in **prett**y matches as well). The result is only one five-letter word: color.

Next, we do the same for seven-letter words. We now get more results. However, because we are only using lowercase letters, we're missing two words that are also seven letters long: Regular and Zealand. We fix this by using [[:alpha:]] instead of [[:lower:]]. (We could have also used the -i option to make everything case-insensitive—egrep -iw [[:lower:]]{7} grep-file.txt.

While this is functionally acceptable, think about it for a second. In that case, you would be searching for *case-insensitive* words made up of exactly seven *lowercase* letters. That doesn't really make any sense. In situations such as these, we always choose logic over functionality, which in this case means changing `[[:lower:]]` to `[[:alpha:]]`, instead of using the `-i` option.

So we know how we can search for words (or lines, if we omit the `-w` option) of a specific length. How about we now look for words longer or shorter than a minimum or maximum length?

Here's an example:

```
reader@ubuntu:~/scripts/chapter_10$ egrep -w '[[:lower:]]{5,}' grep-
file.txt
We can use this regular file for testing grep.
Regular expressions are pretty cool
Did you ever realise that in the UK they say colour,
but in the USA they use color (and realize)!
Also, New Zealand is pretty far away.
reader@ubuntu:~/scripts/chapter_10$ egrep -w '[[:alpha:]]{,3}' grep-
file.txt
We can use this regular file for testing grep.
Regular expressions are pretty cool
Did you ever realise that in the UK they say colour,
but in the USA they use color (and realize)!
Also, New Zealand is pretty far away.
reader@ubuntu:~/scripts/chapter_10$ egrep '.{40,}' grep-file.txt
We can use this regular file for testing grep.
Did you ever realise that in the UK they say colour,
but in the USA they use color (and realize)!
```

This example demonstrates boundary syntax. This first command, `egrep -w '[[:lower:]]{5,}' grep-file.txt`, looks for lowercase words that are five letters or more. If you compare these results to the previous examples, where we were looking for words exactly five letters long, you now see that longer words are also matched.

Next, we reverse the boundary condition: we only want to match on words that are three letters or fewer. We see that all two- and three-letter words are matched (and, because we switched from `[[:lower:]]` to `[[:alpha:]]`, UK and capitalized letters at the beginning of the lines are matched as well).

In the final example, `egrep '.{40,}' grep-file.txt`, we remove the `-w` so we're matching on whole lines. We match on any character (as denoted by the dot), and we want at least 40 characters on a line (as denoted by the `{40,}`). In this case, only three lines of the five are matched (as the other two are shorter).

Quoting is very important for search patterns. If you do not use quotes in your pattern, especially when using special characters, such as { and }, you will need to escape them with a backslash. This can and will lead to confusing situations, where you're staring at the screen wondering why on earth your search pattern is not working, or even throwing errors. Just remember: if you single-quote the search pattern at all times, you will have a much better chance of avoiding these frustrating situations.

The final concept of extended regular expressions we want to show is *alternation*. This uses pipe syntax (not to be confused with pipes used for redirection, which will be further discussed in Chapter 12, *Using Pipes and Redirection in Scripts*) to convey the meaning of *match on xxx OR yyy*.

An example should make this clear:

```
reader@ubuntu:~/scripts/chapter_10$ egrep 'f(a|o)r' grep-file.txt
We can use this regular file for testing grep.
Also, New Zealand is pretty far away.
reader@ubuntu:~/scripts/chapter_10$ egrep 'f[ao]r' grep-file.txt
We can use this regular file for testing grep.
Also, New Zealand is pretty far away.
reader@ubuntu:~/scripts/chapter_10$ egrep '(USA|UK)' grep-file.txt
Did you ever realise that in the UK they say colour,
but in the USA they use color (and realize)!
```

In the case of a single letter difference, we can choose whether we want to use extended alternation syntax, or the earlier-discussed bracket syntax. We would advise using the simplest syntax that accomplishes the goal, which, in this case, is bracket syntax.

However, once we are looking for patterns of more than one character difference, using bracket syntax becomes prohibitively complex. In this case, extended alternation syntax is clear and concise, especially since | or || represents an OR construct in most scripting/programming logic. For this example, this would be like saying: I want to find lines that contain either the word USA or the word UK.

Because this syntax corresponds nicely with a semantic view, it feels intuitive and is understandable, something we should always strive for in our scripts!

sed, the stream editor

Since we're now fully familiar with regular expressions, search patterns, and (extended) grep, it's time to move to one of the most powerful tools in the GNU/Linux landscape: sed. The term is short for **stream ed**itor, and it does exactly what is implied: editing streams.

In this context, a stream can be a lot of things, but in general, it is text. This text may be found within a file, but can also be *streamed* from another process, such as a `cat grep-file.txt | sed ....` In that example, the output of the `cat` command (equal to the content of `grep-file.txt`) serves as input for the `sed` command.

We will look at both in-place file editing and stream editing in our examples.

Stream editing

We'll first look at actual stream editing with `sed`. Stream editing allows us to do really cool stuff: we could, for example, change some words in a text. We could also delete certain lines we do not care about (everything that does not contain the word ERROR, for example).

We'll begin with a simple example, searching for and replacing a word in a line:

```
reader@ubuntu:~/scripts/chapter_10$ echo "What a wicked sentence"
What a wicked sentence
reader@ubuntu:~/scripts/chapter_10$ echo "What a wicked sentence" | sed
's/wicked/stupid/'
What a stupid sentence
```

Just like that, `sed` transformed my positive sentence into something... less positive. The pattern `sed` uses (in `sed` terms, this is just called a *script*) is `s/wicked/stupid/`. The `s` stands for search-replace, and the first word of the *script* is substituted for the second word.

Observe what happens for multiple lines with multiple matches for the search word:

```
reader@ubuntu:~/scripts/chapter_10$ vim search.txt
reader@ubuntu:~/scripts/chapter_10$ cat search.txt
How much wood would a woodchuck chuck
if a woodchuck could chuck wood?
reader@ubuntu:~/scripts/chapter_10$ cat search.txt | sed 's/wood/stone/'
How much stone would a woodchuck chuck
if a stonechuck could chuck wood?
```

From this example, we can learn two things:

- By default, `sed` only replaces the first instance of each word *for each line*.
- `sed` does not match only on whole words, but also on partial words.

What if we wanted to replace all instances within each line? This is called a *global* search-replace, and the syntax is only very slightly different:

```
reader@ubuntu:~/scripts/chapter_10$ cat search.txt | sed 's/wood/stone/g'
How much stone would a stonechuck chuck
if a stonechuck could chuck stone?
```

By adding a g at the end of the sed *script*, we are now globally replacing all instances, instead of just the first instance for each line.

Another possibility is that you would only want to search-replace on the first line. You could use head -1 to only select that line before you send it through sed, but that would mean you would need to append the other lines afterwards.

We can select which lines we want to edit by placing the line numbers in front of the sed script, as follows:

```
reader@ubuntu:~/scripts/chapter_10$ cat search.txt | sed '1s/wood/stone/'
How much stone would a woodchuck chuck
if a woodchuck could chuck wood?
reader@ubuntu:~/scripts/chapter_10$ cat search.txt | sed '1s/wood/stone/g'
How much stone would a stonechuck chuck
if a woodchuck could chuck wood?
reader@ubuntu:~/scripts/chapter_10$ cat search.txt | sed
'1,2s/wood/stone/g'
How much stone would a stonechuck chuck
if a stonechuck could chuck stone?
```

The first script, '1s/wood/stone/', instructs sed to replace the first instance of *wood* on the first line with *stone*. The next script, '1s/wood/stone/g', tells sed to replace all instances of *wood* with *stone*, but only on the first line. The last script, '1,2s/wood/stone/g', makes sed replace all instances of *wood* on all lines between (and including!) 1 and 2.

In-place editing

While it is not *that* big a deal to cat a file before we send it to sed, fortunately, we don't really need to do that. The usage for sed is as follows: sed [OPTION] {script-only-if-no-other-script} [input-file]. As you can see at the end, there is an option for [input-file].

Let's take one of the previous examples, and remove the `cat`:

```
reader@ubuntu:~/scripts/chapter_10$ sed 's/wood/stone/g' search.txt
How much stone would a stonechuck chuck
if a stonechuck could chuck stone?
reader@ubuntu:~/scripts/chapter_10$ cat search.txt
How much wood would a woodchuck chuck
if a woodchuck could chuck wood?
```

As you can see, by using the optional `[input-file]` argument, `sed` processes all lines in that file according to the script. By default, `sed` prints everything it processes. In some cases, this causes lines to be printed twice, namely when using the `print` function of `sed` (which we will see in a bit).

Another very important thing that this example demonstrates: this syntax does not edit the original file; only what is printed out to STDOUT is changed. Sometimes, you will want to edit the file itself—for these scenarios, `sed` has the `--in-place` (`-i`) option.

Make sure you understand that this **irreversibly changes the file on disk**. And, as with most things in Linux, there is no such thing as an undo button or a recycle bin!

Let's see how we can use `sed -i` to persistently change a file (after we make a backup, of course):

```
reader@ubuntu:~/scripts/chapter_10$ cat search.txt
How much wood would a woodchuck chuck
if a woodchuck could chuck wood?
reader@ubuntu:~/scripts/chapter_10$ cp search.txt search.txt.bak
reader@ubuntu:~/scripts/chapter_10$ sed -i 's/wood/stone/g' search.txt
reader@ubuntu:~/scripts/chapter_10$ cat search.txt
How much stone would a stonechuck chuck
if a stonechuck could chuck stone?
```

This time, instead of printing the processed text onto your screen, `sed` quietly changed the file on disk. Because of the destructive nature of this, we created a backup beforehand. However, the `--in-place` option of `sed` can provide that functionality as well, by adding a file suffix:

```
reader@ubuntu:~/scripts/chapter_10$ ls
character-class.txt  error.txt  grep-file.txt  grep-then-else.sh
search.txt   search.txt.bak
reader@ubuntu:~/scripts/chapter_10$ mv search.txt.bak search.txt
reader@ubuntu:~/scripts/chapter_10$ cat search.txt
How much wood would a woodchuck chuck
if a woodchuck could chuck wood?
reader@ubuntu:~/scripts/chapter_10$ sed -i'.bak' 's/wood/stone/g'
```

```
search.txt
reader@ubuntu:~/scripts/chapter_10$ cat search.txt
How much stone would a stonechuck chuck
if a stonechuck could chuck stone?
reader@ubuntu:~/scripts/chapter_10$ cat search.txt.bak
How much wood would a woodchuck chuck
if a woodchuck could chuck wood?
```

sed is a bit stingy with the syntax. If you put a space between −i and '.bak', you will get weird errors (this normally works fine for commands whose options have arguments). In this case, because the script definition follows right after, sed is having trouble differentiating between what is the file suffix and script string.

Just remember that if you want to use this, you need to be careful about this syntax!

Line manipulation

While the word manipulation functionality of sed is great, it also allows us to manipulate whole lines. For example, we can delete certain lines, by number:

```
reader@ubuntu:~/scripts/chapter_10$ echo -e "Hi,\nthis is \nPatrick"
Hi,
this is
Patrick
reader@ubuntu:~/scripts/chapter_10$ echo -e "Hi,\nthis is \nPatrick" | sed
'd'
reader@ubuntu:~/scripts/chapter_10$ echo -e "Hi,\nthis is \nPatrick" | sed
'1d'
this is
Patrick
```

By using echo −e combined with the newline character (\n), we can create multi-line statements. −e is explained on the man echo page as *enable interpretation of backslash escapes*. By piping this multi-line output into sed, we can use the delete functionality, which is a script that simply uses the character d.

If we prefix this with a line number, for example 1d, the first line is deleted. If we do not, all lines are deleted, which results in no output for us.

Another, often more interesting, possibility is deleting lines that contain a certain word:

```
reader@ubuntu:~/scripts/chapter_10$ echo -e "Hi,\nthis is \nPatrick" | sed
'/Patrick/d'
Hi,
this is
```

```
reader@ubuntu:~/scripts/chapter_10$ echo -e "Hi,\nthis is \nPatrick" | sed
'/patrick/d'
Hi,
this is
Patrick
```

In the same way as we used a script with word matching for the search-replace function of sed, so can we also delete a whole line if a word is present. As you can see from the preceding example, this is case-sensitive. Luckily, there's always a solution if we want to do this in a case-insensitive manner. In grep, this would be the -i flag, but for sed this -i is already reserved for --in-place functionality.

How do we do it then? By using our old friends regular expressions, of course! See the following example:

```
reader@ubuntu:~/scripts/chapter_10$ echo -e "Hi,\nthis is \nPatrick" | sed
'/[Pp]atrick/d'
Hi,
this is
reader@ubuntu:~/scripts/chapter_10$ echo -e "Hi,\nthis is \nPatrick" | sed
'/.atrick/d'
Hi,
this is
```

While it's not as graceful as the functionality provided by grep, it does get the job done in most situations. It should at least make you aware of the fact that using regular expressions with sed makes the whole thing much more flexible and much more powerful.

As with most things, with added flexibility and power comes added complexity. However, we hope that with this gentle introduction to regular expressions and sed, the combination of both does not feel unmanageably complex.

Instead of deleting lines from a file or stream, you might have a better use case for just showing a few files. There is a small issue with this, however: by default, sed prints all lines it processes. If you give sed the instruction to print a line (with the p script), it will print that line two times—once for the match on the script, and the other time for the default print.

This looks something like this:

```
reader@ubuntu:~/scripts/chapter_10$ cat error.txt
Process started.
Running normally.
ERROR: TCP socket broken.
ERROR: Cannot connect to database.
Exiting process.
```

```
reader@ubuntu:~/scripts/chapter_10$ sed '/ERROR/p' error.txt
Process started.
Running normally.
ERROR: TCP socket broken.
ERROR: TCP socket broken.
ERROR: Cannot connect to database.
ERROR: Cannot connect to database.
Exiting process.
```

The syntax for the print and delete scripts is similar: `'/word/d'` and `'/word/p'`. To suppress the default behavior of sed, which prints all lines, add a -n (also known as --quiet or --silent):

```
reader@ubuntu:~/scripts/chapter_10$ sed -n '/ERROR/p' error.txt
ERROR: TCP socket broken.
ERROR: Cannot connect to database.
```

You might have figured out that printing and deleting lines with sed scripts shares the same functionality as grep and grep -v. In most cases, you can choose which you prefer to use. However, some advanced functionality, like deleting lines that match, but only from the first 10 lines of a file, can only be done with sed. As a rule of thumb, anything that can be achieved with grep using a single statement should be handled with grep; otherwise, turn to sed.

There is one final use case for sed that we would like to highlight: you have a file or stream, and you need to delete not a whole line, but only some words in those lines. With grep, this cannot be (easily) achieved. sed has a very simple way of doing this, however.

What makes searching and replacing different to just plain deleting a word? Just the replacement pattern!

See the following example:

```
reader@ubuntu:~/scripts/chapter_10$ cat search.txt
How much stone would a stonechuck chuck
if a stonechuck could chuck stone?
reader@ubuntu:~/scripts/chapter_10$ sed 's/stone//g' search.txt
How much  would a chuck chuck
if a chuck could chuck ?
```

By *replacing* the word stone with *nothing* (as that is exactly what is present between the second and third backslash in the sed script), we delete the word stone completely. In this example, however, you can see a common problem you will undoubtedly run across: extra whitespace after deleting a word.

This leads us to one more trick for `sed`, which helps you out in this regard:

```
reader@ubuntu:~/scripts/chapter_10$ sed -e 's/stone //g' -e 's/stone//g'
search.txt
How much would a chuck chuck
if a chuck could chuck ?
```

By supplying −e, followed by a `sed` script, you can make `sed` run multiple scripts (in order!) over your stream. By default, `sed` expects at least one script, which is why you do not need to supply the −e if you're only processing a single script. For more scripts than this, you'll need to add a −e before each.

Final remarks

Regular expressions are **hard**. What makes this even harder on Linux is that regular expressions have been implemented by different programs (which have different maintainers, with different opinions) slightly differently.

To make matters worse, some features of regular expressions have been hidden as extended regular expressions by some programs, whereas they are considered the default by other programs. In past years, the maintainers of these programs seemed to have moved towards a more global POSIX standard for *regular* regular expressions and *extended* regular expressions, but still to this day, there are some discrepancies.

We have some very simple advice for dealing with this: **just try it out**. You might not remember what the asterisk represents in globbing, as opposed to regular expressions, or why the question mark does something different. Perhaps you'll forget to 'activate' extended syntax with −E, and your extended search pattern will return weird errors.

You will definitely forget to quote a search pattern once, and if it contains a character such as a dot or $ (which is interpreted by Bash,) your command will crash and burn, often with a not-too-clear error message.

Just know that we have all made these mistakes, and only experience will make this easier. In fact, in writing this chapter, almost none of the commands as we had them in our heads worked right away! You are not alone in this, and you should not feel bad about it. *Just keep going and keep trying until it works, and until you understand why it did not work the first time.*

Summary

This chapter explained regular expressions, and two common tools that use them under Linux: `grep` and `sed`.

We began by explaining that regular expressions are *search patterns*, used in combination with text to find matches. These search patterns allow us to search very flexibly in text where its contents are not necessarily known at runtime.

Search patterns allow us, for example, to look only for words and not numbers, for words at the beginnings or endings of lines, or for empty lines. Search patterns include wildcards, which can represent one or more of a certain character or character class.

We introduced the `grep` command to show how we can use the basic functionality of regular expressions in Bash.

The second part of this chapter dealt with globbing. Globbing is used as a wildcard mechanism for file names and paths. It has similarities with regular expressions, but also some key differences. Globbing can be used with most commands that deal with files (and, since most *things* under Linux can be considered files, this means almost all commands support some form of globbing).

The last half of the chapter described using regular expressions with `egrep` and `sed`. `egrep`, being a simple wrapper for `grep -E`, allows us to use extended syntax for regular expressions, which we discussed along with some often-used, advanced features of `grep`.

In contrast to default regular expressions, extended regular expressions allow us to specify the length of certain patterns and how often they repeat, as well as allowing us to use alternation.

The final part of this chapter described `sed`, the stream editor. `sed` is a complex but very powerful command, which allows us to do even more exciting stuff than `grep`.

The following commands were introduced in this chapter: `grep`, `set`, `egrep`, and `sed`.

Questions

1. What is a search pattern?
2. Why are regular expressions considered greedy?
3. Which character in search patterns is considered a wildcard for any one character, except newlines?
4. How is the asterisk used in Linux regular expression search patterns?
5. What are line anchors?
6. Name three character types.
7. What is globbing?
8. What is possible in extended regular expression syntax that is not possible with normal regular expressions under Bash?
9. What would be a good rule of thumb for deciding whether to use `grep` or `sed`?
10. Why are regular expressions on Linux/Bash so hard?

Further reading

The following resources might be interesting if you'd like to go deeper into the subjects of this chapter:

- **The Linux Documentation Project on Regular Expressions**: `http://www.tldp.org/LDP/abs/html/x17129.html`
- **The Linux Documentation Project on Globbing**: `http://www.tldp.org/LDP/abs/html/globbingref.html`
- **The Linux Documentation Project on Sed**: `http://tldp.org/LDP/abs/html/x23170.html`

11
Conditional Testing and Scripting Loops

This chapter will begin with a recap on `if-then-else`, before presenting advanced uses of `if-then-else` conditionals. We will introduce scripting loops in the form of `while` and `for`, and we will show how we can control these loops with `exit`, `break`, and `continue`.

The following commands will be introduced in this chapter: `elif`, `help`, `while`, `sleep`, `for`, `basename`, `break`, and `continue`.

The following topics will be covered in this chapter:

- Advanced `if-then-else`
- The `while` loop
- The `for` loop
- The `loop` control

Technical requirements

All scripts for this chapter can be found on GitHub: `https://github.com/PacktPublishing/Learn-Linux-Shell-Scripting-Fundamentals-of-Bash-4.4/tree/master/Chapter11`. All other tools are still valid, both on your host machine as well as on your Ubuntu virtual machine. For the **break-x.sh**, **for-globbing.sh**, **square-number.sh**, **while-interactive.sh** scripts only the final version is found online. Be sure to verify the script version in the header before executing it on your system.

Advanced if-then-else

This chapter is dedicated to everything to do with conditional testing and scripting loops, which are two concepts that are often intertwined. We have already seen the `if-then-else` loop in Chapter 9, *Error Checking and Handling,* which focused on error checking and handling. We'll present a small recap of the things we've described regarding `if-then-else`, before moving on to advanced concepts.

A recap on if-then-else

`If-then-else` logic does almost exactly what the name implies: **if** *something-is-the-case,* **then** *do-something* or **else** *do-something-else.* In practice, this could be **if** *the disk is full,* **then** *delete some files* or **else** *report that the disk space looks great.* In a script, this could look something like this:

```
reader@ubuntu:~/scripts/chapter_09$ cat if-then-else-proper.sh
#!/bin/bash

#####################################
# Author: Sebastiaan Tammer
# Version: v1.0.0
# Date: 2018-09-30
# Description: Use the if-then-else construct, now properly.
# Usage: ./if-then-else-proper.sh file-name
#####################################

file_name=$1

# Check if the file exists.
if [[ -f ${file_name} ]]; then
  cat ${file_name} # Print the file content.
else
  echo "File does not exist, stopping the script!"
  exit 1
fi
```

If a file exists, we print the contents. Otherwise (so, if the file does not exist), we give the user feedback in the form of the error message, then we exit the script with an exit status of 1. Remember, any exit code that is not 0 signifies a *script failure.*

Using regular expressions in tests

A chapter after introducing `if-then-else`, we learned all about regular expressions. That chapter, however, was mostly theoretical and only contained a single script! Now, as you might realize, regular expressions are mostly supporting constructs that are to be used with other scripting tools. In the case of the tests we have described, we can use both globbing and regular expressions within the `[[...]]` blocks! Let's look at this in more depth, as follows:

```
reader@ubuntu:~/scripts/chapter_11$ vim square-number.sh
reader@ubuntu:~/scripts/chapter_11$ cat square-number.sh
#!/bin/bash

#####################################
# Author: Sebastiaan Tammer
# Version: v1.0.0
# Date: 2018-10-26
# Description: Return the square of the input number.
# Usage: ./square-number.sh <number>
#####################################

INPUT_NUMBER=$1

# Check the number of arguments received.
if [[ $# -ne 1 ]]; then
 echo "Incorrect usage, wrong number of arguments."
 echo "Usage: $0 <number>"
 exit 1
fi

# Check to see if the input is a number.
if [[ ! ${INPUT_NUMBER} =~ [[:digit:]] ]]; then
 echo "Incorrect usage, wrong type of argument."
 echo "Usage: $0 <number>"
 exit 1
fi

# Multiple the input number with itself and return this to the user.
echo $((${INPUT_NUMBER} * ${INPUT_NUMBER}))
```

We first check if the user supplied the correct number of arguments (which is what we should always do). Next, we use the `=~` operator within the test `[[..]]` block. This allows us to **evaluate using regular expressions**. In this case, it simply allows us to verify that the user input is a number, and not anything else.

Now, if we call this script, we will see the following:

```
reader@ubuntu:~/scripts/chapter_11$ bash square-number.sh
Incorrect usage, wrong number of arguments.
Usage: square-number.sh <number>
reader@ubuntu:~/scripts/chapter_11$ bash square-number.sh 3 2
Incorrect usage, wrong number of arguments.
Usage: square-number.sh <number>
reader@ubuntu:~/scripts/chapter_11$ bash square-number.sh a
Incorrect usage, wrong type of argument.
Usage: square-number.sh <number>
reader@ubuntu:~/scripts/chapter_11$ bash square-number.sh 3
9
reader@ubuntu:~/scripts/chapter_11$ bash square-number.sh 11
121
```

We can see that both of our input checks work. If we call this script without exactly one argument (`$# -ne 1`), it fails. This is true for both 0 and 2 arguments. Next, if we call the script with a letter instead of a number, we get to the second check and the consequent error message: `wrong type of argument`. Finally, to prove that the script actually does what we want, we will try it with single number: 3 and 11. The returns of 9 and 121 are the squares of these numbers, so it seems we achieved our goal!

However, not everything is always as it seems. This is a common pitfall when using regular expressions, as the following code should illustrate:

```
reader@ubuntu:~/scripts/chapter_11$ bash square-number.sh a3
0
reader@ubuntu:~/scripts/chapter_11$ bash square-number.sh 3a
square-number.sh: line 28: 3a: value too great for base (error token is
"3a")
```

How did this happen? We checked to see if the user input was a number, did we not? Actually, contrary to what you might think, we actually checked if the user input *matched positively against a number*. To say this in simpler terms, if the input contains a number, the check succeeds. What we really want to check is if the input is a number *from the beginning to the end*. Perhaps this sounds familiar, but it definitely smells like line anchors! The following code applies this:

```
reader@ubuntu:~/scripts/chapter_11$ vim square-number.sh
reader@ubuntu:~/scripts/chapter_11$ head -5 square-number.sh
#!/bin/bash

####################################
# Author: Sebastiaan Tammer
# Version: v1.1.0
```

```
reader@ubuntu:~/scripts/chapter_11$ grep 'digit' square-number.sh
if [[ ! ${INPUT_NUMBER} =~ ^[[:digit:]]$ ]]; then
```

We made two changes: the search pattern we're matching against is no longer just
`[[:digit:]]`, but `^[[:digit:]]$`, and we updated the version number (something we
haven't done too much up until now). Because we are now anchoring the digit to both the
beginning and the end of the line, we can no longer inject a letter in a random spot. Run the
script with incorrect input to verify this:

```
reader@ubuntu:~/scripts/chapter_11$ bash square-number.sh a3
Incorrect usage, wrong type of argument.
Usage: square-number-improved.sh <number>
reader@ubuntu:~/scripts/chapter_11$ bash square-number.sh 3a
Incorrect usage, wrong type of argument.
Usage: square-number-improved.sh <number>
reader@ubuntu:~/scripts/chapter_11$ bash square-number.sh 3a3
Incorrect usage, wrong type of argument.
Usage: square-number-improved.sh <number>
reader@ubuntu:~/scripts/chapter_11$ bash square-number.sh 9
81
```

I would love to tell you that we're now perfectly safe. But, alas, as it often is with regular
expressions, it's not that simple. The script now works great for a single number (0–9), but if
you try it with a double-digit number, it fails with `wrong type of argument error` (try
it out!). We need one final tweak to make sure it does exactly what we want: we need to
make sure that the digit also accepts multiple sequential digits. The *one or more* construct in
regular expressions is the + sign, which we can just append to `[[:digit:]]`:

```
reader@ubuntu:~/scripts/chapter_11$ vim square-number.sh
reader@ubuntu:~/scripts/chapter_11$ head -5 square-number.sh
#!/bin/bash

####################################
# Author: Sebastiaan Tammer
# Version: v1.2.0
reader@ubuntu:~/scripts/chapter_11$ grep 'digit' square-number.sh
if [[ ! ${INPUT_NUMBER} =~ ^[[:digit:]]+$ ]]; then
reader@ubuntu:~/scripts/chapter_11$ bash square-number.sh 15
225
reader@ubuntu:~/scripts/chapter_11$ bash square-number.sh 1x5
Incorrect usage, wrong type of argument.
Usage: square-number-improved.sh <number>
```

We changed the pattern, upped the version number, and ran the script with different
inputs. The final pattern of `^[[:digit:]]+$` can be read as *one or more digits from the start
to the end of the line*, which, in this case, means *a number, and nothing else!*

The lesson here is that you really need to test your regular expressions thoroughly. As you know by now, search patterns are greedy, and as soon as a little bit matches, it considers the result a success. As seen in the previous example, this was not specific enough. The only way to implement (and learn!) this is by trying to break your own scripts. Try wrong input, weird input, very specific input, and so on. Unless you try a lot, you can't be sure that it will *probably* work.

You can use all regular expression search patterns in test syntax. Other examples that we will not flesh out, but should definitely be considered, are as follows:

- The variable should start with a / (for a fully qualified path)
- The variable cannot contain whitespace (using the `[[:blank:]]` search pattern)
- The variable should contain only lowercase letters (achievable with the `^[[:lower:]]+$` pattern)
- The variable should contain a file name with an extension (can match on `[[:alnum:]]\.[[:alpha:]]`)

The elif condition

In the scenarios we've seen up until now, there was only ever the need to check for one *if condition*. But as you might expect, sometimes, there are multiple things that you want to check for, each with their own sets of following actions (*then block*). You could solve this by using two full `if-then-else` statements, but at the very least you'd have a duplicate *else block*. Even worse, if you have three or more conditions you want to check for, you'll have more and more duplicate code! Luckily for us, we can solve this by using the `elif` command, which is part of the `if-then-else` logic. As you've probably guessed, `elif` is short for `else-if`. It allows us to do something like the following:

IF condition1, THEN do thing1, ELIF condition2, THEN do thing2, ELSE do final-thing

You can chain as many `elif` commands after the initial `if` command as you want, but there is one important thing to consider: as soon as any condition is true, only that `then` statement is executed; all others are skipped.

If you're thinking of a situation in which multiple conditions can be true, and their `then` statements should be executed, you need to use multiple `if-then-else` blocks. Let's look at a simple example that first checks if the argument given by the user is a file. If it is, we print the file using `cat`. If this is not the case, we check if it is a directory. Should this be the case, we list the directory with `ls`. If this is also not the case, we'll print an error message and exit with a non-zero exit status. Look at the following command:

```
reader@ubuntu:~/scripts/chapter_11$ vim print-or-list.sh
reader@ubuntu:~/scripts/chapter_11$ cat print-or-list.sh
#!/bin/bash

#####################################
# Author: Sebastiaan Tammer
# Version: v1.0.0
# Date: 2018-10-26
# Description: Prints or lists the given path, depending on type.
# Usage: ./print-or-list.sh <file or directory path>
#####################################

# Since we're dealing with paths, set current working directory.
cd $(dirname $0)

# Input validation.
if [[ $# -ne 1 ]]; then
  echo "Incorrect usage!"
  echo "Usage: $0 <file or directory path>"
  exit 1
fi

input_path=$1

if [[ -f ${input_path} ]]; then
  echo "File found, showing content:"
  cat ${input_path} || { echo "Cannot print file, exiting script!"; exit 1;
}
elif [[ -d ${input_path} ]]; then
  echo "Directory found, listing:"
  ls -l ${input_path} || { echo "Cannot list directory, exiting script!";
exit 1; }
else
  echo "Path is neither a file nor a directory, exiting script."
  exit 1
fi
```

As you can see, when we're dealing with file input by users, we need extra sanitation. We make sure to set the current working directory in the script with cd $(dirname $0), and we assume that every command can fail, so we handle these failures with the || construct, as explained in Chapter 9, *Error Checking and Handling*. Let's try and see if we can find most of the paths that this logic can take:

```
reader@ubuntu:~/scripts/chapter_11$ bash print-or-list.sh
Incorrect usage!
Usage: print-or-list.sh <file or directory path>
reader@ubuntu:~/scripts/chapter_11$ bash print-or-list.sh /etc/passwd
File found, showing content:
root:x:0:0:root:/root:/bin/bash
daemon:x:1:1:daemon:/usr/sbin:/usr/sbin/nologin
bin:x:2:2:bin:/bin:/usr/sbin/nologin
<SNIPPED>
reader@ubuntu:~/scripts/chapter_11$ bash print-or-list.sh /etc/shadow
File found, showing content:
cat: /etc/shadow: Permission denied
Cannot print file, exiting script!
reader@ubuntu:~/scripts/chapter_11$ bash print-or-list.sh /tmp/
Directory found, listing:
total 8
drwx------ 3 root root 4096 Oct 26 08:26 systemd-
private-4f8c34d02849461cb20d3bfdaa984c85...
drwx------ 3 root root 4096 Oct 26 08:26 systemd-
private-4f8c34d02849461cb20d3bfdaa984c85...
reader@ubuntu:~/scripts/chapter_11$ bash print-or-list.sh /root/
Directory found, listing:
ls: cannot open directory '/root/': Permission denied
Cannot list directory, exiting script!
reader@ubuntu:~/scripts/chapter_11$ bash print-or-list.sh /dev/zero
Path is neither a file nor a directory, exiting script.
```

In order, we've seen the following scenarios for our script:

1. **No argument**: Incorrect usage error
2. **File argument /etc/passwd**: File content printed
3. **File argument on non-readable file /etc/shadow**: Cannot print file error
4. **Directory argument /tmp/**: List of directory printed
5. **Directory argument on non-listable directory /root/**: Cannot list directory error
6. **Special file (block device) argument /dev/zero**: Path is neither a file nor a directory error

These six input scenarios represent all of the possible paths our script can take. While you might have considered all of the error handling for a (seemingly simple) script a bit over the top, these arguments should validate why we actually need all of this error handling.

While `elif` greatly enhances the possibilities of an `if-then-else` statement, too much `if-elif-elif-elif-.......-then-else` will make your script really hard to read. There is another construct (which is outside the scope of this book), called `case`. This deals with many different, unique conditions. Look at the further reading section at the end of this chapter for a good resource on `case`!

Nesting

Another concept that is very interesting is nesting. In essence, nesting is really simple: it is placing another `if-then-else` statement within either the `then` or `else` of the *outer* `if-then-else`. This allows us to, for example, first determine if a file is readable, before determining what type of file it is. By using nested `if-then-else` statements, we can rewrite the previous code in such a way that we no longer need the `||` construct:

```
reader@ubuntu:~/scripts/chapter_11$ vim nested-print-or-list.sh
reader@ubuntu:~/scripts/chapter_11$ cat nested-print-or-list.sh
#!/bin/bash

#####################################
# Author: Sebastiaan Tammer
# Version: v1.0.0
# Date: 2018-10-26
# Description: Prints or lists the given path, depending on type.
# Usage: ./nested-print-or-list.sh <file or directory path>
#####################################

# Since we're dealing with paths, set current working directory.
cd $(dirname $0)

# Input validation.
if [[ $# -ne 1 ]]; then
  echo "Incorrect usage!"
  echo "Usage: $0 <file or directory path>"
  exit 1
fi

input_path=$1

# First, check if we can read the file.
```

```
if [[ -r ${input_path} ]]; then
  # We can read the file, now we determine what type it is.
  if [[ -f ${input_path} ]]; then
    echo "File found, showing content:"
    cat ${input_path}
  elif [[ -d ${input_path} ]]; then
    echo "Directory found, listing:"
    ls -l ${input_path}
  else
    echo "Path is neither a file nor a directory, exiting script."
    exit 1
  fi
else
  # We cannot read the file, print an error.
  echo "Cannot read the file/directory, exiting script."
  exit 1
fi
```

Try the preceding script with the same input as the previous example. In this case, you'll see much nicer output in the error scenarios, since we now control those (instead of the default output of `cat: /etc/shadow: Permission denied` from `cat`, for example). Functionally, however, nothing has changed! We think that this script, which uses nesting, is more readable than the previous example, because we handle the error scenarios ourselves now instead of relying on the system commands to do it for us.

> We've discussed indentation before, but in our opinion, scripts like this one are where it truly shines. By indenting the inner `if-then-else` statement, it is much more clear that the second `else` belongs to the outer `if-then-else` statement. If you're using multiple levels of indentation (because, in theory, you can nest as often as you'd like), it really helps everyone working on the script to follow this logic.

Nesting is not just reserved for `if-then-else`. The two loops that we will introduce later in this chapter, `for` and `while`, can also be nested. And, what's even more practical, you can nest all of them within all of the others (from a technical perspective; it should make sense from a logical perspective as well, of course!). You will see examples of this when we explain `while` and `for` later.

Getting help

By now, you're probably afraid that you'll never remember all this. While we're sure that in time, given enough practice, you most certainly will, we understand that it is a lot to take in when you're not as experienced. To make this easier, there is another helpful command besides the man pages. As you might have found (and failed when you tried), man if, or man [[, do not work. If you check these commands with type if and type [[, you'll actually see that they are not commands but *shell keywords*. For most of the shell builtins and shell keywords, you can use the help command to print some information on what they do and how to use them! Using help is as simple as help if, help [[, help while, and so on. For if-then-else statements, only help if works:

```
reader@ubuntu:~/scripts/chapter_11$ help if
if: if COMMANDS; then COMMANDS; [ elif COMMANDS; then COMMANDS; ]... [ else
COMMANDS; ] fi
    Execute commands based on conditional.
    The 'if COMMANDS' list is executed. If its exit status is zero,
     then the 'then COMMANDS' list is executed.  Otherwise, each
     'elif COMMANDS' list is executed in turn, and if its
     exit status is zero, the corresponding
    'then COMMANDS' list is executed and the if command completes.
Otherwise,
    the 'else COMMANDS' list is executed, if present.
    The exit status of the entire construct is the
     exit status of the last command executed, or zero
    if no condition tested true.
    Exit Status:
    Returns the status of the last command executed.
```

So, overall, there are three ways to get Linux to print some helpful information for you:

- Man pages with the man command
- Help information with the help command
- Command native help print (often as flag -h, --help, or -help)

Depending on the type of command (binary or shell builtin/keyword), you'll use either man, help, or the --help flag. Remember, by checking which type of command you're dealing with (so that you can make a more educated guess about which method of help you can try first), use type -a <command>.

The while loop

Now that we've got the if-then-else recap and advanced usage out of the way, it is time to discuss the first scripting loop: while. Look at the following definition, which should seem familiar after if-then-else:

WHILE condition-is-true DO thing-to-do DONE

The biggest difference between if and while is that while will perform the action many times, so long as the condition specified is still true. Because it is often not needed to have an unending loop, the action will regularly mutate something related at the condition. This basically means that the action in *do* will eventually cause the while condition to be false instead of true. Let's look at a simple example:

```
reader@ubuntu:~/scripts/chapter_11$ vim while-simple.sh
reader@ubuntu:~/scripts/chapter_11$ cat while-simple.sh
#!/bin/bash

####################################
# Author: Sebastiaan Tammer
# Version: v1.0.0
# Date: 2018-10-27
# Description: Example of a while loop.
# Usage: ./while-simple.sh
####################################

# Infinite while loop.
while true; do
  echo "Hello!"
  sleep 1 # Wait for 1 second.
done
```

This example is the most basic form of while: an unending loop (because the condition is simply true) that prints a message and then sleeps for one second. This new command, sleep, is often used within loops (both while and for) to wait for a specified time. In this case, we run sleep 1, which waits a single second before going back to the top of the loop and printing Hello! again. Be sure to try it out and notice how it will never stop (*Ctrl + C* will, however, kill the process, since it's interactive).

Now we'll create a script that will end at certain time. To do this, we'll define a variable outside of the `while` loop, which we will use as a counter. This counter will be incremented at each run of the `while` loop, until the threshold defined in the condition is reached. Take a look:

```
reader@ubuntu:~/scripts/chapter_11$ vim while-counter.sh
reader@ubuntu:~/scripts/chapter_11$ cat while-counter.sh
cat while-counter.sh
#!/bin/bash

####################################
# Author: Sebastiaan Tammer
# Version: v1.0.0
# Date: 2018-10-27
# Description: Example of a while loop with a counter.
# Usage: ./while-counter.sh
####################################

# Define the counter outside of the loop so we don't reset it for
# every run in the loop.
counter=0

# This loop runs 10 times.
while [[ ${counter} -lt 10 ]]; do
  counter=$((counter+1)) # Increment the counter by 1.
  echo "Hello! This is loop number ${counter}."
  sleep 1
done

# After the while-loop finishes, print a goodbye message.
echo "All done, thanks for tuning in!"
```

This script should be self-explanatory because of the comments we've added. `counter` is added outside the `while` loop, because otherwise every run of the loop would start with `counter=0`, which would reset the progress. As long as the counter is less than 10, we'll keep running the loop. After 10 runs, this is no longer the case, and instead of going back in the loop, we're going to the next instruction in the script, which is printing the goodbye message. Go ahead and run this script. Edit the number after sleep (hint: it also accepts values smaller than a second), or remove sleep altogether.

The until loop

While has a twin: until. An until loop does exactly what while does, with only one difference: the loop only runs as long as the condition is **false**. As soon as the condition becomes **true**, the loop no longer runs. We'll make some minor changes to the previous script and we'll see how until works:

```
reader@ubuntu:~/scripts/chapter_11$ cp while-counter.sh until-counter.sh
reader@ubuntu:~/scripts/chapter_11$ vim until-counter.sh
reader@ubuntu:~/scripts/chapter_11$ cat until-counter.sh
#!/bin/bash

####################################
# Author: Sebastiaan Tammer
# Version: v1.0.0
# Date: 2018-10-27
# Description: Example of an until loop with a counter.
# Usage: ./until-counter.sh
####################################

# Define the counter outside of the loop so we don't reset it for
# every run in the loop.
counter=0

# This loop runs 10 times.
until [[ ${counter} -gt 9 ]]; do
    counter=$((counter+1)) # Increment the counter by 1.
    echo "Hello! This is loop number ${counter}."
    sleep 1
done

# After the while-loop finishes, print a goodbye message.
echo "All done, thanks for tuning in!"
```

As you can see, the changes to this script are very minimal (but important, nonetheless). We replaced while with until, -lt with -gt, and 10 with 9. Now, it reads run the loop until the counter is greater than 9 as opposed to run the loop as long as the counter is lower than 10. Because we are using lower than and greater than, we have to change the number, otherwise we're going to experience the famous *off-by-one* error (which, in this case, means that we'll loop 11 times, should we not have changed the 10 to a 9; try it!).

In essence, the `while` and `until` loops are exactly the same. You will use a `while` loop more often than an until loop: since you can just negate the condition, a `while` loop will always work. However, sometimes, an `until` loop might *feel* more justified. In any case, use the one that is easiest to comprehend for the situation! When in doubt, just using `while` will hardly ever be wrong, as long as you get the condition right.

Creating an interactive while loop

In reality, you will not use a `while` loop that often. In most scenarios, a `for` loop is better (as we will see later on in this chapter). There is, however, one situation where a `while` loop is excellent: dealing with user input. If you use the `while true` construct with an if-then-else block nesting within it, you can keep asking the user for input until you get the answer you're looking for. The following example, which is a simple riddle, should clarify matters:

```
reader@ubuntu:~/scripts/chapter_11$ vim while-interactive.sh
reader@ubuntu:~/scripts/chapter_11$ cat while-interactive.sh
#!/bin/bash

#####################################
# Author: Sebastiaan Tammer
# Version: v1.0.0
# Date: 2018-10-27
# Description: A simple riddle in a while loop.
# Usage: ./while-interactive.sh
#####################################

# Infinite loop, only exits on correct answer.
while true; do
  read -p "I have keys but no locks. I have a space but no room. You can
enter, but can't go outside. What am I? " answer
  if [[ ${answer} =~ [Kk]eyboard ]]; then # Use regular expression so 'a
keyboard' or 'Keyboard' is also a valid answer.
    echo "Correct, congratulations!"
    exit 0 # Exit the script.
  else
    # Print an error message and go back into the loop.
    echo "Incorrect, please try again."
  fi
done

reader@ubuntu:~/scripts/chapter_11$ bash while-interactive.sh
I have keys but no locks. I have a space but no room. You can enter, but
can't go outside. What am I? mouse
```

```
Incorrect, please try again.
I have keys but no locks. I have a space but no room. You can enter, but
can't go outside. What am I? screen
Incorrect, please try again.
I have keys but no locks. I have a space but no room. You can enter, but
can't go outside. What am I? keyboard
Correct, congratulations!
reader@ubuntu:~/scripts/chapter_11$
```

In this script, we use `read -p` to ask the user a question, and we store the reply in the `answer` variable. We then use a nested if-then-else block to check if the user gave the correct answer. We use a simple regular expression if-condition, `${answer} =~ [Kk]eyboard`, which gives a little flexibility to the user with regards to capitals and perhaps the word a in front. For every incorrect answer, the *else* statement prints an error and the loop starts back at `read -p`. If the answer is correct, the *then* block is executed, which ends with `exit 0` to signify the end of the script. As long as the correct answer isn't given, the loop will go on forever.

You might see a problem with this script. If we wanted to do anything after the `while` loop, we'd need to *break* out of it without exiting the script. We will see how we can achieve this with the – wait for it – `break` keyword! But first, we'll check out the `for` loop.

The for loop

The `for` loop can be considered the more powerful loop in Bash scripting. In practice, `for` and `while` are interchangeable, but `for` has better shorthand syntax. This means that to write a loop in `for` often requires much less code than an equivalent `while` loop.

The `for` loop has two different syntaxes: a C-style syntax and the `regular` Bash syntax. We'll first look at the Bash syntax:

FOR value IN list-of-values DO thing-with-value DONE

A `for` loop allows us to *iterate* over a list of things. Each loop will use a different item in that list, in a sequential order. This very simple example should illustrate this behavior:

```
reader@ubuntu:~/scripts/chapter_11$ vim for-simple.sh
reader@ubuntu:~/scripts/chapter_11$ cat for-simple.sh
#!/bin/bash

####################################
# Author: Sebastiaan Tammer
# Version: v1.0.0
```

```
# Date: 2018-10-27
# Description: Simple for syntax.
# Usage: ./for-simple.sh
######################################

# Create a 'list'.
words="house dog telephone dog"

# Iterate over the list and process the values.
for word in ${words}; do
  echo "The word is: ${word}"
done

reader@ubuntu:~/scripts/chapter_11$ bash for-simple.sh
The word is: house
The word is: dog
The word is: telephone
The word is: dog
```

As you can see, for takes a list (in this case, a string delimited by whitespace), and for each value it finds it performs the echo action. We've added some extra text there so that you can see that it actually goes into the loop four times and does not just print the list with extra new lines. The main thing to notice here is that in the echo we use the ${word} variable, which we defined as the second word in the for definition. This means that for every run of the for loop, the value of the ${word} variable is different (which is very much using a variable as it is intended, with a *variable* content!). You can name this anything, but we prefer to give semantically logical names; since we called our list *words*, an item in that list would be a *word*.

If you want to do the same thing with while, things are going to get a lot more complicated. It's definitely possible by using a counter and a command such as cut (which allows you to cut out different parts of a string), but since the for loop does it in this simple manner, why bother?

The second syntax that we can use with for will be more recognizable for those experienced with other scripting programming languages. This C-style syntax uses a counter that increments until a certain point, not unlike the example we saw when we looked at while. The syntax is as follows:

```
FOR ((counter=0; counter<=10; counter++)); DO something DONE
```

Seems pretty similar right? Check out this example script:

```
reader@ubuntu:~/scripts/chapter_11$ vim for-counter.sh
reader@ubuntu:~/scripts/chapter_11$ cat for-counter.sh
#!/bin/bash
```

```
#####################################
# Author: Sebastiaan Tammer
# Version: v1.0.0
# Date: 2018-10-27
# Description: Example of a for loop in C-style syntax.
# Usage: ./for-counter.sh
#####################################

# This loop runs 10 times.
for ((counter=1; counter<=10; counter++)); do
  echo "Hello! This is loop number ${counter}."
  sleep 1
done

# After the for-loop finishes, print a goodbye message.
echo "All done, thanks for tuning in!"

reader@ubuntu:~/scripts/chapter_11$ bash for-counter.sh
Hello! This is loop number 1.
Hello! This is loop number 2.
Hello! This is loop number 3.
Hello! This is loop number 4.
Hello! This is loop number 5.
Hello! This is loop number 6.
Hello! This is loop number 7.
Hello! This is loop number 8.
Hello! This is loop number 9.
Hello! This is loop number 10.
All done, thanks for tuning in!
```

Again, due to the nature of off-by-one errors, we have to use slightly different numbers. Since the counter is incremented *at the end of the loop,* we need to start it at 1 instead of 0 (or we could have done the same in the while loop). In C-style syntax, <= means *smaller than or equal to,* and ++ means *increment by 1.* So, we have a counter that starts at 1, continues until it reaches 10, and is incremented by 1 for each run of the loop. We find this for loop preferable to the equivalent while loop; it needs less code and is more common in other scripting/programming languages.

Even better, there is a way to iterate over a number range (as we did for 1–10 previously), with the for loop Bash syntax as well. Because a number range is nothing more than a *list of numbers,* we can use almost the same syntax as we did in the first example, in which we iterated over a *list of words.* Take a look at the following code:

```
reader@ubuntu:~/scripts/chapter_11$ vim for-number-list.sh
reader@ubuntu:~/scripts/chapter_11$ cat for-number-list.sh
#!/bin/bash
```

```
####################################
# Author: Sebastiaan Tammer
# Version: v1.0.0
# Date: 2018-10-27
# Description: Example of a for loop with a number range.
# Usage: ./for-number-list.sh
####################################

# This loop runs 10 times.
for counter in {1..10}; do
  echo "Hello! This is loop number ${counter}."
  sleep 1
done

# After the for-loop finishes, print a goodbye message.
echo "All done, thanks for tuning in!"

reader@ubuntu:~/scripts/chapter_11$ bash for-number-list.sh
Hello! This is loop number 1.
Hello! This is loop number 2.
Hello! This is loop number 3.
Hello! This is loop number 4.
Hello! This is loop number 5.
Hello! This is loop number 6.
Hello! This is loop number 7.
Hello! This is loop number 8.
Hello! This is loop number 9.
Hello! This is loop number 10.
All done, thanks for tuning in!
```

So, the syntax for <variable> in <list> works with a list of {1..10}. This is called **brace expansion** and was added in Bash version 4. The syntax for brace expansion is quite simple:

```
{<starting value>..<ending value>}
```

Brace expansion can be used in many ways, but printing lists of numbers or characters is the most well-known:

```
reader@ubuntu:~/scripts/chapter_11$ echo {1..5}
1 2 3 4 5
reader@ubuntu:~/scripts/chapter_11$ echo {a..f}
a b c d e f
```

The brace expansion {1..5} returns the string 1 2 3 4 5, which is a whitespace delimited list of values and can thus be used in the Bash-style for loop! Alternatively, {a..f} prints the string a b c d e f. The range is actually determined by ASCII hexadecimal codes; this allows us to do the following as well:

```
reader@ubuntu:~/scripts/chapter_11$ echo {A..z}
A B C D E F G H I J K L M N O P Q R S T U V W X Y Z [ ] ^ _ ` a b c d e f
g h i j k l m n o p q r s t u v w x y z
```

It might seem weird that you'll see some special characters printed halfway, but those are in-between the uppercase and lowercase Latin alphabet characters. Note that this syntax is very similar to getting the value of a variable with ${variable} (however, that is parameter expansion and not brace expansion).

The brace expansion has one other interesting piece of functionality: it allows us to define the increment! Simply put, this allows us to tell Bash how many steps to skip each time we increment. The syntax for this is as follows:

```
{<starting value>..<ending value>..<increment>}
```

By default, the increment value is 1. If this is the desired functionality, we can omit the increment value, as we previously saw. If we do set it, however, we'll see something like the following:

```
reader@ubuntu:~/scripts/chapter_11$ echo {1..100..10}
1 11 21 31 41 51 61 71 81 91
reader@ubuntu:~/scripts/chapter_11$ echo {0..100..10}
0 10 20 30 40 50 60 70 80 90 100
```

Now, the increment is done in steps of 10. As you can see in the previous example, the <ending value> is considered *inclusive*. This means that values that are *lower or equal* will be printed, but others will not. The next value in the first brace expansion in the preceding example. {1..100..10}, would have been 101; since this is not lower or equal to 100, the value is not printed and the expansion is terminated.

Finally, since we promised that anything we could do with while we could also do with for, we'd like to end this part of the chapter by showing you how you would create an infinite loop with for. This is the most common reason to choose while over for, because the for syntax is a little weird:

```
eader@ubuntu:~/scripts/chapter_11$ vim for-infinite.sh
reader@ubuntu:~/scripts/chapter_11$ cat for-infinite.sh
#!/bin/bash
```

```
######################################
# Author: Sebastiaan Tammer
# Version: v1.0.0
# Date: 2018-10-27
# Description: Example of an infinite for loop.
# Usage: ./for-infinite.sh
######################################

# Infinite for loop.
for ((;;)); do
  echo "Hello!"
  sleep 1 # Wait for 1 second.
done

reader@ubuntu:~/scripts/chapter_11$ bash for-infinite.sh
Hello!
Hello!
Hello!
^C
```

We use the C-style syntax, but we omit the initialization, comparison, and incrementing of the counter. Therefore, it reads as follows:

for ((<nothing>;<no-comparison>;<no-increment>)); do

This ends up as `((;;));`, which only makes sense if you put it in the context of the normal syntax, as we did in the previous example. We could also just omit either the increment or the comparison to the same effect, but that would do the same thing with more code. Often, shorter is better, since it will be clearer.

Try to replicate the infinite `for` loop, but only by omitting a single value from the `for` clause. If you get that working, you'll be a step closer to understanding why you have now made it unending. If you need a little nudge, perhaps you'd want to echo the value of `counter` in the loop so that you can see what is happening. Or you could always run it with `bash -x`, of course!

Globbing and the for loop

Now, let's look at a few more practical examples. Most things you will do on Linux will deal with files (remember why?). Imagine that you have a bunch of log files sitting on the server and you'd like to perform some actions on them. If it is just a single action with a single command, you can most probably use a globbing pattern with that command (such as with `grep -i 'error' *.log`). However, imagine a situation where you want to collect log files that contain a certain phrase, or perhaps only the lines from those files. In this case, using a globbing pattern in combination with a `for` loop will allow us to perform many commands on many files, which we can find dynamically! Let's give it a go. Because this script will combine many of the lessons we've covered so far, we'll begin simple and expand it gradually:

```
reader@ubuntu:~/scripts/chapter_11$ vim for-globbing.sh
reader@ubuntu:~/scripts/chapter_11$ cat for-globbing.sh
#!/bin/bash

#####################################
# Author: Sebastiaan Tammer
# Version: v1.0.0
# Date: 2018-10-27
# Description: Combining globbing patterns in a for loop.
# Usage: ./for-globbing.sh
#####################################

# Create a list of log files.
for file in $(ls /var/log/*.log); do
  echo ${file}
done

reader@ubuntu:~/scripts/chapter_11$ bash for-globbing.sh
/var/log/alternatives.log
/var/log/auth.log
/var/log/bootstrap.log
/var/log/cloud-init.log
/var/log/cloud-init-output.log
/var/log/dpkg.log
/var/log/kern.log
```

By using the `$(ls /var/log/*.log)` construct, we can create a list of all files that end in `.log` that are found in the `/var/log/` directory. If you manually run the `ls /var/log/*.log` command, you will notice that the format is the same as the others we've seen when used in the Bash-style for syntax: single words, whitespace delimited. Because of this, we can now manipulate all of the files we found in order! Let's see what happens if we try to grep in these files:

```
reader@ubuntu:~/scripts/chapter_11$ cat for-globbing.sh
#!/bin/bash

######################################
# Author: Sebastiaan Tammer
# Version: v1.1.0
# Date: 2018-10-27
# Description: Combining globbing patterns in a for loop.
# Usage: ./for-globbing.sh
######################################

# Create a list of log files.
for file in $(ls /var/log/*.log); do
  echo "File: ${file}"
  grep -i 'error' ${file}
done
```

Since we changed the content of the script, we've upped the version from `v1.0.0` to `v1.1.0`. If you run this script now, you'll see that some of files return a positive match on the grep, while others do not:

```
reader@ubuntu:~/scripts/chapter_11$ bash for-globbing.sh
File: /var/log/alternatives.log
File: /var/log/auth.log
File: /var/log/bootstrap.log
Selecting previously unselected package libgpg-error0:amd64.
Preparing to unpack .../libgpg-error0_1.27-6_amd64.deb ...
Unpacking libgpg-error0:amd64 (1.27-6) ...
Setting up libgpg-error0:amd64 (1.27-6) ...
File: /var/log/cloud-init.log
File: /var/log/cloud-init-output.log
File: /var/log/dpkg.log
2018-04-26 19:07:33 install libgpg-error0:amd64 <none> 1.27-6
2018-04-26 19:07:33 status half-installed libgpg-error0:amd64 1.27-6
2018-04-26 19:07:33 status unpacked libgpg-error0:amd64 1.27-6
<SNIPPED>
File: /var/log/kern.log
Jun 30 18:20:32 ubuntu kernel: [    0.652108] RAS: Correctable Errors
collector initialized.
Jul  1 09:31:07 ubuntu kernel: [    0.656995] RAS: Correctable Errors
```

```
collector initialized.
Jul  1 09:42:00 ubuntu kernel: [    0.680300] RAS: Correctable Errors
collector initialized.
```

Great, so now we've accomplished the same thing with a complicated for loop that we could have also done directly with grep! Now, let's get our money's worth and do something with the files after we've determined that they contain the word error:

```
reader@ubuntu:~/scripts/chapter_11$ vim for-globbing.sh
reader@ubuntu:~/scripts/chapter_11$ cat for-globbing.sh
#!/bin/bash

#####################################
# Author: Sebastiaan Tammer
# Version: v1.2.0
# Date: 2018-10-27
# Description: Combining globbing patterns in a for loop.
# Usage: ./for-globbing.sh
#####################################

# Create a directory to store log files with errors.
ERROR_DIRECTORY='/tmp/error_logfiles/'
mkdir -p ${ERROR_DIRECTORY}

# Create a list of log files.
for file in $(ls /var/log/*.log); do
 grep --quiet -i 'error' ${file}

 # Check the return code for grep; if it is 0, file contains errors.
 if [[ $? -eq 0 ]]; then
 echo "${file} contains error(s), copying it to archive."
 cp ${file} ${ERROR_DIRECTORY} # Archive the file to another directory.
 fi

done

reader@ubuntu:~/scripts/chapter_11$ bash for-globbing.sh
/var/log/bootstrap.log contains error(s), copying it to archive.
/var/log/dpkg.log contains error(s), copying it to archive.
/var/log/kern.log contains error(s), copying it to archive.
```

The next version, v1.2.0, does a quiet `grep` (no output, since we just want the exit status of 0 when something is found). Directly after the `grep`, we use a nested `if-then` to copy the files to an archive directory that we defined at the beginning of the script. When we run the script now, we can see the same files that generated output in the previous version of the script, but now it copies the entire file. At this point, the `for` loop is proving its value: we're now doing multiple operations on a single file that was found with the globbing pattern. Let's take this one step further and remove all of the lines that do not contain an error from the archived files:

```
reader@ubuntu:~/scripts/chapter_11$ vim for-globbing.sh
reader@ubuntu:~/scripts/chapter_11$ cat for-globbing.sh
#!/bin/bash

######################################
# Author: Sebastiaan Tammer
# Version: v1.3.0
# Date: 2018-10-27
# Description: Combining globbing patterns in a for loop.
# Usage: ./for-globbing.sh
######################################

# Create a directory to store log files with errors.
ERROR_DIRECTORY='/tmp/error_logfiles/'
mkdir -p ${ERROR_DIRECTORY}

# Create a list of log files.
for file in $(ls /var/log/*.log); do
  grep --quiet -i 'error' ${file}

  # Check the return code for grep; if it is 0, file contains errors.
  if [[ $? -eq 0 ]]; then
    echo "${file} contains error(s), copying it to archive
${ERROR_DIRECTORY}."
    cp ${file} ${ERROR_DIRECTORY} # Archive the file to another directory.

    # Create the new file location variable with the directory and basename
of the file.
    file_new_location="${ERROR_DIRECTORY}$(basename ${file})"
    # In-place edit, only print lines matching 'error' or 'Error'.
    sed --quiet --in-place '/[Ee]rror/p' ${file_new_location}
  fi

done
```

Version v1.3.0! To keep it a little readable, we have not included error checking on the `cp` and `mkdir` commands. However, due to the nature of this script (creating a subdirectory in `/tmp/` and copying files there), the chance of issues there is very slim. We added two new interesting things: a new variable called `file_new_location` with the file name of the new location and `sed`, which ensures only the error lines remain in the archived files.

First, let's consider `file_new_location=${ERROR_DIRECTORY}$(basename ${file})`. What we're doing is pasting together two strings: first, the archive directory, followed by the *basename of the processed file*. The `basename` command strips the fully qualified path of a file, and only leaves the file name at the leaf of the path intact. If we were to look at the steps that Bash will undertake to resolve this new variable, it would probably look something like this:

- `file_new_location=${ERROR_DIRECTORY}$(basename ${file})`
  `-> resolve ${file}`
- `file_new_location=${ERROR_DIRECTORY}$(basename`
  `/var/log/bootstrap.log)`
  `-> resolve $(basename /var/log/bootstrap.log)`
- `file_new_location=${ERROR_DIRECTORY}bootstrap.log`
  `-> resolve ${ERROR_DIRECTORY}`
- `file_new_location=/tmp/error_logfiles/bootstrap.log`
  `-> done, final value of variable!`

With that out of the way, we can now run `sed` on that new file. The `sed --quiet --in-place '/[Ee]rror/p' ${file_new_location}` command simply replaces the content of the file with all lines that match the regular expression search pattern of `[Ee]rror`, which is (almost) what we initially grepped for. Remember, we need `--quiet` because, by default, `sed` prints all lines. If we were to omit this, we would end up with all of the lines in the file, but all of the error files would be duplicated: once from the non-quiet output of `sed`, and once from the search pattern match. However, with --quiet active, `sed` only prints the matching lines and writes those to the files. Let's see this in practice and verify the outcome:

```
reader@ubuntu:~/scripts/chapter_11$ bash for-globbing.sh
/var/log/bootstrap.log contains error(s), copying it to archive
/tmp/error_logfiles/.
/var/log/dpkg.log contains error(s), copying it to archive
/tmp/error_logfiles/.
/var/log/kern.log contains error(s), copying it to archive
/tmp/error_logfiles/.
reader@ubuntu:~/scripts/chapter_11$ ls /tmp/error_logfiles/
bootstrap.log  dpkg.log  kern.log
```

```
reader@ubuntu:~/scripts/chapter_11$ head -3 /tmp/error_logfiles/*
==> /tmp/error_logfiles/bootstrap.log <==
Selecting previously unselected package libgpg-error0:amd64.
Preparing to unpack .../libgpg-error0_1.27-6_amd64.deb ...
Unpacking libgpg-error0:amd64 (1.27-6) ...

==> /tmp/error_logfiles/dpkg.log <==
2018-04-26 19:07:33 install libgpg-error0:amd64 <none> 1.27-6
2018-04-26 19:07:33 status half-installed libgpg-error0:amd64 1.27-6
2018-04-26 19:07:33 status unpacked libgpg-error0:amd64 1.27-6

==> /tmp/error_logfiles/kern.log <==
Jun 30 18:20:32 ubuntu kernel: [    0.652108] RAS: Correctable Errors
collector initialized.
Jul  1 09:31:07 ubuntu kernel: [    0.656995] RAS: Correctable Errors
collector initialized.
Jul  1 09:42:00 ubuntu kernel: [    0.680300] RAS: Correctable Errors
collector initialized.
```

As you can see, the three lines at the top of each file all contain the `error` or `Error` string. Actually, all of the lines in all of those files contained either of those strings; be sure to verify this on your own system since the content will undoubtedly be different.

Now that we've finished this example, we have a few challenges for the reader, should you like to take them on:

- Make this script accept input. This could be the archive directory, the path glob, the search pattern, or even all three!
- Make this script more robust by adding exception handling to commands that *could* fail.
- Invert the functionality of this script, by using the `sed '/xxx/d'` syntax (hint: you'll probably need redirection for this).

 While this example should illustrate a lot of things, we realize that just searching on the word `error` does not actually only return errors. Actually, most of what we saw being returned was related to an installed package, `liberror`! In practice, you might be working with log files that have a predefined structure when it comes to errors. In this case, it is much easier to determine a search pattern that only logs real errors.

Loop control

At this point, you should feel comfortable with using `while` and `for` loops. There is one more, rather important, topic to discuss with regards to loops: **loop control**. Loop control is a generic term, for anything that you do to, well, control the loop! However, there are two *keywords* that we'll need if we want to unleash the full power of loops: `break` and `continue`. We'll start with `break`.

Breaking the loop

For some scripting logic, it will prove necessary to break out of the loop. You might imagine that, in one of your scripts, you are waiting for something to finish. As soon as that happens, you want to *do something*. Waiting and periodically checking inside a `while true` loop could be an option for this, but if you recall in the `while-interactive.sh` script, we exited on the successful answer to the riddle. On an exit, we cannot run any more commands that are outside of the `while` loop! This is where `break` comes into play. It allows us to exit the *loop*, but continue the *script*. First, let's update `while-interactive.sh` to make use of this loop control keyword:

```
reader@ubuntu:~/scripts/chapter_11$ vim while-interactive.sh
reader@ubuntu:~/scripts/chapter_11$ cat while-interactive.sh
#!/bin/bash

####################################
# Author: Sebastiaan Tammer
# Version: v1.1.0
# Date: 2018-10-28
# Description: A simple riddle in a while loop.
# Usage: ./while-interactive.sh
####################################

# Infinite loop, only exits on correct answer.
while true; do
  read -p "I have keys but no locks. I have a space but no room. You can
enter, but can't go outside. What am I? " answer
  if [[ ${answer} =~ [Kk]eyboard ]]; then # Use regular expression so 'a
keyboard' or 'Keyboard' is also a valid answer.
    echo "Correct, congratulations!"
    break # Exit the while loop.
  else
    # Print an error message and go back into the loop.
    echo "Incorrect, please try again."
  fi
```

```
done

# This will run after the break in the while loop.
echo "Now we can continue after the while loop is done, awesome!"
```

We made three changes:

- Adopted a higher version number
- Replaced `exit 0` with `break`
- Added a simple `echo` after the while loop

When we still had `exit 0` in place, the final `echo` would never have run (but don't trust us, be sure to verify this yourself!). Now, run it with `break` and watch:

```
reader@ubuntu:~/scripts/chapter_11$ bash while-interactive.sh
I have keys but no locks. I have a space but no room. You can enter, but
can't go outside. What am I? keyboard
Correct, congratulations!
Now we can continue after the while loop is done, awesome!
```

There we go, code execution after a broken `while` loop. Often, after an infinite loop, there is definitely other code that needs to be executed, and this is the way to do it.

We can use `break` not only in a `while` loop, but most certainly in a `for` loop. The following example shows how we can use `break` in a `for` loop:

```
reader@ubuntu:~/scripts/chapter_11$ vim for-loop-control.sh
reader@ubuntu:~/scripts/chapter_11$ cat for-loop-control.sh
#!/bin/bash

#####################################
# Author: Sebastiaan Tammer
# Version: v1.0.0
# Date: 2018-10-28
# Description: Loop control in a for loop.
# Usage: ./for-loop-control.sh
#####################################

# Generate a random number from 1-10.
random_number=$(( ( RANDOM % 10 ) + 1 ))

# Iterate over all possible random numbers.
for number in {1..10}; do
  if [[ ${number} -eq ${random_number} ]]; then
    echo "Random number found: ${number}."
    break # As soon as we have found the number, stop.
  fi
```

```
    # If we get here the number did not match.
    echo "Number does not match: ${number}."
  done
echo "Number has been found, all done."
```

At the top of this script's functionality, a random number between 1 and 10 is determined (don't worry about the syntax). Next, we iterate over the numbers 1 through 10 and for each number, we'll check if it's equal to the randomly generated number. If it is, we print a success message *and we break the loop*. Otherwise, we're going outside of the `if-then` block and printing the failure message. If we did not include the break statement, the output would look like this:

```
reader@ubuntu:~/scripts/chapter_11$ bash for-loop-control.sh
Number does not match: 1.
Number does not match: 2.
Number does not match: 3.
Random number found: 4.
Number does not match: 4.
Number does not match: 5.
Number does not match: 6.
Number does not match: 7.
Number does not match: 8.
Number does not match: 9.
Number does not match: 10.
Number has been found, all done.
```

Not only do we see the number printed as both matching and non-matching (which is a logical error, of course), but the script also continues checking all other numbers when we're certain that those will not match. Now, if we used exit instead of break, the final statement will never be printed:

```
reader@ubuntu:~/scripts/chapter_11$ bash for-loop-control.sh
Number does not match: 1.
Number does not match: 2.
Number does not match: 3.
Number does not match: 4.
Number does not match: 5.
Number does not match: 6.
Random number found: 7.
```

Only by using `break` will we get exactly the amount of output we need; nothing more and nothing less. You might have seen that we could have also used an `else` clause for the `Number does not match:` message. Still, nothing would be stopping the program. So even if the random number was found on the first try (which will happen, eventually), it will still compare all of the values in the list until it reaches the end of that list.

Not only is this a waste of time and resources, but imagine the output if the random number was somewhere between 1 and 1,000,000! Just remember: if you're done with the loop, **break out of it.**

The continue keyword

As with most things in Bash (and life), there is a Yang to the Yin that is `break`: the `continue` keyword. If you use continue, you're telling the loop to stop the current loop, but *continue* with the next run. So, instead of stopping the entire loop, you'll just stop the current iteration. Let's see if another example can make this clear:

```
reader@ubuntu:~/scripts/chapter_11$ vim for-continue.sh
reader@ubuntu:~/scripts/chapter_11$ cat for-continue.sh
#!/bin/bash

#####################################
# Author: Sebastiaan Tammer
# Version: v1.0.0
# Date: 2018-10-28
# Description: For syntax with a continue.
# Usage: ./for-continue.sh
#####################################

# Look at numbers 1-20, in steps of 2.
for number in {1..20..2}; do
  if [[ $((${number}%5)) -eq 0 ]]; then
    continue # Unlucky number, skip this!
  fi

  # Show the user which number we've processed.
  echo "Looking at number: ${number}."

done
```

In this example, all of the numbers that can be divided cleanly by 5 are considered unlucky and should not be processed. This is achieved by the `[[ $((${number}%5)) -eq 0 ]]` condition:

- **[[$(($\{number\}%5)) -eq 0]]** -> test syntax
- [[**$(($\{number\}%5))** -eq 0]] -> arithmetic syntax
- [[$((**$\{number\}**%5)) -eq 0]] -> modulo 5 of the variable **number**

If the number passes this test (and is thus cleanly divisible by 5, such as 5, 10, 15, 20, and so on), continue is executed. When this happens, the next iteration of the loop is run (and echo is **NOT** executed!), as can be seen when running this script:

```
reader@ubuntu:~/scripts/chapter_11$ bash for-continue.sh
Looking at number: 1.
Looking at number: 3.
Looking at number: 7.
Looking at number: 9.
Looking at number: 11.
Looking at number: 13.
Looking at number: 17.
Looking at number: 19.
```

As the list should imply, the numbers 5, 10, and 15 are processed, but we do not see them in echo. We can also see everything after, which would not have happened with break. Verify if this is actually happening with bash -x (warning: loads of output!) and check what happens if you replace continue with break or even exit.

Loop control and nesting

For the final part of this chapter, we'd like to show you how you can influence nested loops with loop control as well. Both break and continue will take an extra argument: a number that specified which loop to break out of. By default, if this argument is omitted, it is assumed to be 1. So, the break command is equal to break 1, and continue 1 is the same as continue. As stated before, we can theoretically nest our loops as deep as we want; you're likely to hit logical issues a lot earlier than problems with the technical capabilities of your modern system! We'll look at a simple example that shows us how we can use a break 2 to not only break out of a for loop, but out of the outer while loop as well:

```
reader@ubuntu:~/scripts/chapter_11$ vim break-x.sh
reader@ubuntu:~/scripts/chapter_11$ cat break-x.sh
#!/bin/bash

####################################
# Author: Sebastiaan Tammer
# Version: v1.0.0
# Date: 2018-10-28
# Description: Breaking out of nested loops.
# Usage: ./break-x.sh
####################################

while true; do
```

```
     echo "This is the outer loop."
     sleep 1

     for iteration in {1..3}; do
       echo "This is inner loop ${iteration}."
       sleep 1
     done
done
echo "This is the end of the script, thanks for playing!"
```

This first version of the script does not contain `break`. When we run this, we never see the final message and we get an endless repeating pattern:

```
reader@ubuntu:~/scripts/chapter_11$ bash break-x.sh
This is the outer loop.
This is inner loop 1.
This is inner loop 2.
This is inner loop 3.
This is the outer loop.
This is inner loop 1.
^C
```

Now, let's break the inner loop when the iteration hits 2:

```
reader@ubuntu:~/scripts/chapter_11$ vim break-x.sh
reader@ubuntu:~/scripts/chapter_11$ cat break-x.sh
#!/bin/bash

#####################################
# Author: Sebastiaan Tammer
# Version: v1.1.0
# Date: 2018-10-28
# Description: Breaking out of nested loops.
# Usage: ./break-x.sh
#####################################
<SNIPPED>
   for iteration in {1..3}; do
     echo "This is inner loop ${iteration}."
     if [[ ${iteration} -eq 2 ]]; then
       break 1
     fi
     sleep 1
   done
<SNIPPED>
```

When we run the script now, we still get infinite loops, but we're cutting the inner for loop short after two iterations instead of three:

```
reader@ubuntu:~/scripts/chapter_11$ bash break-x.sh
This is the outer loop.
This is inner loop 1.
This is inner loop 2.
This is the outer loop.
This is inner loop 1.
^C
```

Now, let's instruct the inner loop to break out of the outer loop by using the `break 2` command:

```
reader@ubuntu:~/scripts/chapter_11$ vim break-x.sh
reader@ubuntu:~/scripts/chapter_11$ cat break-x.sh
#!/bin/bash

####################################
# Author: Sebastiaan Tammer
# Version: v1.2.0
# Date: 2018-10-28
# Description: Breaking out of nested loops.
# Usage: ./break-x.sh
####################################
<SNIPPED>
    if [[ ${iteration} -eq 2 ]]; then
        break 2 # Break out of the outer while-true loop.
    fi
<SNIPPED>
```

Behold, an inner loop breaking out of an outer loop successfully:

```
reader@ubuntu:~/scripts/chapter_11$ bash break-x.sh
This is the outer loop.
This is inner loop 1.
This is inner loop 2.
This is the end of the script, thanks for playing!
```

There we go, full control over our loops, even when we nest as many as we need for our scripting needs. The same theory applies to `continue` as well. If, in this example, we use `continue 2` instead of `break 2`, we would still get an infinite loop (since while true never ends). However, if your other loop was also a `for` or a non-infinite `while` loop (which, in our experience, is more common but does not make for a great simple example), `continue 2` could allow you to execute exactly the logic that the situation desires.

Summary

This chapter was dedicated to conditional testing and scripting loops. Since we had already discussed the `if-then-else` statements, we recapped on this information before going on to showing more advanced uses of the conditional testing toolkit. This advanced information included using regular expressions, which we learned about in the previous chapter, within a conditional testing scenario to allow for more flexible tests. We also showed you how multiple conditions can be tested sequentially, using `elif` (short for `else if`). We explained how multiple `if-then-else` statements can be nested to create advanced logic.

In the second part of this chapter, we introduced the `while` loop. We showed you how we can use this to create a script that will run indefinitely, or how we can use conditions to stop the loop when a certain criteria has been met. We presented the `until` keyword, which has the same functionality as `while` but allows for negative checking instead of positive for `while`. We ended the explanation on `while` by showing you how an interactive script can be created in an unending `while` loop (using our old friend `read`).

After `while`, we introduced the more powerful `for` loop. This loop can do the same things `while` can, but often the shorter syntax allows us to write less code (and more readable code, which is still a very important aspect in scripting!). We showed you how `for` can iterate over a list, and how we can create a list of numbers using *brace expansion*. We ended our discussion on `for` loops by giving a practical example of combining `for` with file globbing patterns to allow us to dynamically find, grab, and process files.

We ended this chapter by explaining loop control, which is achieved in Bash with the `break` and `continue` keywords. These keywords allows us to *break* out of a loop (even from nested loops, as far back outside as we need), and also allow us to stop the current iteration of the loop and *continue* to the next iteration.

The following commands/keywords were introduced in this chapter: `elif`, `help`, `while`, `sleep`, `for`, `basename`, `break`, and `continue`.

Questions

1. How does an `if-then(-else)` statement end?
2. How can we use regular expression search patterns in a conditional evaluation?
3. Why do we need the `elif` keyword?
4. What is *nesting*?
5. How can we get information about how to use shell builtins and keywords?
6. What is the opposite keyword of `while`?
7. Why would we choose the for loop over the `while` loop?
8. What is brace expansion and on which characters can we use it?
9. Which two keywords allow us to have more granular control over loops?
10. If we are nesting loops, how can we employ loop control to influence outer loops from an inner loop?

Further reading

The following resources might be interesting if you'd like to go deeper into the subjects of this chapter:

- **The case statement**: http://tldp.org/LDP/Bash-Beginners-Guide/html/sect_07_03.html
- **Brace expansions**: http://wiki.bash-hackers.org/syntax/expansion/brace
- **The Linux Documentation Project on loops**: http://www.tldp.org/LDP/abs/html/loops1.html

12
Using Pipes and Redirection in Scripts

In this chapter, we'll explain a very important aspect of Bash: *redirection*. We'll start by describing the different types of input and output redirections, and how they are related to Linux file descriptors. After the basics of redirection are covered, we will continue with some advanced uses.

Next up are *pipes*, which is a concept used heavily within shell scripting. We present a few practical examples of pipes. Finally, we show how *here documents* work, which also have some great uses.

The following commands will be introduced in this chapter: `diff`, `gcc`, `fallocate`, `tr`, `chpasswd`, `tee`, and `bc`.

The following topics will be covered in this chapter:

- Input/output redirection
- Pipes
- Here documents

Technical requirements

All scripts for this chapter can be found on GitHub at the following link: `https://github.com/tammert/learn-linux-shell-scripting/tree/master/chapter_12`. For all other exercises, your Ubuntu 18.04 virtual machine is still your best friend.

Input/output redirection

In this chapter, we will discuss redirection in Linux in detail.

Simply put, redirection is pretty much exactly as the word implies: the redirecting of *something* to *something else*. For example, we've already seen that we can use the output of one command as the input for the next command, using pipes. Pipes are implemented in Linux using the | sign.

However, that might raise the question: how does Linux deal with input and output in the first place? We'll begin our journey into redirection with some theory on **file descriptors**, which are what make all redirection possible!

File descriptors

You might be tired of hearing it, but it is still no less true: in Linux, everything is a file. We've seen that a file is a file, a directory is a file, even hard disks are files; but now, we'll take this one step further: your keyboard, which you use for *input*, is also a file!

Complementary to that, your Terminal, which commands use as *output*, is, guess what: a file.

You can find these files, as with most special files, within your Linux filesystem tree. Let's check our virtual machine:

```
reader@ubuntu:~$ cd /dev/fd/
reader@ubuntu:/dev/fd$ ls -l
total 0
lrwx------ 1 reader reader 64 Nov  5 18:54 0 -> /dev/pts/0
lrwx------ 1 reader reader 64 Nov  5 18:54 1 -> /dev/pts/0
lrwx------ 1 reader reader 64 Nov  5 18:54 2 -> /dev/pts/0
lrwx------ 1 reader reader 64 Nov  5 18:54 255 -> /dev/pts/0
```

Out of the four files we find here, three are important: /dev/fd/0, /dev/fd/1, and /dev/fd/2.

As you might suspect from the heading of this text, **fd** stands for **file descriptor**. These file descriptors are used internally to bind input and output from and to the user to a Terminal. You can actually see how this is done with the file descriptors: they are symbolically linked to /dev/pts/0.

In this instance, **pts** stands for **pseudo Terminal slave**, which is the definition given to SSH connections. Look at what happens when we look at `/dev/fd` from three different locations:

```
# SSH connection 1
reader@ubuntu:~/scripts/chapter_12$ ls -l /dev/fd/
total 0
lrwx------ 1 reader reader 64 Nov  5 19:06 0 -> /dev/pts/0
lrwx------ 1 reader reader 64 Nov  5 19:06 1 -> /dev/pts/0
lrwx------ 1 reader reader 64 Nov  5 19:06 2 -> /dev/pts/0

# SSH connection 2
reader@ubuntu:/dev/fd$ ls -l
total 0
lrwx------ 1 reader reader 64 Nov  5 18:54 0 -> /dev/pts/1
lrwx------ 1 reader reader 64 Nov  5 18:54 1 -> /dev/pts/1
lrwx------ 1 reader reader 64 Nov  5 18:54 2 -> /dev/pts/1

# Virtual machine terminal
reader@ubuntu:/dev/fd$ ls -l
total 0
lrwx------ 1 reader reader 64 Nov  5 19:08 0 -> /dev/tty/1
lrwx------ 1 reader reader 64 Nov  5 19:08 1 -> /dev/tty/1
lrwx------ 1 reader reader 64 Nov  5 19:08 2 -> /dev/tty/1
```

Each of these connections has their own `/dev/` mount (which is of `udev` type, stored in memory), which is why we do not see output from one connection into the other one.

Now, we've been talking about input and output. But, as you have no doubt seen, there are three file descriptors allocated in the preceding examples. In a Linux (or Unix/Unix-like system), there are three default **streams** which are exposed by default through file descriptors:

- The *standard input* stream, `stdin`, by default bound to `/dev/fd/0`
- The *standard output* stream, `stdout`, by default bound to `/dev/fd/1`
- The *standard error* stream, `stderr`, by default bound to `/dev/fd/2`

As far as these three streams go, `stdin` and `stdout` should be rather straightforward: input and output. However, as you might have deduced, output is actually split into *normal* output and *error* output. Normal output is sent to the `stdout` file descriptor, while error output is often sent to `stderr`.

Since both of these are symbolically linked to the Terminal, you will see them there no matter what. However, as we will see later on in this chapter, as soon as we start redirecting, this difference becomes important.

You might see some other file descriptors, such as the 255 in the first example. Besides their use in supplying input and output to the Terminal, file descriptors are also used when Linux opens a file in the filesystem. This other use of file descriptors is outside of the scope for this book; we have, however, included a link in the *Further reading* section for those interested.

In a normal interaction, text you type in a Terminal gets written to stdin on /dev/fd/0, which a command can read. Using that input, the command usually does something (otherwise, we wouldn't need the command!) and writes the output to stdout or stderr. where it will be read by the Terminal for display to you. So in short:

- A *Terminal* **writes** to stdin and **reads** from stdout or stderr
- A *command* **reads** from stdin and **writes** to stdout or stderr

Besides the file descriptors Linux uses internally, there are also a few file descriptors reserved for when you want to create really advanced scripts; these are 3 through 9. Any others *might* be used by the system, but these are guaranteed free for your use. As this is, as stated, very advanced and not used too often, we will not go into detail. However, we've found some further reading which might be interesting, which is included at the end of this chapter.

Redirecting output

Now that the theory on input, output, and file descriptors should be clear, we're going to see how we can use these techniques in our command-line and scripting adventures.

It is in fact pretty hard to write shell scripts without using redirection; we've actually used redirection a couple of times in the book before this chapter, because we really needed it to get our stuff done at that time (file-create.sh in Chapter 8, *Variables and User Input*, for example).

Now, let's get some real experience with redirection out of the way!

stdout

Most output from commands will be *standard output*, written to stdout on /dev/fd/1. By using the > symbol, we can redirect this out with the following syntax:

```
command > output-file
```

A redirect will always be made to a file (however, as we know, not all files are equal, so after the regular examples, we'll show you some Bash magic where non-regular files are concerned). If the file does not exist, it will be created. If it does exist, it will be **overwritten**.

In its simplest form, everything that would normally be printed to your Terminal can be redirected to a file:

```
reader@ubuntu:~/scripts/chapter_12$ ls -l /var/log/dpkg.log
-rw-r--r-- 1 root root 737150 Nov  5 18:49 /var/log/dpkg.log
reader@ubuntu:~/scripts/chapter_12$ cat /var/log/dpkg.log > redirected-
file.log
reader@ubuntu:~/scripts/chapter_12$ ls -l
total 724
-rw-rw-r-- 1 reader reader 737150 Nov  5 19:45 redirected-file.log
```

As you know, `cat` prints the whole file content to your Terminal. In reality, it actually sends the whole content to `stdout`, which is bound to `/dev/fd/1`, which is bound to your Terminal; this is why you see it.

Now, if we redirect the content of the file back to another file, we've essentially made a great effort to... copy a file! From the file sizes you can see that it is actually the same file. If you're unsure, you can use the `diff` command to see if the files are the same:

```
reader@ubuntu:~/scripts/chapter_12$ diff /var/log/dpkg.log redirected-
file.log
reader@ubuntu:~/scripts/chapter_12$ echo $?
0
```

If `diff` does not return any output, and it has an exit code of 0, there are no differences in the file.

Back to the redirection example. We used > to redirect the output to the file. In reality, > is shorthand for 1>. You might recognize this 1: it refers to the file descriptor `/dev/fd/1`. As we'll see when we're dealing with `stderr`, which is on `/dev/fd/2`, we will use 2> instead of 1> or >.

First, however, let's build a simple script to illustrate this a little bit further:

```
reader@ubuntu:~/scripts/chapter_12$ vim redirect-to-file.sh
reader@ubuntu:~/scripts/chapter_12$ cat redirect-to-file.sh
#!/bin/bash

#####################################
# Author: Sebastiaan Tammer
# Version: v1.0.0
# Date: 2018-11-05
```

```
# Description: Redirect user input to file.
# Usage: ./redirect-to-file.sh
######################################

# Capture the users' input.
read -p "Type anything you like: " user_input

# Save the users' input to a file.
echo ${user_input} > redirect-to-file.txt
```

Now, when we run this, read will prompt us to input some text. This will be saved in the user_input variable. Then, we'll use echo to send the content of the user_input variable to stdout. But, instead of it reaching the Terminal on /dev/pts/0 via /dev/fd/1, we redirect it to the redirect-to-file.txt file.

All in all, it looks something like this:

```
reader@ubuntu:~/scripts/chapter_12$ bash redirect-to-file.sh
Type anything you like: I like dogs! And cats. Maybe a gecko?
reader@ubuntu:~/scripts/chapter_12$ ls -l
total 732
-rw-rw-r-- 1 reader reader 737150 Nov  5 19:45 redirected-file.log
-rw-rw-r-- 1 reader reader    383 Nov  5 19:58 redirect-to-file.sh
-rw-rw-r-- 1 reader reader     38 Nov  5 19:58 redirect-to-file.txt
reader@ubuntu:~/scripts/chapter_12$ cat redirect-to-file.txt
I like dogs! And cats. Maybe a gecko?
```

Now, this works as advertised. However, if we run it again, we see two things that can go wrong with this script:

```
reader@ubuntu:~/scripts$ bash chapter_12/redirect-to-file.sh
Type anything you like: Hello
reader@ubuntu:~/scripts$ ls -l
<SNIPPED>
drwxrwxr-x 2 reader reader 4096 Nov  5 19:58 chapter_12
-rw-rw-r-- 1 reader reader    6 Nov  5 20:02 redirect-to-file.txt
reader@ubuntu:~/scripts$ bash chapter_12/redirect-to-file.sh
Type anything you like: Bye
reader@ubuntu:~/scripts$ ls -l
<SNIPPED>
drwxrwxr-x 2 reader reader 4096 Nov  5 19:58 chapter_12
-rw-rw-r-- 1 reader reader    4 Nov  5 20:02 redirect-to-file.txt
```

The first thing that goes wrong, which we've warned about before, is that relative paths might mess up where the file is written.

You might have envisioned that the file was created right next to the script; this will only happen if your *current working directory* is in the directory where the script is. Because we call it from lower in the tree, the output is written there (since that is the current working directory).

The other problem is that each time we type something in, we remove the old content of the file! After we type `Hello`, we see that the file is six bytes (one byte for each character, plus a newline), and after we typed `Bye`, we now see that the file is only four bytes (three characters plus the newline).

This might be the desired behavior, but more often than not it is much nicer if the output is *appended* to the file, instead of replacing it.

Let's solve both issues in a new version of the script:

```
reader@ubuntu:~/scripts$ vim chapter_12/redirect-to-file.sh
reader@ubuntu:~/scripts$ cat chapter_12/redirect-to-file.sh
#!/bin/bash

######################################
# Author: Sebastiaan Tammer
# Version: v1.1.0
# Date: 2018-11-05
# Description: Redirect user input to file.
# Usage: ./redirect-to-file.sh
######################################

# Since we're dealing with paths, set current working directory.
cd $(dirname $0)

# Capture the users' input.
read -p "Type anything you like: " user_input

# Save the users' input to a file. > for overwrite, >> for append.
echo ${user_input} >> redirect-to-file.txt
```

Now, if we run it (from wherever), we'll see that new text gets appended to the first sentence, I like dogs! And cats. Maybe a gecko? in the /home/reader/chapter_12/redirect-to-file.txt file:

```
reader@ubuntu:~/scripts$ cd /tmp/
reader@ubuntu:/tmp$ cat /home/reader/scripts/chapter_12/redirect-to-
file.txt
I like dogs! And cats. Maybe a gecko?
reader@ubuntu:/tmp$ bash /home/reader/scripts/chapter_12/redirect-to-
file.sh
```

```
Type anything you like: Definitely a gecko, those things are awesome!
reader@ubuntu:/tmp$ cat /home/reader/scripts/chapter_12/redirect-to-
file.txt
I like dogs! And cats. Maybe a gecko?
Definitely a gecko, those things are awesome!
```

So, `cd $(dirname $0)` helped us with our relative paths, and a >> instead of > ensured appending instead of overwriting. As you might expect, >> is again short for 1>>, as we will see when we start redirecting `stderr` streams in a bit.

A little while back, we promised you some Bash magic. While not exactly magic, it might hurt your head just a little:

```
reader@ubuntu:~/scripts/chapter_12$ cat redirect-to-file.txt
I like dogs! And cats. Maybe a gecko?
Definitely a gecko, those things are awesome!
reader@ubuntu:~/scripts/chapter_12$ cat redirect-to-file.txt > /dev/pts/0
I like dogs! And cats. Maybe a gecko?
Definitely a gecko, those things are awesome!
reader@ubuntu:~/scripts/chapter_12$ cat redirect-to-file.txt > /dev/fd/1
I like dogs! And cats. Maybe a gecko?
Definitely a gecko, those things are awesome!
reader@ubuntu:~/scripts/chapter_12$ cat redirect-to-file.txt > /dev/fd/2
I like dogs! And cats. Maybe a gecko?
Definitely a gecko, those things are awesome!
```

So, we've managed to print our file using `cat` a total of four times. We could have done that with `for` as well, you might be thinking, but the lesson is not the amount of times we printed the message, but how we did it!

First, we just used `cat`; nothing special there. Next, we used `cat` in combination with a redirection of `stdout` to `/dev/pts/0`, our Terminal. Again, the message is printed.

The third and fourth times, we sent the redirected `stdout` of `cat` to `/dev/fd/1` and `/dev/fd/2`. Since these are symlinked to `/dev/pts/0`, it's not really surprising that these also end up on our Terminal.

How then do we actually differentiate between `stdout` and `stderr`?

stderr

If you were confused by the preceding example, that was probably because you misunderstood the flow that stderr messages take (and we don't blame you, we confused ourselves there!). While we sent the output of the cat command to /dev/fd/2, we used >, which sends stdout and not stderr.

So in our example, we just abused the stderr file descriptor to print to the Terminal; bad practice. We promise not to do it again. Now then, how can we *actually* work with stderr messages?

```
reader@ubuntu:/tmp$ cat /root/
cat: /root/: Permission denied
reader@ubuntu:/tmp$ cat /root/ 1> error-file
cat: /root/: Permission denied
reader@ubuntu:/tmp$ ls -l
-rw-rw-r-- 1 reader reader    0 Nov  5 20:35 error-file
reader@ubuntu:/tmp$ cat /root/ 2> error-file
reader@ubuntu:/tmp$ ls -l
-rw-rw-r-- 1 reader reader   31 Nov  5 20:35 error-file
reader@ubuntu:/tmp$ cat error-file
cat: /root/: Permission denied
```

This interaction should illustrate some things. First, when cat /root/ throws a Permission denied error, it sends it to stderr instead of stdout. We can see this, because when we do the same command but we try to redirect the *standard output* with 1> error-file, we still see the output *in the Terminal* and we also see that error-file is empty.

When instead we use 2> error-file, which redirects stderr instead of regular stdout, we do not see the error message in our Terminal anymore.

Even better, we now see that error-file has 31 bytes of content, and when we print it with cat, we once again see our redirected error message! As mentioned before, and in the same spirit as 1>>, if you'd like to *append* instead of *overwrite* the stderr stream to a file, use 2>>.

Now, because it is hard to find a command that prints both stdout and stderr in the same command, we'll create our own: a very simple C program which prints two lines of text, one to stdout and one to stderr.

As a sneak preview into programming and compiling, look at this (don't worry if you don't fully understand this):

```
reader@ubuntu:~/scripts/chapter_12$ vim stderr.c
reader@ubuntu:~/scripts/chapter_12$ cat stderr.c
#include <stdio.h>
int main()
{
  // Print messages to stdout and stderr.
  fprintf(stdout, "This is sent to stdout.\n");
  fprintf(stderr, "This is sent to stderr.\n");
  return 0;
}

reader@ubuntu:~/scripts/chapter_12$ gcc stderr.c -o stderr
reader@ubuntu:~/scripts/chapter_12$ ls -l
total 744
-rw-rw-r-- 1 reader reader 737150 Nov  5 19:45 redirected-file.log
-rw-rw-r-- 1 reader reader    501 Nov  5 20:09 redirect-to-file.sh
-rw-rw-r-- 1 reader reader     84 Nov  5 20:13 redirect-to-file.txt
-rwxrwxr-x 1 reader reader   8392 Nov  5 20:46 stderr
-rw-rw-r-- 1 reader reader    185 Nov  5 20:46 stderr.c
```

The `gcc stderr.c -o stderr` command compiles the source code found in `stderr.c` to the binary `stderr`.

`gcc` is the GNU Compiler Collection, and is not always installed by default. If you want to follow along with this example and you're getting an error about not being able to find `gcc`, install it using `sudo apt install gcc -y`.

If we run our program, we get two lines of output. Because this is not a Bash script, we cannot execute it with `bash stderr`. We need to make the binary executable with `chmod`, and run it with `./stderr`:

```
reader@ubuntu:~/scripts/chapter_12$ bash stderr
stderr: stderr: cannot execute binary file
reader@ubuntu:~/scripts/chapter_12$ chmod +x stderr
reader@ubuntu:~/scripts/chapter_12$ ./stderr
This is sent to stdout.
This is sent to stderr.
```

Now, let's see what happens when we start redirecting part of this output:

```
reader@ubuntu:~/scripts/chapter_12$ ./stderr > /tmp/stdout
This is sent to stderr.
reader@ubuntu:~/scripts/chapter_12$ cat /tmp/stdout
This is sent to stdout.
```

Because we only redirected `stdout` (last reminder: > equals 1>) to the fully-qualified file `/tmp/stdout`, the `stderr` message was still printed to the Terminal.

The other way around gives similar results:

```
reader@ubuntu:~/scripts/chapter_12$ ./stderr 2> /tmp/stderr
This is sent to stdout.
reader@ubuntu:~/scripts/chapter_12$ cat /tmp/stderr
This is sent to stderr.
```

Now, when we only redirect `stderr` using `2> /tmp/stderr`, we see the `stdout` message appear in our Terminal and the `stderr` is correctly redirected to the `/tmp/stderr` file.

I'm sure you're asking yourself this question right now: how can we redirect **all output**, both `stdout` and `stderr`, to a file? If this was a book about Bash 3.x, we'd be having a difficult conversation. That conversation would entail us redirecting `stderr` to `stdout`, after which we could use > to send all output (because we already diverted `stderr` to `stdout` in the first place) to a single file.

Even though that is the logical way to do it, the redirection of `stderr` to `stdout` is actually present at the end of the command. The command ends up like this: `./stderr > /tmp/output 2>&1`. Not *too complex*, but hard enough that you never really remember it in one go (you can trust us on this).

Fortunately, in Bash 4.x we have a new redirection command available to us that can do the same thing, but in a much more understandable fashion: `&>`.

Redirect all output

In most situations, output that is sent to `stderr` instead of `stdout` will contain words that make it clear you're dealing with an error. This will include examples such as `permission denied`, `cannot execute binary file`, `syntax error near unexpected token`, and so on.

Because of this, it is often not really necessary to split output into `stdout` and `stderr` (but, obviously, sometimes it will be great functionality). In these cases, the addition to Bash 4.x that allows us to redirect both `stdout` and `stderr` with a single command is perfect. This redirection, which you can use with the syntax `&>`, does not work differently to the earlier examples we have seen.

Let's review our previous example and see how this makes our lives easier:

```
reader@ubuntu:~/scripts/chapter_12$ ./stderr
This is sent to stdout.
This is sent to stderr.
reader@ubuntu:~/scripts/chapter_12$ ./stderr &> /tmp/output
reader@ubuntu:~/scripts/chapter_12$ cat /tmp/output
This is sent to stderr.
This is sent to stdout.
```

Excellent! With this syntax, we no longer have to worry about the different output streams. This is especially practical when working with commands that are new to you; in this case, you might miss interesting error messages because they got lost when the stderr stream is not saved.

At the risk of sounding repetitive, the syntax for appending both stdout and stderr to a file is again an extra >: &>>.

Go ahead and try it out with the previous example. We won't print it here, because it should be obvious by now how this works.

Unsure about whether to redirect all output, or just stdout or stderr? Our advice: start with redirecting **both** to the same file. If in your use case this gives too much noise (either masking errors or normal log messages), you could always decide to redirect either of them to a file, and get the other printed in your Terminal. Often, in practice, stderr messages need the context provided by stdout messages to make sense of the error anyway, so you may as well have them conveniently located in the same file!

Special output redirection

While sending all output is often a nice thing to do, another thing you will find yourself doing on a regular basis is redirecting errors (which you expect on some commands) to a special device: /dev/null.

The null kind of gives away the functionality: it's somewhere between a trash can and a black hole.

/dev/null

In reality, all data sent (actually, written) to `/dev/null` will be discarded, but nonetheless generate a *write operation succeeded* back to the calling command. In this case, that would be the redirection.

This is important, because look what happens when a redirection is unable to complete successfully:

```
reader@ubuntu:~/scripts/chapter_12$ ./stderr &> /root/file
-bash: /root/file: Permission denied
reader@ubuntu:~/scripts/chapter_12$ echo $?
1
```

This operation fails (because the `reader` user obviously can't write in the home directory of the `root` superuser).

Look at what happens when we try the same thing with `/dev/null`:

```
reader@ubuntu:~/scripts/chapter_12$ ./stderr &> /dev/null
reader@ubuntu:~/scripts/chapter_12$ echo $?
0
reader@ubuntu:~/scripts/chapter_12$ cat /dev/null
reader@ubuntu:~/scripts/chapter_12$
```

That's all there is to it. All the output is gone (both `stdout` and `stderr`, because of the `&>` redirection), but the command still reports the desirable exit status of `0`. When we make sure that the data is gone, we use `cat /dev/null`, which results in nothing.

We'll show you a practical example that you will no doubt find yourself using often in your scripting:

```
reader@ubuntu:~/scripts/chapter_12$ vim find.sh
reader@ubuntu:~/scripts/chapter_12$ cat find.sh
#!/bin/bash

#####################################
# Author: Sebastiaan Tammer
# Version: v1.0.0
# Date: 2018-11-06
# Description: Find a file.
# Usage: ./find.sh <file-name>
#####################################

# Check for the current number of arguments.
if [[ $# -ne 1 ]]; then
  echo "Wrong number of arguments!"
```

```
    echo "Usage: $0 <file-name>"
    exit 1
fi

# Name of the file to search for.
file_name=$1

# Redirect all errors to /dev/null, so they don't clutter the terminal.
find / -name "${file_name}" 2> /dev/null
```

This script contains only constructs we've introduced before, apart from the `/dev/null` redirection of `stderr`. While this `find.sh` script is in fact nothing more than a simple wrapper around the `find` command, it makes a big difference.

Look at what happens when we use `find` to look for the file `find.sh` file (because why not!):

```
reader@ubuntu:~/scripts/chapter_12$ find / -name find.sh
find: '/etc/ssl/private': Permission denied
find: '/etc/polkit-1/localauthority': Permission denied
<SNIPPED>
find: '/sys/fs/pstore': Permission denied
find: '/sys/fs/fuse/connections/48': Permission denied
/home/reader/scripts/chapter_12/find.sh
find: '/data/devops-files': Permission denied
find: '/data/dev-files': Permission denied
<SNIPPED>
```

We've cut out about 95% of the output, since you would probably agree there isn't much merit in five pages of `Permission denied` errors. Because we're running `find` as a normal user, we do not have access to many parts of the system. These errors reflect this.

We did actually locate our script, as highlighted earlier, but it could take a few minutes of scrolling before you encounter it. This is exactly what we meant about error output drowning relevant output.

Now, let's look for the same file with our wrapper script:

```
reader@ubuntu:~/scripts/chapter_12$ bash find.sh find.sh
/home/reader/scripts/chapter_12/find.sh
```

There we go! Same result, but without all those pesky errors confusing us. Since the `Permission denied` errors are sent to the `stderr` stream, we *deleted* them using `2> /dev/null` after the `find` command.

This actually brings us to another point: you can use redirection to silence commands as well. We've seen many commands that incorporate a --quiet or -q flag. Some commands, though, such as find, do not have this flag.

You could argue that it would be weird for find to have this flag (why search for files when you don't want to know where it is, right?), but there might be other commands in which exit codes present enough information, but do not have a --quiet flag; those are great candidates for redirection of everything to /dev/null.

All commands are different. While most have an available --quiet flag by now, there will always be cases in which this does not work for you. Perhaps the --quiet flag only silences stdout and not stderr, or perhaps it only reduces output. In any case, knowledge about redirecting all output to /dev/null when you're really not interested in that output (only in the exit status) is a very good thing to have!

/dev/zero

Another special device we can use is /dev/zero. When we redirect output to /dev/zero, it does exactly the same as /dev/null: the data disappears. However, in practice, /dev/null is most often used for this purpose.

So, why have this special device then? Because /dev/zero can also be used to read null bytes. Out of all possible 256 bytes, the null byte is the first: the hexadecimal 00. A null byte is often used to signify the termination of a command, for example.

Now, we can also use these empty bytes to allocate bytes to the disk:

```
reader@ubuntu:/tmp$ ls -l
-rw-rw-r-- 1 reader reader   48 Nov  6 19:26 output
reader@ubuntu:/tmp$ head -c 1024 /dev/zero > allocated-file
reader@ubuntu:/tmp$ ls -l
-rw-rw-r-- 1 reader reader 1024 Nov  6 20:09 allocated-file
-rw-rw-r-- 1 reader reader   48 Nov  6 19:26 output
reader@ubuntu:/tmp$ cat allocated-file
reader@ubuntu:/tmp$
```

By using head -c 1024, we specify we want the *first 1024 characters from* /dev/zero. Because /dev/zero only supplies null bytes, these will all be the same, but we know for sure that there will be 1024 of them.

We redirect those to a file using `stdout` redirection, and we then see a file with a size of 1024 bytes (how surprising). Now, if we `cat` this file, we see nothing! Again, this should not be a surprise, because null bytes are exactly that: empty, void, null. The Terminal has no way of representing them, so it does not.

Should you ever need to do this in a script, there is another option for you: `fallocate`:

```
reader@ubuntu:/tmp$ fallocate --length 1024 fallocated-file
reader@ubuntu:/tmp$ ls -l
-rw-rw-r-- 1 reader reader 1024 Nov  6 20:09 allocated-file
-rw-rw-r-- 1 reader reader 1024 Nov  6 20:13 fallocated-file
-rw-rw-r-- 1 reader reader   48 Nov  6 19:26 output
reader@ubuntu:/tmp$ cat fallocated-file
reader@ubuntu:/tmp$
```

As you can see from the preceding output, this command does exactly what we already accomplished with our `/dev/zero` read and redirection (we wouldn't be surprised if `fallocate` was actually a fancy wrapper around reading from `/dev/zero`, but we can't say this for sure).

Input redirection

Two other famous special devices, `/dev/random` and `/dev/urandom`, are best discussed in tandem with the next bit of redirection: *input redirection*.

Input normally comes from your keyboard, passed through by the Terminal to the command. The easiest example for this is the `read` command: it reads from `stdin` until it encounters a newline (when the *Enter* key is pressed) and then saves the input to the `REPLY` variable (or anything custom, should you have given that argument). It looks a bit like this:

```
reader@ubuntu:~$ read -p "Type something: " answer
Type something: Something
reader@ubuntu:~$ echo ${answer}
something
```

Easy. Now, let's say we run this command non-interactively, which means we cannot use a keyboard and Terminal to supply the information (not a real use case for `read`, but this makes for a nice example).

In this case, we can use input redirection (of `stdin`) to supply the input to `read`. This is achieved with the < character, which is shorthand for <0. Remember that the `stdin` file descriptor was `/dev/fd/0`? Not a coincidence.

Let's use `read` in a non-interactive manner by redirecting `stdin` to read from a file, instead of the Terminal:

```
reader@ubuntu:/tmp$ echo "Something else" > answer-file
reader@ubuntu:/tmp$ read -p "Type something: " new_answer < answer-file
reader@ubuntu:/tmp$ echo ${new_answer}
Something else
```

To show that we're not cheating and reusing the already stored answer in the `${answer}` variable, we've renamed the variable in which the reply for `read` is stored to `${new_answer}`.

Now, at the end of the command we redirected `stdin` from the `answer-file` file, which we created first using `echo` + redirection of `stdout`. This was as simple as adding `<` `answer-file` after the command.

This redirection makes `read` read from the file until a newline is encountered (which is conveniently what `echo` always ends a string with).

Now that the basics of input redirection should be clear, let's get back to our special devices: `/dev/random` and `/dev/urandom`. These two special files are pseudo-random number generators, which is a complicated word for something that generates *almost* random data.

In the case of these special devices, they gather *entropy* (a complicated word for something like randomness) from things like device drivers, mouse movements, and other things that are mostly random.

There is a slight difference between `/dev/random` and `/dev/urandom`: when there is not enough entropy in the system, `/dev/random` stops generating random output, while `/dev/urandom` keeps going.

If you really need full entropy, `/dev/random` might be the better choice (in all honesty, you're probably taking other measures in that situation anyway), but most often, `/dev/urandom` is the better choice in your scripting, since blocking can create incredible wait times. This comes from first-hand experience and can be very inconvenient!

For our examples, we'll only show `/dev/urandom`; output from `/dev/random` is similar.

In practice, `/dev/urandom` spits out bytes *randomly*. While some bytes are in the printable ASCII character range (1-9, a-z, A-Z), others are used for whitespaces (0x20) or newlines (0x0A).

You can see the randomness by using `head -1` to grab 'the first line' from `/dev/urandom`. Since a line is terminated by a newline, the command `head -1 /dev/urandom` will print everything until the first newline: this can be a few or a lot of characters:

```
reader@ubuntu:/tmp$ head -1 /dev/urandom
~d=G1���RB�Ç��"@
F��OJ2�%�=�8�#,�t�7���M���s��Ov�w��k�q��WWW��E�h��Q"x8��l�d
��P�,�.:�m�[Lb/A�J�ő�M�o�v��
�
reader@ubuntu:/tmp$ head -1 /dev/urandom
��o�u���'��+�)T�M���K�K����Y��G�g".!{R^d8L��s5c*�.d�
```

The first instance we ran printed a lot more characters (not all of them readable) than the second time around; this can be directly linked to the randomness of the bytes generated. The second time we ran `head -1 /dev/urandom`, we encountered the newline byte, 0x0A, faster than the first iteration.

Generating a password

Now, you might be wondering what use random characters might have. A prime example is generating passwords. Long, random passwords are always good; they're resistant to brute-force attacks, cannot be guessed, and, if not reused, are **very** secure. And let's be honest, how cool is it to generate a random password using the entropy from your own Linux system?

Even better, we can use input redirection from `/dev/urandom` to accomplish this, together with the `tr` command. A simple script would look like this:

```
reader@ubuntu:~/scripts/chapter_12$ vim password-generator.sh
reader@ubuntu:~/scripts/chapter_12$ cat password-generator.sh
#!/bin/bash

#####################################
# Author: Sebastiaan Tammer
# Version: v1.0.0
# Date: 2018-11-06
# Description: Generate a password.
# Usage: ./password-generator.sh <length>
#####################################

# Check for the current number of arguments.
if [[ $# -ne 1 ]]; then
  echo "Wrong number of arguments!"
  echo "Usage: $0 <length>"
  exit 1
```

```
fi

# Verify the length argument.
if [[ ! $1 =~ ^[[:digit:]]+$ ]]; then
  echo "Please enter a length (number)."
  exit 1
fi

password_length=$1

# tr grabs readable characters from input, deletes the rest.
# Input for tr comes from /dev/urandom, via input redirection.
# echo makes sure a newline is printed.
tr -dc 'a-zA-Z0-9' < /dev/urandom | head -c ${password_length}
echo
```

The header and input checks, even the one with the regular expression checking for a digit, should be clear by now.

Next, we use the `tr` command with redirected input from `/dev/urandom` to grab readable characters in our set of a-z, A-Z, and 0-9. These are *piped* to `head` (more on pipes later in this chapter), which causes the first *x* characters for be printed to the user (as specified in the argument to the script).

To make sure the Terminal formatting is correct, we throw in a quick `echo` without an argument; this just prints a newline. And just like this, we've built our own *private, secure,* and *offline* password generator. Using input redirection, even!

Advanced redirecting

We've now seen both input and output redirection, and some practical uses for both. We have not, however, combined both forms of redirection yet, and this is very much possible!

You will probably not use this too often, though; most commands accept the input as an argument, and often supply a flag that allows you to specify a file to output to. But knowledge is power, and if you ever come across a command that does not have these arguments, you know you can solve this yourself.

Try the following on your command line, and try to understand why you get the results that you see:

```
reader@ubuntu:~/scripts/chapter_12$ cat stderr.c
#include <stdio.h>
int main()
```

```
{
  // Print messages to stdout and stderr.
  fprintf(stdout, "This is sent to stdout.\n");
  fprintf(stderr, "This is sent to stderr.\n");
  return 0;
}

reader@ubuntu:~/scripts/chapter_12$ grep 'stderr' < stderr.c
  // Print messages to stdout and stderr.
  fprintf(stderr, "This is sent to stderr.\n");
reader@ubuntu:~/scripts/chapter_12$ grep 'stderr' < stderr.c > /tmp/grep-
file
reader@ubuntu:~/scripts/chapter_12$ cat /tmp/grep-file
  // Print messages to stdout and stderr.
  fprintf(stderr, "This is sent to stderr.\n");
```

As you can see, we can use both < and > on the same line to redirect both the input and output. First, we use `grep` with input redirection in the `grep 'stderr' < stderr.c` command (which is technically what `grep 'stderr' stderr.c` does as well). We see the output in our Terminal.

Next, we add `> /tmp/grep-file` right behind that command, which means we'll redirect our `stdout` to that `/tmp/grep-file` file. We no longer see the output in the Terminal, but when we `cat` the file we get it back, so it was successfully written to the file.

Since we're in the advanced part of this chapter, we will demonstrate that it actually doesn't matter where the input redirection is placed:

```
reader@ubuntu:~/scripts/chapter_12$ < stderr.c grep 'stdout' > /tmp/grep-
file-stdout
reader@ubuntu:~/scripts/chapter_12$ cat /tmp/grep-file-stdout
  // Print messages to stdout and stderr.
  fprintf(stdout, "This is sent to stdout.\n");
```

Here, we specified the input redirection at the beginning of our command. For us, this feels like the more logical approach when you consider the flow, but this causes the actual command (`grep`) to appear roughly halfway through the command, which messes up the readability.

This is mostly a moot point because, in practice, we have found very little use for both input and output redirection; even in this example, we would just write the command as `grep 'stdout' stderr.c > /tmp/grep-file-stdout` and the confusing construction is gone.

But really understanding what is going on with input and output, and how some commands do some of the heavy lifting for you, is worth your time! These are exactly the kind of issues you're going to encounter in more complex scripts, and fully understanding this will save you a lot of troubleshooting time.

Redirecting redirections

We already gave you a sneak preview of the process of redirecting redirections. The most famous example, which was mostly used before Bash 4.x, is redirecting the stderr stream to the stdout stream. By doing this, you can redirect *all* output with just the > syntax.

You can achieve it like this:

```
reader@ubuntu:/tmp$ cat /etc/shadow
cat: /etc/shadow: Permission denied
reader@ubuntu:/tmp$ cat /etc/shadow > shadow
cat: /etc/shadow: Permission denied
reader@ubuntu:/tmp$ cat shadow
#Still empty, since stderr wasn't redirected to the file.
reader@ubuntu:/tmp$ cat /etc/shadow > shadow 2>&1
#Redirect fd2 to fd1 (stderr to stdout).
reader@ubuntu:/tmp$ cat shadow
cat: /etc/shadow: Permission denied
```

Remember, you no longer need this syntax with Bash 4.x, but if you ever want to use your own custom file descriptors as input/output streams, this will be useful knowledge. By ending the command with 2>&1, we're writing all stderr output (2>) to the stdout descriptor (&1).

We can also do it the other way around:

```
reader@ubuntu:/tmp$ head -1 /etc/passwd
root:x:0:0:root:/root:/bin/bash
reader@ubuntu:/tmp$ head -1 /etc/passwd 2> passwd
root:x:0:0:root:/root:/bin/bash
reader@ubuntu:/tmp$ cat passwd
#Still empty, since stdout wasn't redirected to the file.
reader@ubuntu:/tmp$ head -1 /etc/passwd 2> passwd 1>&2
#Redirect fd1 to fd2 (stdout to stderr).
reader@ubuntu:/tmp$ cat passwd
root:x:0:0:root:/root:/bin/bash
```

So now, we're redirecting the stderr stream to the passwd file. However, the head -1 /etc/passwd command only delivers an stdout stream; we're seeing it printed to the Terminal instead of to the file.

When we use `1>&2` (which could also be written as `>&2`) we're redirecting `stdout` to `stderr`. Now it is written to the file and we can `cat` it there!

 Remember, this is advanced information, which is mostly useful for your theoretical understanding and when you start working with your own custom file descriptors. For all other output redirections, play it safe and use the `&>` syntax as we discussed earlier.

Command substitution

While not strictly redirection in the Linux sense, *command substitution* in our eyes is a form of functional redirection: you use the output of a command as an argument to another command. If we needed to use output as input for the next command, we'd use a pipe (as we'll see in a few pages), but sometimes we just need that output at a very specific location in our command.

This is where command substitution is used. We've already seen command substitution in some of our scripts: `cd $(dirname $0)`. Simply put, this does something like `cd` to the result of `dirname $0`.

`dirname $0` gives back the directory where the script is located (since `$0` is the fully-qualified path of the script), so when we use this with scripts, we'll make sure all operations are always carried out relative to the directory where the script is located.

If we did not have command substitution, we'd need to store the output somewhere before we could use it again:

```
dirname $0 > directory-file
cd < directory-file
rm directory-file
```

While this *sometimes* works, there are some pitfalls here:

- You need to write a file somewhere where you have write permissions
- You need to clean up the file after the `cd`
- You need to make sure the file does not conflict with other scripts

To cut a long story short, this is a far from ideal solution, and best avoided. And since Bash supplies command substitution, there is no real drawback to using it. As we've seen, the command substitution in `cd $(dirname $0)` handles this for us, without the need for us to track files or variables or any other complicated constructions.

Command substitution is actually used quite a lot in Bash scripting. Take a look at the following example, in which we use command substitution to instantiate and populate a variable:

```
reader@ubuntu:~/scripts/chapter_12$ vim simple-password-generator.sh
reader@ubuntu:~/scripts/chapter_12$ cat simple-password-generator.sh
#!/bin/bash

#####################################
# Author: Sebastiaan Tammer
# Version: v1.0.0
# Date: 2018-11-10
# Description: Use command substitution with a variable.
# Usage: ./simple-password-generator.sh
#####################################

# Write a random string to a variable using command substitution.
random_password=$(tr -dc 'a-zA-Z0-9' < /dev/urandom | head -c 20)

echo "Your random password is: ${random_password}"

reader@ubuntu:~/scripts/chapter_12$ bash simple-password-generator.sh
Your random password is: T3noJ3Udf8a2eQbqPiad
reader@ubuntu:~/scripts/chapter_12$ bash simple-password-generator.sh
Your random password is: wu3zpsrusT5zyvbTxJSn
```

For this example, we reused the logic in our earlier `password-generator.sh` script. This time, we do not give the user the option to supply a length; we keep it simple and assume a length of 20 (which is, at least in 2018, a pretty good length for a password).

We use command substitution to write the result (the random password) to a variable, which we then `echo` to the user.

We actually could have done this in a single line:

```
reader@ubuntu:~/scripts/chapter_12$ echo "Your random password is: $(tr -dc
'a-zA-Z0-9' < /dev/urandom | head -c 20)"
Your random password is: REzCOa11pA2846fvxsa
```

However, as we have discussed many times by now, *readability counts* (still!). We feel that first writing to a variable with a descriptive name, before we actually use it, increases the readability of the script.

Furthermore, if we wanted to use the same random value more than once, we need a variable anyway. So in this case, the extra verbosity in our script helps us and is desirable.

 The predecessor to $(..)$ was the use of backticks, which is the ` character (found next to the 1 on English-International keyboards). `$(cd dirname $0)` was previously written as `` `cd dirname $0` ``. While this mostly does the same as the newer (and better) $(..)$ syntax, there are two things that were often an issue with backticks: word splitting and newlines. These are both issues that are caused by whitespace. It is much easier to use the new syntaxes and not have to worry about things like this!

Process substitution

Something closely related to command substitution is *process substitution*. The syntax is as follows:

```
<(command)
```

It works very similarly to command substitution, but instead of sending the output of a command as a string somewhere, you can reference the output as a file. This means that some commands, which do not expect a string but instead a reference to a file, can be used with dynamic input as well.

While too advanced to discuss in great detail, here's a simple example that should get the point across:

```
reader@ubuntu:~/scripts/chapter_12$ diff <(ls /tmp/) <(ls /home/)
1,11c1
< directory-file
< grep-file
< grep-file-stdout
< passwd
< shadow
---
> reader
```

The `diff` command normally compares two files and prints their differences. Now, instead of files, we used process substitution to have `diff` compare the results from `ls /tmp/` and `ls /home/`, using the `<(ls /tmp/)` syntax.

Pipes

Finally, the moment we've all been waiting for: **pipes**. These near-magical constructs are used so much in Linux/Bash that everyone should know about them. Anything more complex than a single command will almost always use pipes to get to the solution.

And now the big reveal: all a pipe really does is connect the `stdout` of a command to the `stdin` of another command.

Wait, what?!

Binding stdout to stdin

Yes, that is really all that happens. It might be a little disappointing, now that you know all about input and output redirection. However, just because the concept is simple, that doesn't mean that pipes are not **extremely powerful** and very widely used.

Let's look at an example that shows how we can replace input/output redirection with a pipe:

```
reader@ubuntu:/tmp$ echo 'Fly into the distance' > file
reader@ubuntu:/tmp$ grep 'distance' < file
Fly into the distance
reader@ubuntu:/tmp$ echo 'Fly into the distance' | grep 'distance'
Fly into the distance
```

For the normal redirection, we first write some text to a file (using output redirection), which we then use as input for `grep`. Next, we do the exact same functional thing, but without the file as an intermediate step.

Basically, the pipe syntax is as follows:

```
command-with-output | command-using-input
```

You can use multiple pipes on a single line, and you can use any combination of pipes and input/output redirection, as long as it makes sense.

Often, when you get to the point of more than two pipes/redirections, you can increase readability with an extra line, perhaps using command substitution to write the intermediate result to a variable. But, technically, you can make it as *complex* as you want; just be vigilant in not making it too *complicated*.

As stated, pipes bind `stdout` to `stdin`. You might have an idea about the issue coming up: `stderr`! Look at this example of how the separation of output into `stdout` and `stderr` affects pipes:

```
reader@ubuntu:~/scripts/chapter_12$ cat /etc/shadow | grep 'denied'
cat: /etc/shadow: Permission denied
reader@ubuntu:~/scripts/chapter_12$ cat /etc/shadow | grep 'denied' >
/tmp/empty-file
cat: /etc/shadow: Permission denied #Printed to stderr on terminal.
reader@ubuntu:~/scripts/chapter_12$ cat /etc/shadow | grep 'denied' 2>
/tmp/error-file
cat: /etc/shadow: Permission denied #Printed to stderr on terminal.
reader@ubuntu:~/scripts/chapter_12$ cat /tmp/empty-file
reader@ubuntu:~/scripts/chapter_12$ cat /tmp/error-file
```

Now, initially this example might confuse you. Let's go through it step by step to figure it out.

First, `cat /etc/shadow | grep 'denied'`. We try to `grep` the `stdout` of `cat /etc/shadow` for the word `denied`. We do not actually find it, but we see it printed on our Terminal anyway. Why? Because even though `stdout` is piped to `grep`, `stderr` is sent straight to our Terminal (and **not** through `grep`).

If you're connecting via SSH to Ubuntu 18.04, you should see color highlighting by default when a `grep` is successful; in this example, you would not encounter this.

The next command, `cat /etc/shadow | grep 'denied' > /tmp/empty-file`, redirects the `stdout` of `grep` to a file. Since `grep` did not process the error message, the file remains empty.

Even if we try to redirect `stderr` at the end, as can be seen in the `cat /etc/shadow | grep 'denied' 2> /tmp/error-file` command, we still do not get any output in the file. This is because redirections **are sequential**: the output redirection only applies to the `grep`, not the `cat`.

Now, in the same way output redirections have a way to redirect both `stdout` and `stderr`, so does a pipe with the `|&` syntax. Look at the same example again, now using proper redirections:

```
reader@ubuntu:~/scripts/chapter_12$ cat /etc/shadow |& grep 'denied'
cat: /etc/shadow: Permission denied
reader@ubuntu:~/scripts/chapter_12$ cat /etc/shadow |& grep 'denied' >
/tmp/error-file
reader@ubuntu:~/scripts/chapter_12$ cat /tmp/error-file
cat: /etc/shadow: Permission denied
```

```
reader@ubuntu:~/scripts/chapter_12$ cat /etc/shadow |& grep 'denied' 2>
/tmp/error-file
cat: /etc/shadow: Permission denied
reader@ubuntu:~/scripts/chapter_12$ cat /tmp/error-file
```

For the first command, if you have color syntax enabled, you will see the word `denied` is bold and colored (in our case, red). This means that now that we use `|&`, `grep` did successfully process the output.

Next, when we redirect using the `stdout` of `grep`, we see that we successfully write the output to a file. If we try to redirect it with `2>`, we see it printed in the Terminal again, but not in the file. This is because of the sequential nature of redirects: as soon as `grep` successfully processes the input (which came from `stderr`), `grep` outputs this to `stdout`.

`grep` actually does not know that the input was originally an `stderr` stream; as far as it is concerned, it is just `stdin` to process. And since for `grep` a successful process goes to `stdout`, that's where we find it in the end!

If we want to be safe and we do not need to split the functionality of `stdout` and `stderr`, the safest way would be to use the command like this: `cat /etc/shadow |& grep 'denied' &> /tmp/file`. Since both the pipe and output redirections process `stdout` and `stderr`, we'll always end up with all output where we want it.

Practical examples

Because the theory of pipes should now be relatively simple (as we got most of it out of the way when we talked about input and output redirection), we'll present a number of practical examples that really illustrate the power of pipes.

It is good to remember that pipes only work on commands that accept input from `stdin`; not all do. If you pipe something to a command that totally disregards that input, you'll probably be disappointed with the results.

Since we have now introduced pipes, we'll use them more liberally in the rest of the book. While these examples will present some ways of using pipes, the rest of the book will contain many more!

Yet another password generator

So, we've already created two password generators. Since three is the magic number, and this is a really good example to demonstrate chaining pipes, we'll create one more (the last one, promise):

```
reader@ubuntu:~/scripts/chapter_12$ vim piped-passwords.sh
reader@ubuntu:~/scripts/chapter_12$ cat piped-passwords.sh
#!/bin/bash

#####################################
# Author: Sebastiaan Tammer
# Version: v1.0.0
# Date: 2018-11-10
# Description: Generate a password, using only pipes.
# Usage: ./piped-passwords.sh
#####################################

password=$(head /dev/urandom | tr -dc 'a-zA-Z0-9' | head -c20)

echo "Your random password is: ${password}"
```

First, we grab the first 10 lines from /dev/urandom (the default behavior for head). We send this to tr, which trims it to the character sets we want (because it also outputs non-readable characters). Then, when we have a character set that we can use, we grab the first 20 characters from that using head again.

If you run just head /dev/urandom | tr -dc 'a-zA-Z0-9' a few times, you'll see that the length differs; this is because of the randomness of the newline byte. By grabbing 10 lines from /dev/urandom, the chance of not having enough readable characters to create a 20-character password is very small.

(Challenge to the reader: create a script with a loop that does this long enough to encounter this situation!)

This example illustrates a few things. Firstly, we can often achieve a lot of things we want to do with a few smart pipes. Secondly, it is not unusual to use the same command multiple times. We could have also chosen tail -c20 for the final command in the chain, by the way, but this has a nice symmetry to the whole command!

Finally, we have seen three different password generators that do, in reality, the same thing. As always, in Bash there are many ways to accomplish the same goal; it is up to you to decide which is most applicable. Readability and performance should be the two main factors in this decision, as far as we're concerned.

Setting passwords in a script

Another task that you may find yourself wanting to script is setting the password for a local user. While this is not always good practice from a security standpoint (especially for personal user accounts), it is something that is used for functional accounts (users that correspond to software, such as the Apache user running the httpd processes).

Most of these users do not need a password, but sometimes they do. In this case, we can use pipes with the chpasswd command to set their passwords:

```
reader@ubuntu:~/scripts/chapter_12$ vim password-setter.sh
reader@ubuntu:~/scripts/chapter_12$ cat password-setter.sh
#!/bin/bash

#####################################
# Author: Sebastiaan Tammer
# Version: v1.0.0
# Date: 2018-11-10
# Description: Set a password using chpasswd.
# Usage: ./password-setter.sh
#####################################

NEW_USER_NAME=bob

# Verify this script is run with root privileges.
if [[ $(id -u) -ne 0 ]]; then
  echo "Please run as root or with sudo!"
  exit 1
fi

# We only need exit status, send all output to /dev/null.
id ${NEW_USER_NAME} &> /dev/null

# Check if we need to create the user.
if [[ $? -ne 0 ]]; then
  # User does not exist, create the user.
  useradd -m ${NEW_USER_NAME}
fi

# Set the password for the user.
echo "${NEW_USER_NAME}:password" | chpasswd
```

Before you run this script, remember that this adds a user to your system with a very simple (bad) password. We updated our input sanitation a bit for this script: we used command substitution to see if the script was running with root privileges. Because id -u returns the numerical ID for the user, which should be 0 in the case of the root user or sudo privileges, we can compare it using -ne 0.

If we run the script and the user does not exist, we create the user before setting the password for that user. This is done by sending a username:password to the stdin of chpasswd, via a pipe. Do note that we used -ne 0 twice, but for very different things: the first time for comparing a user ID, the second time with an exit status.

You can probably think of multiple improvements for this script. For example, it might be good to be able to specify both the username and password instead of these hardcoded dummy values. Also, a sanity check after the chpasswd command is definitely a good idea. In the current iteration, the script does not give **any** feedback to the user; very bad practice.

See if you can fix these issues, and be sure to remember that any input specified by the user should be checked *thoroughly*! If you really want a challenge, do this for multiple users in a for loop, by grabbing the input from a file.

 An important thing to note is that a process, when running, is visible to any user on the system. This is often not that big a problem, but if you're providing usernames and passwords directly to the script as arguments, those are visible to everyone as well. This is often only for a very short time, but they will be visible nonetheless. Always keep security in mind when dealing with sensitive issues such as passwords.

tee

A command that was seemingly created to work in tandem with a pipe is tee. The description on the man page should tell most of the story:

tee - read from standard input and write to standard output and files

So, in essence, sending something to the stdin of tee (via a pipe!) allows us to save that output to both your Terminal and a file at the same time.

This is often most useful when using interactive commands; it allows you to follow the output live, but also write it to a (log) file for later review. Updating a system provides a good example for the use case of tee:

```
sudo apt upgrade -y | tee /tmp/upgrade.log
```

We can make it even better by sending *all* output to `tee`, including `stderr`:

```
sudo apt upgrade -y |& tee /tmp/upgrade.log
```

The output will look something like this:

```
reader@ubuntu:~/scripts/chapter_12$ sudo apt upgrade -y |& tee
/tmp/upgrade.log
WARNING: apt does not have a stable CLI interface. Use with caution in
scripts.
Reading package lists...
<SNIPPED>
0 upgraded, 0 newly installed, 0 to remove and 0 not upgraded.
reader@ubuntu:~/scripts/chapter_12$ cat /tmp/upgrade.log
WARNING: apt does not have a stable CLI interface. Use with caution in
scripts.
Reading package lists...
<SNIPPED>
0 upgraded, 0 newly installed, 0 to remove and 0 not upgraded.
```

The first line of both the Terminal output and the log file is a `WARNING` which is sent to `stderr`; if you used `|` instead of `|&`, that would not have been written to the log file, only on the screen. If you use `|&` as advised, you will see that the output on your screen and the contents of the file are a perfect match.

By default, `tee` overwrites the destination file. Like all forms of redirection, `tee` also has a way to append instead of overwrite: the `--append` (`-a`) flag. In our experience, this is often a prudent choice, not dissimilar to `|&`.

While `tee` is a great asset for your command-line arsenal, it most definitely has its place in scripting as well. Once your scripts get more complex, you might want to save parts of the output to a file for later review. However, to keep the user updated on the status of a script, printing some to the Terminal might also be a good idea. If these two scenarios overlap, you'll need to use `tee` to get the job done!

Here documents

The final concept we'll introduce in this chapter is the *here document*. Here documents, also called heredocs, are used to supply input to certain commands, slightly different to `stdin` redirection. Notably, it is an easy way to give multiline input to a command. It works with the following syntax:

```
cat << EOF
input
more input
the last input
EOF
```

If you run this in your Terminal, you'll see the following:

```
reader@ubuntu:~/scripts/chapter_12$ cat << EOF
> input
> more input
> the last input
> EOF
input
more input
the last input
```

The << syntax lets Bash know you want to use a heredoc. Right after that, you're supplying a *delimiting identifier*. This might seem complicated, but it really means that you supply a string that will terminate the input. So, in our example, we supplied the commonly used `EOF` (short for **e**nd **o**f **f**ile).

Now, if the heredoc encounters a line in the input that exactly matches the delimiting identifier, it stops listening for further input. Here's another example that illustrates this more closely:

```
reader@ubuntu:~/scripts/chapter_12$ cat << end-of-file
> The delimiting identifier is end-of-file
> But it only stops when end-of-file is the only thing on the line
> end-of-file does not work, since it has text after it
> end-of-file
The delimiting identifier is end-of-file
But it only stops when end-of-file is the only thing on the line
end-of-file does not work, since it has text behind it
```

While using this with `cat` illustrates the point, it is not a very practical example. The `wall` command, however, is. `wall` lets you broadcast a message to everyone connected to the server, to their Terminal. When used in combination with a heredoc, it looks a little like this:

```
reader@ubuntu:~/scripts/chapter_12$ wall << EOF
> Hi guys, we're rebooting soon, please save your work!
> It would be a shame if you lost valuable time...
> EOF

Broadcast message from reader@ubuntu (pts/0) (Sat Nov 10 16:21:15 2018):

Hi guys, we're rebooting soon, please save your work!
It would be a shame if you lost valuable time...
```

In this case, we receive our own broadcast. If you connect multiple times with your user, however, you'll see the broadcast come in there as well.

Give it a try with a Terminal console connection and an SSH connection simultaneously; you'll understand it much better if you see it first-hand.

Heredocs and variables

A source of confusion when using heredocs often arises from using variables. By default, variables are resolved in a heredoc, as can be seen in the following example:

```
reader@ubuntu:~/scripts/chapter_12$ cat << EOF
> Hi, this is $USER!
> EOF
Hi, this is reader!
```

However, this might not always be desirable functionality. You might want to use this to write to a file in which the variables should be resolved later.

In this case, we can quote the delimiting identifier EOF to prevent variables being substituted:

```
reader@ubuntu:~/scripts/chapter_12$ cat << 'EOF'
> Hi, this is $USER!
> EOF
Hi, this is $USER!
```

Using heredocs for script input

Since heredocs allow us to simply pass newline-delimited input to a command, we can use this to run an interactive script in a non-interactive manner! We have used this in practice, for instance, on database installer scripts that could only be run interactively. However, once you know the order of the questions and the input you want to supply, you can use the heredoc to supply this input to that interactive script.

Even better, we have already created a script that uses interactive input, /home/reader/scripts/chapter_11/while-interactive.sh, which we can use to show this functionality:

```
reader@ubuntu:/tmp$ head /home/reader/scripts/chapter_11/while-interactive.sh
#!/bin/bash

######################################
# Author: Sebastiaan Tammer
# Version: v1.1.0
# Date: 2018-10-28
# Description: A simple riddle in a while loop.
# Usage: ./while-interactive.sh
######################################

reader@ubuntu:/tmp$ bash /home/reader/scripts/chapter_11/while-interactive.sh << EOF
a mouse   #Try 1.
the sun   #Try 2.
keyboard  #Try 3.
EOF

Incorrect, please try again. #Try 1.
Incorrect, please try again. #Try 2.
Correct, congratulations!    #Try 3.
Now we can continue after the while loop is done, awesome!
```

We know that the script continues until it gets the right answer, which is either keyboard or Keyboard. We use the heredoc to send three answers, in order, to the script: a mouse, the sun, and finally keyboard. We can correspond the output to the input quite easily.

For more verbosity, run the script with heredoc input with a bash -x, which will show you definitively that there are three tries to the riddle.

You might want to use a here document within a nested function (which will be explained in the next chapter) or within a loop. In both cases, you should already be using indentation to improve readability. However, this impacts your heredoc, because the whitespace is considered part of the input. If you find yourself in that situation, heredocs have an extra option: <<- instead of <<. When supplying the extra -, all *tab characters* are ignored. This allows you to indent the heredoc construction with tabs, which maintains both readability and function.

Here strings

The last thing we'd like to discuss in this chapter is the *here string*. It is very similar to the here document (hence the name), but it deals with a single string, instead of a document (who would have thought!).

This construct, which uses the <<< syntax, can be used to supply text input to a command that perhaps normally only accepts input from stdin or a file. A good example for this is bc, which is a simple calculator (part of the GNU Project).

Normally, you use it in one of two ways: sending input to stdin via a pipe, or by pointing bc to a file:

```
reader@ubuntu:/tmp$ echo "2^8" | bc
256

reader@ubuntu:/tmp$ echo "4*4" > math
reader@ubuntu:/tmp$ bc math
bc 1.07.1
Copyright 1991-1994, 1997, 1998, 2000, 2004, 2006, 2008, 2012-2017 Free
Software Foundation, Inc.
This is free software with ABSOLUTELY NO WARRANTY.
For details type `warranty'.
16
^C
(interrupt) use quit to exit.
quit
```

When used with stdin, bc returns the result of the calculation. When used with a file, bc opens an interactive session, which we need to manually close by entering quit. Both ways seem a little too much work for what we want to achieve.

Let's look at how a here string fixes this:

```
reader@ubuntu:/tmp$ bc <<< 2^8
256
```

There we go. Just a simple here string as input (which is sent to `stdin` of the command), and we get the same functionality as an `echo` with a pipe. However, now it is just a single command, instead of a chain. Simple but effective, just the way we like it!

Summary

This chapter explained almost everything there is to know about *redirection* on Linux. We began with a general description of what redirection is, and how *file descriptors* are used to facilitate redirections. We learned that file descriptors 0, 1, and 2 are used for `stdin`, `stdout`, and `stderr`, respectively.

We then got acquainted with the syntax for redirections. This included >, 2>, &>, and <, and their appending syntaxes, >>, 2>>, &>>, and <<.

We discussed a few special Linux devices, `/dev/null`, `/dev/zero`, and `/dev/urandom`. We showed examples of how we could use these devices to remove output, generate null bytes, and generate random data. In the advanced redirecting section, we showed that we could bind `stdout` to `stderr` and vice versa.

Furthermore, we learned about *command substitution* and *process substitution*, which allows us to use the result of a command in an argument to another command, or as a file.

Next up were *pipes*. Pipes are simple, but very powerful, Bash constructs, which are used to connect the `stdout` (and possibly `stderr`) of one command to the `stdin` of another. This allows us to chain commands, manipulating the data streams further as we go, through as many commands as we want.

We also introduced `tee`, which allows us to send a stream to both our Terminal and a file, a construction often used for log files.

Finally, we explained *here documents* and *here strings*. These concepts allow us to send multiline and single-line input directly from the Terminal into the `stdin` of other commands, something that would otherwise require an `echo` or `cat`.

The following commands were introduced in this chapter: `diff`, `gcc`, `fallocate`, `tr`, `chpasswd`, `tee`, and `bc`.

Questions

1. What are file descriptors?
2. What do the terms `stdin`, `stdout`, and `stderr` mean?
3. How do `stdin`, `stdout`, and `stderr` map to the default file descriptors?
4. What is the difference between the output redirections >, 1>, and 2>?
5. What is the difference between > and >>?
6. How can both `stdout` and `stderr` be redirected at the same time?
7. Which special devices can be used to act as a black hole for output?
8. What does a pipe do, with regards to redirections?
9. How can we send output to both the Terminal and a log file?
10. What is a typical use case for a here string?

Further reading

- **Read more about file descriptors at the following link**: `https://linuxmeerkat.wordpress.com/2011/12/02/file-descriptors-explained/`.
- **Find information about advanced scripts with file descriptors at the following link**: `https://bash.cyberciti.biz/guide/Reads_from_the_file_descriptor_(fd)`.
- **Read more about command substitution at the following link**: `http://www.tldp.org/LDP/abs/html/commandsub.html`.
- **Find information about here documents at the following link**: `https://www.tldp.org/LDP/abs/html/here-docs.html`.

13
Functions

In this chapter, we'll explain a very practical concept of Bash scripting: functions. We'll show what they are, how we can use them, and why we would want to use them.

After the basics of functions have been introduced, we're taking it a step further and we'll show how functions can have their own input and output.

The concept of a function library will be described and we will start to build our own personal function library that will contain various utility functions.

The following commands will be introduced in this chapter: `top`, `free`, `declare`, `case`, `rev`, and `return`.

The following topics will be covered in this chapter:

- Functions explained
- Augmenting functions with parameters
- Function libraries

Technical requirements

All scripts for this chapter can be found on GitHub: `https://github.com/ PacktPublishing/Learn-Linux-Shell-Scripting-Fundamentals-of-Bash-4.4/tree/ master/Chapter13`. Apart from your Ubuntu Linux virtual machine, no other resources are needed to complete the examples in this chapter. For the **argument-checker.sh, functions-and-variables.sh, library-redirect-to-file.sh** scripts only the final version is found online. Be sure to verify the script version in the header before executing it on your system.

Functions explained

In this chapter, we're going to look at functions, and how these can enhance your scripts. The theory of functions is not too complicated: a function is a set of commands grouped together that can be called (executed) multiple times without having to write the whole set of commands again. As always, a good example is worth a thousand words, so let's dive right in with one of our favorite examples: printing `Hello world!`.

Hello world!

We now know it's relatively easy to get the words `Hello world!` to appear on our terminal. A simple `echo "Hello world!"` does just the trick. However, if we wanted to do this multiple times, how would we go about it? You could suggest using any kind of loop, which would indeed allow us to print multiple times. However, that loop also requires some extra code and planning up front. As you will notice, in practice loops are great for iterating over items, but not exactly suitable for reusing code in a predictable manner. Let's see how we can use a function to do this instead:

```
reader@ubuntu:~/scripts/chapter_13$ vim hello-world-function.sh
reader@ubuntu:~/scripts/chapter_13$ cat hello-world-function.sh
#!/bin/bash

#####################################
# Author: Sebastiaan Tammer
# Version: v1.0.0
# Date: 2018-11-11
# Description: Prints "Hello world!" using a function.
# Usage: ./hello-world-function.sh
#####################################

# Define the function before we call it.
hello_world() {
  echo "Hello world!"
}

# Call the function we defined earlier:
hello_world

reader@ubuntu:~/scripts/chapter_13$ bash hello-world-function.sh
Hello world!
```

As you see, we first defined the function, which is nothing more than writing the commands that should be executed once the function is called. At the end of the script, you can see we execute the function by just entering the function name, as we would any other command. It is important to note that you can only call a function *if you have previously defined it*. This means that the entire function definition needs to be higher in the script than its call. For now, we'll place all functions as the first items in our scripts. Later on in this chapter, we'll show you how we can be more efficient with this.

What you saw in the previous example was the first of two possible syntaxes for function definition in Bash. If we extract just the function, the syntax is as follows:

```
function_name() {
    indented-commands
    further-indented-commands-as-needed
  }
```

The second possible syntax, which we like less than the previous one, is this:

```
function function_name {
    indented-commands
    further-indented-commands-as-needed
  }
```

The difference between the two syntaxes is the absence of either the word `function` at the beginning or `()` after the function name. We prefer the first syntax, which uses the `()` notation, as it is much closer to the notation of other scripting/programming languages and should thus be much more recognizable for most. And, as an added bonus, it is shorter and simpler than the second notation. As you might expect, we'll continue using only the first notation in the rest of the book; the other was presented for completeness (and it is always convenient to understand it if you come across it online when researching for your scripting!).

Remember, we use indentation to relay information about where commands are nested to the reader of a script. In this case, since all commands within a function are only run when the function is called, we indent them with two spaces so it's clear we're inside the function.

More complexity

A function can have as many commands as needed. In our simple example, we only added a single echo, which we then only called once. While this is nice for abstraction, it does not really warrant creating a function (yet). Let's look at a more complex example that will give you a better idea why abstraction of commands in functions is a good idea:

```
reader@ubuntu:~/scripts/chapter_13$ vim complex-function.sh
reader@ubuntu:~/scripts/chapter_13$ cat complex-function.sh
#!/bin/bash

#####################################
# Author: Sebastiaan Tammer
# Version: v1.0.0
# Date: 2018-11-11
# Description: A more complex function that shows why functions exist.
# Usage: ./complex-function.sh
#####################################

# Used to print some current data on the system.
print_system_status() {
  date # Print the current datetime.
  echo "CPU in use: $(top -bn1 | grep Cpu | awk '{print $2}')"
  echo "Memory in use: $(free -h | grep Mem | awk '{print $3}')"
  echo "Disk space available on /: $(df -k / | grep / | awk '{print $4}')"
  echo # Extra newline for readability.
}

# Print the system status a few times.
for ((i=0; i<5; i++)); do
  print_system_status
  sleep 5
done
```

Now we're talking! This function has five commands, three of which include command substitution with chained pipes. Now, our scripts are starting to become complex yet powerful. As you can see, we define the function using the () notation. We then call this function in a C-style for loop, which causes the script to print the system status five times with a five-second pause in between (due to sleep, which we saw earlier in *Chapter 11, Conditional Testing and Scripting Loops*). When you run this, it should look like this:

```
reader@ubuntu:~/scripts/chapter_13$ bash complex-function.sh
Sun Nov 11 13:40:17 UTC 2018
CPU in use: 0.1
Memory in use: 85M
Disk space available on /: 4679156
```

```
Sun Nov 11 13:40:22 UTC 2018
CPU in use: 0.2
Memory in use: 84M
Disk space available on /: 4679156
```

Apart from the date, the chance of the other output changing significantly is slim, unless you have other processes running. However, the purpose of functions should be clear: define and abstract a set of functionalities in a transparent manner.

 While not the topic of this chapter, we used a few new commands here. The `top` and `free` commands are often used to check how the system is performing, and can be used without any arguments (`top` opens full screen, which you can exit with *Ctrl + C*). In the *Further reading* section of this chapter, you can find more on these (and other) performance monitoring tools in Linux. We've also included a primer on `awk` there.

There are many advantages to using functions; these include but are not limited to the following:

- Easy to reuse code
- Allows sharing of code (via libraries, for example)
- Abstract confusing code to a simple function call

An important thing in functions is naming. A function name should be as concise as possible, but still needs to tell the user what it does. For example, if you call a function something non-descriptive such as `function1`, how will anyone know what it does? Compare this to a name like we saw in the example: `print_system_status`. While perhaps not perfect (what is system status?), it at least points us in the right direction (if you agree that CPU, memory, and disk usage are considered part of system status, that is). Perhaps a better name for the function would be `print_cpu_mem_disk`. It is up to you to decide! Make sure you consider who the target audience is when making this choice; this often has the greatest impact.

While descriptiveness is very important in function naming, so is adhering to a naming convention. We've already presented this same consideration in Chapter 8, *Variables and User Input*, when we dealt with variable naming. To reiterate: the most important rule is to *be consistent*. If you want our advice for a function naming convention, stick with the one we laid out for variables: lowercase, separated by underscores. This is what we used in the previous examples, and is what we will continue to show in the rest of the book.

Variable scopes

While functions are great, there are some things we have previously learned that we'll need to reconsider in the scope of functions, most notably variables. We know that variables store information that can be accessed or mutated multiple times and at multiple points in our scripts. However, something we have not yet learned is that a variable always has a *scope*. By default, variables are scoped *globally*, which means they can be used throughout the script at any point. With the introduction of functions also comes a new scope: *local*. Local variables are defined within a function and live and die with the function call. Let's see this in action:

```
reader@ubuntu:~/scripts/chapter_13$ vim functions-and-variables.sh
reader@ubuntu:~/scripts/chapter_13$ cat functions-and-variables.sh
#!/bin/bash
#####################################
# Author: Sebastiaan Tammer
# Version: v1.0.0
# Date: 2018-11-11
# Description: Show different variable scopes.
# Usage: ./functions-and-variables.sh <input>
#####################################

# Check if the user supplied at least one argument.
if [[ $# -eq 0 ]]; then
  echo "Missing an argument!"
  echo "Usage: $0 <input>"
  exit 1
fi

# Assign the input to a variable.
input_variable=$1
# Create a CONSTANT, which never changes.
CONSTANT_VARIABLE="constant"

# Define the function.
hello_variable() {
  echo "This is the input variable: ${input_variable}"
  echo "This is the constant: ${CONSTANT_VARIABLE}"
}

# Call the function.
hello_variable
reader@ubuntu:~/scripts/chapter_13$ bash functions-and-variables.sh
teststring
This is the input variable: teststring
This is the constant: constant
```

So far, so good. We can use our *global* constants in a function. This is not surprising, since it is not called a global variable lightly; it can be used anywhere in the script. Now, let's see what happens when we add some extra variables in the function:

```
#!/bin/bash

#####################################
# Author: Sebastiaan Tammer
# Version: v1.1.0
# Date: 2018-11-11
# Description: Show different variable scopes.
# Usage: ./functions-and-variables.sh <input>
#####################################
<SNIPPED>
# Define the function.
hello_variable() {
  FUNCTION_VARIABLE="function variable text!"
  echo "This is the input variable: ${input_variable}"
  echo "This is the constant: ${CONSTANT_VARIABLE}"
  echo "This is the function variable: ${FUNCTION_VARIABLE}"
}

# Call the function.
hello_variable

# Try to call the function variable outside the function.
echo "Function variable outside function: ${FUNCTION_VARIABLE}"
```

What do you think happens now? Give it a try:

```
reader@ubuntu:~/scripts/chapter_13$ bash functions-and-variables.sh input
This is the input variable: input
This is the constant: constant
This is the function variable: function variable text!
Function variable outside function: function variable text!
```

Contrary to what you might have suspected, the variable we defined inside the function is actually still a global variable (sorry for tricking you!). If we wanted to use locally scoped variables, we need to add the built-in local shell:

```
#!/bin/bash
#####################################
# Author: Sebastiaan Tammer
# Version: v1.2.0
# Date: 2018-11-11
# Description: Show different variable scopes.
# Usage: ./functions-and-variables.sh <input>
#####################################
```

```
<SNIPPED>
# Define the function.
hello_variable() {
  local FUNCTION_VARIABLE="function variable text!"
  echo "This is the input variable: ${input_variable}"
  echo "This is the constant: ${CONSTANT_VARIABLE}"
  echo "This is the function variable: ${FUNCTION_VARIABLE}"
}
<SNIPPED>
```

Now, if we execute it this time, we'll actually see the script misbehaving at the final command:

```
reader@ubuntu:~/scripts/chapter_13$ bash functions-and-variables.sh more-input
input
This is the input variable: more-input
This is the constant: constant
This is the function variable: function variable text!
Function variable outside function:
```

Because of the local addition, we can now only use the variable and its content inside of the function. So, when we call the `hello_variable` function, we see the content of the variable, but when we try to print it outside of the function in `echo "Function variable outside function: ${FUNCTION_VARIABLE}"`, we see it is empty. This is the expected and desirable behavior. What you can actually do, and is sometimes really convenient, is the following:

```
#!/bin/bash

#####################################
# Author: Sebastiaan Tammer
# Version: v1.3.0
# Date: 2018-11-11
# Description: Show different variable scopes.
# Usage: ./functions-and-variables.sh <input>
#####################################
<SNIPPED>
# Define the function.
hello_variable() {
  local CONSTANT_VARIABLE="maybe not so constant?"
  echo "This is the input variable: ${input_variable}"
  echo "This is the constant: ${CONSTANT_VARIABLE}"
}

# Call the function.
hello_variable
```

```
# Try to call the function variable outside the function.
echo "Function variable outside function: ${CONSTANT_VARIABLE}"
```

Now, we've defined a locally scoped variable *with the same name* as a globally scoped one we have already initialized! You might have an idea about what happens next, but be sure to run the script and understand why this happens:

```
reader@ubuntu:~/scripts/chapter_13$ bash functions-and-variables.sh last-input
This is the input variable: last-input
This is the constant: maybe not so constant?
Function variable outside function: constant
```

So, when we used the `CONSTANT_VARIABLE` variable (remember, constants are still considered variables, albeit special ones) within the function, it printed the value of the locally scoped one: `maybe not so constant?`. When outside the function, in the main body of the script, we printed the value for the variable again, and we were presented with the value as we had originally defined it: `constant`.

You might be having a hard time imagining a use case for this. While we agree that you will probably not use this often, it does have its place. For example, imagine a complex script where a global variable is used by multiple functions and commands sequentially. Now, you might come across a situation where you need the value of the variable, but slightly modified to use it correctly in a function. You also know that functions/commands further on need the original value. Now, you could copy the contents to a new variable and use that, but by *overriding* the variable within a function you make it much clearer to the reader/user that you have a purpose for this; that it is a well-informed decision and you're aware you need that exception *for just that function*. Using a locally scoped variable (preferably with a comment, as always) will ensure readability!

 Variables can be set read-only by using the `declare` built-in shell. If you check the help, with `help declare`, you'll see it described as `'Set variable values and attributes'`. A read-only variable such as a constant can be created by replacing `CONSTANT=VALUE` with `declare -r CONSTANT=VALUE`. If you do this, you can no longer (temporarily) override a variable with a local instance; Bash will give you an error. In practice, the `declare` command is not used too much as far as we have encountered, but it can serve useful purposes besides read-only declarations, so be sure to give it a look!

Practical examples

Before we introduce function parameters in the next part of this chapter, we'll first look into a practical example of functions that do not need parameters. We'll go back to previous scripts we've created, and see if there is some functionality we can abstract as a function. Spoiler alert: there is a great one, which deals with a little something called error handling!

Error handling

In Chapter 9, *Error Checking and Handling*, we created the following construction: command || { echo "Something went wrong."; exit 1; }. As you (hopefully) remember, the || syntax means that everything on the right-hand side will only be executed if the command on the left-hand side has an exit status that is not 0. While this setup worked fine, it did not exactly increase readability. It would be much better if we could abstract our error handling to a function, and call that function instead! Let's do just that:

```
reader@ubuntu:~/scripts/chapter_13$ vim error-functions.sh
reader@ubuntu:~/scripts/chapter_13$ cat error-functions.sh
#!/bin/bash

#####################################
# Author: Sebastiaan Tammer
# Version: v1.0.0
# Date: 2018-11-11
# Description: Functions to handle errors.
# Usage: ./error-functions.sh
#####################################

# Define a function that handles minor errors.
handle_minor_error() {
  echo "A minor error has occured, please check the output."
}

# Define a function that handles fatal errors.
handle_fatal_error() {
  echo "A critical error has occured, stopping script."
  exit 1
}

# Minor failures.
ls -l /tmp/ || handle_minor_error
ls -l /root/ || handle_minor_error

# Fatal failures.
cat /etc/shadow || handle_fatal_error
```

```
cat /etc/passwd || handle_fatal_error
```

This script defines two functions: `handle_minor_error` and `handle_fatal_error`. For a minor error, we will print a message but the script execution does not stop. A fatal error, however, is considered so severe that the flow of the script is expected to be disrupted; in this case, it is of no use to continue the script so we'll make sure the function stops it. By using the functions combined with the `||` construct, we do not need to check for exit codes inside the functions; we only end up inside the functions if the exit code was not 0, so we already know we're in an error situation. Before we execute this script, take a moment to reflect *how much we improved the readability* with these functions. When you're done with that, run this script with debug output, so you can follow the entire flow:

```
reader@ubuntu:~/scripts/chapter_13$ bash -x error-functions.sh
+ ls -l /tmp/
total 8
drwx------ 3 root root 4096 Nov 11 11:07 systemd-private-869037dc...
drwx------ 3 root root 4096 Nov 11 11:07 systemd-private-869037dc...
+ ls -l /root/
ls: cannot open directory '/root/': Permission denied
+ handle_minor_error
+ echo 'A minor error has occured, please check the output.'
A minor error has occured, please check the output.
+ cat /etc/shadow
cat: /etc/shadow: Permission denied
+ handle_fatal_error
+ echo 'A critical error has occured, stopping script.'
A critical error has occured, stopping script.
+ exit 1
```

As you see, the first command, `ls -l /tmp/`, succeeds and we see its output; we do not enter the `handle_minor_error` function. The next command, which we do expect to fail, does indeed. We see that we now go into the function and the error message we specified there is printed. But, since it is only a minor error, we continue the script. However, when we get to `cat /etc/shadow`, which we consider a vital component, we encounter a `Permission denied` message that causes the script to execute `handle_fatal_error`. Because this function has an `exit 1`, the script is terminated and the fourth command is never executed. This should illustrate another point: an `exit`, even from inside a function, is global and terminates the script (not just the function). If you wish to see this script succeed, run it with `sudo bash error-functions.sh`. You will see that neither of the error functions is executed.

Augmenting functions with parameters

Just as a script can accept input in the form of arguments, so can a function. In reality, most functions will use parameters. Static functions, such as the error handling example from earlier, are not as powerful or flexible as their counterparts to accept arguments.

Colorful

In the next example, we'll create a script that allows us to print text to our terminals in a few different colors. It does this based on a function that has two parameters: string and color. Take a look at the following commands:

```
reader@ubuntu:~/scripts/chapter_13$ vim colorful.sh
reader@ubuntu:~/scripts/chapter_13$ cat colorful.sh
#!/bin/bash

#####################################
# Author: Sebastiaan Tammer
# Version: v1.0.0
# Date: 2018-11-17
# Description: Some printed text, now with colors!
# Usage: ./colorful.sh
#####################################

print_colored() {
  # Check if the function was called with the correct arguments.
  if [[ $# -ne 2 ]]; then
    echo "print_colored needs two arguments, exiting."
    exit 1
  fi

  # Grab both arguments.
  local string=$1
  local color=$2

  # Use a case-statement to determine the color code.
  case ${color} in
  red)
    local color_code="\e[31m";;
  blue)
    local color_code="\e[34m";;
  green)
    local color_code="\e[32m";;
  *)
    local color_code="\e[39m";; # Wrong color, use default.
```

```
  esac

  # Perform the echo, and reset color to default with [39m.
  echo -e ${color_code}${string}"\e[39m"
}

# Print the text in different colors.
print_colored "Hello world!" "red"
print_colored "Hello world!" "blue"
print_colored "Hello world!" "green"
print_colored "Hello world!" "magenta"
```

A lot is happening in this script. To help with your understanding, we'll go through it piece by piece, starting with the first part of the function definition:

```
print_colored() {
  # Check if the function was called with the correct arguments.
  if [[ $# -ne 2 ]]; then
    echo "print_colored needs two arguments, exiting."
    exit 1
  fi

  # Grab both arguments.
  local string=$1
  local color=$2
```

The first thing we do within the function body is check the number of arguments. The syntax is the same as the checks we normally do for arguments passed to the entire script, which might be helpful or perhaps confusing. A good thing to realize is that the $# construct applies to the scope in which it is used; if it is used within the main script, it checks the arguments passed there. If it is used, like it is here, within a function, it checks the number of arguments passed to the function. The same goes for $1, $2, and so on: if used within a function, they refer to the ordered arguments passed to the function, and not the script in general. When we grab the arguments, we write them to *local* variables; we don't strictly need to do that in this simple script, but it is always good practice to mark variableses local when you only use them in the local scope. You might imagine that in larger, more complex scripts many functions use variables that might accidentally be called the same thing (in this case, string is a very common word). By marking them local, you're not only improving readability, but also preventing errors caused by variables that have the same name; all in all, a very good idea. Let's get back to the next part of our script, the case-statement:

```
  # Use a case-statement to determine the color code.
  case ${color} in
  red)
    color_code="\e[31m";;
```

```
blue)
  color_code="\e[34m";;
green)
  color_code="\e[32m";;
*)
  color_code="\e[39m";; # Wrong color, use default.
esac
```

Now is an excellent time to introduce `case`. A case-statement is basically a very long `if-then-elif-then-elif-then...` chain. The more options there are for a variable, the longer the chain would become. With `case`, you can just say `for certain values in ${variable}, do <something>`. In our example, that means that if the `${color}` variable is `red`, we'll set another `color_code` variable to `\e[31m` (more on that in a bit). If it is `blue`, we'll do something else, and the same goes for `green`. Finally, we'll define a wildcard; any value for the variable that was not specified will go through there, as a sort of catch-all construction. If the color specified is something incompatible, such as **dog**, we'll just set the default color. The alternative would be breaking off the script, which is a bit of an overreaction to a wrong color. To terminate a `case`, you'll use the `esac` keyword (which is the reverse of `case`), in a similar manner to `if`, which is terminated by its reverse, `fi`.

Now, on to the technical aspect of *colors on your terminal*. While most things we've been learning about are Bash or Linux specific, printed colors are actually defined by your terminal emulator. The color codes we're using are pretty standard and should be interpreted by your terminal as *do not print this character literally, but instead change the color to <color>*. The terminal sees an *escape sequence*, \e, followed by a *color code*, [31m, and knows you're instructing it to print a different color than previously defined (often defaults for that terminal emulator, unless you've changed the color scheme yourself). You can do many more things (as long as your terminal emulator supports this, of course) with escape sequences, such as creating bold text, blinking text, and another background color for your text. For now, remember *the \e[31m sequence is not printed but interpreted.* For the catch-all in `case`, you do not want to explicitly set a color, but instead signal the terminal to print in the *default* color. This means that for every compatible terminal emulator, the text is printed in the color the user has chosen (or got assigned by default).

Now for the final part of the script:

```
# Perform the echo, and reset color to default with [39m.
echo -e ${color_code}${string}"\e[39m"
}

# Print the text in different colors.
print_colored "Hello world!" "red"
print_colored "Hello world!" "blue"
```

```
print_colored "Hello world!" "green"
print_colored "Hello world!" "magenta"
```

The last part of the `print_colored` function actually prints the colored text. It does this by using the good old `echo` with the `-e` flag. `man echo` reveals that `-e` *enables interpretation of backslash escapes*. If you do not specify this option, your output will just be something like `\e[31mHello world!\e[39m`. A good thing to know in this situation is that as soon as your terminal encounters a color code escape sequence, *all subsequent text will be printed in that color!* Because of this, we end the echo with `"\e[39m"`, which resets the color for all following text back to default.

Finally, we call the function multiple times, with the same first argument, but a different second argument (the color). If you run the script, the output should look similar to this:

```
reader@ubuntu:~/scripts/chapter_13$ bash colorful.sh
Hello world!
Hello world!
Hello world!
Hello world!
```

In the preceding screenshot, my color scheme is set to green-on-black, which is why the last `Hello world!` is bright green. You can see it is the same color as `bash colorful.sh`, which should be all the confirmation you need to be sure the `[39m` color code is actually default.

Returning values

Some functions follow the *processor* archetype: they take input, do something with it, and return the result back to the caller. This is something of a classic function: depending on the input, different output is generated. We'll show this with an example that reverses the input the user specifies to the script. This is normally done with the `rev` command (and will actually be accomplished with `rev` in our function as well), but we're creating a wrapper function around this with a little extra functionality:

```
reader@ubuntu:~/scripts/chapter_13$ vim reverser.sh
reader@ubuntu:~/scripts/chapter_13$ cat reverser.sh
#!/bin/bash

#####################################
# Author: Sebastiaan Tammer
# Version: v1.0.0
# Date: 2018-11-17
# Description: Reverse the input for the user.
```

```
# Usage: ./reverser.sh <input-to-be-reversed>
####################################
 
# Check if the user supplied one argument.
if [[ $# -ne 1 ]]; then
  echo "Incorrect number of arguments!"
  echo "Usage: $0 <input-to-be-reversed>"
  exit 1
fi

# Capture the user input in a variable.
user_input="_${1}_" # Add _ for readability.

# Define the reverser function.
reverser() {
  # Check if input is correctly passed.
  if [[ $# -ne 1 ]]; then
    echo "Supply one argument to reverser()!" && exit 1
  fi

  # Return the reversed input to stdout (default for rev).
  rev <<< ${1}
}

# Capture the function output via command substitution.
reversed_input=$(reverser ${user_input})

# Show the reversed input to the user.
echo "Your reversed input is: ${reversed_input}"
```

As this is again a longer, more complex script, we're going to look at it bit by bit to make sure you understand it all. We even sneaked a little surprise in there that proves one of our earlier statements, but we'll get to that in a bit. We'll skip the header and input check and move to capturing the variable:

```
# Capture the user input in a variable.
user_input="_${1}_" # Add _ for readability.
```

In most of the earlier examples, we've always directly mapped input to a variable. However, this time we're showing that you can actually also add some extra text. In this case, we're taking the input by the user and we add an underscore before and after. If the user inputs rain, the variable will actually contain _rain_. This will prove insightful later. Now, for the function definition, we use the following code:

```
# Define the reverser function.
reverser() {
  # Check if input is correctly passed.
```

```
if [[ $# -ne 1 ]]; then
  echo "Supply one argument to reverser()!" && exit 1
fi

# Return the reversed input to stdout (default for rev).
rev <<< ${1}
}
```

The `reverser` function requires a single argument: the input to be reversed. As always, we first check if the input is correct, before we actually do anything. Next, we use `rev` to reverse the input. However, `rev` normally expects input from a file or `stdin`, not a variable as an argument. Because we do not want to add an extra echo and pipe, we use a here string (as explained in `Chapter 12`, *Using Pipes and Redirection in Scripts*), which allows us to directly use the variable content as `stdin`. Since `rev` already outputs the result to `stdout`, we do not need to provide anything, such as an echo, at that point.

We told you we'd prove a previous statement, which in this case relates to `$1` in the previous snippet. If `$1` within the function related to the first argument *of the script* and not the first argument *of the function*, we would not see the underscores we added when we wrote the `user_input` variable. For the script, `$1` could equal `rain`, where in the function, `$1` equals `_rain_`. When you run the script, you'll definitely see the underscores, which means that each function really has its own set of arguments!

Tying it all together is the final piece of the script:

```
# Capture the function output via command substitution.
reversed_input=$(reverser ${user_input})

# Show the reversed input to the user.
echo "Your reversed input is: ${reversed_input}"
```

Since the `reverser` function sends the reversed input to `stdout`, we'll use command substitution to capture it in a variable. Finally, we print some clarifying text and the reversed input to the user with `echo`. The result will look like this:

```
reader@ubuntu:~/scripts/chapter_13$ bash reverser.sh rain
Your reversed input is: _niar_
```

Underscores and all, we get the reverse of `rain`: `_nair_`. Nice!

To avoid too much complexity, we split the final part of this script in two lines. However, once you feel comfortable with command substitutions, you could save yourself the intermediate variable and use the command substitution directly within the echo, like so: `echo "Your reversed input is: $(reverser ${user_input})"`. We would recommend not making it much more complex than this, however, since that will start to affect the readability.

Function libraries

When you get to this part of the book, you'll have seen well over 50 example scripts. Many of these scripts have some shared components: input checking, error handling, and setting the current working directory have been used in multiple scripts. This code doesn't really change; perhaps the comments or echoes were slightly different, but in reality it's just duplicated code. Pair this with the problem of having to define functions at the top of your script (or, at the very least, before you start using them) and your maintainability is beginning to suffer. Luckily for us all, there is a great solution for this: **creating your own function library!**

Source

The idea of a function library is that you define functions that are *shared* between different scripts. These are repeatable, generic functions that do not care too much about the specific script to work. When you create a new script, the first thing you'll do, right after the header, is *include the function definitions from the library*. The library is nothing more than another shell script: however, it is only used to define functions, so it never calls anything. If you were to run it, the end result would be the same as if you had run an empty script. We'll start creating our very own function library first, before we look at how we can include it.

There is only one real consideration when creating a function library: where to put it. You want to have it present just once in your filesystem, preferably in a predictable location. Personally, we prefer the `/opt/` directory. However, by default `/opt/` is only writable to the `root` user. In a multiuser system, it's probably not a bad idea to place it there, owned by `root` and readable by everyone, but since this is a single-user situation, we'll place it directly in our home directory. Let's make a humble beginning with our library there:

```
reader@ubuntu:~$ vim bash-function-library.sh
reader@ubuntu:~$ cat bash-function-library.sh
#!/bin/bash

#####################################
# Author: Sebastiaan Tammer
# Version: v1.0.0
# Date: 2018-11-17
# Description: Bash function library.
# Usage: source ~/bash-function-library.sh
#####################################

# Check if the number of arguments supplied is exactly correct.
check_arguments() {
  # We need at least one argument.
  if [[ $# -lt 1 ]]; then
    echo "Less than 1 argument received, exiting."
    exit 1
  fi

  # Deal with arguments
  expected_arguments=$1
  shift 1 # Removes the first argument.

  if [[ ${expected_arguments} -ne $# ]]; then
    return 1 # Return exit status 1.
  fi
}
```

Because this is a generic function, we need to first supply the number of arguments we're expecting, followed by the actual arguments. After we save the expected number of arguments, we use `shift` to *shift* all arguments one place to the left: $2 becomes $1, $3 becomes $2, and $1 is removed entirely. Doing this, only the number of arguments to check remains, with the expected number safely stored inside a variable. We then compare the two values, and if they're not the same, we return an exit code of 1. `return` is similar to `exit`, but it does not stop the script execution: if we want to do that, the script calling the function should take care of this.

To use this library function within another script, we'll need to include it. In Bash, this is called *sourcing*. Sourcing is achieved with the `source` command:

```
source <file-name>
```

The syntax is simple. As soon as you source a file, all its contents will be processed. In our library case, when we only define functions, nothing will be executed but we'll have the functions available. If you're sourcing a file that contains actual commands, such as echo, cat, or mkdir, these commands *will be executed.* As always, an example is worth a thousand words, so let's see how we can use source to include the library functions:

```
reader@ubuntu:~/scripts/chapter_13$ vim argument-checker.sh
reader@ubuntu:~/scripts/chapter_13$ cat argument-checker.sh
#!/bin/bash

####################################
# Author: Sebastiaan Tammer
# Version: v1.0.0
# Date: 2018-11-17
# Description: Validates the check_arguments library function
# Usage: ./argument-checker.sh
####################################

source ~/bash-function-library.sh

check_arguments 3 "one" "two" "three" # Correct.
check_arguments 2 "one" "two" "three" # Incorrect.
check_arguments 1 "one two three" # Correct.
```

Pretty simple right? We source the file using a fully qualified path (yes, even though ~ is shorthand, this is still fully qualified!) and go right on with using the function that was defined in the other script. If you run this with debug, you'll see that the function works as we expect:

```
reader@ubuntu:~/scripts/chapter_13$ bash -x argument-checker.sh
+ source /home/reader/bash-function-library.sh
+ check_arguments 3 one two three
+ [[ 4 -lt 1 ]]
+ expected_arguments=3
+ shift 1
+ [[ 3 -ne 3 ]]
+ check_arguments 2 one two three
+ [[ 4 -lt 1 ]]
+ expected_arguments=2
+ shift 1
+ [[ 2 -ne 3 ]]
+ return 1
+ check_arguments 1 'one two three'
+ [[ 2 -lt 1 ]]
+ expected_arguments=1
+ shift 1
+ [[ 1 -ne 1 ]]
```

The first and third function call are expected to be correct, whereas the second should fail. Because we used `return` and not `exit` in our function, the script continues even after the second function call returns an exit status of 1. As the debug output shows, the second time we call the function, the evaluation 2 not equals 3 is performed and succeeds, which results in `return 1`. For the other calls, the arguments are correct and the default return code of 0 is returned (not shown from output, but this is really what happens; add `echo $?` if you want to verify for yourself).

Now, to use this in an actual script, we'll need to pass all arguments the user gives us to our function. This can be done using the `$@` syntax: where `$#` corresponds to the number of arguments, `$@` simply prints all arguments. We'll update `argument-checker.sh` to check arguments to the script as well:

```
reader@ubuntu:~/scripts/chapter_13$ vim argument-checker.sh
reader@ubuntu:~/scripts/chapter_13$ cat argument-checker.sh
#!/bin/bash

#####################################
# Author: Sebastiaan Tammer
# Version: v1.1.0
# Date: 2018-11-17
# Description: Validates the check_arguments library function
# Usage: ./argument-checker.sh <argument1> <argument2>
#####################################

source ~/bash-function-library.sh

# Check user input.
# Use double quotes around $@ to prevent word splitting.
check_arguments 2 "$@"
echo $?
```

We pass the expected amount of arguments, 2, and all arguments received by the script, `$@`, to our sourced function. Run it with a few different inputs and see what happens:

```
reader@ubuntu:~/scripts/chapter_13$ bash argument-checker.sh
1
reader@ubuntu:~/scripts/chapter_13$ bash argument-checker.sh 1
1
reader@ubuntu:~/scripts/chapter_13$ bash argument-checker.sh 1 2
0
reader@ubuntu:~/scripts/chapter_13$ bash argument-checker.sh "1 2"
1
reader@ubuntu:~/scripts/chapter_13$ bash argument-checker.sh "1 2" 3
0
```

Excellent, everything seems to be working! The most interesting tries are probably the last two, since they illustrate the problem often posed by *word splitting*. By default, Bash will interpret every piece of whitespace as a separator. In the fourth example, we pass the "1 2" string, which is actually *a single argument because of the quotes*. If we did not use double quotes around $@, this would happen:

```
reader@ubuntu:~/scripts/chapter_13$ tail -3 argument-checker.sh
check_arguments 2 $@
echo $?

reader@ubuntu:~/scripts/chapter_13$ bash argument-checker.sh "1 2"
0
```

In this example, Bash passes the arguments to the function without preserving the quotes. The function would then receive "1" and "2", instead of "1 2". Something to watch out for, always!

Now, we can use a predefined function to check if the number of arguments is correct. However, currently we do not use our return code for anything. We're going to make one final adjustment to our `argument-checker.sh` script, which will stop script execution if the number of arguments is not correct:

```
reader@ubuntu:~/scripts/chapter_13$ vim argument-checker.sh
reader@ubuntu:~/scripts/chapter_13$ cat argument-checker.sh
#!/bin/bash

####################################
# Author: Sebastiaan Tammer
# Version: v1.2.0
# Date: 2018-11-17
# Description: Validates the check_arguments library function
# Usage: ./argument-checker.sh <argument1> <argument2>
####################################

source ~/bash-function-library.sh

# Check user input.
# Use double quotes around $@ to prevent word splitting.
check_arguments 2 "$@" || \
{ echo "Incorrect usage! Usage: $0 <argument1> <argument2>"; exit 1; }

# Arguments are correct, print them.
echo "Your arguments are: $1 and $2"
```

Because of the page width of this book, we've broken the line with `check_arguments` in two by using `\`: this signals to Bash to continue on the next line. You can omit this and have the full command on a single line, if you prefer. If we run the script now, we'll see desirable script execution:

```
reader@ubuntu:~/scripts/chapter_13$ bash argument-checker.sh
Incorrect usage! Usage: argument-checker.sh <argument1> <argument2>
reader@ubuntu:~/scripts/chapter_13$ bash argument-checker.sh dog cat
Your arguments are: dog and cat
reader@ubuntu:~/scripts/chapter_13$ bash argument-checker.sh dog cat mouse
Incorrect usage! Usage: argument-checker.sh <argument1> <argument2>
```

Congratulations, we have begun the creation of a function library and have successfully used it in one of our scripts!

There is a somewhat confusing shorthand syntax for source: a single dot (`.`). If we wanted to use that shorthand in our scripts, it would simply be `. ~/bash-function-library.sh`. We are, however, not big fans of this syntax: the `source` command is not long or complicated, while a single `.` can easily be missed or misused if you forget a space after it (which can be hard to see!). Our advice: know the shorthand exists if you encounter it somewhere in the wild, but use the full built-in source when writing scripts.

More practical examples

We're going to spend the last part of this chapter expanding your function library with commonly used actions from earlier scripts. We'll copy a script from one of the earlier chapters and use our function library to replace functionality that can then be handled with a function from our library.

Current working directory

The first candidate for inclusion in our own private function library is correctly setting the current working directory. This is a pretty simple function, so we'll add it without too much explanation:

```
reader@ubuntu:~/scripts/chapter_13$ vim ~/bash-function-library.sh
reader@ubuntu:~/scripts/chapter_13$ cat ~/bash-function-library.sh
#!/bin/bash
#####################################
# Author: Sebastiaan Tammer
```

```
# Version: v1.1.0
# Date: 2018-11-17
# Description: Bash function library.
# Usage: source ~/bash-function-library.sh
####################################
<SNIPPED>
# Set the current working directory to the script location.
set_cwd() {
  cd $(dirname $0)
}
```

Because a function library is something that is potentially updated quite frequently, correctly updating the information in the header is very important. Preferably (and most likely in an enterprise environment), you will commit new versions of your function library to a version control system. Using proper Semantic Version in the header will help you keep a clean history. Particularly, if you combine this with configuration management tooling such as Chef.io, Puppet, and Ansible, you will keep a good overview of what you've changed and deployed to where.

Now, we'll update our script from the previous chapter, `redirect-to-file.sh`, with our library inclusion and function call. The end result should be the following:

```
reader@ubuntu:~/scripts/chapter_13$ cp ../chapter_12/redirect-to-file.sh
library-redirect-to-file.sh
reader@ubuntu:~/scripts/chapter_13$ vim library-redirect-to-file.sh
reader@ubuntu:~/scripts/chapter_13$ cat library-redirect-to-file.sh
#!/bin/bash

####################################
# Author: Sebastiaan Tammer
# Version: v1.0.0
# Date: 2018-11-17
# Description: Redirect user input to file.
# Usage: ./library-redirect-to-file.sh
####################################

# Load our Bash function library.
source ~/bash-function-library.sh

# Since we're dealing with paths, set current working directory.
set_cwd

# Capture the users' input.
read -p "Type anything you like: " user_input

# Save the users' input to a file. > for overwrite, >> for append.
echo ${user_input} >> redirect-to-file.txt
```

For teaching purposes, we've copied the file to the directory of the current chapter; normally, we would just update our original file. We've only added the inclusion of our function library and replaced the magical cd $(dirname $0) with our set_cwd function call. Let's run it from a location where the script is not and see if the directory is correctly set:

```
reader@ubuntu:/tmp$ bash ~/scripts/chapter_13/library-redirect-to-file.sh
Type anything you like: I like ice cream, I guess
reader@ubuntu:/tmp$ ls -l
drwx------ 3 root root 4096 Nov 17 11:20 systemd-private-af82e37c...
drwx------ 3 root root 4096 Nov 17 11:20 systemd-private-af82e37c...
reader@ubuntu:/tmp$ cd ~/scripts/chapter_13
reader@ubuntu:~/scripts/chapter_13$ ls -l
<SNIPPED>
-rw-rw-r-- 1 reader reader 567 Nov 17 19:32 library-redirect-to-file.sh
-rw-rw-r-- 1 reader reader 26 Nov 17 19:35 redirect-to-file.txt
-rw-rw-r-- 1 reader reader 933 Nov 17 15:18 reverser.sh
reader@ubuntu:~/scripts/chapter_13$ cat redirect-to-file.txt
I like ice cream, I guess
```

So, even though we used the $0 syntax (which, as you remember, prints the fully qualified path of the script), we see here that it refers to the path of library-redirect-to-file.sh and not, as you might have reasonably assumed, to the location of the bash-function-library.sh script. This should confirm our explanation that only function definitions are included, and when the functions are called at runtime they take on the environment of the script that includes them.

Type checking

Something we've done in many of our scripts is checking arguments. We started our library with a function that allowed checking the number of arguments the user gave as input. Another action we frequently performed on user input was validating the input type. If our script requires a number, for example, we'd like the user to actually enter a number and not a word (or a written out number, such as 'eleven'). You might remember the approximate syntax, but I'm sure that by now if you needed it again, you would look through our older scripts to find it. Doesn't that sound like the ideal candidate for a library function? We create and thoroughly test our function once, and then we can feel safe just sourcing and using it! Let's create a function that checks if a passed argument is actually an integer:

```
reader@ubuntu:~/scripts/chapter_13$ vim ~/bash-function-library.sh
reader@ubuntu:~/scripts/chapter_13$ cat ~/bash-function-library.sh
#!/bin/bash
```

```
#####################################
# Author: Sebastiaan Tammer
# Version: v1.2.0
# Date: 2018-11-17
# Description: Bash function library.
# Usage: source ~/bash-function-library.sh
#####################################
<SNIPPED>

# Checks if the argument is an integer.
check_integer() {
  # Input validation.
  if [[ $# -ne 1 ]]; then
    echo "Need exactly one argument, exiting."
    exit 1 # No validation done, exit script.
  fi

  # Check if the input is an integer.
  if [[ $1 =~ ^[[:digit:]]+$ ]]; then
    return 0 # Is an integer.
  else
    return 1 # Is not an integer.
  fi
}
```

Because we're dealing with a library function, we can be a little more verbose for the sake of readability. Too much verbosity in a regular script will reduce readability, but as soon as someone is looking at the function library for understanding, you can assume they'll like some more verbose scripting. After all, when we call the function in a script we'll only see `check_integer ${variable}`.

On to the function. We first check if we've received a single argument. If we did not receive that, we exit instead of return. Why would we do this? The script that calls should not be confused about what a return code of 1 means; if it can mean that we either did not check anything, but also that the check itself failed, we're bringing ambiguity where we don't want it. So simply said, return always tells the caller something about the passed argument, and if the script calls the function wrong, it will see the full script exit with an error message.

Next, we use the regular expression we constructed in `Chapter 10`, *Regular Expressions*, to check if the argument is in fact an integer. If it is, we return `0`. If it is not, we'll hit the `else` block and `1` will be returned. To emphasize this point to someone reading the library, we included the `# Is an integer` and `# Is not an integer` comments. Why not make it easy on them? Remember, you do not always write it for someone else, but if you look at your own code a year later, you will definitely also feel like *someone else* (again, you can trust us on this!).

We'll do another search-replace from one of our earlier scripts. A suitable one from the previous chapter, `password-generator.sh`, will serve this purpose nicely. Copy it to a new file, load the function library with source, and replace the argument checks (yes, both!):

```
reader@ubuntu:~/scripts/chapter_13$ vim library-password-generator.sh
reader@ubuntu:~/scripts/chapter_13$ cat library-password-generator.sh
#!/bin/bash

######################################
# Author: Sebastiaan Tammer
# Version: v1.0.0
# Date: 2018-11-17
# Description: Generate a password.
# Usage: ./library-password-generator.sh <length>
######################################

# Load our Bash function library.
source ~/bash-function-library.sh

# Check for the correct number of arguments.
check_arguments 1 "$@" || \
{ echo "Incorrect usage! Usage: $0 <length>"; exit 1; }

# Verify the length argument.
check_integer $1 || { echo "Argument must be an integer!"; exit 1; }

# tr grabs readable characters from input, deletes the rest.
# Input for tr comes from /dev/urandom, via input redirection.
# echo makes sure a newline is printed.
tr -dc 'a-zA-Z0-9' < /dev/urandom | head -c $1
echo
```

We're replaced both the number of arguments check and the integer check with our library functions. We've also removed the variable declaration and used $1 directly in the functional part of the script; this is not always the best thing to do. However, when input is only used once, first storing it in a named variable creates some overhead which we might skip. Even with all the whitespace and comments, we still managed to reduce the script lines from 31 to 26 by using function calls. When we call our new and improved script, we see the following:

```
reader@ubuntu:~/scripts/chapter_13$ bash library-password-generator.sh
Incorrect usage! Usage: library-password-generator.sh <length>
reader@ubuntu:~/scripts/chapter_13$ bash library-password-generator.sh 10
50BCuB8351
reader@ubuntu:~/scripts/chapter_13$ bash library-password-generator.sh 10
20
Incorrect usage! Usage: library-password-generator.sh <length>
reader@ubuntu:~/scripts/chapter_13$ bash library-password-generator.sh bob
Argument must be an integer!
```

Great, our checks are working as expected. Looks much better too, doesn't it?

Yes-no check

We'll show one more check before we finish this chapter. Halfway through the book, in Chapter 9, *Error Checking and Handling*, we presented a script that dealt with a user that could supply either a 'yes' or a 'no'. But, as we explained there, the user might also use 'y' or 'n', and perhaps even a capital letter in there somewhere. By secretly using a little Bash expansion, which you will see properly explained in Chapter 16, *Bash Parameter Substitution and Expansion*, we were able to make a relatively clear check for user input. Let's get that thing in our library!

```
reader@ubuntu:~/scripts/chapter_13$ vim ~/bash-function-library.sh
reader@ubuntu:~/scripts/chapter_13$ cat ~/bash-function-library.sh
#!/bin/bash

####################################
# Author: Sebastiaan Tammer
# Version: v1.3.0
# Date: 2018-11-17
# Description: Bash function library.
# Usage: source ~/bash-function-library.sh
####################################
<SNIPPED>

# Checks if the user answered yes or no.
check_yes_no() {
```

```
# Input validation.
if [[ $# -ne 1 ]]; then
  echo "Need exactly one argument, exiting."
  exit 1 # No validation done, exit script.
fi

# Return 0 for yes, 1 for no, exit 2 for neither.
if [[ ${1,,} = 'y' || ${1,,} = 'yes' ]]; then
  return 0
elif [[ ${1,,} = 'n' || ${1,,} = 'no' ]]; then
  return 1
else
  echo "Neither yes or no, exiting."
  exit 2
fi
}
```

We've got a little advanced scripting cooked up for you with this example. Instead of a binary return, we now have four possible outcomes:

- Function incorrectly called: `exit 1`
- Function found a yes: `return 0`
- Function found a no: `return 1`
- Function found neither: `exit 2`

With our new library function, we'll take the `yes-no-optimized.sh` script and replace the complex logic with (almost) a single function call:

```
reader@ubuntu:~/scripts/chapter_13$ cp ../chapter_09/yes-no-optimized.sh
library-yes-no.sh
reader@ubuntu:~/scripts/chapter_13$ vim library-yes-no.sh
reader@ubuntu:~/scripts/chapter_13$ cat library-yes-no.sh
#!/bin/bash

#####################################
# Author: Sebastiaan Tammer
# Version: v1.0.0
# Date: 2018-11-17
# Description: Doing yes-no questions from our library.
# Usage: ./library-yes-no.sh
#####################################

# Load our Bash function library.
source ~/bash-function-library.sh

read -p "Do you like this question? " reply_variable
```

```
check_yes_no ${reply_variable} && \
echo "Great, I worked really hard on it!" || \
echo "You did not? But I worked so hard on it!"
```

Take a minute to look at the preceding script. It will probably be a little confusing at first, but try to remember what && and || do. Because of some smart ordering we applied, we can use && and || in sequence to achieve our result. Look at it like this:

1. If check_yes_no returns an exit status of 0 (when a **yes** is found), the command after && is executed. Since that echoes the success, and echo has an exit code of 0, the failure echo after the next || is not executed.

2. If check_yes_no returns an exit status of 1 (when a **no** is found), the command after && is not executed. However, it continues until it reaches ||, which goes on to the failure echo since the return code was still *not* 0.

3. If check_yes_no exits on either the lack of argument or lack of yes/no, the commands after both && and || are not executed (because the script is given an exit instead of return, so code execution is stopped immediately).

Pretty clever right? However, we must admit, it's a little against most things we've been teaching you with regards to readability. Consider this a teaching exercise for chaining && and || instead. If you'd want to implement the yes-no check yourself, it would probably be better to create dedicated check_yes() and check_no() functions. In any case, let's see if our tricked out script actually works as we hope it does:

```
reader@ubuntu:~/scripts/chapter_13$ bash library-yes-no.sh
Do you like this question? Yes
Great, I worked really hard on it!
reader@ubuntu:~/scripts/chapter_13$ bash library-yes-no.sh
Do you like this question? n
You did not? But I worked so hard on it!
reader@ubuntu:~/scripts/chapter_13$ bash library-yes-no.sh
Do you like this question? MAYBE
Neither yes or no, exiting.
reader@ubuntu:~/scripts/chapter_13$ bash library-yes-no.sh
Do you like this question?
Need exactly one argument, exiting.
```

All scenarios as we've defined them in the check work out. Great success!

Normally, you do not want to mix exit and return codes too much. Also, using a return code to convey anything other than pass or fail is also pretty uncommon. However, since you can return 256 different codes (from 0 up to 255), this is at least possible by design. Our yes-no example was a good candidate for showing how this could be used. However, as a general tip, you're probably better off by using it in a pass/fail way, as currently you place the burden of knowing the different return codes on the caller. Which is, to say the least, not always a fair thing to ask of them.

We'd like to end this chapter with a small exercise for you. In this chapter, before we introduced the function library, we already created a few functions: two for error handling, one for colored printing, and one for reversing text. Your exercise is simple: grab those functions and add them to your personal function library. Make sure to keep the following things in mind:

- Are the functions verbose enough to be included in the library as is, or could they use more?
- Can we call the functions and deal with the output as is, or would an edit be preferable?
- Are returns and exits properly implemented, or do they need to be adjusted to work as a generic library function?

There are no right or wrong answers here, just things to consider. Good luck!

Summary

In this chapter, we have presented Bash functions. Functions are generic chains of commands that can be defined once, before being called multiple times. Functions are reusable and can be shared between multiple scripts.

Variable scopes were introduced. The variables we've seen thus far were always *globally* scoped: they were available to the entire script. However, with the introduction of functions, we encounter *locally* scoped variables. These are only accessible within a function and marked with the `local` keyword.

We learned that functions can have their own independent set of parameters, which can be passed as arguments when the function is called. We proved that these are in fact different from the global arguments passed to the script (unless all arguments are passed through to the function, of course). We gave an example about returning output from a function using `stdout`, which we could capture by encapsulating the function call in a command substitution.

In the second half of this chapter, we turned our attention to creating a function library: an independent script without actual commands, which can be included (via the source command) in another script. As soon as the library is sourced in another script, all functions defined in the library can then be used by the script. We spent the remainder of this chapter showing how this was done, while simultaneously expanding our function library with some practical utility functions.

We ended the chapter with an exercise for the reader, to make sure all functions defined in this chapter are included in their own personal function library.

The following commands were introduced in this chapter: top, free, declare, case, rev, and return.

Questions

1. In which two ways can we define a function?
2. What are some advantages of functions?
3. What is the difference between a globally scoped variable and a locally scoped one?
4. How can we set values and attributes to variables?
5. How can a function use arguments passed to it?
6. How can we return a value from a function?
7. What does the source command do?
8. Why would we want to create a function library?

Further reading

- **Linux performance monitoring**: https://linoxide.com/monitoring-2/linux-performance-monitoring-tools/
- **AWK basic tutorial**: https://mistonline.in/wp/awk-basic-tutorial-with-examples/
- **Advanced Bash variables**: https://www.thegeekstuff.com/2010/05/bash-variables/
- **Sourcing**: https://bash.cyberciti.biz/guide/Source_command

Scheduling and Logging
14

In this chapter, we'll teach you the basics of scheduling and logging the results of your scripts. We'll begin by explaining how both `at` and `cron` can be used to schedule commands and scripts. In the second part of the chapter, we will describe how we can log the results of our scripts. We can use both the local mail functionality of Linux and redirection to achieve this purpose.

The following commands will be introduced in this chapter: `at`, `wall`, `atq`, `atrm`, `sendmail`, `crontab`, and `alias`.

The following topics will be covered in this chapter:

- Scheduling with `at` and `cron`
- Logging script results

Technical requirements

All scripts for this chapter can be found on GitHub: `https://github.com/PacktPublishing/Learn-Linux-Shell-Scripting-Fundamentals-of-Bash-4.4/tree/master/Chapter14`. The rest of the examples and exercises should be performed on your Ubuntu virtual machine.

Scheduling with at and cron

We've learned about many things in the world of shell scripting so far: variables, conditionals, loops, redirections, and even functions. In this chapter, we'll explain another important concept that is closely related to shell scripting: scheduling.

Simply put, scheduling is making sure your commands or scripts run at certain times, without the need for you to personally start them every time. A classic example can be found in cleaning up logs; often, older logs are no longer useful and take up too much space. For example, you could fix this with a cleanup script that removes logs older than 45 days. However, such a script should probably be run once a day. On a workday, this shouldn't pose the biggest problem, but having to log in during the weekend is no fun. Actually, we should not even consider this, since scheduling allows us to define *when* or *how often* a script should run!

In Linux scheduling, the most commonly used tools are at and cron. We'll first describe the principles of scheduling using at, before we continue with the much more powerful (and because of that, more widely used) cron.

at

The at command is used mostly for ad hoc scheduling. The syntax for at is very close to our natural language. This is easiest explained with an example, as follows:

```
reader@ubuntu:~/scripts/chapter_14$ date
Sat Nov 24 11:50:12 UTC 2018
reader@ubuntu:~/scripts/chapter_14$ at 11:51
warning: commands will be executed using /bin/sh
at> wall "Hello readers!"
at> <EOT>
job 6 at Sat Nov 24 11:51:00 2018
reader@ubuntu:~/scripts/chapter_14$ date
Sat Nov 24 11:50:31 UTC 2018

Broadcast message from reader@ubuntu (somewhere) (Sat Nov 24 11:51:00
2018):

Hello readers!

reader@ubuntu:~/scripts/chapter_14$ date
Sat Nov 24 11:51:02 UTC 2018
```

In essence, you're telling the system: *at <timestamp>, do something*. When you enter the at 11:51 command, you will be placed in an interactive prompt that will allow you to enter the commands you want executed. After that, you exit the prompt with *Ctrl + D*; if you use *Ctrl + C*, the job will not be saved! For reference, we use a simple command here, wall, which allows you to broadcast a message to everyone that is logged in to the server at that time.

Time syntax

When you use `at`, you can specify the time absolutely, like we did in the previous example, or relatively. An example of relative would be *in 5 minutes* or *after 24 hours*. This is often easier than checking the current time, adding your desired interval to it, and passing it to `at`. This works with the following syntax:

```
reader@ubuntu:~/scripts/chapter_14$ at now + 1 min
warning: commands will be executed using /bin/sh
at> touch /tmp/at-file
at> <EOT>
job 10 at Sun Nov 25 10:16:00 2018
reader@ubuntu:~/scripts/chapter_14$ date
Sun Nov 25 10:15:20 UTC 2018
```

You always need to specify relative to which time you want to add the minute, hour, or day. Fortunately, we can use **now** as a keyword for the current time. Do note that when dealing with minutes, `at` will always round to the nearest full minute. Besides minutes, the following are also valid (as found in `man at`):

- Hours
- Days
- Weeks

You can even create more complex solutions, such as *4 pm three days from now*. However, we feel like `cron` is better suited for these kinds of situations. With regards to `at`, the best use seems to be one-off jobs at a time that is *near*.

The at queue

As soon as you start scheduling jobs, you'll find yourself in a situation where you either messed up the time or the content for a job. For some jobs, you can just add a new one and let the other fail. However, there are certainly instances where the original job will wreak havoc on your system. In this case, it would be a great idea to delete the incorrect job. Luckily, the creators of `at` foresaw this problem (and probably experienced it too!) and created this functionality. The `atq` command (short for **at queue**), shows you the jobs currently in the pipeline. With `atrm` (don't think we need to explain that one), you can remove jobs by number. Let's look at an example of multiple jobs in the queue, and removing one:

```
reader@ubuntu:~/scripts/chapter_14$ vim wall.txt
reader@ubuntu:~/scripts/chapter_14$ cat wall.txt
wall "Hello!"
```

```
reader@ubuntu:~/scripts/chapter_14$ at now + 5 min -f wall.txt
warning: commands will be executed using /bin/sh
job 12 at Sun Nov 25 10:35:00 2018
reader@ubuntu:~/scripts/chapter_14$ at now + 10 min -f wall.txt
warning: commands will be executed using /bin/sh
job 13 at Sun Nov 25 10:40:00 2018
reader@ubuntu:~/scripts/chapter_14$ at now + 4 min -f wall.txt
warning: commands will be executed using /bin/sh
job 14 at Sun Nov 25 10:34:00 2018
reader@ubuntu:~/scripts/chapter_14$ atq
12      Sun Nov 25 10:35:00 2018 a reader
13      Sun Nov 25 10:40:00 2018 a reader
14      Sun Nov 25 10:34:00 2018 a reader
reader@ubuntu:~/scripts/chapter_14$ atrm 13
reader@ubuntu:~/scripts/chapter_14$ atq
12      Sun Nov 25 10:35:00 2018 a reader
14      Sun Nov 25 10:34:00 2018 a reader
```

As you can see, we've used a new flag for `at`: `-f`. This allows us to run commands defined
in a file, instead of having to use the interactive shell. This file, which we ended with **.txt**
(for clarity, no extension is needed), contains the commands to be executed. We use this file
to schedule three jobs: after 5 minutes, after 10 minutes, and after 4 minutes. After doing
that, we use `atq` to see the current queue: all three jobs, numbered 12, 13, and 14. At this
point in time, we realize we only want the jobs to run after 4 and 5 minutes, and not after
10. We can now use `atrm` to remove job number 13 by simply adding that number to the
command. When we look at the queue again right afterward, we see that only jobs 12 and
14 remain. After a few minutes, the first two **Hello!** messages are printed onto our screen. If
we wait the full 10 minutes, we will see... nothing, as we've successfully deleted our job:

```
Broadcast message from reader@ubuntu (somewhere) (Sun Nov 25 10:34:00
2018):

Hello!


Broadcast message from reader@ubuntu (somewhere) (Sun Nov 25 10:35:00
2018):

Hello!


reader@ubuntu:~/scripts/chapter_14$ date
Sun Nov 25 10:42:07 UTC 2018
```

Instead of using `atq` and `atrm`, `at` also has flags we can use for those functions. For `atq`, this is `at -l` (*list*). `atrm` even has two possible alternatives: `at -d` (*delete*) and `at -r` (*remove*). It does not matter whether you use the supporting commands or the flags; under the hood, the same thing will be executed. Use whatever is easiest to remember for you!

at output

As you might have noticed, up until now we've only used commands that did not rely on stdout (a little sneaky, we know). However, once you think about it, this poses a real problem. Normally, when we deal with commands and scripts, we use stdout/stderr to get a feeling about the result of our actions. The same goes for interactive prompts: we use our keyboards to supply input via stdin. Now that we're scheduling *non-interactive jobs*, things will be different. For starters, we cannot use interactive constructs such as `read` anymore. Scripts will simply fail because there is no stdin available. But, again, there is no stdout available either, so we do not even see the scripts fail! Or is there?

Somewhere in the manpage of `at`, you can find the following text:

> *"The user will be mailed standard error and standard output from his commands, if any. Mail will be sent using the command /usr/sbin/sendmail. If at is executed from a su(1) shell, the owner of the login shell will receive the mail."*

It would seem that the creators of `at` thought of this problem as well. However, if you do not have a lot of experience with Linux (yet!), you're probably confused about the mail portion of the preceding text. If you're thinking about the kind that has stamps, you're pretty far off. However, if you think *email*, you're a bit warmer.

Without going into too much detail (which is definitely outside the scope of this book), Linux has a local *mail spool,* which allows you to send emails within your local system. If you configure this with an upstream server, you can actually send an actual email as well, but for now, remember that an internal email on a Linux system is available. With this mail spool, emails are (perhaps unsurprisingly) files on the filesystem. These can be found at **/var/spool/mail**, which is actually a symbolic link to **/var/mail**. If you followed along with the installation of an Ubuntu 18.04 machine, these directories will be empty. This is easily explained: by default, `sendmail` is not installed. When it is not installed, and you schedule a job that has stdout, this happens:

```
reader@ubuntu:/var/mail$ which sendmail # No output, so not installed.
reader@ubuntu:/var/mail$ at now + 1 min
warning: commands will be executed using /bin/sh
at> echo "Where will this go?"
```

```
at> <EOT>
job 15 at Sun Nov 25 11:12:00 2018
reader@ubuntu:/var/mail$ date
Sun Nov 25 11:13:02 UTC 2018
reader@ubuntu:/var/mail$ ls -al
total 8
drwxrwsr-x  2 root mail 4096 Apr 26  2018 .
drwxr-xr-x 14 root root 4096 Jul 29 12:30 ..
```

Yep, exactly nothing happens. Now, if we install `sendmail` and try this again, we should see a different result:

```
reader@ubuntu:/var/mail$ sudo apt install sendmail -y
[sudo] password for reader:
Reading package lists... Done
<SNIPPED>
Setting up sendmail (8.15.2-10) ...
<SNIPPED>
reader@ubuntu:/var/mail$ which sendmail
/usr/sbin/sendmail
reader@ubuntu:/var/mail$ at now + 1 min
warning: commands will be executed using /bin/sh
at> echo "Where will this go?"
at> <EOT>
job 16 at Sun Nov 25 11:17:00 2018
reader@ubuntu:/var/mail$ date
Sun Nov 25 11:17:09 UTC 2018
You have new mail in /var/mail/reader
```

Mail, just for you! If we inspect **/var/mail/**, we'll see just a single file that contains our output:

```
reader@ubuntu:/var/mail$ ls -l
total 4
-rw-rw---- 1 reader mail 1341 Nov 25 11:18 reader
reader@ubuntu:/var/mail$ cat reader
From reader@ubuntu.home.lan Sun Nov 25 11:17:00 2018
Return-Path: <reader@ubuntu.home.lan>
Received: from ubuntu.home.lan (localhost.localdomain [127.0.0.1])
    by ubuntu.home.lan (8.15.2/8.15.2/Debian-10) with ESMTP id wAPBH0Ix003531
    for <reader@ubuntu.home.lan>; Sun, 25 Nov 2018 11:17:00 GMT
Received: (from reader@localhost)
    by ubuntu.home.lan (8.15.2/8.15.2/Submit) id wAPBH0tK003528
    for reader; Sun, 25 Nov 2018 11:17:00 GMT
Date: Sun, 25 Nov 2018 11:17:00 GMT
From: Learn Linux Shell Scripting <reader@ubuntu.home.lan>
Message-Id: <201811251117.wAPBH0tK003528@ubuntu.home.lan>
Subject: Output from your job 16
```

```
To: reader@ubuntu.home.lan
```

Where will this go?

It even looks like a real email, with a **Date:**, a **Subject:**, a **To:**, and **From:** (and so on). If we schedule more jobs, we'll see new mails appended to this single file. Linux has some simple, text-based mail clients that allow you to treat this single file as multiple emails, (one example of this is `mutt`); however, we do not need these for our purposes.

 One thing of note when dealing with notifications from the system, such as the **You have new mail** one, is that it does not always get pushed to your Terminal (while some others, such as `wall`, do). These messages are printed the next time your Terminal is updated; this is often done when you enter a new command, (or just an empty *Enter*). If you're working on these examples and waiting for the output, don't hesitate to press *Enter* a few times and see whether something comes up!

While it is sometimes great to get the output of commands we're running as jobs, more often than not it can be very annoying, since many processes can send you local mail. Often, this will result in a situation where you do not look at the mail, or even actively suppress output for commands, so you do not receive more mails. Further on in this chapter, after we introduce `cron`, we'll spend some time describing how we can deal with output *the right way*. As a small preview, this means we won't rely on inbuilt capabilities like this, but we'll use redirection to **write the output we need to a place where we know to find it.**

cron

Now that the basics of scheduling via `at` have been discussed, let's take a look at the real powerhouse for scheduling on Linux: `cron`. Aptly named from the Greek word *chronos*, which translates to *time*, `cron` is a job scheduler, which consists of two main components: the *cron daemon* (sometimes referred to as *crond*), and the *crontab*. The cron daemon is the background process that runs the scheduled jobs. These jobs are scheduled using the crontab, which is simply a file on the filesystem that is most often edited with a command by the same name: `crontab`. We'll start by looking at the `crontab` command and syntax.

crontab

Every user on a Linux system can have their own crontab. There is also a system-wide crontab (not to be confused with the crontab that can run under the **root** user!), which is used for periodic tasks; we'll get to those later in this chapter. For now, we'll start by exploring the crontab syntax, and create our first crontab for our **reader** user.

Syntax for the crontab

While the syntax may initially seem confusing, it is actually not that hard to understand but extremely flexible:

> *<timestamp> command*

Wow, that was easy! If this were really the case, then yes. However, what we described above as <timestamp> is actually composed of five different fields, which make up the combined period for running jobs multiple times. In reality, the timestamp is defined as follows (in order):

1. Minute-of-the-hour
2. Hour-of-the-day
3. Day-of-the-month
4. Month
5. Day-of-the-week

In any of these values, we can substitute a number for a wildcard, which indicates *all values*. Look at the following table to get a feeling about how we combine these five fields for precise times:

Crontab syntax	Semantic meaning
15 16 * * *	Every day at 16:15.
30 * * * *	Once every hour, at xx:30 (because every hour is valid due to the wildcard).
* 20 * * *	60 times per day, between 20:00 and 20:59 (hour is fixed, minutes have a wildcard).
10 10 1 * *	Once on the first of every month, at 10:10.
00 21 * * 1	Once per week, 21:00 on Monday (1-7 is Monday through Sunday, Sunday is also 0).
59 23 31 12 *	Right before the new year, 23:59 on December 31st.

| 01 00 1 1 3 | On 00:01 on January 1st, but only if that takes place on a Wednesday (which will happen in 2020). |

You might be a little confused by this syntax. Since many of us normally write time as 18:30, reversing the minutes and the hour seems a little counter intuitive. However, this is just the way it is (and trust us, you will get used to the crontab format soon enough). Now, there are a few advanced tricks that work with this syntax as well:

- 8-16 (hyphens allows multiple values, so `00 8-16 * * *` would mean every full hour from 08:00 to 16:00).
- */5 allows every 5 *units* (most often used in the first location, for every 5 minutes). The value */6 for hours is useful as well, for four times a day.
- 00,30 for two values, such as every 30 minutes on the hour or half hour (which could also be written as */30).

Before we get too bogged down in the theory, let's create a simple first crontab for our user using the `crontab` command. The `crontab` command has three interesting flags you'll use most often: `-l` for list, `-e` for edit, and `-r` for remove. Let's create (and remove) our very first crontab using these three commands:

```
reader@ubuntu:~$ crontab -l
no crontab for reader
reader@ubuntu:~$ crontab -e
no crontab for reader - using an empty one

Select an editor.  To change later, run 'select-editor'.
  1. /bin/nano        <---- easiest
  2. /usr/bin/vim.basic
  3. /usr/bin/vim.tiny
  4. /bin/ed

Choose 1-4 [1]: 2
crontab: installing new crontab
reader@ubuntu:~$ crontab -l
# m h  dom mon dow   command
* * * * * wall "Crontab rules!"

Broadcast message from reader@ubuntu (somewhere) (Sun Nov 25 16:25:01
2018):

Crontab rules!

reader@ubuntu:~$ crontab -r
reader@ubuntu:~$ crontab -l
no crontab for reader
```

As you can see, we start by listing the current crontab using the `crontab -l` command. Since we do not have one, we see the message **no crontab for reader** (no surprises there). Next, when we use `crontab -e` to start editing the crontab, we'll get a choice: which editor do we want to use? As always, do whatever works best for you. We have enough experience with `vim` to prefer it over `nano`. We only have to do that once for each user, because Linux will save our preference (check out the ~/**.selected_editor** file). Then, finally, we're presented with a text editor screen, which, on our Ubuntu machine, is filled with a little tutorial on crontabs. Since all these lines start with a #, all are considered comments and do not interfere with execution. Usually, we delete everything *except the syntax hint*: **m h dom mon dow command**. You can expect to forget this syntax a few times, which is why that little hint helps a lot when you need to do a quick edit, especially if it has been a while since you've interacted with a crontab.

We create a crontab with the simplest time syntax of all: wildcards in all five positions. Simply said, that means the command specified after is run *every minute*. After we save and exit, we wait a maximum of one minute before we see the result of the `wall "Crontab rules!";` command a broadcast from our own user, visible to all users on the system. Because this construction spams up the system pretty badly, we remove the crontab after a single broadcast by using `crontab -r`. Alternatively, we could have also removed just that line or commented it out.

A crontab can have many entries. Each entry has to be placed on its own line, with its own time syntax. This allows for a user to have many different jobs scheduled, at different frequencies. Because of this, `crontab -r` is not often used, and by itself is pretty destructive. We would advise you to always use `crontab -e` to ensure you do not accidentally delete your whole job schedule, but just the bits that you want.

As stated, all crontabs are saved as files in the filesystem. You can find them in the **/var/spool/cron/crontabs/** directory. This directory is accessible to the root user only; it would have some big privacy concerns if all users could see each other's job schedules. If you use `sudo` to become **root**, however, you would see the following:

```
reader@ubuntu:~$ sudo -i
[sudo] password for reader:
root@ubuntu:~# cd /var/spool/cron/crontabs/
root@ubuntu:/var/spool/cron/crontabs# ls -l
total 4
-rw------- 1 reader crontab 1090 Nov 25 16:51 reader
```

If we were to open this file (vim, less, cat, whatever you prefer), we'd see the same as a crontab -e for the **reader** user would show us. As a general rule, though, always use the available tools to edit files like these! The primary added benefit of this is that these tools do not allow you to save an incorrect format. If we were to edit the crontab file by hand and get the time syntax wrong, the entire crontab will no longer work. If you do the same with crontab -e, you will see an error and the crontab will not be saved, as follows:

```
reader@ubuntu:~$ crontab -e
crontab: installing new crontab
"/tmp/crontab.ABXIt7/crontab":23: bad day-of-week
errors in crontab file, can't install.
Do you want to retry the same edit? (y/n)
```

In the preceding example, we entered the line * * * * true. As can be seen from the error, where cron expects a digit or wildcard, it finds the command true (which, as you might recall, is a command which simply returns an exit code of 0). It presents the user with an error, and refuses to save the new edit, which means all previous scheduled jobs are safe and will continue to run, even though we messed it up this time.

> The time syntax for crontab allows pretty much any combination you could think of. However, sometimes you do not really care about an exact time, but are more interested in making sure something runs *hourly*, *daily*, *weekly*, or even *monthly*. Cron has some special time syntaxes for this: instead of the five values you normally insert, you can tell the crontab @hourly, @daily, @weekly, and @monthly.

Logging script results

Running scripts on a schedule is a great way to automate repetitive tasks. There is one big consideration when doing this though: logging. Normally, when you run a command, the output will be visible to you directly. If something seems wrong, you are there behind the keyboard to investigate the issue. However, once we start using cron (and even at), we no longer see the direct output of the commands. We can only check the results once we log in, and, if we do not make arrangements, we can only look for the *result of the script* (for example, cleaned up log files). What we need is logging for our script, so we have a simple way to periodically verify whether our script is running successfully.

Crontab environment variables

In our crontab, we can define environment variables, which will be used by our commands and scripts. This function of the crontab is used quite frequently, but mostly only for three environment variables: **PATH**, **SHELL**, and **MAILTO**. We'll look at the use case/necessity for these variables.

PATH

Normally, when you login to a Linux system, you are given a *login shell*. A login shell is a fully interactive shell that does some cool stuff for you: it sets the **PS1** variable (which determines how your prompt looks), correctly sets your **PATH**, and so on. Now, as you might imagine, there is also something other than a login shell. Technically, there are two dimensions that make up four different kinds of shells:

	Login	Non-login
Interactive	Interactive login shell	Interactive non-login shell
Non-interactive	Non-interactive login shell	Non-interactive non-login shell

Most of the time, you'll use an *interactive login shell*, such as when you connect via (SSH) or directly via the Terminal console. The other often encountered shell is the *non-interactive non-login shell*, which is what is used when commands are run via at or cron. The other two are possible, but we will not be going into the details of when you would get those.

So, now that you know we get a different type of shell in at and cron, we're sure you'd like to know what the difference is (as in, why do you care about this?). There are a number of files that set your profile in Bash. Some of these are listed here:

- /etc/profile
- /etc/bash.bashrc
- ~/.profile
- ~/.bashrc

The first two, located in **/etc/**, are system-wide files, and are thus the same for all users. The latter two, which are found in your home directory, are personal; these can be edited to, for example, add aliases that you'd like to use. The alias command is used to create a shorthand for commands with flags. The **~/.bashrc** file contains the line alias ll='ls -alF' by default on Ubuntu 18.04, which means you can type ll and have ls -alF executed instead.

Without going into too much detail (and oversimplifying quite a bit), an interactive login shell reads and parses all these files, while a non-interactive non-login shell does not (for more in-depth information, see the *Further reading* section). As always, a picture is worth a thousand words, so let's check out the differences ourselves:

```
reader@ubuntu:~$ echo $PATH
/usr/local/sbin:/usr/local/bin:/usr/sbin:/usr/bin:/sbin:/bin:/usr/games:/us
r/local/games:/snap/bin
reader@ubuntu:~$ echo $PS1
\[\e]0;\u@\h:
\w\a\]${debian_chroot:+($debian_chroot)}\[\033[01;32m\]\u@\h\[\033[00m\]:\[
\033[01;34m\]\w\[\033[00m\]\$
reader@ubuntu:~$ echo $0
-bash
reader@ubuntu:~$ at now
warning: commands will be executed using /bin/sh
at> echo $PATH
at> echo $PS1
at> echo $0
at> <EOT>
job 19 at Sat Dec  1 10:36:00 2018
You have mail in /var/mail/reader
reader@ubuntu:~$ tail -5 /var/mail/reader
/usr/local/sbin:/usr/local/bin:/usr/sbin:/usr/bin:/sbin:/bin:/usr/games:/us
r/local/games:/snap/bin
$
sh
```

As we can see here, the values differ between a normal (SSH) shell and `at` executed commands. This goes for both **PS1** and the shell itself (which we can find with **$0**). However, for `at`, the **PATH** is the same as for an interactive login session. Now, take a look at what happens if we do this in a crontab:

```
reader@ubuntu:~$ crontab -e
crontab: installing new crontab
reader@ubuntu:~$ crontab -l
# m h  dom mon dow   command
* * * * * echo $PATH; echo $PS1; echo $0
You have mail in /var/mail/reader
reader@ubuntu:~$ tail -4 /var/mail/reader
/usr/bin:/bin
$
/bin/sh
reader@ubuntu:~$ crontab -r # So we don't keep doing this every minute!
```

Starting off, **PS1** is equal to what at sees. Since **PS1** controls the way the shell looks, this is only interesting for interactive sessions; both at and cron are non-interactive. If we move on to **PATH**, we see a very different story: when running in cron, we get **/usr/bin:/bin** instead of
/usr/local/sbin:/usr/local/bin:/usr/sbin:/usr/bin:/sbin:/bin:/usr/games:/usr/local/games:/snap/bin! Simply put, this means for all commands that are outside of **/bin/** and **/usr/bin/**, we need to use the fully qualified filename. This even manifests itself in the **$0** difference (**sh** versus **/bin/sh**). While this is not strictly necessary (since **/bin/** is actually part of the **PATH**), it is still typical to see fully qualified paths for anything cron related.

Now, we have two options to deal with this, if we want to prevent errors such as **sudo: command not found**. We can either make sure we always use fully qualified paths for all commands (which, in practice, will definitely fail a few times), or we can make sure we set a **PATH** for the crontab. The first option gives us a lot more extra work for all things we'll ever do with cron. The second option is actually a really easy way to make sure we negate this problem. We can simply include a PATH=... at the top of the crontab, and all things executed by the crontab use that **PATH**. Give the following a try:

```
reader@ubuntu:~$ crontab -e
no crontab for reader - using an empty one
crontab: installing new crontab
reader@ubuntu:~$ crontab -l
PATH=/usr/local/sbin:/usr/local/bin:/usr/sbin:/usr/bin:/sbin:/bin:/usr/game
s:/usr/local/games:/snap/bin
# m h  dom mon dow   command
* * * * * echo $PATH
reader@ubuntu:~$
You have new mail in /var/mail/reader
reader@ubuntu:~$ crontab -r
reader@ubuntu:~$ tail -2 /var/mail/reader
/usr/local/sbin:/usr/local/bin:/usr/sbin:/usr/bin:/sbin:/bin:/usr/games:/us
r/local/games:/snap/bin
```

Easy-peasy. If you want to verify this for yourself, you could keep the default **PATH** and run something from **/sbin/** (such as the blkid command, which shows information on your disks/partitions). Since this isn't on the **PATH**, if you do not run it fully qualified, you'll encounter the error **/bin/sh: 1: blkid: not found** in your local mail. Pick any command that you could normally run and try it!

With this simple addition to a crontab, you can save yourself a lot of time and effort troubleshooting errors. As with all things in scheduling, you often have to wait at least a few minutes for each script attempt to run, making troubleshooting a time-intensive practice. Do yourself a favor and always make sure to include a relevant PATH as the first line of your crontab.

SHELL

It should be clear from looking at the outputs we saw for **PATH**, both `at` and `cron` by default use **/bin/sh**. You might get lucky and have a distribution where **/bin/sh** defaults to Bash, but this is not necessarily the case, especially not if you followed along with our Ubuntu 18.04 installation! In this case, if we check out **/bin/sh**, we see something different entirely:

```
reader@ubuntu:~$ ls -l /bin/sh
lrwxrwxrwx 1 root root 4 Apr 26  2018 /bin/sh -> dash
```

Dash is the *Debian Almquist shell*, which is the default system shell on recent Debian systems (Ubuntu, as you might remember, belongs to the Debian distribution family). While Dash is a wonderful shell with its own set of advantages and disadvantages, this book is written for Bash. So, for our use case, it is not practical to have `cron` default to using a Dash shell, since that would not allow us to use cool Bash 4.x functions such as advanced redirections, certain expansions, and so on. Fortunately, we can easily set the shell that `cron` should use when we run our commands: we use the **SHELL** environment variable. Setting this is really simple:

```
reader@ubuntu:~$ crontab -e
crontab: installing new crontab
reader@ubuntu:~$ crontab -l
SHELL=/bin/bash
PATH=/usr/local/sbin:/usr/local/bin:/usr/sbin:/usr/bin:/sbin:/bin:/snap/bin
# m h  dom mon dow   command
* * * * * echo $0
reader@ubuntu:~$
You have mail in /var/mail/reader
reader@ubuntu:~$ tail -3 /var/mail/reader
/bin/bash
reader@ubuntu:~/scripts/chapter_14$ crontab -r
```

With just the simple addition of the **SHELL** environment variable, we made sure we do not have mind-boggling issues about why certain Bash functionality is not working. It is always a good idea to prevent these issues rather than hope you catch them quickly, especially if you're still mastering shell scripting.

MAILTO

Now that we've determined we can use environment variables in our crontab by checking out both **PATH** and **SHELL**, let's look at the other very important one, **MAILTO**. As you might guess from the name, this variable controls where mails will be sent. As you remember, mails are sent when a command has stdout (which are pretty much all commands). That means that for every command the crontab executes, you'll probably get a local email. This, as you might suspect, can become annoying very quickly. We could suffix a nice little `&> /dev/null` to all commands we place in the crontab (remember, `&>` is Bash-specific, and would not have worked for the default Dash shell). However, this would mean that we never have any output at all, mailed or otherwise. Besides that problem, we'll also need to add it to all our lines; not really a real practical, workable solution. In a few pages, we're going to discuss how we can redirect our output to somewhere we want. Before we get to that point, however, we need to be able to manipulate the default emails as well.

One option would be to either not install or uninstall `sendmail`. This might be a good solution for some of you, but for others there is another need to have `sendmail` on the system, so it cannot be removed. What then? We can use the **MAILTO** variable in the same way as we use the **PATH**; we set it in the beginning of the crontab, and mails will be properly redirected. If we empty this variable, by assigning it the empty string `""`, no mail will be sent. This looks something like this:

```
reader@ubuntu:~$ crontab -e
no crontab for reader - using an empty one
crontab: installing new crontab
reader@ubuntu:~$ crontab -l
SHELL=/bin/bash
PATH=/usr/local/sbin:/usr/local/bin:/usr/sbin:/usr/bin:/sbin:/bin:/usr/game
s:/usr/local/games:/snap/bin
MAILTO=""
# m h dom mon dow command
* * * * * echo "So, I guess we'll never see this :("
```

We've used the `tail` command a lot up until now, but it actually has a great little flag `--follow` (`-f`), which allows us to see if any new lines are being written to a file. This is normally used to *tail a logfile*, but in this case allows us to see whether we get mail by tailing the **/var/mail/reader** file:

```
reader@ubuntu:~$ tail -f /var/mail/reader
MIME-Version: 1.0
Content-Type: text/plain; charset=UTF-8
Content-Transfer-Encoding: 8bit
X-Cron-Env: <SHELL=/bin/sh>
X-Cron-Env: <HOME=/home/reader>
X-Cron-Env: <PATH=/usr/bin:/bin>
X-Cron-Env: <LOGNAME=reader>

/bin/bash: 1: blkid: not found
```

If everything went as we expected it to, this is the only thing you will see. Since the **MAILTO** variable was declared as the empty string, `""`, `cron` knows not to send out mails. Exit the `tail -f` with *Ctrl + C* (but remember the command), and rest easy now that you've prevented yourself from being spammed by your crontab!

Logging with redirection

While the mail spam has been eliminated, now you find yourself without any output at all, which is definitely not a good thing either. Luckily for us, we've learned all about redirection in `Chapter 12`, *Using Pipes and Redirection in Scripts*. Just as we can use *redirect within scripts* or *on the command-line*, we can use the same constructs in a crontab. The same rules for ordering of pipes and stdout/stderr apply, so we can chain whatever command we want. Before we show this, however, we'll show one more cool functionality of crontab: instantiating a crontab from a file!

```
reader@ubuntu:~/scripts/chapter_14$ vim base-crontab
reader@ubuntu:~/scripts/chapter_14$ cat base-crontab
SHELL=/bin/bash
PATH=/usr/local/sbin:/usr/local/bin:/usr/sbin:/usr/bin:/sbin:/bin:/snap/bin
MAILTO=""
# m h  dom mon dow   command
reader@ubuntu:~/scripts/chapter_14$ crontab base-crontab
reader@ubuntu:~/scripts/chapter_14$ crontab -l
PATH=/usr/local/sbin:/usr/local/bin:/usr/sbin:/usr/bin:/sbin:/bin:/snap/bin
MAILTO=""
# m h  dom mon dow   command
```

First, we create the **base-crontab** file, which contains our Bash **SHELL**, the **PATH** (which we trimmed a little), the **MAILTO** variable, and our syntax header. Next, we use the `crontab base-crontab` command. Simply put, this replaces the current crontab with the contents from the file. This means we can manage the crontab as a file now; this includes support for version control systems and other backup solutions. Even better, when using the `crontab <filename>` command, syntax checking is intact. If the file isn't proper crontab format, you'll see the error **errors in crontab file, can't install.** Should you wish to save the current crontab to a file, the `crontab -l > filename` command will do the trick for you.

Now that that's out of the way, we'll give some examples of redirection for commands run by the crontab. We'll always instantiate from a file, so that you can easily find these materials on the GitHub page:

```
reader@ubuntu:~/scripts/chapter_14$ cp base-crontab date-redirection-
crontab
reader@ubuntu:~/scripts/chapter_14$ vim date-redirection-crontab
reader@ubuntu:~/scripts/chapter_14$ cat date-redirection-crontab
SHELL=/bin/bash
PATH=/usr/local/sbin:/usr/local/bin:/usr/sbin:/usr/bin:/sbin:/bin:/snap/bin
MAILTO=""
# m h  dom mon dow   command
* * * * * date &>> /tmp/date-file
reader@ubuntu:~/scripts/chapter_14$ crontab date-redirection-crontab
reader@ubuntu:~/scripts/chapter_14$ tail -f /tmp/date-file
Sat Dec 1 15:01:01 UTC 2018
Sat Dec 1 15:02:01 UTC 2018
Sat Dec 1 15:03:01 UTC 2018
^C
reader@ubuntu:~/scripts/chapter_14$ crontab -r
```

Now, that was pretty easy. As long as our **SHELL**, **PATH**, and **MAILTO** are properly set, we have avoided a lot of issues that are normally experienced when people start working with scheduling via the crontab.

One thing we have not done yet is run a script with the crontab. So far, only single commands have been run. However, a script will run just as great. We'll use a script from the previous chapter, **reverser.sh**, which will show that we can supply arguments to scripts via the crontab as well. Furthermore, it will show that the redirection we just learned works for script output just as well:

```
reader@ubuntu:~/scripts/chapter_14$ cp base-crontab reverser-crontab
reader@ubuntu:~/scripts/chapter_14$ vim reverser-crontab
reader@ubuntu:~/scripts/chapter_14$ cat reverser-crontab
SHELL=/bin/bash
```

```
PATH=/usr/local/sbin:/usr/local/bin:/usr/sbin:/usr/bin:/sbin:/bin:/snap/bin
MAILTO=""
# m h dom mon dow command
* * * * * /home/reader/scripts/chapter_13/reverser.sh 'crontab' &>>
/tmp/reverser.log
reader@ubuntu:~/scripts/chapter_14$ crontab reverser-crontab
reader@ubuntu:~/scripts/chapter_14$ cat /tmp/reverser.log
/bin/bash: /home/reader/scripts/chapter_13/reverser.sh: Permission denied
reader@ubuntu:~/scripts/chapter_14$ crontab -r
```

Ouch! After all our careful preparation, we still messed up here. Fortunately, the output file we created (which functions as a log file, and has the **.log** extension because of it) also has stderr redirected (because of our Bash 4.x &>> syntax) and we see what the error is. A classic error, **Permission denied** in this case simply means that we are trying to execute a non-executable file:

```
reader@ubuntu:~/scripts/chapter_14$ ls -l
/home/reader/scripts/chapter_13/reverser.sh
-rw-rw-r-- 1 reader reader 933 Nov 17 15:18
/home/reader/scripts/chapter_13/reverser.sh
```

So, we need to fix this. We can do two things:

- Make the file executable with (for example) chmod 755 reverser.sh.
- Change the crontab from reverser.sh to bash reverser.sh.

In this case, there is not really a good or bad solution. On the one hand, it is always a good idea to mark files that need to be executed as executable; this conveys to someone seeing the system that you intended this. On the other hand, if the extra bash command in the crontab can save you from these types of issues, what is the harm in that?

In our opinion, there is slightly more merit in making the file executable and omitting the bash command in your crontab. This keeps the crontab cleaner, (and, from experience, crontabs can easily become a mess if mishandled, so this is a very big plus), and shows someone else looking at the script that it should be executed because of the permissions. Let's apply this fix to our machine:

```
reader@ubuntu:~/scripts/chapter_14$ chmod 755 ../chapter_13/reverser.sh
reader@ubuntu:~/scripts/chapter_14$ crontab reverser-crontab
reader@ubuntu:~/scripts/chapter_14$ tail -f /tmp/reverser.log
/bin/bash: /home/reader/scripts/chapter_13/reverser.sh: Permission denied
Your reversed input is: _batnorc_
^C
reader@ubuntu:~/scripts/chapter_14$ crontab -r
```

There, much better. The full command that we run in the crontab is `/home/reader/scripts/chapter_13/reverser.sh 'crontab' &>>` `/tmp/reverser.log`, which includes the word **crontab** as the first argument to the script. The output, **_batnorc_**, is indeed the reversed word. It would seem that we can correctly pass arguments via the crontab! While this example illustrates the point, it might not get across while this might be significant. However, if you imagine a generic script that is normally used multiple times with different arguments, it could be present with those different arguments in the crontab as well (on multiple lines, perhaps with different schedules). Very useful indeed!

> If you ever need to quickly look up what the deal with the crontab was, you would of course check out `man crontab`. However, what we haven't told you yet is that some commands actually have more than one man page! By default, `man crontab` is shorthand for `man <first-manpage> crontab`. On that page, you'll see the sentence, "SEE ALSO crontab(5), cron(8)". By supplying this number with `man 5 crontab`, you'll see a different page where many of the concepts of this chapter (syntax, environment variables, and examples) are easily accessible to you.

Final logging considerations

You might consider having your script take care of its own logging. While this is certainly possible, (although a little complex and not very readable), we feel strongly that **it is the responsibility of the caller to take care of logging**. If you find a script that takes care of its own logging, you might encounter some of the following issues:

- Multiple users run the same script at different intervals, to a single log file
- The log file needs to have robust user permissions to ensure correct exposure
- Both ad hoc and scheduled runs will appear in the log file

Simply put, delegating the responsibility of logging to the script itself is asking for trouble. For an ad hoc command, you get the output right in your Terminal. If you need it for any other purpose, you can always copy and paste it somewhere, or redirect it. Even more probable is running the script with a pipe to `tee`, so output is shown to your Terminal *and* saved to a file at the same time. For scheduled runs from `cron`, you need to think once about redirection: when you create the schedule. In this case, especially if you use the Bash 4.x construct of `&>>`, you will always see all output (stdout and stderr) appended to the file you specify. In this, there is almost no risk of missing any output. Remember: `tee` and redirections are your friends, and when used properly they make a great addition to any script scheduling!

If you want your cron logging mechanism to be *really fancy*, you can set up `sendmail` (or other software such as `postfix`) as an actual Mail Transfer Agent (very out of the scope of this book, but check the *Further reading* section!). If that is correctly configured, you can set the **MAILTO** variable in the crontab to an actual email address (perhaps `yourname@company.com`), and receive the reports from scheduled jobs in your normal email box. This is best used with important scripts that do not run too often; otherwise, you will just end up with an annoying amount of email.

A note on verbosity

It is important to realize that, just as it is on the command-line directly, only output (stdout/stderr) is logged. By default, most commands that run successfully do not have any output; examples of these are `cp`, `rm`, `touch`, and so on. If you want informative logging in your scripts, it is your responsibility to add output where you see fit. The easiest way to accomplish this is by simply using an `echo` here and there. The easiest way to make a log file give confidence to the user is by having the final command in your scripts be `echo` `"Everything went well, exiting script."`. As long as you handle all potential errors properly during your script, you can safely say that once it reaches the final command the execution has succeeded, and you can notify the user of this. If you do not do this, the log file might stay empty, which can be kind of scary; is it empty because everything succeeded *or because the script did not even run*? This is not something you want to take a chance on, especially not when a simple `echo` can save you all that trouble.

Summary

We started this chapter by showing the new `at` command and explaining how we can use `at` for scheduling scripts. We described the timestamp syntax for `at` and how it contains a queue for all scheduled jobs. We explained how `at` is mostly used for ad hoc scheduled commands and scripts, before we continued to the more powerful `cron` scheduler.

The `cron` daemon, responsible for most scheduled tasks on a system, is a very powerful and flexible scheduler, which is most often used via the so-called crontab. This is a user-bound file, which contains instructions for `cron` on when and how to run commands and scripts. We presented the timestamp syntax that is used in a crontab.

The second part of the chapter dealt with logging our scheduled commands and scripts. When a command is run interactively on the command line, there is no need for dedicated logging, but scheduled commands are not interactive, and thus need additional mechanisms. Output from scheduled commands can either be mailed to a local file with the `sendmail` process, or redirected to a log file using the redirection possibilities we outlined earlier.

We ended the chapter with some final considerations on logging: how it should always be the responsibility of the caller to arrange logging, and how it is the responsibility of the script author to make sure a script is verbose enough to be used non-interactively.

The following commands were introduced in this chapter: `at`, `wall`, `atq`, `atrm`, `sendmail`, `crontab`, and `alias`.

Questions

1. What is scheduling?
2. What do we mean by ad hoc scheduling?
3. Where does the output of commands run with `at` normally go?
4. How is scheduling for the `cron` daemon most often implemented?
5. Which commands allow you to edit your personal crontab?
6. Which five fields are present in the crontab timestamp syntax?
7. Which are the three most important environment variables for the crontab?
8. How can we inspect the output for scripts or commands we have scheduled with `cron`?
9. If our scheduled scripts do not have enough output for us to effectively work with log files, how should we remedy this?

Further reading

The following resources might be interesting if you'd like to go deeper into the subjects of this chapter:

- **Profile and Bashrc**: https://bencane.com/2013/09/16/understanding-a-little-more-about-etcprofile-and-etcbashrc/
- **Set up a Mail Transfer Agent with postfix**: https://www.hiroom2.com/2018/05/06/ubuntu-1804-postfix-en/

Parsing Bash Script Arguments with getopts

15

In this chapter, we'll discuss the different ways of passing arguments to a script, with a special focus on flags. We will start by recapping positional arguments, before continuing with arguments passed as flags. After this, we will talk about how to use flags in your own scripts using the `getopts` shell builtin.

The following commands will be introduced in this chapter: `getopts` and `shift`.

The following topics will be covered in this chapter:

- Positional parameters versus flags
- The `getopts` shell builtin

Technical requirements

All scripts for this chapter can be found on GitHub at the following link: `https://github.com/PacktPublishing/Learn-Linux-Shell-Scripting-Fundamentals-of-Bash-4.4/tree/master/Chapter15`. Follow along with the examples on your Ubuntu Linux virtual machine—no other resources are needed. For the **single-flag.sh** script only the final version is found online. Be sure to verify the script version in the header before executing it on your system.

Positional parameters versus flags

We'll start this chapter off with a short recap on positional arguments. As you might remember from Chapter 8, *Variables and User Input*, we are able to use positional parameters to pass arguments to our scripts.

To put this simply, the following syntax is used:

```
bash script.sh argument1 argument2 ...
```

Inside the preceding (fictive) `script.sh`, we can then grab the values supplied by the user by looking at the positions the arguments are supplied in: `$1` is the first argument, `$2` is the second, and so on. Remember that `$0` is a special argument, which relates to the name of the script: in this case, `script.sh`.

This approach is relatively simple, but also susceptible to errors. When you write this script, you need to check extensively for the input supplied by the user; did they give enough arguments, but not too many? Or, perhaps some arguments are optional, so a few combinations are possible? All these things need to be considered and, if possible, dealt with.

Besides the script writer (you!), there is also the burden on the script caller. Before they can successfully call your script, they need to be aware of how to pass the needed information. For our scripts, we've applied two practices which are meant to minimize the burden on the user:

- Our script header contains a `Usage:` field
- When our scripts are called incorrectly, we print an error message with a *usage hint* similar/equal to the header

Still, this approach is error-prone and not always very user-friendly. There is another option though: *options*, more commonly known as *flags*.

Using flags on the command line

Perhaps you haven't realized it yet, but most commands you use on the command line use a combination of positional arguments and flags. The most basic command in Linux, `cd`, uses a single positional argument: the directory you want to move to.

It does actually have two flags that you can use as well: `-L` and `-P`. The purpose of these flags is niche and not worth explaining here. Almost all commands use both flags and positional arguments complementarily.

So then, when do we use which? As a rule of thumb, flags are often used for *modifiers*, while positional arguments are used for *targets*. A target is simple this is: the thing you want to manipulate with the command. In the case of `ls`, this means that the positional arguments are the files or directories that should be listed (manipulated) by the command.

For the `ls -l /tmp/` command, `/tmp/` is the target, and `-l` is the flag used to modify the behavior of `ls`. By default, `ls` lists all files without extra information such as ownership, permissions, size, and so on. If we want to modify the behavior of `ls`, we add one or more flags: `-l` tells `ls` to use the long listing format, which prints each file on its own line, and prints the extra information about the file too.

Do note that between `ls /tmp/` and `ls -l /tmp/`, the target does not change, but the output does, since we *modified* it with the flag!

Some flags are even more special: they require their own positional argument! So not only can we use the flag to modify the command, but the flag itself has multiple options for how to modify the command's behavior.

A good example of this is the `find` command: by default, it finds all files within a directory, as follows:

```
reader@ubuntu:~/scripts/chapter_14$ find
.
./reverser-crontab
./wall.txt
./base-crontab
./date-redirection-crontab
```

Alternatively, we can use `find` with a positional argument to search not in the current working directory, but somewhere else, as follows:

```
reader@ubuntu:~/scripts/chapter_14$ find ../chapter_10
../chapter_10
../chapter_10/error.txt
../chapter_10/grep-file.txt
../chapter_10/search.txt
../chapter_10/character-class.txt
../chapter_10/grep-then-else.sh
```

Now, `find` also allows us to use the `-type` flag to only print files of a certain type. But by only using the `-type` flag, we have not yet specified what file type we want to print. By specifying the file type directly after the flag (ordering is *critical* here), we tell the flag what to look for. It looks something like the following:

```
reader@ubuntu:/$ find /boot/ -type d
/boot/
/boot/grub
/boot/grub/i386-pc
/boot/grub/fonts
/boot/grub/locale
```

Here we looked for a type of d (directory) within the /boot/ directory. Other arguments to the –type flag include f (file), l (symbolic link), and b (block device).

As always, ordering is important, and something like this will happen if you do not get it right:

```
reader@ubuntu:/$ find -type d /boot/
find: paths must precede expression: '/boot/'
find: possible unquoted pattern after predicate '-type'?
```

Unfortunately for us, not all commands are created equal. Some are more forgiving on the user, and try their hardest to make sense of what has been given as input. Others are much more strict: they will run whatever is passed, even if it does not make any functional sense. Always make sure you verify whether you are using the command and its modifiers correctly!

 The preceding examples use flags differently to how we'll learn to use them with getopts. These examples should only serve to illustrate the concepts of script arguments, flags, and flags-with-arguments. These implementations are written without the use of getopts and thus do not map precisely to what we'll be doing later.

The getopts shell builtin

Now the real fun begins! In this second part of this chapter, we'll explain the getopts shell builtin. The getopts command is used in the beginning of your script to **get the options** you supplied in the form of flags. It has a very specific syntax that will seem confusing at first, but, once we've looked at it fully, it should not be too complicated for you to understand.

Before we dive in, though, we'll need to discuss two things:

- The difference between getopts and getopt
- Short versus long options

As stated, getopts is a *shell builtin*. It is available in both the regular Bourne shell (sh) and in Bash. It originated around 1986, as a replacement for getopt, which was created sometime before 1980.

In contrast to `getopts`, `getopt` is not built into the shell: it is a standalone program that has been ported to many different Unix and Unix-like distributions. The main differences between `getopts` and `getopt` are as follows:

- `getopt` does not handle empty flag arguments well; `getopts` does
- `getopts` is included in the Bourne shell and Bash; `getopt` needs to be installed separately
- `getopt` allows for the parsing of long options (`--help` instead of `-h`); `getopts` does not
- `getopts` has a simpler syntax; `getopt` is more complicated (mainly because it is an external program and not a builtin)

In general, the consensus seems to be that for most cases, using `getopts` is preferable (unless you really want long options). Since `getopts` is a Bash builtin, we'll use it as well, especially since we do not have the need for long options.

Most commands you use on the Terminal have both the short option (which is used almost always when interactively working at the Terminal to save time) and the long option (which is more descriptive and is more suitable for creating better readable scripts). In our experience, short options are more prevalent and, when used correctly, more recognizable as well.

The following list shows the most common short flags, which do the same to most commands:

- `-h`: Prints the help/usage for a command
- `-v`: Makes the command verbose
- `-q`: Makes the command quiet
- `-f <file>`: Passes a file to the <indexentry content="getopts shell builtin, flags:-f ">command
- `-r`: Performs the operation recursively
- `-d`: Runs the command in debug mode

Do not assume all commands parse the short flags, as specified previously. While this is true for most commands, don't all follow these trends. What is printed here has been found from personal experience and should always be verified by you before running a command that is new to you. That being said, running a command without arguments/flags or with a `-h` will, at least 90% of the time, print the correct usage for you to admire.

Even though it would have been nice to have long options available to us for our `getopts` scripting, even long options are never a substitute for writing readable scripts and creating good hints for the user that is using your script. We feel that that's much more important than having long options! Besides, the `getopts` syntax is much cleaner than a comparable `getopt`, and adhering to the KISS principle is still one of our goals.

The getopts syntax

Instead of spending any more time in this chapter not seeing actual code, we're going to jump right in and show a very simple example of a `getopts` script. Of course, we'll walk you through step by step so that you have the chance to understand it all.

The script we're creating does just a few simple things: if it finds the `-v` flag, it prints a *verbose* message, telling us it found the flag. If it does not find any flags, it prints nothing. If it finds any other flag, it prints an error for the user. Simple, right?

Let's take a look:

```
reader@ubuntu:~/scripts/chapter_15$ vim single-flag.sh
reader@ubuntu:~/scripts/chapter_15$ cat !$
cat single-flag.sh
#!/bin/bash

####################################
# Author: Sebastiaan Tammer
# Version: v1.0.0
# Date: 2018-12-08
# Description: Shows the basic getopts syntax.
# Usage: ./single-flag.sh [flags]
####################################

# Parse the flags in a while loop.
# After the last flag, getopts returns false which ends the loop.
optstring=":v"
while getopts ${optstring} options; do
  case ${options} in
    v)
      echo "-v was found!"
      ;;
    ?)
      echo "Invalid option: -${OPTARG}."
      exit 1
      ;;
  esac
done
```

If we run this script, we'll see the following happening:

```
reader@ubuntu:~/scripts/chapter_15$ bash single-flag.sh # No flag, do
nothing.
reader@ubuntu:~/scripts/chapter_15$ bash single-flag.sh -p
Invalid option: -p. # Wrong flag, print an error.
reader@ubuntu:~/scripts/chapter_15$ bash single-flag.sh -v
-v was found! # Correct flag, print the message.
```

So, our script at least works as expected! But why does it work like that? Let's take a look. We'll skip the header, as that should be very clear by now. We'll start with the `while` line, which contains the `getopts` command and `optstring`:

```
# Parse the flags in a while loop.
# After the last flag, getopts returns false which ends the loop.
optstring=":v"
while getopts ${optstring} options; do
```

`optstring`, which is likely short for **opt*ions* string**, tells `getopts` which options should be expected. In this case, we expect only v. However, we start the `optstring` with a colon (:), which is a special character for `optstring` that sets `getopts` in *silent error reporting* mode.

Since we prefer to handle error situations ourselves, we will always start our `optstring` with a colon. However, feel free to see what happens when you remove the colon.

After that, the syntax for `getopts` is pretty simple, as follows:

```
getopts optstring name [arg]
```

We can see the command, followed by the `optstring` (which we abstracted to a separate variable to improve readability), ending with the name of the variable in which we'll store the parsed results.

The final, optional, aspect of `getopts` allows us to pass our own set of arguments, instead of defaulting to everything passed to the script (**$0** through **$9**). We will not be needing/using this in our exercises, but this is definitely good to know. As always, because this is a shell builtin, you can find information on it by executing `help getopts`.

We place this command within a `while` loop so that it iterates over all arguments we passed to the script. If there are no more arguments to be parsed by `getopts`, it returns an exit status other than 0, which causes the `while` loop to exit.

While we're inside the loop, though, we'll hit the `case` statement. As you know, the `case` statement is basically better syntax for a longer `if-elif-elif-elif-else` statement. In our example script, this looks like this:

```
case ${options} in
  v)
    echo "-v was found!"
    ;;
  ?)
    echo "Invalid option: -${OPTARG}."
    exit 1
    ;;
esac
done
```

Notice how the `case` statement ends with the word `esac` (case in reverse). For all our defined flags (currently only `-v`), we have a block of code that will execute only for that flag.

The other thing we find when we look at the `${options}` variable (which we have because we specified it for *name* in the `getopts` command) is the `?` wildcard. We place that at the end of the case statement as a means of catching errors. If it hits the `?)` code block, we've presented `getopts` with a flag it does not understand. In this case, we print an error and exit the script.

The `done` on the last line ends the `while` loop, and signals that all of our flags should have been handled.

> It might seem a bit unnecessary to have both an `optstring` and a case for all possible options. For now, this is indeed the case, but a bit further on in this chapter we'll show you how the `optstring` is used to specify things beyond just the letter; at that point, it should be clear why the `optstring` is here. For now, don't worry about it too much and just enter the flags in both locations.

Multiple flags

Fortunately for us, we do not have to be content with just a single flag: we can define many (right up until we run out of alphabet!).

We'll create a new script that will print a message to the reader. If no flags are specified, we'll print a default message. If we encounter either flag –b or flag –g, we'll print a different message, depending on the flag. We'll also include instructions for the –h flag, which will print a help message when encountered.

A script with these requirements could look something like this:

```
reader@ubuntu:~/scripts/chapter_15$ vim hey.sh
reader@ubuntu:~/scripts/chapter_15$ cat hey.sh
#!/bin/bash

#####################################
# Author: Sebastiaan Tammer
# Version: v1.0.0
# Date: 2018-12-14
# Description: Getopts with multiple flags.
# Usage: ./hey.sh [flags]
#####################################

# Abstract the help as a function, so it does not clutter our script.
print_help() {
  echo "Usage: $0 [flags]"
  echo "Flags:"
  echo "-h for help."
  echo "-b for male greeting."
  echo "-g for female greeting."
}

# Parse the flags.
optstring=":bgh"
while getopts ${optstring} options; do
  case ${options} in
    b)
      gender="boy"
      ;;
    g)
      gender="girl"
      ;;
    h)
      print_help
      exit 0 # Stop script, but consider it a success.
      ;;
    ?)
      echo "Invalid option: -${OPTARG}."
      exit 1
      ;;
  esac
```

```
done

# If $gender is n (nonzero), print specific greeting.
# Otherwise, print a neutral greeting.
if [[ -n ${gender} ]]; then
  echo "Hey ${gender}!"
else
  echo "Hey there!"
fi
```

This script should be readable to you at this point, especially with the included comments. From the top, we start with the header and follow up with the `print_help()` function, which prints our help message when the −h flag is encountered (as we see a few lines further on).

Next up is the `optstring`, which still starts with a colon so that verbose errors from `getopts` is turned off (as we will handle this ourselves). In the `optstring`, all three flags that we will handle, that is −b, −g, and −h, are defined as a single string: bgh.

For each of these flags, we have an entry in the `case` statement: for b) and g), the `gender` variable is set to boy or girl, respectively. For h), the function we defined is called, before calling `exit 0`. (Think about why we would do this! If you're not sure, run the script without the exit.)

We always end a `getopts` block by handling unknown flags with the ?) syntax.

Moving on, after our `case` statements ends with `esac`, we get to the actual functionality. We check whether the `gender` variable is defined: if it is, we print a message that contains the value set according to the flag. If it is not set (that is the case if neither −b and −g are specified), we print a generic greeting that omits gender.

This is also why we `exit 0` after we find −h: otherwise both the help message and the greeting would be given to the user (which is weird, since the user asks *just* for the help page with −h).

Let's see our script in action:

```
reader@ubuntu:~/scripts/chapter_15$ bash hey.sh -h
Usage: hey.sh [flags]
Flags:
-h for help.
-b for male greeting.
-g for female greeting.
reader@ubuntu:~/scripts/chapter_15$ bash hey.sh
Hey there!
```

```
reader@ubuntu:~/scripts/chapter_15$ bash hey.sh -b
Hey boy!
reader@ubuntu:~/scripts/chapter_15$ bash hey.sh -g
Hey girl!
```

So far, so good! If we call it with –h, we see the multi-line help message printed. By default, each echo ends with a newline character, so our five echoes are printed on five lines. We could have worked with a single echo and the \n characters, but this is more readable

If we run our script without flags, we'll see the generic greeting. Running it with either –b or –g will give the gender-specific greeting. Wasn't that easy?

It actually was! However, it is about to get a little bit more complicated. As we've explained before, users tend to be rather unpredictable, and would perhaps use too many flags, or the same flags multiple times.

Let's take a look at how our script reacts to this:

```
reader@ubuntu:~/scripts/chapter_15$ bash hey.sh -h -b
Usage: hey.sh [flags]
Flags:
-h for help.
-b for male greeting.
-g for female greeting.
reader@ubuntu:~/scripts/chapter_15$ bash hey.sh -b -h
Usage: hey.sh [flags]
Flags:
-h for help.
-b for male greeting.
-g for female greeting.
reader@ubuntu:~/scripts/chapter_15$ bash hey.sh -b -h -g
Usage: hey.sh [flags]
Flags:
-h for help.
-b for male greeting.
-g for female greeting.
```

So, regardless of how many flags are specified, as long as the script encounters the –h flag, it will print the help message and exit (due to exit 0). For your understanding, run the preceding commands in debug with bash –x to see that they do actually differ, even though the user does not see this (hint: check for assignments of gender=boy and gender=girl).

This brings us to an important point: *flags are parsed in the order they are supplied by the user!* To further illustrate this point, let's look at another example of a user messing with flags:

```
reader@ubuntu:~/scripts/chapter_15$ bash hey.sh -g -b
Hey boy!
reader@ubuntu:~/scripts/chapter_15$ bash hey.sh -b -g
Hey girl!
```

When the user supplies both the -b and -g flag, both variable assignments for gender are performed by the system. However, it seems as though the final flag is the one that wins, even though we just stated that the flags are parsed in order! Why would that be?

As always, a nice bash -x gives us a good idea of this situation:

```
reader@ubuntu:~/scripts/chapter_15$ bash -x hey.sh -b -g
+ optstring=:bgh
+ getopts :bgh options
+ case ${options} in
+ gender=boy
+ getopts :bgh options
+ case ${options} in
+ gender=girl
+ getopts :bgh options
+ [[ -n girl ]]
+ echo 'Hey girl!'
Hey girl!
```

Initially, the gender variable is assigned the value of boy. However, when the next flag is parsed, the value of the variable is *overwritten with a new value*, girl. Since the -g flag is the final one, the gender variable ends as girl, and thus that is what is printed.

As you will see in the next part of this chapter, it is possible to supply an argument to a flag. For flags without arguments, though, there is a really cool feature that many commands use: flag chaining. It might sound complicated, but it is actually pretty simple: if you have multiple flags, you can place them all behind a single dash.

For our script, it looks like this:

```
reader@ubuntu:~/scripts/chapter_15$ bash -x hey.sh -bgh
+ optstring=:bgh
+ getopts :bgh options
+ case ${options} in
+ gender=boy
+ getopts :bgh options
+ case ${options} in
+ gender=girl
+ getopts :bgh options
```

```
+ case ${options} in
+ print_help
<SNIPPED>
```

We specified all flags as one bunch: instead of -b -g -h, we used -bgh. As we concluded before, the flags are processed in order, which is still the case in our concatenated example (as the debug instruction clearly shows). This is not much different to an ls -al, for example. Again, this only works if a flag does not have an argument.

Flags with arguments

In an optstring, the colon has an extra meaning beyond turning off verbose error logging: when placed after a letter, it signals to getopts that an *option argument* is expected.

If we look back at our first example, the optstring was simply :v. If we wanted the -v flag to accept an argument, we would place a colon behind the v, which would result in the following optstring: :v:. We can then use a special variable we've seen before, OPTARG, to grab that *option argument*.

We'll make a revision to our single-flag.sh script to show you how this works:

```
reader@ubuntu:~/scripts/chapter_15$ vim single-flag.sh
reader@ubuntu:~/scripts/chapter_15$ cat single-flag.sh
#!/bin/bash

######################################
# Author: Sebastiaan Tammer
# Version: v1.1.0
# Date: 2018-12-14
# Description: Shows the basic getopts syntax.
# Usage: ./single-flag.sh [flags]
######################################

# Parse the flags in a while loop.
# After the last flag, getopts returns false which ends the loop.
optstring=":v:"
while getopts ${optstring} options; do
  case ${options} in
    v)
      echo "-v was found!"
      echo "-v option argument is: ${OPTARG}."
      ;;
    ?)
      echo "Invalid option: -${OPTARG}."
      exit 1
```

```
          ;;
     esac
  done
```

The changed lines have been highlighted for your convenience. By adding a colon to the optstring and using the OPTARG variable in the v) block, we now see the following behavior when running the script:

```
reader@ubuntu:~/scripts/chapter_15$ bash single-flag.sh
reader@ubuntu:~/scripts/chapter_15$ bash single-flag.sh -v Hello
-v was found!
-v option argument is: Hello.
reader@ubuntu:~/scripts/chapter_15$ bash single-flag.sh -vHello
-v was found!
-v option argument is: Hello.
```

As you can see, as long as we supply the flag and flag argument, our script works just fine. We do not even need a space between the flag and flag argument; since getopts knows an argument is expected, it can handle either a space or no space. We'd always recommend including the space in any case, to ensure readability, but it is not technically needed.

Also, this proves why we need a separate optstring: the case statement is the same, but getopts now expects an argument, something we could not have done if the creators had omitted the optstring.

As with all things that seem too good to be true, this is one of those situations. While it works fine if the user is nice to your script, if he/she is not, the following might happen:

```
reader@ubuntu:~/scripts/chapter_15$ bash single-flag.sh -v
Invalid option: -v.
reader@ubuntu:~/scripts/chapter_15$ bash single-flag.sh -v ''
-v was found!
-v option argument is:
```

Now that we've told getopts to expect an argument to the -v flag, it will actually not correctly identify the flag if there is no argument. An empty argument, as denoted by the '' in the second script call, is fine, however. (Technically fine, that is, since no user would ever do that.)

Fortunately, there is a solution for this—the :) block, as follows:

```
reader@ubuntu:~/scripts/chapter_15$ vim single-flag.sh
reader@ubuntu:~/scripts/chapter_15$ cat single-flag.sh
#!/bin/bash

####################################
```

```
# Author: Sebastiaan Tammer
# Version: v1.2.0
# Date: 2018-12-14
# Description: Shows the basic getopts syntax.
# Usage: ./single-flag.sh [flags]
####################################

# Parse the flags in a while loop.
# After the last flag, getopts returns false which ends the loop.
optstring=":v:"
while getopts ${optstring} options; do
  case ${options} in
    v)
      echo "-v was found!"
      echo "-v option argument is: ${OPTARG}."
      ;;
    :)
      echo "-${OPTARG} requires an argument."
      exit 1
      ;;
    ?)
      echo "Invalid option: -${OPTARG}."
      exit 1
      ;;
  esac
done
```

It might be a little confusing that both a wrong flag and a missing option argument are resolved as the OPTARG. Without making this situation more complicated than it has to be, it all depends on whether the case statement block contains ?) or :) at that moment. For ?) blocks, everything that is not recognized (the whole flag) is seen as the option argument, and :) blocks only trigger when the optstring contains the proper instruction for an option with an argument.

Everything should work just as intended now:

```
reader@ubuntu:~/scripts/chapter_15$ bash single-flag.sh
reader@ubuntu:~/scripts/chapter_15$ bash single-flag.sh -v
-v requires an argument.
reader@ubuntu:~/scripts/chapter_15$ bash single-flag.sh -v Hi
-v was found!
-v option argument is: Hi.
reader@ubuntu:~/scripts/chapter_15$ bash single-flag.sh -x Hi
Invalid option: -x.
reader@ubuntu:~/scripts/chapter_15$ bash single-flag.sh -x -v Hi
Invalid option: -x.
```

Again, because of the sequential processing of flags, the final call never gets to the −v flag due to the exit 1 in the ?) block. However, all other situations are now properly resolved. Nice!

> The actual processing that getopts does involves multiple passes and the use of shift. This is a little too technical for this chapter, but for those curious among you, the *Further reading* section includes a *very* in-depth explanation of this mechanism that you can read at your leisure.

Combining flags with positional arguments

It is possible to combine positional arguments (in the way we've been using them before this chapter) with options and option arguments. There are some things to consider in this scenario:

- By default, Bash recognizes flags such as −f as positional parameters
- Just as there is an order to flags and flag arguments, there is an order for flags and positional parameters

When dealing with a mix of getopts and positional arguments, the *flags and flag options should always be provided before the positional arguments!* This is because we want to parse and handle all flags and flag arguments before we get to the positional parameters. This is a fairly typical scenario for both scripts and command-line tools, but it is still something we have to consider.

All of the preceding points are best illustrated with an example, as always. We're going to create a simple script that serves as a wrapper for common file operations. With this script, file-tool.sh, we will be able to do the following things:

- List a file (default behavior)
- Delete a file (with the −d option)
- Empty a file (with the −e option)
- Rename a file (with the −m option, which includes another filename)
- Call the help function (with −h)

Take a look at the script:

```
reader@ubuntu:~/scripts/chapter_15$ vim file-tool.sh
reader@ubuntu:~/scripts/chapter_15$ cat file-tool.sh
#!/bin/bash
```

```
#####################################
# Author: Sebastiaan Tammer
# Version: v1.0.0
# Date: 2018-12-14
# Description: A tool which allows us to manipulate files.
# Usage: ./file-tool.sh [flags] <file-name>
#####################################

print_help() {
  echo "Usage: $0 [flags] <file-name>"
  echo "Flags:"
  echo "No flags for file listing."
  echo "-d to delete the file."
  echo "-e to empty the file."
  echo "-m <new-file-name> to rename the file."
  echo "-h for help."
}

command="ls -l" # Default command, can be overridden.

optstring=":dem:h" # The m option contains an option argument.
while getopts ${optstring} options; do
  case ${options} in
    d)
      command="rm -f";;
    e)
      command="cp /dev/null";;
    m)
      new_filename=${OPTARG}; command="mv";;
    h)
      print_help; exit 0;;
    :)
      echo "-${OPTARG} requires an argument."; exit 1;;
    ?)
      echo "Invalid option: -${OPTARG}." exit 1;;
  esac
done

# Remove the parsed flags from the arguments array with shift.
shift $(( ${OPTIND} - 1 )) # -1 so the file-name is not shifted away.

filename=$1

# Make sure the user supplied a writable file to manipulate.
if [[ $# -ne 1 || ! -w ${filename} ]]; then
  echo "Supply a writable file to manipulate! Exiting script."
  exit 1
fi
```

```
# Everything should be fine, execute the operation.
if [[ -n ${new_filename} ]]; then # Only set for -m.
  ${command} ${filename} $(dirname ${filename})/${new_filename}
else # Everything besides -m.
  ${command} ${filename}
fi
```

That's a big one, isn't it? We've shortened it just a little bit by compacting multiple lines into single lines (within the `case` statement), but it's still not a short script. While it might seem intimidating at first, we're sure that with your exposure up until now, and the comments in the script, this should be understandable to you. If it is not fully understandable just yet, don't worry—we're going to explain all the new and interesting lines now.

We're skipping the header, the `print_help()` function, and the default command of `ls -1`. The first interesting bit will be the `optstring`, which now contains options with and without option arguments:

```
optstring=":dem:h" # The m option contains an option argument.
```

When we get to the `m)` block, we save the option argument in the `new_filename` variable for later use.

When we're done with the `case` statement for `getopts`, we run into a command that we've briefly seen before: `shift`. This command allows us to move our positional arguments around: if we do `shift 2`, the argument `$4` becomes `$2`, the argument `$3` becomes `$1`, and the old `$1` and `$2` are removed.

When dealing with a positional parameter behind flags, all flags and flag arguments are seen as positional arguments as well. In this case, if we call the script as `file-tool.sh -m newfile /tmp/oldfile`, the following will be interpreted by Bash:

- `$1`: Interpreted as `-m`
- `$2`: Interpreted as a new file
- `$3`: Interpreted as `/tmp/oldfile`

Fortunately, `getopts` saves the options (and option arguments) it has processed in a variable: `$OPTIND` (from *options index*). To be even more precise, after it has parsed an option, it sets `$OPTIND` to the next possible option or option argument: it starts at 1 and ends when it finds the first non-option argument passed to the script.

In our example, once `getopts` reaches our positional parameter of `/tmp/oldfile`, the `$OPTIND` variable will be 3. Since we just need to `shift` everything before that point away, we subtract 1 from the `$OPTIND`, as follows:

```
shift $(( ${OPTIND} - 1 )) # -1 so the file-name is not shifted away.
```

Remember, `$(( ... ))` is shorthand for arithmetic; the resulting number is used in the `shift` command. The rest of the script is pretty straightforward: we'll do some checks to ensure we only have one positional parameter left (the filename of the file that we want to manipulate), and whether we have write permissions on that file.

Next, depending on which operations we have selected, we'll either do a complex one for the `mv`, or a simple one for all the others. For the rename command, we'll use a bit of command substitution to determine the directory name of the original filename, which we will then reuse in the rename.

If we did our tests like we should, the script should be fully functional with all the requirements we set out. We encourage you to give it a try.

Even better, see if you can come up with a situation that we have not thought of that breaks the script's functionality. If you do find something (spoiler alert: we know of a few shortcomings!), try to fix them yourself.

As you may start to realize, we're entering territory in which it is very hard to harden scripts for every user input. For example, in the last example, if we supply the -m option but omit the content, the filename we supply will be seen as the option argument. In this case, instead of throwing an error for a missing option argument, our script will `shift` the filename away and complain that it doesn't have it. While this script should serve for educational purposes, it is not something that we would trust for our workplace scripting. It is often better not to mix `getopts` with positional arguments, as you would avoid many of the complexities we've faced here. Just have the user supply the filename as another option argument (-f, anyone?) and you'll be much happier!

Summary

This chapter started with a recap of how positional parameters are used in Bash. We continued by showing you how most command-line tools we've introduced up until this point (and those we haven't) use flags, often as *modifiers* for script functionality, whereas positional parameters are used to indicate *targets* for the commands.

We then introduced a way for the reader to incorporate options and option arguments within their own scripts: by using the getopts shell builtin. We kicked this off by discussing the differences between the legacy program getopt and the newer builtin getopts, which we focused on for the rest of this chapter.

Since getopts only allows us to use short options (whereas getopt and some other command-line tools also use long options, denoted by double dashes), we showed you how this is not an issue due to the recognition of common short options such as -h, -v, and so on.

We properly introduced the getopts syntax with a few examples. We showed how you can use flags with and without flag arguments, and how we need an optstring to signal to getopts which options have arguments (and which options to even expect).

We ended this chapter by showing you how options and option arguments could be combined with positional parameters by cleverly using the shift command to deal with this.

The following commands were introduced in this chapter: getopts and shift.

Questions

1. Why are flags often used as modifiers whereas positional parameters are used as targets?
2. Why do we run getopts in a while loop?
3. Why do we need ?) in the case statement?
4. Why do we (sometimes) need :) in the case statement?
5. Why do we need a separate optstring if we're resolving all options anyway?
6. Why do we need to subtract 1 from the OPTIND variable when we use it in shift?
7. Is it a good idea to mix options with positional arguments?

Further reading

Pleas refer to the following links for more information on the topics in this chapter:

- Bash-hackers on `getopts`: `http://wiki.bash-hackers.org/howto/getopts_tutorial`
- `getopts` in depth: `https://www.computerhope.com/unix/bash/getopts.htm`

16
Bash Parameter Substitution and Expansion

This chapter is dedicated to a special feature of Bash: parameter expansion. Parameter expansion allows us to do many interesting things with variables, which we will cover extensively.

We will first discuss default values of variables, input checking, and variable length. In the second part of this chapter, we will look more closely at how we can manipulate variables. This includes replacing and removing patterns from text, modifying the case of variables, and using substrings.

The following commands will be introduced in this chapter: `export` and `dirname`.

The following topics will be covered in this chapter:

- Parameter expansion
- Variable manipulation

Technical requirements

All scripts for this chapter can be found on GitHub at the following link: `https://github.com/PacktPublishing/Learn-Linux-Shell-Scripting-Fundamentals-of-Bash-4.4/tree/master/Chapter16`. For this last regular chapter, your Ubuntu virtual machine should see you through once again.

Parameter expansion

In this second-to-last chapter, with the final chapter being tips and tricks, we will deal with a very cool feature of Bash: *parameter expansion*.

We'll begin with a few notes on terminology. First of all, what's considered *parameter expansion* in Bash deals with more than just parameters/arguments supplied to a script: all special operations we'll be discussing in this chapter are applicable to Bash *variables*. In the official Bash manual page (`man bash`), these are all referred to as parameters.

For positional arguments to scripts, or even options with arguments, this makes sense. However, once we enter the territory of constants defined by the script creator, the distinction between a constant/variable and a parameter gets a bit muddy. This is of no further consequence; just remember that when you see the word *parameter* in a `man page`, it might be referring to variables in general.

Secondly, people tend to be a bit confused about the terms *parameter expansion* and *parameter substitution*, and you'll see these terms used interchangeably on the internet. In the official documentation, the word *substitution* is only used in *command substitution* and *process substitution*.

Command substitution is something we've discussed: it's the `$(...)` syntax. Process substitution is pretty advanced and has not been described: if you ever come across `<(...)` syntax, you're dealing with process substitution. We've included an article on process substitution in the *Further reading* section of this chapter, so be sure to give it a look.

The confusion, we think, stems from the fact that *parameter substitution*, that is, the replacing of the variable name with its value at runtime, is considered only a small part of the greater *parameter expansion* in Bash. That is why you will see some articles or sources refer to all the great features of parameter expansion (default values, case manipulation, and pattern removal, to name a few) as parameter substitution.

Again, just remember that these terms are often interchanged, and people are (probably) talking about the same thing. If you are ever in doubt yourself, we would advise opening up the Bash `man page` on any of your machines, and sticking with the official designation: *parameter expansion*.

Parameter substitutions – recap

While it probably isn't necessary at this point for you, we'd like to quickly recap parameter substitutions so that we can place it within the greater context of parameter expansion.

As we stated in the introduction, and as you've seen throughout this book, parameter substitution is nothing more than replacing a variable with its value at runtime. On the command line, this looks a little like the following:

```
reader@ubuntu:~/scripts/chapter_16$ export word=Script
reader@ubuntu:~/scripts/chapter_16$ echo ${word}
Script
reader@ubuntu:~/scripts/chapter_16$ echo "You're reading: Learn Linux Shell
${word}ing"
You're reading: Learn Linux Shell Scripting
reader@ubuntu:~/scripts/chapter_16$ echo "You're reading: Learn Linux Shell
$wording"
You're reading: Learn Linux Shell
```

Normally in a recap you don't learn any new things, but because we're using this just for context we've managed to sneak some new stuff in here: the `export` command. `export` is a shell builtin (as found with `type -a export`), which we can read about using `help export` (which is the way to get information for all shell builtins).

We don't always need to use `export` when setting a variable value: in this instance, we could have also just used `word=Script`. Normally, when we set a variable, it is only available in our current shell. Any processes that run in a fork of our shell do not have that piece of the environment forked with them: they cannot see the value we have assigned to the variable.

While it is not always necessary, you might encounter the use of `export` when looking for answers online, so it is good to know what it does!

The rest of the example should speak for itself. We assign a value to a variable, and we use parameter substitution at runtime (in this case, with an `echo`) to replace the variable name with the actual value.

As a reminder, will we show you why we advise you to *always* include the curly braces around your variable: it makes sure Bash knows where the name of the variable starts and ends. In the last `echo`, where we can forget to do this, we see that the variable is resolved incorrectly, and the text does not get printed correctly. While not necessary for all scripts, we think it looks better and is a good practice that you should always follow.

As far as we're concerned, only what we've covered here falls under *parameter substitution*. All other features in this chapter are *parameter expansion*, and we will refer to them accordingly!

Default values

On to parameter expansion! As we've hinted, Bash allows us to do many cool things directly with variables. We'll start with the seemingly simple example of defining a default value for your variables.

When dealing with user input, this makes both your life and the script user's life much easier: as long as there is a reasonable default value, we can make sure that we use that instead of throwing an error when the user does not supply the information we want.

We will reuse one of our earliest scripts, `interactive.sh`, from Chapter 8, *Variables and User Input*. It was a very simple script that did not verify user input, and was thus prone to all sorts of problems. Let's get it up-to-date and include our new default values for our parameters, as follows:

```
reader@ubuntu:~/scripts/chapter_16$ cp ../chapter_08/interactive-
arguments.sh default-interactive-arguments.sh
reader@ubuntu:~/scripts/chapter_16$ vim default-interactive-arguments.sh
reader@ubuntu:~/scripts/chapter_16$ cat default-interactive-arguments.sh
#!/bin/bash

#####################################
# Author: Sebastiaan Tammer
# Version: v1.0.0
# Date: 2018-12-16
# Description: Interactive script with default variables.
# Usage: ./interactive-arguments.sh <name> <location> <food>
#####################################

# Initialize the variables from passed arguments.
character_name=${1:-Sebastiaan}
location=${2:-Utrecht}
food=${3:-frikandellen}

# Compose the story.
echo "Recently, ${character_name} was seen in ${location} eating ${food}!"
```

Instead of just grabbing user input with `$1`, `$2` and `$3`, we will now create a more complicated syntax, defined by `man bash`, as follows:

${parameter:-word}
Use Default Values. *If parameter is unset or null, the expansion of word is substituted. Otherwise, the value of parameter is substituted.*

Again, you should read the word *parameter* as *variable* in this context (even though, when user-supplied, it is actually an argument to a parameter, but it could very well be a constant as well). With this syntax, if the variable is either not set or null (empty), the value supplied after the dash (called *word* in the `man page`) will be inserted instead.

We've done this for all three parameters, so let's check out how this works in practice:

```
reader@ubuntu:~/scripts/chapter_16$ bash default-interactive-arguments.sh
Recently, Sebastiaan was seen in Utrecht eating frikandellen!
reader@ubuntu:~/scripts/chapter_16$ bash default-interactive-arguments.sh
'' Amsterdam ''
Recently, Sebastiaan was seen in Amsterdam eating frikandellen!
```

If we do not supply any values to the script, all the defaults are inserted. If we supply three arguments, of which two are just empty strings (''), we can see that Bash will still substitute the defaults for us for the empty string. However, the actual string, Amsterdam, is correctly entered into the text, instead of Utrecht.

While dealing with empty strings in this manner is often desirable behavior, you can also write your scripts to allow for empty strings as a variable default. That looks like the following:

```
reader@ubuntu:~/scripts/chapter_16$ cat /tmp/default-interactive-
arguments.sh
<SNIPPED>
character_name=${1-Sebastiaan}
location=${2-Utrecht}
food=${3-frikandellen}
<SNIPPED>

reader@ubuntu:~/scripts/chapter_16$ bash /tmp/default-interactive-
arguments.sh '' Amsterdam
Recently,  was seen in Amsterdam eating frikandellen!
```

Here, we created a temporary copy to illustrate this functionality. When you remove the colon from the default declaration (`${1-word}` instead of `${1:-word}`), it no longer inserts the default for empty strings. It does, however, for values that are not set at all, as can be seen when we call it with `'' Amsterdam` instead of `'' Amsterdam ''`.

In our experience, in most cases, the default should ignore empty strings, so the syntax as presented in the `man page` is more desirable. If you have a niche case, though, you are now aware of this possibility!

For some of your scripts, you might find that just substituting a default is not enough: you'd rather have the variable set to a value that can then be evaluated with more granularity. This is also possible with parameter expansion, as follows:

> *${parameter:=word}*
> **Assign Default Values.** *If parameter is unset or null, the expansion of word is assigned to parameter. The value of parameter is then substituted. Positional parameters and special parameters may not be assigned to in this way.*

We've never seen the need to use this function, especially since it is not compatible with positional parameters (and as such, we only mention it here and do not go into detail). But, as with all things, it is good to be aware of the possibilities parameter expansion provides in this area.

Input checking

Closely related to setting default values with parameter expansion, we can also use parameter expansion to display an error if a variable is null or empty. Up until now, we've done this by implementing if-then logic within our scripts. While this is an excellent and flexible solution, it is a little verbose—especially if the only thing you're interested in is the user supplying the parameters.

Let's create a new version of our previous example: this one does not supply default values, but will alert the user if positional arguments are missing.

We'll use the following syntax:

> *${parameter:?word}*
> **Display Error if Null or Unset.** *If parameter is null or unset, the expansion of word (or a message to that effect if word is not present) is written to the standard error and the shell, if it is not interactive, exits. Otherwise, the value of parameter is substituted.*

When we use this in our script, it might look something like this:

```
reader@ubuntu:~/scripts/chapter_16$ cp default-interactive-arguments.sh
check-arguments.sh
reader@ubuntu:~/scripts/chapter_16$ vim check-arguments.sh
eader@ubuntu:~/scripts/chapter_16$ cat check-arguments.sh
#!/bin/bash

###################################
# Author: Sebastiaan Tammer
# Version: v1.0.0
# Date: 2018-12-16
```

```
# Description: Script with parameter expansion input checking.
# Usage: ./check-arguments.sh <name> <location> <food>
######################################

# Initialize the variables from passed arguments.
character_name=${1:?Name not supplied!}
location=${2:?Location not supplied!}
food=${3:?Food not supplied!}

# Compose the story.
echo "Recently, ${character_name} was seen in ${location} eating ${food}!"
```

Note the colon again. In the same way the colon worked in the previous example, it also forces this parameter expansion to consider an empty string as a null/unset value.

When we run this script, we see the following:

```
reader@ubuntu:~/scripts/chapter_16$ bash check-arguments.sh
check-arguments.sh: line 12: 1: Name not supplied!
reader@ubuntu:~/scripts/chapter_16$ bash check-arguments.sh Sanne
check-arguments.sh: line 13: 2: Location not supplied!
reader@ubuntu:~/scripts/chapter_16$ bash check-arguments.sh Sanne Alkmaar
check-arguments.sh: line 14: 3: Food not supplied!
reader@ubuntu:~/scripts/chapter_16$ bash check-arguments.sh Sanne Alkmaar
gnocchi
Recently, Sanne was seen in Alkmaar eating gnocchi!
reader@ubuntu:~/scripts/chapter_16$ bash check-arguments.sh Sanne Alkmaar
' '
check-arguments.sh: line 14: 3: Food not supplied!
```

While this works like a charm, it doesn't really look that great, does it? The script name and line numbers are printed, which seems like a bit too much in-depth information for a user of the script.

It is up to you to decide if you think these are acceptable looking feedback messages to your users; personally, we think a nice if-then is often better, but with regards to concise scripting, this cannot be beaten.

> There is another parameter expansion closely related to these:
> ${parameter:+word}. This allows you to use *word* only if the parameter
> is NOT null or empty. In our experience, this isn't a common occurrence,
> but for your scripting needs it might be; look for the words Use
> Alternate Value in man bash to get more information.

Parameter length

We've done a lot of checks in the book so far. One we haven't carried out, however, is on the length of the supplied parameter. What will probably not surprise you at this point is how we can achieve this: with parameter expansion, of course. The syntax is really simple, too:

> *${#parameter}*
> *Parameter length. The length in characters of the value of parameter is substituted. If parameter is * or @, the value substituted is the number of positional parameters.*

So, instead of printing `${variable}`, which will substitute the value at runtime, we will use `${#variable}`, which will give us a number: the number of characters in our value. This might be a little tricky, as things such as whitespaces can also be considered characters.

Take a look at the following example:

```
reader@ubuntu:~/scripts/chapter_16$ variable="hello"
reader@ubuntu:~/scripts/chapter_16$ echo ${#variable}
5
reader@ubuntu:~/scripts/chapter_16$ variable="hello there"
reader@ubuntu:~/scripts/chapter_16$ echo ${#variable}
11
```

As you can see, the word `hello` is identified as five characters; so far, so good. When we look at the sentence `hello there`, we can see two words of five letters each. While you might expect the parameter expansion to return `10`, it actually returns `11`. Since the words are separated by a space, you should not be surprised: this space is the 11th character.

If we take a look back at the syntax definition from the `man bash` page, we'll see the following interesting tidbit:

> *If parameter is * or @, the value substituted is the number of positional parameters.*

Remember how we used `$#` to determine how many arguments are passed to the script in the rest of this book? This is actually Bash parameter expansion at work, as `${#*}` is equal to `$#`!

To drive these points home, let's create a quick script that deals with three-letter acronyms (our personal favorite type of acronym). For now, the functionality of this script will be limited to verifying and printing the user input, but when we get to the end of this chapter, we'll amend it a bit to make it even cooler:

```
reader@ubuntu:~/scripts/chapter_16$ vim acronyms.sh
reader@ubuntu:~/scripts/chapter_16$ cat acronyms.sh
#!/bin/bash

######################################
# Author: Sebastiaan Tammer
# Version: v1.0.0
# Date: 2018-12-16
# Description: Verify argument length.
# Usage: ./acronyms.sh <three-letter-acronym>
######################################

# Use full syntax for passed arguments check.
if [[ ${#*} -ne 1 ]]; then
  echo "Incorrect number of arguments!"
  echo "Usage: $0 <three-letter-acronym>"
  exit 1
fi

acronym=$1 # No need to default anything because of the check above.

# Check acronym length using parameter expansion.
if [[ ${#acronym} -ne 3 ]]; then
  echo "Acronym should be exactly three letters!"
  exit 2
fi

# All checks passed, we should be good.
echo "Your chosen three letter acronym is: ${acronym}. Nice!"
```

We did two interesting things in this script: we used the full syntax of ${#*} to determine the number of arguments passed to our script, and we checked the acronym length with ${#acronym}. Because we used two different checks, we used two different exit codes: exit 1 for the wrong number of arguments, and exit 2 for incorrect acronym length.

In larger, more complex scripts, using different exit codes might save you a significant amount of troubleshooting, so we've included it here for information.

If we now run our script with different incorrect and correct input, we can see it works as planned:

```
reader@ubuntu:~/scripts/chapter_16$ bash acronyms.sh
Incorrect number of arguments!
Usage: acronyms.sh <three-letter-acronym>
reader@ubuntu:~/scripts/chapter_16$ bash acronyms.sh SQL
Your chosen three letter acronym is: SQL. Nice!
reader@ubuntu:~/scripts/chapter_16$ bash acronyms.sh SQL DBA
Incorrect number of arguments!
Usage: acronyms.sh <three-letter-acronym>
reader@ubuntu:~/scripts/chapter_16$ bash acronyms.sh TARDIS
Acronym should be exactly three letters
```

No arguments, too many arguments, arguments of incorrect length: we're equipped to handle everything the user might throw at us. As always, never expect the user to do what you hope, just ensure your script will only execute if the input is correct!

Variable manipulation

Parameter expansion in Bash deals with more than just default values, input checking, and parameter length. It actually also allows us to manipulate the variables before we use them. In this second part of this chapter, we'll explore the capabilities within parameter expansion that deal with *variable manipulation* (our terminology; as far as Bash is concerned, these are just normal parameter expansions).

We'll kick this off with *pattern substitution*, something you should be familiar with after our explanation of sed in Chapter 10, *Regular Expressions*.

Pattern substitution

Simply said, pattern substitution allows us to substitute a pattern with something else (who would have thought!). This is what we could already do with sed:

```
reader@ubuntu:~/scripts/chapter_16$ echo "Hi"
Hi
reader@ubuntu:~/scripts/chapter_16$ echo "Hi" | sed 's/Hi/Bye/'
Bye
```

Initially, our echo contains the word Hi. We then pipe it through sed, in which we look for the *pattern* Hi, which we will *substitute* with Bye. The s at the front of the instruction to sed signals that we're searching and replacing.

Behold, after `sed` is done parsing the stream, we end up with `Bye` on our screen.

If we want to do the same when using a variable, we have two options: we'll either parse it through `sed` as we did previously, or we'll turn to our new best friend for another great parameter expansion:

> *${parameter/pattern/string}*
> **Pattern substitution.** *The pattern is expanded to produce a pattern just as in pathname expansion. Parameter is expanded and the longest match of pattern against its value is replaced with string. If pattern begins with /, all matches of pattern are replaced with string.*

So, for the `${sentence}` variable, we could replace the first instance of a pattern with `${sentence/pattern/string}`, or all instances of the pattern with `${sentence//pattern/string}` (notice the extra forward slash).

On the command line, it might look something like this:

```
reader@ubuntu:~$ sentence="How much wood would a woodchuck chuck if a
woodchuck could chuck wood?"
reader@ubuntu:~$ echo ${sentence}
How much wood would a woodchuck chuck if a woodchuck could chuck wood?
reader@ubuntu:~$ echo ${sentence/wood/stone}
How much stone would a woodchuck chuck if a woodchuck could chuck wood?
reader@ubuntu:~$ echo ${sentence//wood/stone}
How much stone would a stonechuck chuck if a stonechuck could chuck stone
reader@ubuntu:~$ echo ${sentence}
How much wood would a woodchuck chuck if a woodchuck could chuck wood?
```

Once again, this is pretty self-explanatory and simple to use.

One important thing to realize is that this parameter expansion doesn't actually edit the value of the variable: it only affects the current substitution. If you wanted to do a permanent manipulation of the variable, you'd need to write the result to a variable again, as follows:

```
reader@ubuntu:~$ sentence_mutated=${sentence//wood/stone}
reader@ubuntu:~$ echo ${sentence_mutated}
How much stone would a stonechuck chuck if a stonechuck could chuck stone?
```

Or, if you'd prefer to keep the variable name after the mutation, you can assign the mutated value back to the variable in one go, as follows:

```
reader@ubuntu:~$ sentence=${sentence//wood/stone}
reader@ubuntu:~$ echo ${sentence}
How much stone would a stonechuck chuck if a stonechuck could chuck stone?
```

It should not be too difficult to imagine using this syntax in a script. As a simple example, we've created a little interactive quiz in which we'll *help* the user if they happen to give the wrong answer to our very non-opinionated question:

```
reader@ubuntu:~/scripts/chapter_16$ vim forbidden-word.sh
#!/bin/bash

#####################################
# Author: Sebastiaan Tammer
# Version: v1.0.0
# Date: 2018-12-16
# Description: Blocks the use of the forbidden word!
# Usage: ./forbidden-word.sh
#####################################

read -p "What is your favorite shell? " answer

echo "Great choice, my favorite shell is also ${answer/zsh/bash}!"

reader@ubuntu:~/scripts/chapter_16$ bash forbidden-word.sh
What is your favorite shell? bash
Great choice, my favorite shell is also bash!
reader@ubuntu:~/scripts/chapter_16$ bash forbidden-word.sh
What is your favorite shell? zsh
Great choice, my favorite shell is also bash!
```

In this script, if the user is temporarily *confused* and does not give the wanted answer, we'll simply replace their *wrong* answer (zsh) with the *correct* answer, bash.

All jokes aside, other shells such as zsh, ksh, and even the newer fish have their own unique selling points and strengths that makes some users prefer them over Bash for daily work. This is obviously great, and a big part of the mentality of using Linux: you have the freedom to choose whichever software you prefer!

When it comes to scripting, however, we are (obviously) of the opinion that Bash is still the king of shells, if only for the very simple reason that it has become the de facto shell for most distributions. This is very helpful when it comes to portability and interoperability, qualities that are often beneficial for scripts.

Pattern removal

A topic closely related to pattern substitution is *pattern removal*. Let's face it, pattern removal is basically the same as replacing a pattern with nothing.

If pattern removal had exactly the same functionality as pattern substitution, we would not need it. However, pattern removal has a few cool tricks that would be difficult or even impossible to do with pattern substitution.

Pattern removal has two options: removing matched pattern *prefixes* or *suffixes*. In simpler words, it allows you to remove stuff either from the beginning or the end. It also has an option to stop after the first matched pattern, or to continue up until the last.

Without a good example, this might be a bit too abstract (it definitely was for us the first time we encountered this). However, there is an excellent example here: it all has to do with files:

```
reader@ubuntu:/tmp$ touch file.txt
reader@ubuntu:/tmp$ file=/tmp/file.txt
reader@ubuntu:/tmp$ echo ${file}
/tmp/file.txt
```

We've created a variable that contains a reference to a file. If we wanted the directory, or the file without the directory, we could use either basename or dirname, as follows:

```
reader@ubuntu:/tmp$ basename ${file}
file.txt
reader@ubuntu:/tmp$ dirname ${file}
/tmp
```

We could also achieve this with parameter expansions. The syntax for prefix and suffix removal is as follows:

> *${parameter#word}*
> *${parameter##word}*
> **Remove matching prefix pattern.**
>
> *${parameter%word}*
> *${parameter%%word}*
> **Remove matching suffix pattern.**

For our ${file} variable, we can use parameter expansion to remove all directories and only keep the filename, as follows:

```
reader@ubuntu:/tmp$ echo ${file#/}
tmp/file.txt
reader@ubuntu:/tmp$ echo ${file#*/}
tmp/file.txt
reader@ubuntu:/tmp$ echo ${file##/}
tmp/file.txt
reader@ubuntu:/tmp$ echo ${file##*/}
file.txt
```

The difference between the first and second command is minimal: we're using the asterisk wildcard that can match on anything, zero or more times. In this case, since the value of the variable starts with a forward slash, it does not match. However, as soon as we get to the third command, we see the need to include it: we need to match *everything we want to delete*.

In this case, the */ pattern matches on /tmp/, whereas the / pattern only matches on the first forward slash (as the result of the third command clearly shows).

It is good to remember that in this instance, we're merely using parameter expansion to replace the functionality of the basename command. However, if we were not dealing with file references, but (for example) underscore delimited files, we could not achieve this with basename, and parameter expansion would come in quite handy!

Now that we've seen what we can do with prefixes, let's look at suffixes. The functionality is of the same order, but instead of parsing from the start of a value, we're now looking at the end of the value first. We could use this, for example, to remove the extension from the file:

```
reader@ubuntu:/tmp$ file=file.txt
reader@ubuntu:/tmp$ echo ${file%.*}
file
```

This allows us to grab the filename, without the extension. This might be desirable if there is some logic in your script that can be applied to this part of the file. In our experience, this is more common than you think!

For example, you might imagine backups that have a date in the filename that you'd like to compare to today's date, to ensure a backup was successful. A little bit of parameter expansion can get you to your desired format, so the comparison of dates is then trivial.

Just as we were able to replace the `basename` command, we can do the reverse with suffix pattern removal to find the `dirname`, as follows:

```
reader@ubuntu:/tmp$ file=/tmp/file.txt
reader@ubuntu:/tmp$ echo ${file%/*}
/tmp
```

Again, these examples mostly serve for educational purposes. There are many situations in which this could be useful; since these are very diverse, it is hard to give an example that is interesting for everyone.

The situation we introduced regarding backups, however, might be relevant for you. As a basic script, it would look something like this:

```
reader@ubuntu:~/scripts/chapter_16$ vim check-backup.sh
reader@ubuntu:~/scripts/chapter_16$ cat check-backup.sh
#!/bin/bash

###################################
# Author: Sebastiaan Tammer
# Version: v1.0.0
# Date: 2018-12-16
# Description: Check if daily backup has succeeded.
# Usage: ./check-backup.sh <file>
###################################

# Format the date: yyyymmdd.
DATE_FORMAT=$(date +%Y%m%d)

# Use basename to remove directory, expansion to remove extension.
file=$(basename ${1%%.*}) # Double %% so .tar.gz works too.

if [[ ${file} == "backup-${DATE_FORMAT}" ]]; then
  echo "Backup with todays date found, all good."
  exit 0 # Successful.
else
  echo "No backup with todays date found, please double check!"
  exit 1 # Unsuccessful.
fi

reader@ubuntu:~/scripts/chapter_16$ touch /tmp/backup-20181215.tar.gz
reader@ubuntu:~/scripts/chapter_16$ touch /tmp/backup-20181216.tar.gz
reader@ubuntu:~/scripts/chapter_16$ bash -x check-backup.sh
/tmp/backup-20181216.tar.gz
++ date +%Y%m%d
+ DATE_FORMAT=20181216
++ basename /tmp/backup-20181216
```

```
+ file=backup-20181216
+ [[ backup-20181216 == backup-20181216 ]]
+ echo 'Backup with todays date found, all good.'
Backup with todays date found, all good.
+ exit 0
reader@ubuntu:~/scripts/chapter_16$ bash check-backup.sh
/tmp/backup-20181215.tar.gz
No backup with todays date found, please double check!
```

To illustrate this, we're touching dummy backup files. For a real situation, you'd be more likely to pick up the newest file in a directory (with `ls -ltr /backups/ | awk '{print $9}' | tail -1`, for example) and compare that to the current date.

As with most things in Bash scripting, there are other ways to accomplish this date checking. You could argue that we could leave the extension in the file variable and use a regular expression that parses the date: that would work just as well, with pretty much the same amount of work.

The takeaway from this example (and the whole book, really) should be to use something *that works for you and your organization*, as long as you've built it in a robust manner and added the necessary comments for everyone to understand what you did!

Case modification

Next up is another parameter expansion we've already briefly seen: *case modification.* In this instance, case refers to lowercase and uppercase letters.

In the `yes-no-optimized.sh` script we originally created in `Chapter 9`, *Error Checking and Handling*, we had the following instructions:

```
reader@ubuntu:~/scripts/chapter_09$ cat yes-no-optimized.sh
<SNIPPED>
read -p "Do you like this question? " reply_variable

# See if the user responded positively.
if [[ ${reply_variable,,} = 'y' || ${reply_variable,,} = 'yes' ]]; then
  echo "Great, I worked really hard on it!"
  exit 0
fi

# Maybe the user responded negatively?
if [[ ${reply_variable^^} = 'N' || ${reply_variable^^} = 'NO' ]]; then
  echo "You did not? But I worked so hard on it!"
  exit 0
fi
```

As you might expect, the , , and ^^ found within the curly braces of the variable are the parameter expansions we're talking about.

The syntax, as found on man bash, is as follows:

${parameter^pattern}
${parameter^^pattern}
${parameter,pattern}
${parameter,,pattern}
Case modification. *This expansion modifies the case of alphabetic characters in parameter. The pattern is expanded to produce a pattern just as in pathname expansion. Each character in the expanded value of parameter is tested against pattern, and, if it matches the pattern, its case is converted. The pattern should not attempt to match more than one character.*

In our first script, we haven't used a pattern. When not using a pattern, it is implied that the pattern is a wildcard (in this case, the ?), which means everything matches.

A quick command-line example of both lowercase and uppercase modification should clear this up. First, let's take a look at how we can uppercase a variable:

```
reader@ubuntu:~/scripts/chapter_16$ string=yes
reader@ubuntu:~/scripts/chapter_16$ echo ${string}
yes
reader@ubuntu:~/scripts/chapter_16$ echo ${string^}
Yes
reader@ubuntu:~/scripts/chapter_16$ echo ${string^^}
YES
```

If we use a single caret (^), we can see that the first letter of our variables' value will be uppercased. If we use a double caret, ^^, we now have the full value in uppercase.

In a similar manner, commas do the same thing for lowercasing:

```
reader@ubuntu:~/scripts/chapter_16$ STRING=YES
reader@ubuntu:~/scripts/chapter_16$ echo ${STRING}
YES
reader@ubuntu:~/scripts/chapter_16$ echo ${STRING,}
yES
reader@ubuntu:~/scripts/chapter_16$ echo ${STRING,,}
yes
```

Because we can choose to uppercase or lowercase the entire value, we can now much more easily compare user input to a predefined value. Regardless of whether the user inputs YES, Yes, or yes, we can verify all these situations with a single check: ${input,,} == 'yes'.

This gives the user fewer headaches, and a happy user is what we want (remember, you are often the user of your own scripts, and you deserve happiness!).

Now, for the *pattern*, as the man page specifies it. In our personal experience, we have not had to use this option yet, but it is powerful and flexible, so it never hurts to get a little bit more explanation on this.

Basically, the case modification will only be performed if the pattern matches. It can get a little tricky, but you can see how it works here:

```
reader@ubuntu:~/scripts/chapter_16$ animal=salamander
reader@ubuntu:~/scripts/chapter_16$ echo ${animal^a}
salamander
reader@ubuntu:~/scripts/chapter_16$ echo ${animal^^a}
sAlAmAnder
reader@ubuntu:~/scripts/chapter_16$ echo ${animal^^ae}
salamander
reader@ubuntu:~/scripts/chapter_16$ echo ${animal^^[ae]}
sAlAmAndEr
```

The first command we run, ${animal^a}, only uppercases the first letter if it matches the pattern: a. Since the first letter is actually an s, the entire word is printed as lowercase.

For the next command, ${animal^^a}, *all matching letters* are uppercased. So, all three instances of a in the word salamander are given in uppercase.

On the third command, we try to add an extra letter to the pattern. Since this is not the correct way of doing this, the parameter expansion is (likely) trying to find a single letter to match two letters in the pattern. Spoiler alert: this is very much impossible. As soon as we bring some of our regular expression expertise in the mix, we can do what we want: by using [ae], we're specifying that both a and e are valid targets for the case modification operation.

In the end, the animal returned is now sAlAmAndEr, with all vowels uppercased using a custom pattern in combination with the case modification parameter expansion!

As a little bonus, we'd like to share a case modification that is not even present on the man bash page! It is not that complicated, either. If you replace either , or ^ with a tilde, ~, you will get a *case reversal*. As you might expect, a single tilde will operate only on the first letter (if it matches the pattern, if specified), while a double tilde will match on all instances of the pattern (or everything, if no pattern is specified and the default ? is used).

Take a look:

```
reader@ubuntu:~/scripts/chapter_16$ name=Sebastiaan
reader@ubuntu:~/scripts/chapter_16$ echo ${name}
Sebastiaan
reader@ubuntu:~/scripts/chapter_16$ echo ${name~}
sebastiaan
reader@ubuntu:~/scripts/chapter_16$ echo ${name~~}
sEBASTIAAN
reader@ubuntu:~/scripts/chapter_16$ echo ${name~~a}
SebAstiAAn
```

This should be a sufficient explanation of case modification, as all syntaxes are similar and predictable.

Now that you know how to lowercase, uppercase, and even reverse the case of your variables, you should be able to mutate them in any way you like, especially if you add a pattern into the mix, this parameter expansion provides many possibilities!

Substring expansion

Only a single topic with regards to parameter expansion remains: substring expansion. While you might have heard of a substring, it could also be a very complex-sounding term.

Fortunately, it is actually *really really* simple. If we take a string, such as *Today is a great day*, then any part of that sentence that is in the correct order but not the full sentence can be considered a substring of the full string. Examples of this are as follows:

- Today is
- a great day
- day is a gre
- Today is a great da
- o
- (<- there is a space here, you just can't see it)

As you can see from these examples, we're not looking at the semantic meaning of the sentence, but simply at the characters: any number of characters in the correct order can be considered a substring. This includes the entire sentence minus one letter, but also includes just a single letter, or even a single space character.

So, let's look at the syntax for this parameter expansion one last time:

> *${parameter:offset}*
> *${parameter:offset:length}*
> **Substring Expansion.** *Expands to up to length characters of the value of parameter starting at the character specified by offset.*

Basically, we specify where we should start our substring, and what length (in characters) it should have. As with most things computers, the first character will be considered a 0 (and not a 1, as any non-technical person might expect). If we omit the length, we will get everything after the offset; if we do specify it, we get exactly that number of characters.

Let's take a look at how this would work for our sentence:

```
reader@ubuntu:~/scripts/chapter_16$ sentence="Today is a great day"
reader@ubuntu:~/scripts/chapter_16$ echo ${sentence}
Today is a great day
reader@ubuntu:~/scripts/chapter_16$ echo ${sentence:0:5}
Today
reader@ubuntu:~/scripts/chapter_16$ echo ${sentence:1:6}
oday is
reader@ubuntu:~/scripts/chapter_16$ echo ${sentence:11}
great day
```

In our command-line example, we first create the ${sentence} variable containing our previously-given text. First, we echo it fully, before we use ${sentence:0:5} to only print the first five characters (remember, strings start at 0!).

Next, we print the first six characters, starting from the second character (as denoted by the :1:6 notation). In the final command, echo ${sentence:11} shows that we can also use substring expansion without specifying a length. In this case, Bash will simply print everything from the offset until it reaches the end of the variable's value.

We'd like to end this chapter with a promise we made earlier: our three-letter acronym script. Now that we know how to easily extract separate letters from the user input, it would be fun to create a chant!

Let's revise the script:

```
reader@ubuntu:~/scripts/chapter_16$ cp acronyms.sh acronym-chant.sh
reader@ubuntu:~/scripts/chapter_16$ vim acronym-chant.sh
reader@ubuntu:~/scripts/chapter_16$ cat acronym-chant.sh
#!/bin/bash

#####################################
# Author: Sebastiaan Tammer
# Version: v1.0.0
# Date: 2018-12-16
# Description: Verify argument length, with a chant!
# Usage: ./acronym-chant.sh <three-letter-acronym>
#####################################
<SNIPPED>

# Split the string into three letters using substring expansion.
first_letter=${acronym:0:1}
second_letter=${acronym:1:1}
third_letter=${acronym:2:1}

# Print our chant.
echo "Give me the ${first_letter^}!"
echo "Give me the ${second_letter^}!"
echo "Give me the ${third_letter^}!"

echo "What does that make? ${acronym^^}!"
```

We threw in a few case modifications in there for good measure. After we split the letters using substring expansion, we cannot be sure of the casing the user has presented us with. Since this is a chant, we'll assume that uppercase is a not a bad idea, and we'll uppercase everything.

For the single letter, a single caret will do the trick. For the full acronym, we use double carets so that all three characters are uppercase. Using the substring expansions of ${acronym:0:1}, ${acronym:1:1} and ${acronym:2:1}, we are able to get single letters (because the *length* is always 1, but the offset is different).

For the ever-important readability, we assign these letters to their own variables before using them. We could have also used ${acronym:0:1} directly in the echo, but since this script isn't too long, we have chosen the more verbose option of extra variables, in which the names give away what we achieve with the substring expansion.

Finally, let's run this last script and enjoy our personal chant:

```
reader@ubuntu:~/scripts/chapter_16$ bash acronym-chant.sh Sql
Give me the S!
Give me the Q!
Give me the L!
What does that make? SQL!
reader@ubuntu:~/scripts/chapter_16$ bash acronym-chant.sh dba
Give me the D!
Give me the B!
Give me the A!
What does that make? DBA!
reader@ubuntu:~/scripts/chapter_16$ bash acronym-chant.sh USA
Give me the U!
Give me the S!
Give me the A!
What does that make? USA!
```

Mixed-case, lowercase, uppercase, it does not matter: whatever the user inputs, as long as it is three characters, our chant will work just fine. Good stuff! Who knew substring expansion could be so convenient?

One very advanced parameter expansion feature is so-called *parameter transformation*. Its syntax, `${parameter@operator}`, allows some complex operators to be performed on the parameter. To get an idea of what this can do, head over to `man bash` and look for **Parameter transformation**. You'll probably never need it, but the functionality is really cool, so it is definitely worth a look!

Summary

In this chapter, we've discussed everything parameter expansion in Bash. We started by recapping how we've used parameter substitution throughout most of this book, and how parameter substitution is only a small part of Bash parameter expansion.

We moved on to show you how we can use parameter expansion to include default values for variables, in case the user does not supply their own. This functionality also allows us to present the user with an error message if input is missing, although not in the cleanest way.

We ended this introduction to parameter expansion by showing you how we could use this to determine the length of variable values, and we showed you how we've actually used that extensively in the book already, in the form of the $# syntax.

We continued with describing parameter expansions under the heading of *Variable manipulation*. This includes the functionality of *pattern substitution*, which allows us to replace a part of the variable's value (the *pattern*) with another string. In very similar functionality, *pattern removal* allows us to remove some of the value that matches a pattern.

Next up, we showed you how we can manipulate characters from lowercase to uppercase, and vice versa. This functionality was already mentioned earlier in this book, but we have now explained it in more depth.

We ended this chapter with *substring expansion*, which allows us to take parts of variables from an *offset* and/or with a specified *length*.

The following commands were introduced in this chapter: `export` and `dirname`.

Questions

1. What is parameter substitution?
2. How can we include default values for our defined variables?
3. How can we use parameter expansion to handle missing parameter values?
4. What does `${#*}` do?
5. How does pattern substitution work when talking about parameter expansions?
6. How is pattern removal related to pattern substitution?
7. What types of case modifications can we perform?
8. Which two things can we use to get a substring from a variable's value?

Further reading

Please refer to the following links for more information on the topics in this chapter:

- **TLDP on process substitution**: `http://www.tldp.org/LDP/abs/html/process-sub.html`
- **TLDP on parameter substitution**: `https://www.tldp.org/LDP/abs/html/parameter-substitution.html`
- **GNU on parameter expansion**: `https://www.gnu.org/software/bash/manual/html_node/Shell-Parameter-Expansion.html`

Tips and Tricks with Cheat Sheet

17

In this final chapter, we have collected some tips and tricks to help you on your scripting journey. First, we'll touch on some subjects that are important, but weren't directly referenced in our earlier chapters. Then, we'll show you some practical shortcuts for the command line, which should help you improve your speed when doing Terminal work. Finally, we will end with a cheat sheet for the most important interactive commands we have discussed in this book.

The following commands will be introduced in this chapter: `history` and `clear`.

The following topics will be covered in this chapter:

- General tips and tricks
- Command-line shortcuts
- Cheat sheet for interactive commands

Technical requirements

Since this chapter consists mostly of tips, there are no scripts as we have seen in earlier chapters. To really get a feeling for these tricks, you should try them out yourself. As a final goodbye, your Ubuntu virtual machine can serve you well this one last time!

General tips and tricks

For the first part of this chapter, we'll describe a few things we could not place properly in others parts of the book. With the exception of the first subject, *arrays*, both `history` and `alias` are not really used in a scripting context so we elected to present them here. But first, arrays!

Arrays

If you come from a developer background or have dabbled in programming, you will have (probably) come across the term *array*. If we needed to explain arrays in a single sentence, it would look like this: Arrays allow us to store a *collection of data of the same type*. To make this a little less abstract, we'll show you how we can create an *array of strings* in Bash:

```
reader@ubuntu:~$ array=("This" "is" "an" "array")
reader@ubuntu:~$ echo ${array[0]}
This
reader@ubuntu:~$ echo ${array[1]}
is
reader@ubuntu:~$ echo ${array[2]}
an
reader@ubuntu:~$ echo ${array[3]}
array
```

In this string array, we place four elements:

- This
- is
- an
- array

If we want to print the string in the first place in the array, we need to specify that we want the *zeroth position* with the `echo ${array[0]}` syntax. Remember, as is common in IT, the first item in a list is often found at the 0th position. Now, look at what happens if we try to grab the fourth position, and thus the fifth value (that is not there):

```
reader@ubuntu:~$ echo ${array[4]}
 # <- Nothing is printed here.
reader@ubuntu:~$ echo $?
0
reader@ubuntu:~$ echo ${array[*]}
This is an array
```

Weirdly enough, even though we're asking for the value in a position of the array that does not exist, Bash does not consider this an error. If you did the same in some programming languages, such as Java, you'd see an error akin to **ArrayIndexOutOfBoundsException**. As you can see after the exit status of 0, if we want to print *all the values in the array*, we use the asterisk (as a wildcard).

In our scripting example, to keep it a little simpler, we've used *whitespace delimited strings* when we needed to create a list (for reference, look at the script **for-simple.sh** from Chapter 11, *Conditional Testing and Scripting Loops* again). In our experience, for most purposes, this is often easier to work with and powerful enough. Should this not seem the case for your scripting challenges, however, remember that such a thing as arrays in Bash exist and that, perhaps, these might work for you.

The history command

A very powerful and cool command in Bash is history. Simply put, by default, Bash *will store a history of all the commands you type*. These are saved up to a certain threshold, and for our Ubuntu 18.04 installation this is 1,000 commands *in memory* and 2,000 commands *on disk*. Every time you do a clean exit/logout of your terminal, Bash will write the command history from memory to disk, taking both limits into account.

Before we dive (a little) deeper, let's take a look at our personal history for the **reader** user:

```
reader@ubuntu:~$ history
 1013  date
 1014  at 11:49 << wall "Hi"
 1015  at 11:49 <<< wall "Hi"
 1016  echo 'wall "Hi"' | at 11:49
<SNIPPED>
 1998  array=("This" "is" "an" "array")
 1999  echo ${array[0]}
 2000  echo ${array[1]}
 2001  echo ${array[2]}
 2002  echo ${array[3]}
 2003  echo ${array[4]}
 2004  echo ${array[*]}
```

Even though our history is very interesting, it is not interesting enough to print it fully here. Often, if you use this in practice, it can easily become an overload of information as well. We suggest you use the history command in the following manners:

- history | less
- history | grep sed

If you pipe it to less, you'll end up with a nice pager that you can scroll through leisurely and use the search function in. When you exit it using **q**, you will be back at your uncluttered Terminal. If you're looking for a specific command (such as sed), you could also pipe the output of history through the grep command to make a course filter. If that's still too rough, consider adding | less behind the grep to make use of the pager once again.

The configuration for history is found in a few environment variables, which are often set in your **~/.bashrc** file:

```
reader@ubuntu:~$ cat .bashrc
<SNIPPED>
# for setting history length see HISTSIZE and HISTFILESIZE in bash(1)
HISTSIZE=1000
HISTFILESIZE=2000
<SNIPPED>
```

Here, you see the two defaults we had already announced (and which, if you want, can be edited!). For the others, man bash will inform you about the following:

- HISTCONTROL
- HISTFILE
- HISTTIMEFORMAT

Be sure to give those a quick read. Do not underestimate how convenient the history command can be; you will most certainly find yourself *almost* remembering how you used a command before, and if you remember enough you can use history to find out what you did so you can do it again.

Creating your own aliases

Bash allows you to create your own aliases for commands. We've seen this introduced in Chapter 14, *Scheduling and Logging*, but for day-to-day tasks, it is worth exploring a little bit further. The syntax is pretty straightforward:

```
alias name=value
```

In this syntax, alias is the command, name is how the alias will be called by you on the Terminal, and value is what is actually called when you call the alias. For interactive work, this could look like the following:

```
reader@ubuntu:~$ alias message='echo "Hello world!"'
reader@ubuntu:~$ message
Hello world!
```

We created the alias `message`, which actually does `echo "Hello world!"` for us when called. For those of you with a little bit more experience, you've no doubt been using the "command" `ll` for some time now. As you might (or might not) remember, this is a common default `alias`. We can print currently set aliases with the `-p` flag:

```
reader@ubuntu:~$ alias -p
<SNIPPED>
alias grep='grep --color=auto'
alias l='ls -CF'
alias la='ls -A'
alias ll='ls -alF'
alias ls='ls --color=auto'
alias message='echo "Hello world!"'
```

As you can see, by default we have some aliases set and the one we just created is there as well. What is even more interesting, is the fact that we can use `alias` to *override a command*, such as `ls` above. All the times we used `ls` in the book's examples, we've actually been executing `ls --color=auto`! The same goes for `grep`, as the print clearly shows. The `ll` alias quickly allows us to use common, almost essential flags for `ls`. However, you would do well to realize that these aliases are distribution-specific. Take a look at the `ll` alias on my Arch Linux host machine for example:

```
[tammert@caladan ~]$ alias -p
alias ll='ls -lh'
<SNIPPED>
```

This is different from our Ubuntu machine. At the very least, that begs the question: where are these default aliases set? If you remember our explanation about **/etc/profile**, **/etc/bash.bashrc**, **~/.profile**, and **~/.bashrc** (in Chapter 14, *Scheduling and Logging*), we know that these files are the most likely candidates. From experience, you can expect most aliases to be in the **~/.bashrc** file:

```
reader@ubuntu:~$ cat .bashrc
<SNIPPED>
# some more ls aliases
alias ll='ls -alF'
alias la='ls -A'
alias l='ls -CF'
<SNIPPED>
```

If you have commands that you often use, or flags that you would like to include "by default," you can edit your **~/.bashrc** file and add as many `alias` commands as you like. Any commands in the .bashrc file are run when you log in. If you want to make an alias available system-wide, the **/etc/profile** or **/etc/bash.bashrc** files would be better choices to include your `alias` command in. Otherwise, you'd have to edit the personal .bashrc files of all users, current and future (which is not efficient, so you shouldn't even consider this).

Command-line shortcuts

Besides the convenience of the commands in the first part of this chapter, there is another type of time-saver, which does not necessarily need to be discussed in the context of shell scripting, but is still such a great asset that we'd feel bad if we did not share it with you: command-line shortcuts.

Fun with exclamation marks

Exclamations marks are normally used to give text some emphasis, but under Bash they are actually a `shell` keyword:

```
reader@ubuntu:~$ type -a !
! is a shell keyword
```

While the term "shell keyword" does not really give us a great indication of what it does, there are multiple things we can accomplish with the exclamation mark. One we have already seen: if we want to negate a `test`, we can supply the exclamation mark within the check. If you'd like to verify this on your Terminal, try the following with either `true` or `false`:

```
reader@ubuntu:~$ true
reader@ubuntu:~$ echo $?
0
reader@ubuntu:~$ ! true
reader@ubuntu:~$ echo $?
1
```

As you can see, the exclamation mark reverses the exit status: true becomes false, and false becomes true. Another cool feature of the exclamation mark is that a double exclamation mark will be substituted on the command line with the full previous command, like so:

```
reader@ubuntu:~$ echo "Hello world!"
Hello world!
reader@ubuntu:~$ !!
echo "Hello world!"
Hello world!
```

To ensure you're clear about what you're repeating, the command is printed to stdout alongside the output of the command. What's more, we can also choose which part of the command to repeat by using numbers and a colon in combination with an exclamation mark. As always, 0 is reserved for the first argument, 1 for the second, and so on. A good example of this is as follows:

```
reader@ubuntu:/tmp$ touch file
reader@ubuntu:/tmp$ cp file new_file # cp=0, file=1, new_file=2
reader@ubuntu:/tmp$ ls -l !:1 # Substituted as file.
ls -l file
-rw-r--r-- 1 reader reader 0 Dec 22 19:11 file
reader@ubuntu:/tmp$ echo !:1
echo -l
-l
```

The preceding example shows that we used `!:1` to substitute the second word of the previous command. Note that if we repeat this for the `ls -l file` command, the second word is actually the `-l` flag of the `ls` command, so don't assume only full commands are parsed; this is a simple whitespace delimited index.

There is one killer feature with exclamation marks, as far as we're concerned: the `!$` construct. It is the same type of substitution, and as you might guess from how **$** works in `vim`, it substitutes the last word of the previous command. While this might not seem like that big a deal, take a look at how often the last word of the previous command is something you can reuse:

```
reader@ubuntu:/tmp$ mkdir newdir
reader@ubuntu:/tmp$ cd !$
cd newdir
reader@ubuntu:/tmp/newdir
```

Or, when copying a file you want to edit:

```
reader@ubuntu:/tmp$ cp file new_file
reader@ubuntu:/tmp$ vim !$
vim new_file
```

Once you start using it in practice, you'll find that this trick applies to so many commands that it will start saving you time almost immediately. In these examples, the names were short, but if we're talking long pathnames, we'd either have to take our hands away from the keyboard to do a copy/paste with the help of our mouse, or type everything again. And why would you, when a simple !$ does the trick?

In the same way this can quickly become a lifesaver, there is one extremely good example of when to use !!. Take a look at the following situation, which everyone has encountered or will encounter sooner or later:

```
reader@ubuntu:~$ cat /etc/shadow
cat: /etc/shadow: Permission denied
reader@ubuntu:~$ sudo !!
sudo cat /etc/shadow
[sudo] password for reader:
root:*:17647:0:99999:7:::
daemon:*:17647:0:99999:7:::
bin:*:17647:0:99999:7:::
<SNIPPED>
```

When you forget to add a sudo in front of your command (because it is a privileged command or manipulates a privileged file), you can either:

- Type the whole command again
- Copy and paste the command using the mouse
- Use the up arrow, followed by the Home key, and type sudo
- Or simply type sudo !!

It should be clear which is the shortest and easiest, and thus has our preference. Do realize that with this simplicity also comes responsibility: if you try to remove files you should not remove, and you're quickly using sudo !! without fully thinking it through, your system could be gone in an instant. The warning still stands: when interacting as **root** or with sudo, always think twice before running a command.

Running commands from the history

The final thing we find noteworthy to describe in regards to exclamation marks is interacting with the history. As you learned just a few pages ago, the history saves your commands. With the exclamation mark, you can quickly run commands from your history: either by supplying the number of the command (for example, !100) or by entering part of the command (for example: !ls). In our experience, these functions are not used as much as the *reverse search* we'll explain shortly, but it is still good to be aware of this functionality.

Let's take a look at how this looks in practice:

```
reader@ubuntu:~$ history | grep 100
 1100   date
 2033   history | grep 100
reader@ubuntu:~$ !1100
date
Sat Dec 22 19:27:55 UTC 2018
reader@ubuntu:~$ !ls
ls -al
total 152
drwxr-xr-x  7 reader  reader  4096 Dec 22 19:20 .
drwxr-xr-x  3 root    root    4096 Nov 10 14:35 ..
-rw-rw-r--  1 reader  reader  1530 Nov 17 20:47 bash-function-library.sh
<SNIPPED>
```

By supplying the number, !1100 ran the command date again. You should realize that the history, once it reaches its maximum, will change. The command that is today equal to !1100 might next week be a different command altogether. In practice, this is considered a risky move and is often best avoided, because you do not get a confirmation: you see what is being executed, while it is running (or probably, it is done by the time you have seen what you ran). You can only be sure if you check the history first, and in that case you're not saving any time, only using extra.

What is interesting, though, is repeating a command based on the command itself, such as !ls shows. It is still somewhat risky, especially if used in combination with destructive commands such as rm, but if you're sure what the last command was that matches your exclamation mark query, you should be relatively safe (especially for nondestructive commands such as cat or ls). Again, before you start incorporating this practice into your daily life, be sure to keep reading until we've explained reverse searching. At that point, we expect/hope that those are much more interesting to you, and then you can file away the information here as *good to know*.

Keyboard shortcuts

The next class of shortcuts we want to discuss is *keyboard shortcuts*. In contrast to the previous commands and shell keywords, these are simply key combinations that modify things on the command line. The combinations we're discussing all work by using the *CTRL* key as a modifier: you hold down *CTRL* and press another key, for example the *t*. We'll describe this as *CTRL+t*, as we have done in the rest of the book as well. Speaking of **CTRL+t**, this is actually the first shortcut we'd like to address! You can use CTRL+t when you've made a *typo*:

```
reader@ubuntu:~$ head /etc/passdw
# Last two letters are swapped, press CTRL+t to swap them:
reader@ubuntu:~$ head /etc/passwd
```

Because the terminal is modified, it is kind of hard to get an accurate representation for these pages. We've included a comment between the lines, to show what we do and what changes when we do it. However, in your Terminal, you will only ever see one line. Go ahead and try it out. By pressing *CTRL+t*, you can swap the last two characters around as often as you'd like. Do note that it takes whitespace into account as well: if you've already pressed the spacebar, you'll swap the whitespace with the last letter, like so:

```
reader@ubuntu:~$ sl
# CTRL+t
reader@ubuntu:~$ s l
```

If you start using this shortcut, you will soon realize that swapping two letters is a much more common occurrence than you might initially expect. As with most things in Bash, this functionality is present because people use it, so you do not need to feel bad about yourself if this happens to you a bit too often! At least with this shortcut, you'll be able to mitigate the errors quickly.

Next up is the **CTRL+l** shortcut (lowercase *L*), which is actually a shortcut for a command: clear. The functionality of clear is almost as simple as the name of the command: clear - *clear the terminal screen* (from man clear). This is actually a shortcut (and by extension, a command) that we use extensively for every Terminal session. As soon as you get to the *bottom* of your Terminal emulator screen, with a lot of clutter above, you might notice this isn't as nice to work with as the empty Terminal you start with (our personal opinion, perhaps shared by you). If you want to clear this up, you can either use the *CTRL+l* shortcut, or simply type the command clear. When you clear your Terminal, the output is not gone: you can always scroll up (often via mouse wheel or *SHIFT+page-up*) to see what was cleared. But at least your cursor is on a nice, clean screen at the top!

There is also a shortcut for the `exit` command, **CTRL+d**. Not only does this work great for when you want to *exit an SSH session*, but it works for many other interactive prompts as well: a great example for this is `at` (in reality, you *need* to use *CTRL+d* to exit from the `at` prompt, as `exit` will just be interpreted as a command to run!). As you know, **CTRL+c** sends a cancel to a running command (technically a SIGINT, as there are many intensities of cancel/kill under Linux), so be sure not to confuse *CTRL+d* with *CTRL+c*.

With regards to navigation, there are two CTRL-based shortcuts which are often easier to reach than their alternatives: **CTRL+e** and **CTRL+a**. **CTRL+e** moves the cursor to the end of the line, in a similar way to what the END key accomplishes. As you might expect, **CTRL+a** does the reverse: it functions as an alternative to the HOME key. Especially for those of you that are proficient in touch typing, these shortcuts are faster than moving your right hand away from the home row to find the *END/HOME* keys.

Copying and pasting from the terminal

A very common thing to do with GUI-based systems is cutting and pasting text. You'll select text, often with the mouse, and either use the right mouse button to copy and paste, or hopefully you've found the good old **CTRL+c** and **CTRL+v** (for Windows, Command key for macOS). As we explained before and reminded you of two paragraphs ago, *CTRL+c* under Linux is definitely not a *copy*, but a *cancel*. Similarly, *CTRL+v* will most likely not paste text either. So, how then, under Linux, do we copy and paste?

First of all, if you're using SSH and a Terminal emulator from within a GUI desktop, you have the right mouse button available to accomplish this (or, if you're feeling really fancy, pressing the middle mouse button often defaults to paste as well!). You can select text from somewhere on the internet, for example, copy it, and paste it into your Terminal emulator with either button. However, we always strive to optimize our processes, and as soon as you need to grab the mouse, you're losing valuable time. For text you have already copied, there is (for most Terminal emulators!) a shortcut to paste: **SHIFT+insert**. Just so you know, this paste shortcut is not limited to Linux or most Terminal emulators: it seems to be pretty universal, working on Windows and Linux with GUIs as well. Personally, we have replaced *CTRL+v* almost completely with *SHIFT+insert* for our pasting needs.

Obviously, if we can paste in this manner, there must also be a similar way for copying. This is very similar: instead of *SHIFT+insert*, copying can be done with **CTRL+insert**. Again, this is not limited to Linux or Terminals: it works just fine on Windows as well. For those of us working with Linux and Windows, replacing *CTRL+c* and *CTRL+v* with *CTRL+insert* and *SHIFT+insert* ensures that we are always properly copying and pasting, no matter what environment we're working in. Personally, we use Linux at home but Windows at work, which means our time is spent about 50/50 between the operating systems: trust us, it is very nice to have shortcuts that always work!

Now, the method above still sort of relies on having a mouse. Most of the time (think more than 95%, depending on your job) this will be the case, but sometimes you will simply not have a mouse (when connected directly to a Terminal of a server in a data center, for example). Fortunately for us, there are three shortcuts that work in Bash and will allow us to cut and paste directly on the command line:

- **CTRL+w**: Cut the word before the cursor
- **CTRL+u**: Cut everything on the line before the cursor
- **CTRL+y**: Paste everything that was cut (using the two commands above, not the general OS clipboard!)

Besides being able to cut and paste, *CTRL+w* is also great to remove a single whole word from the command line. Look at the following example:

```
reader@ubuntu:~$ sudo cat /etc/passwd # Wrong file, we meant /etc/shadow!
root:x:0:0:root:/root:/bin/bash
daemon:x:1:1:daemon:/usr/sbin:/usr/sbin/nologin
bin:x:2:2:bin:/bin:/usr/sbin/nologin
<SNIPPED>
# Up-arrow
reader@ubuntu:~$ sudo cat /etc/passwd
# CTRL+w
reader@ubuntu:~$ sudo cat # Ready to type /etc/shadow here.
```

Something that tends to happen is giving an incorrect final argument to a command. If you want to revise this real quickly, a simple *up-arrow* followed by a *CTRL+w* will place the previous command minus the final argument back on your Terminal. Now, you just have to give it the correct argument to run it again. Alternatively, you could either:

- Retype the whole command
- Scroll, copy and paste using the mouse
- *Up-arrow* followed by a number of backspaces

In our experience, a double keystroke is always faster than all other possible solutions. Only if the last argument was a single character would using *up-arrow* and *backspace* be *equally fast*, which is kind of a stretch.

Now, in the previous example, we did not actually only *remove* the final argument, we actually *cut* it. When you cut an argument, it gives you the ability to *paste* it back again. As stated, this is a Bash-specific clipboard which is not tied to the system clipboard; while you might think that paste is always done with *SHIFT+insert*, in this case we use *CTRL+y* for the Bash-specific clipboard. The best example to show this is with a full line cut, using **CTRL+u**:

```
root@ubuntu:~# systemctl restart network-online.target # Did not press
ENTER yet.
# Forgot to edit a file before restart, CTRL+u to cut the whole line.
root@ubuntu:~# vim /etc/sysctl.conf # Make the change.
# CTRL+y: paste the cut line again.
root@ubuntu:~# systemctl restart network-online.target # Now we press
ENTER.
```

This is, for us, a typical scenario in which we are one step ahead of ourselves. We have already typed a command we need to execute, but before we press *ENTER* we realize we forgot to do something that needs to be done before our current command can succeed. In this scenario, we use **CTRL+u** to cut the entire command, continue with the prerequisite command, and when we're ready we paste the line with **CTRL+y** again. Again, you might think this will not happen to you, but you might be surprised at how often you will encounter this precise pattern.

Reverse search

As far as keyboard shortcuts go, we believe we have saved the best for last. Out of all the time-savers we have so far introduced, this is by far the coolest as far as we're concerned: *reverse searching*.

A reverse search allows you to go back through your history, and search for a string within your executed commands. You can think of this as similar to `history | grep cat`, but much more interactive and much faster. To enter the reverse search prompt, the keys **CTRL+r** are used:

```
reader@ubuntu:~$ # CTRL+r
(reverse-i-search)'': # Start typing now.
(reverse-i-search)'cat': cat /var/log/dpkg.log # Press CTRL+r again for
next match.
(reverse-i-search)'cat': sudo cat /etc/shadow # When match is found, press
ENTER to execute.
reader@ubuntu:~$ sudo cat /etc/shadow
```

```
root:*:17647:0:99999:7:::
daemon:*:17647:0:99999:7:::
bin:*:17647:0:99999:7:::
<SNIPPED>
```

Please go ahead and give it a try. It is hard to get these interactive prompts down on paper, so we hope the comments above give a good indication of how a reverse search works. You can reverse search all the way up to the beginning of your history. If, at that point, you press *CTRL+r* again, you'll see something like the following:

(failed reverse-i-search)`'cat': cat base-crontab.txt`

This signifies to you that there are no more matches for reverse search to find. At this point, or before if you think you're taking too long, you can always press *CTRL+c* to stop reverse searching.

By contrast with the `!ls` syntax, reverse search will not start looking for the keywords only from the beginning of the line:

`reverse-i-search)`**`'ls'`**`: cat grep-then-else.sh`

This means that it is both more powerful (it just matches anywhere in the command) and more complicated to use (it does not match just the command). However, if you're smart about this and you just want commands, you can always use a well-placed whitespace to make sure situations like the example above do not happen:

`(reverse-i-search)`**`'ls '`**`: ls -al /tmp/new # Note the whitespace after ls.`

While we'd love to talk more about reverse searching, the only true way for you to learn it properly is to start using it. Rest assured, if you get proficient in its use (and also know when to stop searching and just type in the command you're looking for), you'll be sure to impress your peers with your efficient Terminal work!

Cheat sheet for interactive commands

We're going to end this book with a simple cheat sheet used for interactive commands. Getting proficient in Bash is a matter of practice. However, over the years, we have found ourselves stumbling upon new ways to use commands, or flags we weren't aware of, that made our lives much easier. Even during the writing of this book, we encountered things we did not know about before that were pretty helpful. In the process of writing about commands and constructs, you are looking more closely at manual pages and resources than you do when you're simply using them in your day-to-day business.

Please take advantage of these cheat sheets, as they include not only the basic syntax but also flags and tips we think are great to know about (we wish we'd found them earlier in our career)!

Out of scope for these cheat sheets are things such as find/locate, redirection, tests, and loops: these have (hopefully) been adequately described in their own respective chapters.

Navigation

These commands are used for navigation.

cd

Description	Change the shell working directory.
Syntax	cd [dir]
Practical uses	• cd: Navigate to the home directory (as specified in HOME). • cd -: Navigate back to the previous directory (as saved in OLDPWD).

ls

Description	List directory contents.
Syntax	ls [OPTION]... [FILE]...
Practical uses	• ls -a: Do not ignore entries starting with dots (. and ..). • ls -l: Use a long listing format. • ls -h: With -l and/or -s, print human readable sizes (for example, 1K 234M 2G). • ls -R: List subdirectories recursively. • ls -S: Sort by file size, largest first. • ls -t: Sort by modification time, newest first. • ls -ltu: Sort by, and show, access time. • ls -Z: Print any security context of each file.

pwd

Description	Print name of current/working directory.
Syntax	pwd [OPTION]...

File manipulation

These commands are used for file manipulation.

cat

Description	Concatenate files and print on the standard output.
Syntax	cat [OPTION]... [FILE]...
Practical uses	• `cat` or `cat` `-`: With no FILE, or when FILE is -, read standard input. • `cat` `-n`: Number all output lines.

less

Description	Page through text one screen at a time using a pager.
Syntax	less [OPTION]... [FILE]...
Practical uses	• `less` `-S`: Chop long lines. Lines do not wrap around, but can be seen with the left-right arrow keys. • `less` `-N`: Show line numbers.

touch

Description	Change file timestamps and/or create empty files.
Syntax	touch [OPTION]... FILE...
Practical uses	• `touch` `<non-existent-file>`: Create an empty file.

mkdir

Description	Make directories.
Syntax	mkdir [OPTION]... DIRECTORY...
Practical uses	• `mkdir` `-m750` `<dirname>`: Create directory with specified octal permissions. • `mkdir` `-Z`: Set SELinux security context of each created directory to the default type.

cp

Description	Copy files and directories.
Syntax	cp [OPTION]... SOURCE... DIRECTORY

Practical uses	• cp −a: Archive mode, preserve all permissions, links, attributes and so on. • cp −i: Prompt before overwrite (overrides a previous −n option). • cp −r and cp −R: Copy directories recursively. • cp −u: Copy only when the SOURCE file is newer than the destination file or when the destination file is missing.

rm

Description	Remove files or directories.
Syntax	rm [OPTION]... [FILE]...
Practical uses	• rm −f: Ignore nonexistent files and arguments, never prompt. • rm −i: Prompt before every removal. • rm −I (capital i): Prompt once before removing more than three files, or when removing recursively; less intrusive than -i, while still giving protection against most mistakes. • rm −r and rm −R: Remove directories and their contents recursively.

mv

Description	Move (rename) files.
Syntax	mv [OPTION]... SOURCE... DIRECTORY
Practical uses	• mv −f: Do not prompt before overwriting. • mv −n: Do not overwrite an existing file. • mv −u: Move only when the SOURCE file is newer than the destination file or when the destination file is missing.

ln

Description	Make links between files. Defaults to hard links.
Syntax	ln [OPTION]... [-T] TARGET LINK_NAME
Practical uses	• ln −s: Make symbolic links instead of hard links. • ln −i: Prompt whether to remove destinations.

head

Description	Output the first part of files.
Syntax	head [OPTION]... [FILE]...
Practical uses	• head: Print the first 10 lines of each FILE to standard output. • head −n20 or head −20: Print the first NUM lines instead of the first 10. • head −c20: Print the first NUM bytes of each file. • head −q: Never print headers giving file names.

tail

The `tail` command has the same options as `head`, but as seen from the end of the file instead of the beginning.

Description	Output the last part of files.
Syntax	tail [OPTION]... [FILE]...

Permissions and ownership

These commands are used for permission and ownership manipulation.

chmod

Description	Change file mode bits. Can be specified as either rwx or octal mode.
Syntax	chmod [OPTION]... OCTAL-MODE FILE...
Practical uses	• `chmod -c`: Like verbose but report only when a change is made. • `chmod -R`: Change files and directories recursively. • `chmod --reference=RFILE`: Copy the mode from a reference file.

umask

Description	Set file mode creation mask. Since this is a *mask*, it is the reverse of a normal octal mode.
Syntax	umask [octal-mask]

chown

Description	Change file owner and group. Only executable with root permissions.
Syntax	chown [OPTION]... [OWNER][:[GROUP]] FILE...
Practical uses	• `chown user: <file>`: Change ownership to the user and their default group. • `chown -c`: Like verbose, but report only when a change is made. • `chown --reference=RFILE`: Copy the ownership from a reference file. • `chown -R`: Operate on files and directories recursively.

chgrp

Description	Change group ownership.
Syntax	chgrp [OPTION]... GROUP FILE...
Practical uses	• `chgrp -c`: Like verbose, but report only when a change is made. • `chgrp --reference=RFILE`: Copy the group ownership from a reference file. • `chgrp -R`: Operate on files and directories recursively.

sudo

Description	Execute a command as another user.
Syntax	sudo [OPTION]...
Practical uses	• `sudo -i`: Become the root user. • `sudo -l`: List the allowed (and forbidden) commands for the invoking user. • `sudo -u <user> <command>`: Run a <command> as the specified <user>. • `sudo -u <user> -i`: Login as the specified <user>.

su

Description	Change user ID or become superuser.
Syntax	su [options] [username]
Practical uses	• `sudo su -`: Switch to root user. Requires sudo, optionally with your own password. • `su - <user>`: Switch to <user>. Requires password entry for <user>.

useradd

Description	Create a new user or update default new user information.
Syntax	useradd [options] LOGIN
Practical uses	• `useradd -m`: Create the user's home directory if it does not exist. • `useradd -s <shell>`: The name of the user's login shell. • `useradd -u <uid>`: The numerical value of the user's ID. • `useradd -g <group>`: The group name or number of the user's initial login group.

groupadd

Description	Create a new group.
Syntax	groupadd [options] group
Practical uses	• `groupadd -g <gid>`: The numerical value of the group's ID. • `groupadd -r`: Create a system group. These have GIDs which are (normally) lower than users.

usermod

Description	Modify a user account.
Syntax	usermod [options] LOGIN
Practical uses	• `usermod -g <group> <user>`: Change the primary group of the \<user> to \<group>. • `usermod -aG <group> <user>`: Add the \<user> to the \<group>. For the user, this will be a supplementary group. • `usermod -s <shell> <user>`: Set the login shell for the \<user>. • `usermod -md <homedir> <user>`: Move the \<user>s home directory to \<homedir>.

Summary

We started this final chapter with general tips and tricks. This part of the chapter dealt with arrays, the `history` command, and the ability to use `alias` to set up aliases for your favorite commands and their flags.

We continued with keyboard shortcuts. We started that part by talking about exclamation marks and how versatile their use can be in Bash: it is used for negation of exit codes, substituting parts of previous commands, and even for running commands from history by matching either the line number or line content. After that, we showed how a few interesting keyboard shortcuts for Bash allow us to save some time on common operations and usage patterns (such as typos and forgotten intermediate commands). We saved the best keyboard shortcut for last: reverse searches. These allow you to interactively go through your personal history to find just the right command to execute again.

We ended this chapter and the book with a cheat sheet for most of the commands we introduced in this book. This cheat sheet contains the basic syntax for all commands, as well as our favorite flags and combinations with regards to the commands.

The following commands were introduced in this chapter: `history` and `clear`.

Final words

If you have managed to make it this far: thank you for reading our book. We hope you enjoyed reading it as much as we enjoyed creating it. Keep on scripting and learning: practice makes perfect!

Assessments

Chapter 2

1. **What are some of the reasons running a virtual machine would be preferable to a bare-metal installation?**
    - The virtual machine can run inside the current preferred operating system, instead of replacing it or setting up a complicated dual-boot solution.
    - A virtual machine can be snapshotted, which means the entire state of the machine is preserved and can be restored.
    - Many different operation systems can run on a single machine, concurrently.

2. **What are some of the downsides of running a virtual machine as opposed to a bare-metal installation?**
    - There is a little overhead from the virtualization.
    - More resources (CPU/RAM/disk) will always be used compared to running a bare-metal installation.

3. **What is the difference between a type-1 and type-2 hypervisor?**
    Type-1 hypervisors are installed directly on the physical machine (e.g. VMWare vSphere, KVM, Xen), while type-2 hypervisors are installed in an already running operating system (for example, VirtualBox, VMWare Workstation Player).

4. **In which two ways can we start a virtual machine on VirtualBox?**
    - Normally, which opens a new window with the terminal console (or GUI, if a desktop environment is installed).
    - Headless, which runs the virtual machine as a server, without a GUI.

5. **What makes an Ubuntu LTS version special?**
    LTS stands for Long Term Support. Ubuntu LTS versions are guaranteed updates for five years, instead of the nine months for regular Ubuntu releases.

6. **What should we do if, after the Ubuntu installation, the virtual machine boots to the Ubuntu installation screens again?**
    We should check if either the virtual hard disk in higher in the boot order than the optical drive, or we unmount the ISO from the optical drive so only the virtual hard disk is a valid boot target.

7. **What should we do if we accidentally reboot during installation, and we never end up at the Ubuntu installation (but instead see an error)?**
   We should ensure the optical disk is higher in the boot order than the virtual hard disk AND we need to make sure the ISO is mounted on the optical disk.

8. **Why did we setup NAT forwarding for the virtual machine?**
   So we're not limited to using the terminal console, but instead we can use richer SSH tooling such as PuTTY or MobaXterm.

Chapter 3

1. **Why is syntax highlighting an important feature for text editors?**
   It makes it easy to spot syntax error, by using colors.

2. **How can we extend the functionality already provided by Atom?**
   We can install extra Packages, or even write our own.

3. **What are the benefits of autocomplete when writing shell scripts?**
   - It reduces typing, especially for multi-line constructs.
   - It makes it easier to find commands.

4. **How could we describe the difference between Vim and GNU nano?**
   Nano is simple, Vim is powerful.

5. **Which are the two most interesting modes in Vim?**
   Normal mode and Insert mode.

6. **What is the .vimrc file?**
   It is used to configure persistent options for Vim, such as the color scheme and how to handle tabs.

7. **What do we mean when we call nano a WYSIWYG editor?**
   WYSIWYG stands for What You See Is What You Get, which means you can start typing at your cursor.

8. **Why would we want to combine GUI editors with command-line editors?**
   Because it's easier to write in GUI editors, but easier to troubleshoot with command-line editors.

Chapter 4

1. **What is a file system?**
   A software implementation of the way data is stored on and retrieved from a physical medium.

2. **Which Linux specific file systems are most common?**
   - ext4
   - XFS
   - Btrfs

3. **True of false: multiple file system implementations can be used concurrently on Linux?**
   True; the root file system is always a single type, but different parts of the file system tree can be used to mount other file system types on.

4. **What is the journaling feature present on most Linux file system implementations?**
   Journaling is the mechanism which ensures writes to disks cannot fail halfway. It greatly improves reliability of the file system.

5. **On which point in the tree is the root file system mounted?**
   At the highest point, on / .

6. **What is the PATH variable used for?**
   It is used to determine from which directory binaries can be used. You can check the contents of the PATH variable with the command 'echo $PATH'.

7. **In which top-level directory are configuration files stored according to the Filesystem Hierarchy Standard?**
   In /etc/.

8. **Where are process logs commonly saved?**
   In /var/log/.

9. **How many file types does Linux have?**
   7

10. **How does the Bash autocomplete function work?**
    For commands that support the autocomplete function, you can use TAB once to get the correct argument (if there is a single possibility), or TAB twice for a list of possible arguments.

Chapter 5

1. **Which three permissions are used for Linux files?**
   - Read
   - Write
   - Execute

2. **Which three types of ownership are defined for Linux files?**
   - User
   - Group
   - Others

3. **Which command is used to change the permissions on a file?**
   `chmod`

4. **What mechanism controls the default permissions for newly created files?**
   `umask`

5. **How is the following symbolic permission described in octal: rwxrw-r--**
   0764. 7 from rwx on the first three places (user), 6 from `rw-` on the second three places (group), and 4 from `r--` on the last three places (others).

6. **How is the following octal permission described symbolically: 0644**
   rw-r--r--. First 6 is ReadWrite, then two 4s which are just Reads.

7. **Which command allows us to gain superuser privileges?**
   `sudo`

8. **Which commands can we use to change ownerships for a file?**
   - `chown`
   - `chgrp`

9. **How can we arrange for multiple users to share access to files?**
   We make sure they share group membership, and create a directory in which only members of those groups are allowed.

10. **Which types of Advanced Permissions does Linux have?**
    - File Attributes
    - Special File Permissions
    - Access Control Lists

Chapter 6

1. **Which command do we use to copy files in Linux?**
   `cp`.

2. **What is the difference between moving and renaming files?**
   Technically, there is no difference. Functionally, moving changes the directory a file is in, while renaming keeps the file in the same directory. Both are handled in Linux by the `mv` command.

3. **Why is the** `rm` **command, used to remove files under Linux, potentially dangerous?**
    - It can be used to recursively delete directories and anything in them
    - It does not (by default) present an 'Are you sure?' prompt
    - It allows you to delete files using wildcards

4. **What is the difference between a hard link and a symbolic (soft) link?**
   Hard links refer to the data on the filesystem, while symbolic links refer to the file (which, in turn, refers to the data on the filesystem).

5. **What are the three most important operating modes of** `tar`**?**
    - Archiving mode
    - Extracting mode
    - Printing mode

6. **Which option is used by** `tar` **to select the output directory?**
   `-C`

7. **What is the biggest difference between** `locate` **and** `find` **when searching on filename?**
   Locate allows partly named matches by default, while find requires specifying wildcards if that partial matches are desired.

8. **How many options of** `find` **can be combined?**
   As many as the search requires! This is exactly what makes `find` so incredibly powerful.

Chapter 7

1. **What do we, by convention, do as the first thing when we learn a new programming or scriping language?**
   We print the string "Hello World".

2. **What is the shebang for Bash?**
   #!/bin/bash

3. **Why is the shebang needed?**
   If we're running the script without specifying which program we should use, the shebang will allow Linux to use the correct one.

4. **In what three ways can we run a script?**
    - By using the program which we want to run it with: `bash script.sh`
    - By setting the executable permission and prefixing the scriptname with ./: `./script.sh`

- By setting the executable permission and using the fully qualified path to the file: `/tmp/script.sh`

5. **Why do we place such emphasis on readability when creating shell scripts?**
    - Scripts are much easier to use if the person using them can easily understand what the script does
    - If anyone other than yourself needs to edit the script (and you can consider yourself 'someone else' too after a few months!) it helps tremendously if it's simple to understand

6. **Why do we use comments?**
   So we can explain things in the script which might not be obvious by just looking at the commands. Furthermore, it also allows us to give some design rationale if that helps clarify the script.

7. **Why do we recommend including a script header for all shell scripts you write?**
   If gives a bit of information on the author, age and description to the script. It helps give context to the script, which can be very helpful when the script is not working as expected, or needs to be modified.

8. **Which three types of verbosity have we discussed?**
    - Verbosity in comments
    - Verbosity in commands
    - Verbosity in command output

9. **What is the KISS principle?**
   KISS, which stands for *Keep It Simple, Stupid*, is a design recommendation which helps us to remember that we should keep things simple, as that often increases usability and readability, while even being the best solution most of the times as well.

Chapter 8

1. **What is a variable?**
   A variable is a basic building block for programming languages, which is used to store run-time values that can be referenced multiple times in the application.

2. **Why do we need variables?**
   Variables are great for storing information you need multiple times. In this case, if you need to change the information, it's a single operation (in the case of a constant). In the case of a real variable, it allows us to reference run-time information in the program.

Lastly, proper variable naming allow us to grant extra context to our script, increasing readability.

3. **What is a constant?**
A constant is a special type of variable, since its value is determined is fixed and used throughout the script. Normal variables are often mutated multiple times during execution.

4. **Why are naming conventions especially important for variables?**
Bash allows us to name our variables almost anything. Because this can become confusing (which is never a good thing!) it is important to pick one naming convention and stick to it: this increases consistency and coherence for our scripts.

5. **What are positional arguments?**
When you call a Bash script, any other text passed after the `bash scriptname.sh` command can be accessed in the script, as this text is considered the *arguments* to the script. Each word not enclosed in quotes is handled as a single argument: a multi-word argument should be enclosed in quotes!

6. **What is the difference between a parameter and an argument?**
Arguments are used to fill the parameters of a script. Parameters are the *static variable names* which are used in the script logic, whereas the arguments are the *run-time values* used as the parameters.

7. **How can we make a script interactive?**
By using the `read` command. We can store the values that the users gives in a variable of our choice, otherwise we can use the default **$REPLY** variable.

8. **How can we create a script that we can use both non-interactive and interactively?**
By combining (optional) positional arguments with the `read` command. To verify that we have all the information we need before starting the logic of the script, we use the `if-then` construct coupled with the `test` command to see if all our variables are populated.

Chapter 9

1. **Why do we need an exit status?**
So commands can signal to their callers if they succeeded or failed in a simple manner.

2. **What is the difference between exit status, exit code and return code?**
An exit code and return code refer to the same thing. An exit status is a *concept*, which is brought to life by the exit/return code.

3. **Which flag do we use with test to test for:**
   - *An existing directory*
   -d
   - *A writable file*
   -w
   - *An existing symbolic link*
   -h (or -L)

4. **What is the preferred shorthand syntax for** test -d /tmp/**?**
   [[-d /tmp/]]. Note that a space after [[and before]] is mandatory, or the command will fail!

5. **How can we print debug information in a Bash session?**
   Set the -x flag, either in the shell with set -x or when calling a script with bash -x.

6. **How can we check if a variable has content?**
   - if [[-n ${variable}]] to check if the variable is non-zero
   - if [[! -z ${variable}]] to check if the variable is not zero

7. **What is the Bash format for grabbing a return code?**
   $?.

8. **Of || and &&, which is the logical AND and which the OR?**
   || is OR, && is AND.

9. **What is the Bash format for grabbing the number of arguments?**
   $#.

10. **How can we make sure it does not matter from which working directory the user calls the script?**
    By providing a cd $(dirname $0) at the beginning of the script.

11. **How do Bash parameter expansions help us when dealing with user input?**
    It allows us to remove capital letters so we can more easily compare to expected values.

Chapter 10

1. **What is a search pattern?**
   A regular expression syntax which allows us to find pieces of text with specified characteristics, such as length, content and location on a line.

2. **Why are regular expressions considered greedy?**
Most regular expression try to find as much data as they can that match the search pattern. This includes whitespace and other punctuation, which is a logical separation for humans but not necessarily for a machine.

3. **Which character in search patterns is considered a wildcard for any one character, except newlines?**
The dot (.).

4. **How is the asterisk used in Linux regular expression search patterns?**
The * is used in combination with another character to allow it to form a repeating character. Example search pattern: **spe*d** will match spd, sped, speed, speeeeeeeed, and so on.

5. **What are line anchors?**
The special characters used to denote line beginnings and endings. ^ for the beginning of the line, $ for the line end.

6. **Name three character types.**
Any of these are correct:
   - alphanumeric
   - alphabet
   - lowercase
   - uppercase
   - digits
   - blanks

7. **What is globbing?**
Globbing is accomplished when you use a * or ? on the command-line when interacting with files or file paths. Globbing allows us to easily manipulate (move, copy, delete, and so on) files that are matched on the globbing pattern.

8. **What is possible in the extended regular expression syntax, that is not possible with normal regular expressions under Bash?**
   - One or more repeating characters
   - Exact number of repeating characters
   - Range of repeating characters
   - Alternation with more than a single character

9. **What would be a good rule of thumb between deciding to use `grep` or `sed`?**
If your goal can be achieved with a single `grep` statement, choose simplicity. If it cannot be achieved in that manner, choose `sed` for more powerful syntax.

10. **Why are regular expressions on Linux/Bash so hard?**
    There are many different implementations that are similar. With regular expressions and their difficulty as-is, this confusion does not help. Only practice and experience will remedy this!

Chapter 11

1. **How does an if-then(-else) statement end?**
   With the reverse of the word if: `fi`

2. **How can we use regular expression search patterns in a conditional evaluation?**
   By employing the =~ comparison symbol. For example: `[[ ${var} =~ [[:digit:]] ]]`

3. **Why do we need the** `elif` **keyword?**
   If we want to sequentially test for more than one condition, we can use else if (`elif`).

4. **What is** *nesting*?
   Using an `if-then-else` statement or loop within another if-then-else statement or loop.

5. **How can we get information about how to use shell builtins and keywords?**
   By using the command `help`, followed by the builtin or keyword we want information about. For example: `help [[`

6. **What is the opposite keyword of** `while`?
   `until`. A while loop runs until the condition is no longer *true*, an until loop runs until the condition is no longer *false*.

7. **Why would we choose the for loop over the while loop?**
   `for` is more powerful and has many convenient shorthand syntaxes which would be hard or unreadable with `while`.

8. **What is brace expansion and on which characters can we use it?**
   Brace expansion allows us to write very short code, which generates a whitespace delimited list based on ASCII characters. For example: `{1..10}` prints the numbers 1 through 10, with spaces in between. We can also use this for uppercase or lowercase letters, or any range in the ASCII character set.

9. **Which two keywords allows us to have more granular control over loops?**
   `break` and `continue`. `break` stops the current loop, while `continue` jumps to the next iteration in the loop.

10. **If we are nesting loops, how can we employ loop control to influence outer loops from an inner loop?**
By adding a number higher than 1 to the `break` or `continue` keyword. Example: `break 2` exits from both the inner and one outer loop.

Chapter 12

1. **What are file descriptors?**
A handle to files or devices used by Linux as an interface for input/output.

2. **What do the terms stdin, stdout and stderr mean?**
    - stdin, standard input. Used for input to commands.
    - stdout, standard output. Used for normal output of commands.
    - stderr, standard error. Used for error output of commands.

3. **How to stdin, stdout and stderr map to the default file descriptors?**
stdin is bound to fd0, stdout to fd1, and stderr to fd2.

4. **What is the difference between the output redirections >, 1> and 2>?**
> and 1> are equal, and refer to redirecting stdout. 2> is used to redirect stderr.

5. **What is the difference between > and >>?**
> will overwrite the file if it already has content, while >> will append to the file.

6. **How can both stdout and stderr be redirected at the same time?**
    - By using `&>` (and `&>>`)
    - By binding stderr to stdout, using `2>&1`
    - By piping with `|&`

7. **Which special devices can be used to act as a black hole for output?**
/dev/null and **/dev/zero**.

8. **What does a pipe do, with regards to redirections?**
It binds the stdout/stderr of a command to the stdin of another command.

9. **How can we send output to both the terminal and a log file?**
By piping through the `tee` command, preferably with `|&` so both stdout and stderr is forwarded.

10. **What is a typical use-case for a *here string*?**
We can use a here string if we want to supply input directly to stdin of a command. `bc` is a good example of this.

Chapter 13

1. **In which two ways can we define a function?**
   - name() {
     }
   - function name {
     }

2. **What are some advantages of functions?**
   - Easy to reuse code
   - Facilitates code sharing
   - Abstracting complex code

3. **What is the difference between a globally scoped variable and a locally scoped one?**
   Locally scoped variables are only valid within a function, globally scoped variables can be used throughout the entire script (even in functions).

4. **How can we set values and attributes on variables?**
   By using the `declare` command.

5. **How can a function use arguments passed to it?**
   In the same way as a script can: by using $1, $#, $@, and so on.

6. **How can we return a value from a function?**
   By outputting it to stdout. The command that calls the function should know to capture the output, using command substitution.

7. **What does the `source` command do?**
   It executes commands from a file in the current shell. If the sourced file contains only function definitions, these are loaded to be used later (but still only in the current shell).

8. **Why would we want to create a function library?**
   A lot of utility functions, such as argument checking, error handling and color setting, never change and can sometimes be complex to figure out. If we do this once properly, we can then use the predefined functions from our library without needing to duplicate code from older scripts.

Chapter 14

1. **What is scheduling?**
   Scheduling allows us to define when and how a script should run, without the need for the user to be interactive at that time.

2. **What do we mean with ad-hoc scheduling?**
   Ad-hoc scheduling, which we normally do with `at` on Linux, is scheduling that is not periodically repeated, but often a one-time job at a fixed time.

3. **Where does the output of commands run with `at` normally go?**
   By default, `at` tries to use `sendmail` to send a local mail to the user who owns the queue/job. If sendmail is not installed, the output is gone.

4. **How is scheduling for the `cron` daemon most often implemented?**
   As a user-bound crontab.

5. **Which commands allows you to edit your personal crontab?**
   The command `crontab -e`. Furthermore, you can list the current crontab with `crontab -l` and remove the current crontab with `crontab -r`.

6. **Which five fields are present in the crontab timestamp syntax?**
   1. minute
   2. hour
   3. day-of-month
   4. month-of-year
   5. day-of-week

7. **Which are the three most important environment variables for the crontab?**
   1. PATH
   2. SHELL
   3. MAILTO

8. **How can we inspect the output for scripts or commands we have scheduled with `cron`?**
   We can either use redirection in the crontab to write the output to a file, or we can use the Linux local mail functionality to send us the output. Most of the times, redirecting output to a log file is the way to go.

9. **If our scheduled scripts do not have enough output for us to effectively work with log files, how should we remedy this?**
   Use the echo command in multiple places in your script, to signal a message to the reader that execution is doing what is expected. Example of this are: 'Step 1 completed successfully, continuing.' and 'Script execution was a success, exiting.'.

Chapter 15

1. **Why are flags often used as *modifiers* whereas positional parameters are used as *targets*?**
   Flags often modify the behavior: it can make a script more or less verbose, or perhaps write the output somewhere. Often, a command manipulates a file, which is then considered the primary *target* for what the command actually tries to achieve.

2. **Why do we run** getopts **in a** while **loop?**
   All flags are parsed sequentially, and when getopts can no longer find new flags it will return an exit code different from 0, which will exit the while loop at exactly the right moment.

3. **Why do we need a ?) in the case statement?**
   We cannot trust the user to correctly use all flags all the time. **?)** matches any flag we have not specified, which we can then use to inform the user of incorrect usage.

4. **Why do we (sometimes) need a :) in the case statement?**
   The **:)** is used when the optstring specifies an argument for an option, but the user has not given it. It allows you to inform the user of the missing information (and you will most probably abort the script at this point).

5. **Why do we need a separate optstring is we're resolving all options anyway?**
   Because the optstring will tell getopts which options have arguments and which do not.

6. **Why do we need to substract 1 from the OPTIND variable when we use it in** shift**?**
   The OPTIND variable always refers to the *next possible index*, which means it is always 1 ahead of the final flag that was found. Because we only need to shift away the flags (which are seen as positional arguments!), we need to make sure we reduce the OPTIND by 1 before we shift.

7. **Is it a good idea to mix options with positional arguments?**
   Because of the added complexity of dealing with both options and positional arguments, it is often better to specify the *target* of your operation as a flag argument for the −f flag; -f is almost universally excepted as a file reference, which will always be considered as a logical target for most operations.

Chapter 16

1. **What is *parameter substitution*?**
   Nothing more than the run-time substitution of the variable name with its value at that moment.

2. **How can we include default values for our defined variables?**
   With the ${variable:-value} syntax, where *variable* is the name and *value* the default value. This will only be used if the value is null or empty (").

3. **How can we use parameter expansion to handle missing parameter values?**
   While you would normally use an `if [[ -z ${variable} ]]; then`, parameter expansion allows you to use the following syntax to generate an error message and `exit 1`: **${1:?Name not supplied!}**

4. **What does ${#*} do?**
   It is the same as $#, which we use to determine the number of arguments passed to our shell script. The general **${#name}** syntax allows us to get the length of the value of the *name* variable.

5. **How does *pattern substitution* work when talking about parameter expansions?**
   Pattern substitution allows us to take the value of a variable and modify it slightly, by doing a search/replace for a *pattern*.

6. **How is *pattern removal* related to *pattern substitution*?**
   Removing a pattern is the same as replacing a pattern with nothing. With pattern removal, we get the added flexibility of search both from the beginning of the text (prefix) and from the end (suffix). Pattern removal is great when working with file paths.

7. **What types of case modifications can we perform?**
   - Lowercasing
   - Upercasing
   - Reversing the casing

8. **Which two things can we use to get a substring from a variables' value?**
   We need an *offset*, or a *lenght*, or the combination of both (most common).

Other Books You May Enjoy

If you enjoyed this book, you may be interested in these other books by Packt:

Mastering Linux Shell Scripting - Second Edition
Mokhtar Ebrahim, Andrew Mallett

ISBN: 978-1-78899-055-4

- Make, execute, and debug your first Bash script
- Create interactive scripts that prompt for user input
- Foster menu structures for operators with little command-line experience
- Develop scripts that dynamically edit web configuration files to produce a new virtual host
- Write scripts that use AWK to search and reports on log files
- Draft effective scripts using functions as building blocks, reducing maintenance and build time
- Make informed choices by comparing different script languages such as Python with BASH

Linux Shell Scripting Cookbook - Third Edition
Clif Flynt, Sarath Lakshman, Shantanu Tushar

ISBN: 978-1-78588-198-5

- Interact with websites via scripts
- Write shell scripts to mine and process data from the Web
- Automate system backups and other repetitive tasks with crontab
- Create, compress, and encrypt archives of your critical data.
- Configure and monitor Ethernet and wireless networks
- Monitor and log network and system activity
- Tune your system for optimal performance
- Improve your system's security
- Identify resource hogs and network bottlenecks
- Extract audio from video files
- Create web photo albums
- Use git or fossil to manage revision control and interact with FOSS projects
- Create and maintain Linux containers and Virtual Machines
- Run a private Cloud server

Leave a review - let other readers know what you think

Please share your thoughts on this book with others by leaving a review on the site that you bought it from. If you purchased the book from Amazon, please leave us an honest review on this book's Amazon page. This is vital so that other potential readers can see and use your unbiased opinion to make purchasing decisions, we can understand what our customers think about our products, and our authors can see your feedback on the title that they have worked with Packt to create. It will only take a few minutes of your time, but is valuable to other potential customers, our authors, and Packt. Thank you!

Index

crontab environment variables
  about 334
  MAILTO 338, 339
  PATH 334, 336
  SHELL 337, 338
crontab
  about 330
  syntax 330, 332, 333

D

Debian 8
default values, parameter expansion
  input, checking 372, 373
  length 374, 375
description header 77
directory structure 51

E

egrep 202, 203, 204, 205, 206
elif condition 222, 224, 225
error checking
  about 148
  exit status 148, 150
  functional checks 150, 152
  test shorthand 152, 153
error handling
  about 155
  if-then-else 160, 162, 163
  if-then-exit 156, 158, 160
  shorthand syntax 164, 166
error prevention
  about 166
  absolute path, managing 170, 172
  arguments, checking 166, 169, 170
  relative paths, managing 170, 172
  y/n, dealing with 172, 175
exclamation marks 396, 398
exclamation marks, Bash
  commands, running form history 398
execute 72
extended file system (ext) 50

F

Fedora 8
file attributes 90

file descriptors 254, 256
file ownership
  manipulating 76
file permissions
  chgrp 82, 84, 85
  chmod 76, 78, 79, 80, 81
  chown 82, 84, 85
  manipulating 76
  sudo 82, 83
  umask 76, 78, 79, 80, 81
file
  copying 96, 98
  find command, using 107, 110
  finding 106
  linking 99, 101
  locate command, using 106
  moving 99, 101
  operations 95
  removing 98
  renaming 99, 101
Filesystem Hierarchy Standard (FHS) 51
flags
  combining, with positional arguments 360, 363
  using, on command line 346, 347
  versus positional parameters 345, 346
  with arguments 357, 360
for loop
  about 232, 233, 234, 236
  globbing 238, 239, 241, 242
function libraries
  about 308
  practical examples 313
  source command 308, 310, 312, 313
functions
  about 292
  abstraction of commands, complex example
    294, 295
  augmenting, with parameters 302
  practical examples 300
  script, creating for printing text in different color
    302, 304
  used, for printing Hello world! 292, 293
  values, returning 305, 307
  variable scopes 296, 298, 299

G

getopts shell builtin, flags
  -d 349
  -f 349
  -h 349
  -q 349
  -r 349
  -v 349
getopts shell builtin
  about 348, 349, 350
  flags, combining with positional arguments 360,
    363
  flags, with arguments 357, 360
  multiple flags 352, 353, 356
getopts
  syntax 350, 351, 352
  versus getopt 349
globbing
  about 192, 193, 194, 195
  disabling 197, 198
  for loop 238, 239, 241, 242
GNU zip 102
graphical editors
  Atom 34
  combining, with command-line editor 46, 47
  Notepad++ 38
graphical user interfaces (GUIs) 8
grep 181
Group ID (GID) 73
groups 73, 74, 75

H

help
  obtaining 227
here documents 284, 285
heredocs
  strings 287
  using, for script input 286
  variables, using 285
history command 393, 394
hypervisor 13

I

if-then-else 218
in-place editing 209
input redirection
  about 254, 268, 270
  password, generating 270, 271
integrated development environment (IDE) 38
interactive commands 404
interactive commands, for file manipulation
  about 406
  cat command 406
  cp command 407
  head command 407
  less command 406
  ln command 407
  mkdir command 406
  mv command 407
  rm command 407
  tail command 408
  touch command 406
interactive commands, for navigation
  about 405
  cd command 405
  ls command 405
  pwd command 405
interactive commands, for permission and
    ownership manipulation
  about 408
  chgrp command 409
  chmod command 408
  chown command 408
  groupadd command 409
  su command 409
  sudo command 409
  umask command 408
  useradd command 409
  usermod command 410
interactive scripts
  versus non-interactive scripts 138, 140
interactive while loop
  creating 231, 232
ISO image
  download link 14

dealing with 134
parameters 137
users 73, 74, 75

V

variable manipulation
 about 376
 case modification 382, 383, 385
 pattern removal 379, 380, 382
 pattern substitution 376, 377, 378
 substring expansion 385, 386, 387, 388
variables
 about 61, 128, 129
 naming 132, 134
 need for 130, 131
VDI (VirtualBox Disk Image) 16
verbosity
 about 343
 in comments 120
 of command output 122, 123

of commands 121, 122
VHD (Virtual Hard Disk) 16
Vim
 .vimrc 42
 about 39, 41, 42
 cheat sheet 43
vimtutor 42
virtual machine
 about 12
 accessing, via SSH 29
 Ubuntu, installing 21, 24, 28
VirtualBox
 reference 13
 setting up 13
 virtual machine, creating 14, 19, 20

W

What You See Is What You Get (WYSIWYG) 44
while loop 228, 229
write 72